Who Ran the Citi

Historical Urban Studies

Series editors: *Richard Rodger and Jean-Luc Pinol*

Titles in this series include:

Who Ran the Cities?

City Elites and Urban Power Structures in
Europe and North America, 1750–1940

Edited by

RALF ROTH AND ROBERT BEACHY

Routledge
Taylor & Francis Group

LONDON AND NEW YORK

First published 2007 by Ashgate Publishing

Published 2016 by Routledge
2 Park Square, Milton Park, Abingdon, Oxfordshire OX14 4RN
711 Third Avenue, New York, NY 10017, USA

First issued in paperback 2016

Routledge is an imprint of the Taylor & Francis Group, an informa business

British Library Cataloguing in Publication Data
Who ran the cities? : city elites and urban power structures in Europe and North America, 1750–1940. (Historical urban studies)
   1. Elite (Social sciences) – Great Britain – History   2. Elite (Social sciences) – Europe – History   3. Cities and towns – Great Britain – History   4. Cities and towns – Europe – History   5. Municipal government – Great Britain – History   6. Municipal government – Europe – History
   I. Roth, Ralf   II. Beachy, Robert
   305.5'24'091732

Library of Congress Cataloging-in-Publication Data
Who ran the cities? : city elites and urban power structures in Europe and North America, 1750–1940 / edited by Ralf Roth and Robert Beachy.
   p. cm. – (Historical urban studies series)
   Includes bibliographical references and index.
   ISBN 978-0-7546-5153-6 (alk. paper)
   1. Municipal government – Europe – History.   2. Municipal government – North America – History.   3. Elite (Social sciences) – Europe – History.   4. Elite (Social sciences) – North America – History.   5. Europe – Politics and government.   6. North America – Politics and government. I. Roth, Ralf. II. Beachy, Robert.

   JS3000.W46 2007
   320.8'509409034dc22

                                                                    2006038644

   ISBN 13: 978-1-138-27405-1 (pbk)
   ISBN 13: 978-0-7546-5153-6 (hbk)

Contents

PART II: DIVERSITY – FORMAL AND INFORMAL STRUCTURES OF CONTINENTAL EUROPE'S CITY ELITES

PART III: DEMOCRATIC METROPOLISES – CITY ELITES IN NORTH AMERICA

List of Figures and Tables

Figures

Tables

List of Abbreviations

CIHM	Canadian Institute for Historical Microreproductions
CFC	*Commercial and Financial Chronicle*
edn.	edition
esp.	especially
GGF	Grant Francis Collection
IfSG	Institut für Stadtgeschichte Frankfurt am Main
ILP	Independent Labour Party
IUP	Irish University Press
KLA	King's Lynn Borough Archive
LA	Lincolnshire Archives
LCC	London County Council
LGB	Local Government Board
MOH	Medical Officer of Health
MP	Member of Parliament
n. a.	not available
NLW	National Library of Wales
NRO	Norfolk Record Office
NYDT	*New-York Daily Tribune*
NYH	*New York Herald*
NYT	*New York Times*
PCWS	Pest Charitable Women's Society
PP	Parliamentary Papers
repr.	reprint
SL	Swansea Library Collection
SPD	Sozialdemokratische Partei Deutschlands
UWSA	University of Wales Swansea Archive
vol.	volume
vols.	volumes
WGAS	West Glamorgan Archive Service
YIM	Yorkshire Imperial Metals
YMCA	Young Men's Christian Association
YWCA	Young Women's Christian Association

Notes on Contributors

Robert Beachy is Associate Professor of History at Goucher College, where he teaches European history. His publications include *The Soul of Commerce: Credit, Property, and Politics in Leipzig, 1750–1840* (Leiden 2005) and *Women, Business and Finance in Nineteenth Century Europe* (Oxford 2005). He is coauthoring *German Civil Wars: Constructing and Commemorating the Nation, 1756–1914*, to be published with Oxford University Press. He is now working on a new project, *Berlin: Gay Metropolis, 1860–1933*.

Sven Beckert is Professor of History at Harvard University where he teaches the history of the United States in the nineteenth century. His publications include *The Monied Metropolis: New York City and the Consolidation of the American Bourgeoisie* (Cambridge 2001). He is currently writing *The Empire of Cotton: A Global History*, to be published by Alfred A. Knopf.

Marcus Gräser is Private Docent of Modern History at the Department of History and Research Associate at the Center for North American Studies at the University of Frankfurt am Main, Germany. The present article is based on extensive research on the history of middle class(es), cities, and welfare state building in the USA and in Germany from 1880–1940.

Denise McHugh is a research fellow at the Centre for Urban History, University of Leicester and a tutor in urban history at the universities of Leicester and Cambridge, United Kingdom. The present article is based on her doctoral dissertation, 'Remaking the Victorian County Town, 1860–1910' (University of Leicester Ph.D. thesis, 2002). Her current research focuses on imperialism and urban change.

Emi Konishi is Associate Professor of British Studies at the School of Economics, Senshu University, Japan. The present article is based on her doctoral dissertation, 'The Age of Pluralist Power: The Urban Elite and the Public Sphere in King's Lynn, 1750–1835' (Keio University Ph.D. thesis, 2000). She has also published a series of other articles on the same subject.

Louise Miskell is Lecturer in History at the Department of History, University of Wales Swansea, United Kingdom. The research for her chapter was carried out as part of a project on Swansea's industrial and urban development in the eighteenth and nineteenth centuries. The volume *Intelligent Town: An Urban History of Swansea 1780–1850*, was published by the University of Wales Press in 2006.

James Moore is deputy director of the Centre for Metropolitan History at the Institute of Historical Research, London. He specialises in the comparative urban history of nineteenth-century Britain and has published articles on many aspects of urban and regional politics, local government and civic culture. He has recently completed a book, *The Transformation of Urban Liberalism*, on the changing structure of urban Liberal politics in the late-nineteenth century. His ongoing work includes a new study of London Progressivism, that will examine the role of political ideology in shaping London's modern metropolitan identity.

Dobrinka Parusheva is Research Associate at the Institute of Balkan Studies, Bulgarian Academy of Sciences in Sofia, Bulgaria. Her interests also include research on urban elites and government in the Balkans upon which the present article is based. She has published numerous articles in this field.

Richard Rodger is Professor of Economic and Social History at the University of Edinburgh, United Kingdom. As Editor of *Urban History* and General Editor (with Jean-Luc Pinol) of 30 books in the series *Historical Urban Studies*, Rodger has encouraged new work and innovative approaches to urban history. His most recent books include *The Transformation of Edinburgh: Land Property and Trust in the Nineteenth Century* (Cambridge 2001), *Cities of Ideas: Civil Society and Urban Governance in Britain 1800–2000* (with R. Colls) (Aldershot 2004) and with J. Herbert, *Testimonies of the City: Identity, Community and Change in a Contemporary Urban World* (Aldershot 2006). In 2004 he was elected to membership of the British Academy of Social Sciences.

Ralf Roth is Private Docent of History at the Department of History at the University of Frankfurt am Main, Germany, and Research Fellow at the Royal Holloway College at the University of London. His numerous articles published in German, British and Spanish journals focus on the social and cultural history of cities and communication networks. After his research on the development of urban elites he completed a project about the impact of the railways on German society, which he published as *Das Jahrhundert der Eisenbahn. Die Herrschaft über Raum und Zeit, 1800–1914* (Ostfildern 2005).

Michael Schäfer is Private Docent at Bielefeld University and Research Fellow at Chemnitz University of Technology, Germany. The present article is based on a comparative research project on urban middle classes in Germany and Britain before, during, and after World War One. Results of this project have already been published in several German articles and in a monographic study, *Bürgertum in der Krise. Städtische Mittelklassen in Edinburgh und Leipzig von 1890 bis 1930* (Göttingen 2003).

Steinar Supphellen is Professor of History in the Department of History at The Norwegian University of Science and Technology (NTNU), Trondheim, and President of The Royal Norwegian Society of Sciences and Letters. He has written books on administration and urban history and articles on a variety of topics, mostly in early modern European history.

Árpád Tóth is Lecturer in the Department of Modern and Contemporary Hungarian History, at the University of Miskolc, Hungary, where he lectures on the social and urban history of Hungary. He received his MA degree at the University ELTE of Budapest in history and sociology and at the University of Leicester, United Kingdom in urban history. The present article is based on his Ph.D. thesis about the social history of the earliest voluntary societies in Hungary, published recently in Hungarian. His research also considers social networks, schooling, professionalisation and demographic behaviour in greater Hungarian towns.

Brian Young is James McGill Professor of History at McGill University in Montreal, Canada. He has published books and articles on Canadian and French-Canadian legal and cultural history. His article is part of a larger study of the role of the elite bourgeoisie in the culture and social landscape of nineteenth-century urban Quebec.

Historical Urban Studies
General Editors' Preface

Density and proximity are two of the defining characteristics of the urban dimension. It is these that identify a place as uniquely urban, though the threshold for such pressure points varies from place to place. What is considered an important cluster in one context – may not be considered as urban elsewhere. A third defining characteristic is functionality – the commercial or strategic position of a town or city which conveys an advantage over other places. Over time, these functional advantages may diminish, or the balance of advantage may change within a hierarchy of towns. To understand how the relative importance of towns shifts over time and space is to grasp a set of relationships which is fundamental to the study of urban history.

Towns and cities are products of history, yet have themselves helped to shape history. As the proportion of urban dwellers has increased, so the urban dimension has proved a legitimate unit of analysis through which to understand the spectrum of human experience and to explore the cumulative memory of past generations. Though obscured by layers of economic, social and political change, the study of the urban milieu provides insights into the functioning of human relationships and, if urban historians themselves are not directly concerned with current policy studies, few contemporary concerns can be understood without reference to the historical development of towns and cities.

This longer historical perspective is essential to an understanding of social processes. Crime, housing conditions and property values, health and education, discrimination and deviance, and the formulation of regulations and social policies to deal with them were, and remain, amongst the perennial preoccupations of towns and cities – no historical period has a monopoly of these concerns. They recur in successive generations, albeit in varying mixtures and strengths; the details may differ

The central forces of class, power and authority in the city remain. If this was the case for different periods, so it was for different geographical entities and cultures. Both scientific knowledge and technical information were available across Europe and showed little respect for frontiers. Yet despite common concerns and access to broadly similar knowledge, different solutions to urban problems were proposed and adopted by towns and cities in different parts of Europe. This comparative dimension informs urban historians as to which were systematic factors and which were of a purely local nature: general and particular forces can be distinguished.

These analytical and comparative frameworks inform this book. Indeed, thematic, comparative and analytical approaches to the historical study of towns and cities is the hallmark of the Historical Urban Studies series which now extends to over 30 titles, either already published or currently in production. European urban historiography has been extended and enriched as a result and this book makes another important addition to an intellectual mission to which we, as General Editors, remain firmly committed.

Richard Rodger   *University of Edinburgh*
Jean-Luc Pinol   *Université de Lyon II*

Preface

This book has its origin in the fruitful discussions of the Sixth International Conference on Urban History: 'Power, Knowledge and Society in the City' which was hosted by the *European Association of Urban Historians* (EAUH) in Edinburgh in September 2002. The session 'Who Ran the Cities? Elites and Urban Power Structures, 1700–2000', chaired by Sven Beckert (*Harvard University*, Cambridge), Marcus Gräser (*Johann Wolfgang Goethe-Universität*, Frankfurt am Main), and Ralf Roth (*Johann Wolfgang Goethe-Universität*, Frankfurt am Main), opened new perspectives on elites and urban history. We thank the EAUH for having included it in the programme of the conference.

All papers presented there and others solicited after the conference have been extensively rewritten and enlarged for inclusion in this book. We thank the authors for having answered our questions and for the productive dialogues about their work. The book broadens our view of the Transatlantic world. It considers eight countries and covers a region that reaches from Norway to Hungary, from the United Kingdom and Germany to the United States of America and Canada. We believe that some breakthroughs in comparative social and urban history may result from what is still a first step in a very promising field.

We wish to extend our thanks to Professors Jean-Luc Pinol and Richard Rodger for having included this book in the *Historical Urban Studies* series, to Ashgate Publishing and to Thomas Gray for his patient help.

Sinntal and Baltimore in July 2007

Ralf Roth
Robert Beachy

Introduction:
Who Ran the Cities?

Ralf Roth and Robert Beachy

Methodolocical problems of defining an elite

How do we begin to understand the relationship between 'elites' and the exercise of 'power' in cities? How can we determine who really took decisions? These and many other questions animated one of the main sessions, 'Who Ran the Cities? Elite and Urban Power Structures in Europe and North America', at the 2002 European Association of Urban Historians Conference 'Power, Knowledge and Society in the City'. Since an estimated 80 per cent of the world's population will inhabit an urban environment in the not too-distant future, the debates raised in the papers presented at this panel deserve the attention of social scientists of all kinds. For this reason, too, the field of urban studies will continue to gain interest as a 'crossroads' between urban, cultural and social history.

Of course, it is notoriously difficult to analyse the distribution of political power in modern cities. With the rise of broad political participation through the course of the nineteenth century, the questions of how and whether traditional elites maintained influence in municipal government are not easily answered. It is therefore necessary to combine several fields of research, which have otherwise often remained separate: the economic, social and cultural history of elite groups, on the one hand, and the political history of power resources and decision-making on the other.

It is easy to assume that a 'natural' relationship existed between elites and power resources – one that guided urban decision-making and determined its outcome. Of course wealth and education (as major forms of 'capital' and pillars of the elite) were concentrated in the hands of a small group. But was political power similarly concentrated or was it distributed more broadly along the entire spectrum of the urban population? Was it perhaps the case that economic, social and cultural elites were isolated from political decision-making and therefore not identical with the political elite? Is it possible that philanthropy, educational attainment, and support for the arts were used to exert influence without the direct control of political institutions? Did economic, social and political changes strengthen the power of established elites or did these processes generate new elites who could challenge those with inherited wealth and position? What about the power of working-class movements and their influence on municipal government and the strategic thinking of elite groups? Did these reciprocal influences significantly change the political culture? The anthology also addresses more 'structural' aspects, such as the role of coalition-building among various classes and elite groups and their ability to place their representatives in positions of power and influence.

Establishing the character of an urban ruling elite is the central methodological challenge and requires fundamental theories of historical research. One aspect of such research is identifying the individuals that constituted an elite group, a methodology that contrasts sharply with much social history dominated by the study of 'structures'. This is a long-standing question that animated the German 'Lamprecht' debate of the late nineteenth century, when historian Karl Lamprecht challenged historians to place greater emphasis on social processes. According to Lamprecht, instead of focusing on 'great events and great men', historians should 'base [their research] on the long-term movements of economic conditions and social institutions'.[1] Instead of the actions of individuals, this new social history emphasised power relationships, whose investigation received priority over individuals or power elites. Viewed less as powerful actors, these elite groups represented a subordinate historical agency, subject to the influences of social relationships and social change.[2]

As profitable as this theory has proven to be for investigating general social contexts and especially for considering mass movements, these views have also thwarted the empirical research of elite groups. For this reason, theories of elite groups have remained abstract and hypothetical.[3] French

---

[1]   K. Lamprecht, 'Der Ausgang des geschichtswissenschaftlichen Kampfes', *Die Zukunft,* 31 Juli 1897. See also K. Lamprecht, 'Halbwahrheiten', in K. Lamprecht, ed., *Zwei Streitschriften den Herren H. Oncken, H. Delbrück, M. Lenz zugeeignet* (Berlin 1897), 39–77, esp. 51. On Lamprecht and his influence in German history see H.-U. Wehler, 'Theorieprobleme der modernen deutschen Wirtschaftsgeschichte', in H.-U. Wehler, ed., *Historische Sozialwissenschaft und Geschichtsschreibung. Studien zu Aufgaben und Traditionen deutscher Geschichtswissenschaft* (Göttingen 1980), 106–25, esp. 108–10.

[2]   See K. U. Mayer, 'Struktur und Wandel der politischen Eliten in der Bundesrepublik', in R. Lasserre et al., eds, *Deutschland – Frankreich, Bausteine zu einem Strukturvergleich* (Stuttgart 1980), 165–95, esp. 192, and T. Parsons, 'Evolutionäre Universalien der Gesellschaft', in W. Zapf, ed., *Theorien des sozialen Wandels* (Königstein/Ts. 1979), 75–94, esp. 64. In this tradition Thorstein Veblen developed the position that the global economy, technology, science and emancipation should be seen as a single entity. See E. K. Scheuch, 'Continuity and Change in German Social Structure', *Historical Social Research* 46, 1988, 31–121, esp. 31–3. This was one reason that research on elites was considered unattractive. In contrast to these reductive models, Heinrich Best has argued that the political sphere enjoyed a relative autonomy from the social order. See H. Best, *Die Männer von Besitz und Bildung. Struktur und Handeln parlamentarischer Führungsgruppen in Deutschland und Frankreich 1848/49* (Düsseldorf 1990), 15.

[3]   On this debate, see H. P. Dreitzel, *Elitebegriff und Sozialstruktur. Eine soziologische Begriffsanalyse* (Stuttgart 1962), and on the principles of a Marxist elite theory see N. Poulantzas, *Politische Macht und gesellschaftliche Klassen*, 2. ed.

historical research at the beginning of the nineteenth century viewed history as the product of class conflict and investigated primarily the factors that determine the actions of individuals. This perspective gained currency in Germany through the work of Karl Marx and Friedrich Engels and was transformed by the application of Weberian theory to the study of major social movements. Only much later was attention given to the processes mediating economic and social relationships, political power and cultural factors, and along with this the latitude for the actions of individuals. This prepared the context for a study of elite groups based on individuals, for which historians have attempted to develop viable research methods since the 1960s. Down to the present, the results of this research remain contradictory since the very question of who belongs to an elite is contested. Under the influence of American urban sociology, a number of competing theories have emerged. One approach has attempted to identify the offices and functions relevant to social change and the corresponding individuals who held these positions. In contrast, another approach places great importance on the measurement of reputation or stature.[4] Attempts to apply these models to historical research have quickly demonstrated the limits of these one-dimensional theories.

At first blush the theoretical approach of considering formal office-holding appears to offer a simple and elegant solution to the problem. However, it is not clear how to delineate an elite in relation to its respective 'positions' or political offices. Especially larger cities with their sophisticated administrative structures and various informal communication networks present tremendous difficulties. Even studies of officeholders based on prosopographical methods fall short, since they exclude a large proportion of those elite groups who held political power. The ruling council of a German or British city, for example, was never the unique representative of its burghers, respective citizens, or an independent executive within the republican commune. Many of the council's objectives were defeated to

---

(Frankfurt am Main 1975). A prime example is Karl Marx's analysis of the political rule of Napoleon III, which Marxist social science has taken as a model for the interpretation of the Bismarck state and the Third Reich. The proponents of this paradigm have failed, however, to develop a concrete description of the leading groups. See K. Marx, 'Der achtzehnte Brumaire des Louis Bonaparte', in Marx-Engels Werke, vol. 8 (Berlin 1975), 111–207; H.-U. Wehler, *Das Deutsche Kaiserreich 1871–1918*, 5. ed. (Göttingen 1983), 63–6; L. Gall, 'Bismarck und Bonapartismus', *Historische Zeitschrift*, 223, 1976, 618–37, and O. Pflanze, 'Bismarcks Herrschaftstechnik als Problem der gegenwärtigen Historiographie', *Historische Zeitschrift*, 234, 1982, 562–99.

[4]   For empirical studies of regional elites see O. Stammer and P. Weingart, *Politische Soziologie* (Munich 1972), 145–147. See also D. Herzog, *Politische Karrieren. Selektion und Professionalisierung politischer Führungsgruppen* (Opladen 1975), 94–7. For methodological suggestions see W. A. Welsh, *Leaders and Elites* (New York 1979), 47–9 and 59–61.

some extent by other burgher committees, and the execution of decisions was always carefully controlled. The thesis has still other problems. How do we weight the importance of different positions? Attempts to establish a point system that considers the web of political committees and offices and likewise accounts for the inexact values of qualitative factors necessarily fails. Certainly efforts to quantify such disparate factors demonstrate the absurdity of this approach. The results would be determined in large part by the assignment of values to diverse factors and ultimately by the arbitrary analysis of the historian.[5]

The theoretical approach of the office-holding model is not without value for the study of elite groups, however, as long as its limitations are recognised. The approach outlined here certainly allows us to identify elements of an urban elite, particularly those present in political corporations, namely council members and the members of burgher committees. In some German studies these have been analysed and described as the *politische Führungsschicht* ('group of political leaders').[6] These and other studies have additionally identified and shed light on a second group consisting of the *wirtschaftliche Oberschicht* ('economic upper class'), described as the highest tax payers.[7] For the example of New York Sven Beckert provides

---

[5]   On the critique of prosopographical methods see L. Stone, 'Prosopographie – englische   Erfahrungen',   in   K.   Jarausch,   ed.,   *Quantifizierung   und Geschichtswissenschaft. Probleme und Möglichkeiten* (Düsseldorf 1976), 64–97. See also J. D. Nagle, *System and succession. The social bases of political recruitment* (Austin 1977), 229–31, and H.-G. Schumann, 'Die soziale und politische Funktion lokaler Eliten', in B. Kirchgässner and J. Schadt, eds, *Kommunale Selbstverwaltung – Idee und Wirklichkeit* (Sigmaringen 1983), 30–38. For the example of Reutlingen see H.-J. Siewert, *Lokale Elitensysteme. Ein Beitrag zur Theoriediskussion in der Community-Power-Forschung und ein Versuch zur empirischen Überprüfung* (Tübingen 1979), and for Cologne see C. v. Looz-Corswarem, 'Die politische Elite Kölns im Übergang vom 18. zum 19. Jahrhundert', in H. Schilling and H. Diederiks, eds, *Bürgerliche Eliten in den Niederlanden und in Nordwestdeutschland. Studien zur Sozialgeschichte des europäischen Bürgertums und in der Neuzeit* (Cologne and Vienna 1985), 421–44.

[6]   For important suggestions for studying political elites see R. Jeske, 'Kommunale Amtsinhaber und Entscheidungsträger – die politische Elite', in L. Gall, ed., *Stadt und Bürgertum im Übergang von der traditionalen zur modernen Gesellschaft.* (Munich 1993), 273–94. On the topic of the identification and description of elites see D. Herzog, *Politische Führungsgruppen. Probleme und Ergebnisse der modernen Elitenforschung* (Darmstadt 1982). For similar studies see H.-W. Schmuhl, *Die Herren der Stadt. Bürgerliche Eliten und städtische Selbstverwaltung in Nürnberg und Braunschweig vom 18. Jahrhundert bis 1918* (Gießen 1998), and M. Schäfer, *Bürgertum in der Krise. Städtische Mittelklassen in Edinburgh und Leipzig 1890 bis 1930* (Göttingen 2003).

[7]   For the debate on economic elites see A. Schulz, 'Wirtschaftlicher Status und Einkommensverteilung – die ökonomische Oberschicht', in: L. Gall, ed., *Stadt und Bürgertum im Übergang von der traditionalen zur modernen Gesellschaft* (Munich 1993), 249–71.

important fundamental research on this issue in his book *The Monied Metropolis*, which is augmented by additional research presented in an essay in this volume.[8] In German commercial cities such as Frankfurt, Leipzig, Cologne, Hamburg, or Bremen these two groups were by no means identical nor can their relationship to one another be described as static. The same can be said for British cities such as Edinburgh, Lincoln, Swansea or King's Lynn, for Norwegian towns like Trondheim, or for American and Canadian cities including New York, Chicago, Montreal and Quebec. Neither can an elite be reduced to those holding the greatest political or economic power. Indeed, the question of power becomes more dynamic as one uncovers the complex structures and role of culture within the system of a bourgeois society.

It was Jürgen Habermas who emphasised the genesis of a public sphere as a constitutive element of modern civil society and as a critical institution for the dominance of the middle class.[9] Thomas Nipperdey used Habermas's sociological concept to develop a groundbreaking historical interpretation in which he identified four main factors for explaining the successful spread of voluntary societies in late eighteenth and early nineteenth-century Europe. The first of these elements was the manner in which free associations allowed their members to meet each other independent of the social restrictions of traditional old regime corporations. The new clubs also served an ideological purpose by allowing members to forge political identities and interests and establish a new spirit for a modern civil society. Many of the associations also had practical ambitions, which they pursued successfully without the support of the state or other traditional institutions. Finally, the new clubs and societies served to promote patronage of the fine arts and can be seen as agencies for the creation of 'art'.[10] Nipperdey applied these four functions of free associations in his interpretation of the origin of modern middle-class society. He further analysed bourgeois society according to its three main characteristics: as a social, a political and a cultural entity. It was Nipperdey's view that voluntary societies served primarily a cultural function, and were responsible for establishing the cultural sphere of early middle-class society.[11] The associational movement increased tremendously within the first decades of the nineteenth century, and with this popularity helped to organise elements of the enlightened nobility and even the under classes.[12] Nipperdey concluded that

---

[8]   S. Beckert, *The Monied Metropolis. New York City and the Consolidation of the American Bourgeoisie, 1850–1896* (Cambridge and New York 2001).

[9]   Jürgen Habermas, *Strukturwandel der Öffentlichkeit. Untersuchungen zu einer Kategorie der bürgerlichen Gesellschaft* (Frankfurt am Main 1962), esp. chapter 5 'Institutionen der Öffentlichkeit', 90–107.

[10]   Th. Nipperdey, 'Verein als soziale Struktur in Deutschland im späten 18. und frühen 19. Jahrhundert', in H. Heimpel, ed., *Geschichtswissenschaft und Vereinswesen im 19. Jahrhundert* (Göttingen 1972), 1–44.

[11]   Ibid. 27.

[12]   Ibid. 39–41.

'The association is the most important medium for the formation of civil society'.[13] Like Habermas and Nipperdey David Blackbourn and Geoff Eley have considered the growth of the German bourgeoisie in the context of the

> development of a public sphere (*Öffentlichkeit*), separate from and independent of the state: a sphere of activity and discourse through the press, and through legally guaranteed rights of association and assembly. These "bourgeois freedoms" together with the rights of free speech and petition, constituted the formal attributes of equality before the law within a *Rechtsstaat*.[14]

The development Habermas, Nipperdey, Blackbourn and Eley have identified in German history has a close British counterpart, anlysed by Robert J. Morris, and to a lesser extent Peter Clark. Not only the timing of but also the major dynamics in the development of British associational culture were very similar to German conditions. As Morris notes, the period up to 1780 was a formative one in which the first British 'clubs' formed as eating and drinking societies or informal coffee shop gatherings. Most of these societies still lacked much formal organisational structure and could strive for little more than conviviality. The groups that coalesced after 1780, however, often responded to a sense of instability or crisis – political, ideological, epidemiological, or religious – and assimilated formal associational trappings including extensive byelaws, constitutions and a leadership structure. This period to the end of the nineteenth century was one characterised by the increasing assertion of British middle-class dominance, which often relied on close relations with Christian evangelicalism as well as the burgeoning 'free' professions of the natural and academic sciences. The British club also proved an important instrument for the assertion of marginalised groups including the working classes and women as well as cultural and ethnic minorities. Marked by secularisation, increased state involvement, and growing leisure and consumption, the twentieth century represented a period in which the club became a central pillar of British civil society and social structure.[15]

---

[13] 'Der Verein ist das entscheidende Medium zur Formung der bürgerlichen Gesellschaft', Th. Nipperdey, *Deutsche Gesellschaft 1800–1866. Bürgerwelt und starker Staat* (Munich 1983), 268. See also Nipperdey, Verein, 42.

[14] D. Blackbourn and G. Eley, *The Peculiarities of German History: Bourgeois Society and Politics in Nineteenth-Century Germany* (Oxford and New York 1984), 192.

[15] R. J. Morris, 'Clubs, societies and associations' in F. M. L. Thompson, ed., *The Cambridge Social History of Britain. vol. 3: Social Agencies and Institutions* (Cambridge 1990), 395–443; R. J. Morris, 'The middle class and British towns and cities of the Industrial Revolution, 1780–1870', in D. Fraser and A. Sutcliffe, eds, *The pursuit of Urban History* (London 1983), 286–306, and P. Clark, *British Clubs and Societies, 1580–1800. The Origins of an Associational World* (Oxford 2000).

Both English and German scholarship constitute an important background for the interpretation of European civil society, which has informed, in turn, many studies on the emergence of new urban elites. Generally, this work proceeds from the assumption that the constitution of urban elites represented processes of concrete social interaction and exclusion and depended therefore on the specific individuals or social groups that were active in city governance, in church boards, in economic interest groups, and not least, in the important cultural and social activities of associations. Not only political rulers but also leading economic, social, and cultural actors must be identified, and especially in their relationships to each other. Here reputation plays a tremendous role. One important index for the standing of individuals within the burgher community is election or appointment to one of the many informal bodies within the web of urban administration. These indices are especially well suited for conducting a value neutral analysis. In this sense, the elite is not constructed by the arbitrary categories of the historian but rather through the assessment of burgher contemporaries.[16] The goal of some German elite studies has been to characterise these circles, to analyse their social components, their economic positions, their political orientations, and their cultural activities. Another element of this analysis has considered the relationships of individual groups to the political and economic leadership as well as to the participation of elite members in both associational culture and religious organisations.

In view of these considerations, we would like to propose the following topics as a framework for our anthology. 1. One critical factor is the role of wealth and economic power in determining elite status and how this is expressed through specific city constitutions as well as the peculiarities of national law with respect to the relationship between city and state. This complex of relations will animate the first section of the book, which presents the examples of several British cities. 2. The meaning of cultural institutions and informal networks for urban political culture will be of importance in various chapters of the second section, which concentrate on elites in continental Europe. 3. The role of the masses and their influence on urban politics play a key role in the third section, which examines North American cities.

---

[16] For information on the groups considered in this analysis of Frankfurt elites see R. Roth, *Stadt und Bürgertum in Frankfurt am Main. Ein besonderer Weg von der ständischen zur modernen Bürgergesellschaft 1760 bis 1914* (Munich 1996), table attachments A and B. On the methodological principles of this study see Th. Maentel, 'Reputation und Einfluß – die gesellschaftlichen Führungsgruppen', in Gall, *Stadt und Bürgertum*, 295–314. For different views on the research of historical elites see E. Weyrauch, 'Zur sozialen und wirtschaftlichen Situation Kitzingens im 16. Jahrhundert', in I. Bátori and E. Weyrauch, eds, *Die bürgerliche Elite der Stadt Kitzingen. Studien zur Sozial- und Wirtschaftsgeschichte einer landesherrlichen Stadt im 16. Jahrhundert* (Stuttgart 1982), 27–90.

Some results from our collection of essays

To answer the problems discussed above our anthology collects case studies about the processes of decision-making in modern cities throughout Western Europe and North America. The authors of the twelve contributions represent eight different countries and deal with the cities of eight nations. Our hope is that the anthology encourages scholars to replace common stereotypes of a monolithic elite with a more complicated view of urban power dynamics as an interplay between various economic, social, political and cultural elite groups. To contribute to this complex account of cities, elites, and the exercise of power, the anthology brings together different methodological approaches in studying European as well as North-American cities; the anthology should thus facilitate methodological as well as international comparison.

To simplify the presentation of this research we have divided the anthology into three parts. The first five chapters examine the urban elites of the United Kingdom, which are considered together as the 'British Model'. The first essay, Emil Konishi's 'Pluralist Power in Eighteenth-Century English Towns' turns directly to the question of the character and function of an urban elite in a changing milieu. In light of the concentration of office holders on political boards, Konishi pays attention to the nature of power in the non-political social and cultural spheres. Using the example of the port town King's Lynn, Konishi focuses on the 'individual careers of persons who possessed significant cultural and social influence but no political power' (5). Indeed, she finds that Quaker bankers did not join the traditional political institutions but performed services for the county (instead of the municipality) and participated in the system of voluntary associations. Also women played a greater role in public and social activities. Generally within the cultural sphere the spectrum of social groups was much wider than within the sphere of traditional politics. 'Through common experiences' forged in the network of voluntary associations and committees, according to Konishi, a stratum of 'new political leaders' learned to co-operate 'with the old political leaders' (19) and thus prepared the constitution of a new elite.

Turning our attention to the nineteenth century Louise Miskell stresses the importance of the 1835 municipal reform act in her contribution, 'Urban Power, Industrialisation and Political Reform'. She raises the problem of how elite urban groups used regional power structures for their own purposes. Focusing on the Welsh city Swansea, an industrial town and sea-bathing resort, Miskell identifies, in addition to the hinterland gentry and a commercial middle class, a dynamic group of industrialists who migrated in from other regions but were excluded from key posts in the city administration. As a consequence, these industrialists had minimal impact on local municipal policy. They focused on the wider region, however, and established a range of county contacts that allowed them to achieve the office of high sheriff. Opportunity came with the 1835 Municipal Reform Act, which 'brought an end to the reign of the old, self-elected corporations' (32) and allowed prominent industrialists to seek political offices within the town.

The third contribution 'Who Really Ran the Cities? Municipal Knowledge and Policy Networks in British Local Government, 1832–1914' by James Moore and Richard Rodger deals with the problem of administrative power and knowledge about the services of modern city government. Moore and Rodger observe that 'the elected business class' withdrew from city government after 'municipal functions' had been significantly expanded in the second half of the nineteenth century, and they claim that 'the ascent of the expert with his professional qualifications was consequently assured' (39). Like Miskell, Moore and Rodger identify the beginning of this process in Great Britain with the Municipal Corporation Act of 1835. In the following decades this tendency continued with the Local Government Act of 1859 and the Local Management Act of 1885. These new urban regulations quickly created new centres of power. They were anchored by a network of committees which provided the city administration with specific knowledge about the manifold problems of expanding municipal activities. Further sources of knowledge included the information provided in reports, by local statistical societies and by professional organisations. This system of urban policy changed with 'the growth of political parties within local government' (69), and both liberals and conservatives began to change fundamentally the source of policy initiative. Moore and Rodger conclude that

> Ideological and local differences were still important and local government did retain a great deal of independence. Yet the nationalisation of municipal knowledge and information networks, assisted by the rise of social sciences, helped create growing consensus and policy convergence (69).

In chapter four, 'The Unregulated Town: Strategies of Lincoln's Municipal Elite', Denise McHugh addresses important elements of the questions raised by Moore and Rodger. McHugh examines in detail the composition of a municipal elite and its urban management policy in the years after the Municipal Reform Act of 1835. Focusing on Lincoln, a former church centre and market town that languished as a provincial city in the nineteenth century, McHugh identifies a big shift from an old to a new elite, arguing that 'Patricians, often Anglican and Tory, were usurped by a more commercial, Liberal and often non-conformist middle-class elite' (72). Some small manufacturers survived and the railways helped to establish an industry of machine construction. It was this dynamic group that would dominate Lincoln's municipal elite in the decades between 1860 and 1910. They did not rule alone, however, but shared their power with an important group of professionals. Both groups were linked by an important though informal network. McHugh argues: 'The elite was formed from the intense network of social, familial, business and occupational connections operating within the county town' (91). Although it was a relatively small elite, characterised by an astonishingly longevity of service, it incorporated new members of the middle class. While the 'inner circle remained relatively inaccessible to newly elected councillors' (80) this could not prevent a shift in the elite's confessional composition from Anglican to Methodist. The new elite used its control of the corporation, according to McHugh, to promote 'a low cost, low tax business environment', and they 'exhibited a strong local resistance to central government "interference" and statutory authority; and finally, they established high levels of elite cohesion and advantage' (91).

In the final essay of the first section, Michael Schäfer compares Edinburgh and Leipzig, and – unlike Konishi, Miskell, Moore and Rodger, and McHugh, who focus on the nineteenth century – considers the development of urban political elites in the twentieth century. Schäfer's main question concerns the impact of democratisation on city elites in Great Britain and Germany. Countering a common preconception that there were vast differences between the two countries, Schäfer identifies many interesting similarities. Both Edinburgh's and Leipzig's urban political bodies were rooted in local government reforms of the 1830s, and both shared a restrictive municipal franchise. A significant variation was the piecemeal extension of suffrage rights in Britain, compared to many German cities (and Leipzig in particular), where suffrage remained restricted until the introduction of a radically democratic franchise after the Revolution of November 1918. Strikingly, the social composition of the Leipzig and Edinburgh city parliaments was nearly identical. Both were dominated by wealthy, middle-class, house owners and master artisans, while educated middle-class members played only a minor role. One great difference between the two cities, however, was their respective relationships to the state. While city administrations in Germany were tightly controlled by state government, the British state possessed few means of direct control over municipalities. Astonishingly enough, German cities often gained a greater practical autonomy because they received in principle a universal competence that superseded the authority of British local governments, which required formal state sanction for virtually every single administrative act. While local policy in German cities like Leipzig was dominated by the magistrate, the city parliament of Edinburgh embodied the power centre of British cities. Moreover, the political climate of the two cities differed radically. Voters' rights represented one of these distinctions. In Edinburgh the labour movement developed close ties over decades to the liberal party. In contrast, Leipzig became the birthplace of a German labour movement that distanced itself from liberal policy and the liberal parties of the German middle classes. Schäfer analyses what this meant for political action at the municipal level and demonstrates distinctions between the two with the example of municipal public housing. As Schäfer explains

> The case of Edinburgh represents in many ways a British pattern of piece-meal reform and gradual expansion of participation rights, leaving urban elites ample time to adapt to democratic change. (...) Leipzig's civic elite had lost much of its credibility long before the 1918 revolution. In many respects the Leipzig urban bourgeoisie tried to meet the challenge of urban democracy by authoritarian measures (113).

Schäfer's chapter closes the first section but also offers a valuable segue to the second on the 'Formal and Informal Structures of Continental Europe's City Elites'. Steinar Supphellen's study of the Norwegian town Trondheim, one of the largest towns in eighteenth-century Norway, demonstrates the continuity of a mercantile political elite until well into the nineteenth century. Trondheim was ruled by a group composed of wealthy merchants who were engaged in a Europe-wide trading network, which reached from Dublin to London and Amsterdam, as well as to Hamburg, Königsberg and Riga. The ruling Trondheim merchants were rarely Norwegian natives, however, and most had immigrated from The Netherlands or Germany. Supphellen argues that 'The social elite also included the bishop and a few other prelates, the leading civil administrators, and a few officers. Craftsmen and artisans had little chance of entering this social stratum dominated by the merchants' (119). This power structure survived all municipal reforms in the nineteenth century. Although top administrators came increasingly from outside, the leading figures of the magistrate had little chance of opposing the group of elite merchants, who not only had contacts in high places but also possessed an economic monopoly for financing local projects. The Trondheim magistrate depended on the will of the largest tax payers, leading Supphellen to conclude that the merchants 'formed the economic and social elite and in practice they were the political elite, directly and indirectly' (126).

What seems clear and unambiguous in a Norwegian city becomes disturbingly contradictory in Ralf Roth's chapter 'German Urban Elites in the Eighteenth and Nineteenth Centuries'. Roth stresses the significant fragmentation within German urban elite groups, which requires careful consideration of not only social, political, and confessional distinctions within the power structures of traditional and reformed political bodies but also the roles of independent and self-administered organisations, foundations and associations. Many aspects of city life were self-regulated by special institutions, which were not always closely connected to the political sphere. In short, German city elites included many citizens who were not formally political leaders. Roth first considers the trade and banking city of Frankfurt am Main and then compares this with a series of other German cities including the industrial city of Dortmund in the Ruhr region, the port city Bremen, the manufacturing city Augsburg, the Bavarian residence Munich and the Rhenish trading centre Cologne. One striking conclusion drawn by Roth is that the political climate differed markedly from city to city. While the main characteristics of the Frankfurt elite could be described as liberal, consensus-driven and integrative, Dortmund's elites experienced harsh policy confrontations very similar to Schäfer's description of Leipzig. In Bremen social openness was combined with a predominance of traditional culture and resistance to the widening of political participation. Augsburg shared with Frankfurt and Bremen the characteristic of a socially mixed elite. However, Augsburg's Catholic patricians experienced a sharp loss of influence to the city's Protestant merchants. As in Dortmund, the Augsburg elite preferred a confrontational policy that excluded craftsmen from any higher political position. Munich's elites faced many more political conflicts with the Bavarian state and tended to embrace a unifying policy that considered the interests of different social groups. As in Frankfurt, the Cologne elite was socially heterogeneous. But in contrast to Frankfurt, Cologne's elite included no patricians and a much weaker educated middle class. Additionally the Cologne merchants had a more dominant position. Like Munich, Cologne also embraced a unifying policy, the result of opposition to the Prussian state.

Although the political climate differed from city to city, Germany's urban elite groups shared a number of important structural features. First, most were composed of different social groups and this composition changed during the decades of the nineteenth century. These groups also developed an important network of non-political societies. Roth examines the role of the societies as well the activities of their elite members and argues that over centuries the elite 'formed a complex self-governing regime with a city government and distinct control institutions'. Roth also considers how this associational network interacted with 'guilds, boards of trade, foundations and the boards of religious communities, in addition to the city regime itself. Around 1800, sometimes earlier, sometimes later, these networks were complemented by a cultural network of the associational movement that gave the elite a further platform for its activities'. Roth concludes that the elite in German cities 'was a permanently changing group, including and excluding persons according to the roles they played in political and non-political networks' (160).

Árpád Tóth also emphasises the importance of voluntary societies and informal power structures in his study of the Hungarian city Pest. In Tóth's view associations were of tremendous importance for the emergence of the middle class. At the beginning of the nineteenth century, the domination of oligarchic groups limited political participation but in the 1830s the situation changed dramatically. It was not only protest against corruption but also the emergence of voluntary societies that could be seen as a forerunner of a new city elite dominated by the middle class, which heralded the social shift in urban power. At this point, Pest also emerged as the centre of Hungary's most important associations. Like Roth, Tóth discusses the system of associations and especially the Casino clubs and shows the key role they played in the formation of a new elite. As in German cities, the Pest associations were important instruments for the solution of growing social problems that sprang up at the end of the eighteenth and beginning of the nineteenth centuries. Societies broke down the walls between burghers and non burghers, as well between confessions and social groups. Tóth summarises that voluntary societies recruited 'members from various classes, encouraged the integration of a diverse urban society' (175) and they also 'played a distinctive role in the formation of urban life in Pest' (177).

The relative urbanity of Hungarian Pest stands in sharp contrast to the traditional world of Balkan cities, the topic of Dobinka Parusheva's contribution. This region of Europe was dominated by a peasant culture, and lacked traditional landed elites as well as a bourgeoisie. Even by the end of the nineteenth century end only 20 per cent of the total population lived in towns. Only the capitals and some port cities including Bucharest, Athens and Pireus had populations in excess of 100,000 inhabitants. Municipal government and administration followed the principles of Islam, though this system was speedily undermined by new social forces that emerged from the economic development and the construction of transportation networks. Balkan cities increased in size and complexity 'and then began the transformation of power structures' (184). While the traditional city elite remained in power new actors appeared on the scene including a 'nascent bourgeoisie' and artisan guilds. A new Western European style culture developed and contributed to the disintegration of Balkan society. Parusheva argues that this culture 'ran across religious boundaries. Patterns of settlement changed and were now based on class rather than religion. Muslims, Christians and Jews mingled in the labour unions, guilds and bourgeois clubs' (189). According to Parusheva, 'This was the breeding ground for the emergence of a certain "Balkan bourgeoisie" that achieved a serious "rationalisation of city power"' (192).

This account from the edge of Europe stands in sharp contrast to the anthology's third section, which focuses on city elites in the big metropolises of North America. These concluding chapters demonstrate the dramatic impact of mass democracy and the inherent problems of integrating bourgeois rule with a power structure based on democratic principles. Sven Beckert's chapter on class and politics in New York demonstrates how the wealthy middle class voted for a restricted and antidemocratic franchise in the late 1870s. This was a direct reaction to the political success of working-class and lower middle-class movements. Beckert discusses the fundamental question of a bourgeoisie's rule when its traditional political bastions in the city administration experienced a slow but steady erosion. Significantly, 'the city's economic elite' supported a 'constitutional amendment limiting suffrage rights in New York City' and forced 'citizens of working- and middle-class background' to defend 'an expansive democracy' (212). But this attack was not very successful and New York's city elite changed strategies and embraced the same methods as its Continental European counterparts. In short, they increased their influence through a dense social network of clubs, trade associations, union organisations, all means of promoting a specific bourgeois cultural politics. Although the influence of New York's bourgeoisie over the political machine declined, it was able to maintain its power. As Beckert explains, this influence 'rested to a very large degree on the control of capital, networks and information, not on class identities, class organisations and class mobilisations' (212). This was the reason why 'bourgeois New Yorkers remained politically powerful throughout the nineteenth century despite the changing forms of their political activism' (204).

Somewhat different was the development in Chicago, which Marcus Gräser demonstrates in his contribution on Chicago's educated middle class. Like Beckert, Gräser analyses the relationship of social class to politics and questions why the University of Chicago school of sociology and the progressive movement did not exert greater influence on municipal policies. According to Gräser, although progressive reformers initiated efficient public debates for hygienic and social reforms, their voices did not reach city hall. For example, when Mary McDowell promoted reforms to counter the dirt and smell of Chicago's meat-packing district, the reception of her ideas among intellectuals was striking but politically she was 'unable to penetrate an invisible cordon which seemed to encircle decision-makers in City Hall' (219). Gräser ascribes this to the rapid growth of American cities: 'quick naturalisation and undisputed general male suffrage resulted in the emergence of a political mass-market and the rise of party machines'. And this 'machine politics partially replaced the traditional system of municipal administration' (221). This was very different from the administration of German cities with their close ties to the (upper) middle classes. It also differed sharply from the corporations of British cities where representatives of the (upper) middle class continued to hold key positions. American cities, and especially Chicago, were soon run by lower-middle-class politicians and not by intellectuals or professional administrators. As a consequence, many progressives became dubious of mass democracy. But unlike New York, Chicago's machine-style democracy did not lead to an anti-democratic political backlash. As Gräser explains, 'The de-facto exclusion of the educated middle class from political decision-making significantly distinguished Chicago as well as other American cities from northern and western European cities' (228).

The concluding chapter by Brian Young investigates the patrician culture of Quebec and Montreal. More European than US-American, the elites of these French-Canadian cities enjoyed landed wealth in the Francophone regions of Quebec and a special status that Young describes as 'patrician': 'As a social construction, patricians are characterised more by family, birth, status, and respectability than by enormous capitalist wealth' (236). As a group, of course, patricians more than others transmitted certain pre-industrial legal and feudal relics. Although both Montreal and Quebec were deeply marked by immigration, the 'seigniorial power exercised by both clergy and grande bourgeoisie was equally prominent' (240). From a very early period, the Canadian patricians influenced town development, and they also joined the militia and were connected with British military forces in the struggle against France. The patricians entered the associational world and formed a distinctive milieu: 'Often associated with feudalisation, titles, honorary degrees, chancellorships, and positioning in ceremonies formed an integral part of patrician culture' (246). To explain this growing milieu, Young argues that 'the slower advance of industrial capitalism in Quebec may have permitted its patrician group to persist more effectively using anchors in the church, militia, justice, and land-owning sectors' (247).

What Young's analysis demonstrates for Francophone Canada – that seemingly pre-modern elites maintained their urban hegemony much longer than anticipated – illustrates one of the larger points of the anthology as a whole. Namely, there was rarely if ever a transparent relationship between elite status and urban political control. Indeed, while traditional and new urban elites often dominated political machinery and other resources, this was almost always mediated by a range of cultural, sociological, and historical forces, including the activities of clubs and associations, arts patronage, the contributions of urban planners and professionals, industrialisation and democratisation. As the essays on US-American cities demonstrate so well, the extension of suffrage to most adult males including recent immigrants created working- and lower-middle-class political machines that could easily thwart the designs of cultural and economic elites. Those continental European cities represented in this collection depict an even more complex set of relations where old and new elites vied for urban political control, sometimes cooperating to exclude working class formations or to counter the influences of a princely court, while other times developing more collaborative or integrative models that extended political opportunities to non-elite factions. This latter pattern corresponded closest to the strategies of British urban elites who succeeded in mollifying and pre-empting militant labour and lower-middle-class protest through cooptation.

What the broad geographic and historic comparison of this anthology is able to conclude is that there is no straightforward or simple answer to the question 'Who Ran the Cities?' and instead what historians, sociologists and urban geographers must recognise is the incredible complexity involved in the exercise of modern urban political power. The forces of industry, population growth and immigration have rendered the relatively clear political relations of the pre-modern town strikingly opaque. This presents a formidable challenge for scholars of urban history but also a remarkable and exciting set of research opportunities.

PART I

The British Model – City Elites in the United Kingdom

Elite and Pluralist Power in Eighteenth-Century English Towns: A Case Study of King's Lynn

Emi Konishi

The long eighteenth-century in England (1660–1830) was an age of urbanisation.[1] Not only metropolitan areas but also many provincial towns thrived during this period, buttressed by the political stability that followed the Restoration as well as by the commercial and consumer revolutions and improved agricultural techniques. The provincial towns increased not only in size and number, moreover, but they also became more diversified than before. New types of towns with spa or resort functions appeared, and older towns were refashioned socially and culturally as well as materially.

Originally towns were settlements where most or the majority of the inhabitants were employed in non-agricultural sectors such as commerce or manufacturing. The critical task of a town government, therefore, was to guarantee the inhabitants the ability to maintain their trades and basic living needs. In order to realise this purpose, town authorities and a minority of townsmen were often conferred with some form of political or legal privilege.

From these relatively simple economic and politico-legal bodies, eighteenth-century English towns were transformed into more complicated entities. As the term 'Urban Renaissance' conveys, towns became not only legally-privileged spaces for trade and industry but also venues for social and cultural activities.[2] In provincial towns, especially regional capitals, new types of social organisations like clubs and voluntary associations began to appear, which provided charitable services or organised cultural activities

---

[1] This paper is one of the results of a project funded by the Senshu University Research Grant (2004). I would like to thank Prof. Penelope J. Corfield and Prof. Tadashi Nakano for their critical reading of this paper. I also thank Susan Maddock, the principal archivist of Norfolk Record Office for all her help concerning manuscripts, and Sir Jeremy Bagge for permitting access to his family records.

[2] P. Borsay, *English Urban Renaissance: Culture and Society in the Provincial Town, 1660–1820* (Oxford 1989).

including balls, theatre, or music concerts.[3] With the allure of fashion, shopping, sightseeing and 'modernity', towns attracted people living outside the town, and the influence of an urban lifestyle gradually permeated the surrounding countryside. This urban transformation was caused partly by the pressure of city dwellers who demanded a more comfortable and refined setting. The town government had to meet these expectations for urban amenities, and at the same time to address various 'urban problems' such as crime, poverty, inadequate housing, transport and public hygiene, which grew with the progress of urbanisation. Existing organisations and the financial capacity of traditional government could not deal satisfactorily with these problems and, therefore, new types of 'political' organisations and new ways of financing became necessary.

In this chapter, I will discuss the character and function of the urban elite in this changing *milieu*. I understand the urban elite to be a group of leaders who can wield power or influence over the positions and the decision-making process of town government. Of course, power can be exerted in private domains such as the exercise of paternal power in the family. However, in the context of town governance, power is primarily a 'public' matter and must be exercised and displayed in the 'public sphere', themes that have been broadly discussed by Jürgen Habermas.[4] In contrast to Habermas's politically oriented argument, however this paper will stress other aspects of power and the public sphere: the non-political nature of power including its social and cultural uses in the public sphere, and the reciprocal aspect of power.[5]

With rapid urbanisation, town government could no longer make decisions or implement its projects without the help or co-operation from a wider group of townsmen. Social and cultural venues became parts of the 'public sphere', in that the activities and communication performed there influenced, directly or indirectly, town governance. As the public sphere became more diverse, power also became pluralistic, and so did the elite. Generally speaking, power is not exercised by leaders in a simple top-down process. In order for power to be stably and effectively maintained, it needs the explicit or implicit affirmation of the governed.[6] Power is, therefore, a product of a two-way process between the leaders and the governed, and this process is continually displayed and reproduced in the 'public sphere'. This is particularly true of power exercised in social and cultural spheres, like

---

[3]   P. Clark, *British Clubs and Societies c. 1580–1800: The Origins of an Associational World* (Oxford 2000).

[4]   J. Habermas, *The Structural Transformation of the Public Sphere: An Inquiry into a Category of Bourgeois Society*, translated by T. Burger (Cambridge 1989).

[5]   For further discussion, see E. Konishi, 'The Age of Pluralist Power: The Urban Elite and the Public Sphere in King's Lynn, 1750–1835', Keio University Ph.D. thesis, 2000.

[6]   P. J. Corfield, *Power and the Professions in Britain, 1700–1850* (London 1995).

voluntary associations and fashionable events, which lack the legal support provided for 'political' power.

Taking King's Lynn as an example, this paper will examine the individual careers of persons who possessed significant cultural and social influence but no political power. The stereotyped image of the English urban elite seems to be that of wealthy, male, urban inhabitants, often merchants and Anglicans, with political power as freemen or town burgesses. In order to challenge this common image, in section two, I propose a wider, multi-dimensional interpretation of a 'new' urban elite in King's Lynn, which relies on a pluralist approach. The relationship between the traditional older elite and the new rising one is often said to have been antagonistic and competitive.[7] However, this claim does not apply to King's Lynn in the long eighteenth-century, as I will discuss in section three. Keeping this in mind, the concluding section will reappraise the historical impact that the 1835 Municipal Corporation Act had on the town government of King's Lynn.

Multi-dimensional interpretation

King's Lynn was the third largest town in the county of Norfolk, in the east of England. The estimated population of 5,000–6,000 in 1700 did not change significantly for a half century, but by 1789 the population had increased to 9,089.[8] According to the national census, it rose more gradually to 10,096 in 1801, 10,259 in 1811, 12,253 in 1821 and 13,370 in 1831.[9] Surrounded by rich agricultural terrain, King's Lynn had been a prosperous port town from the medieval period into the nineteenth century, exporting mainly corn. Compared with the rapidly developing industrial towns in the North and the Midlands, King's Lynn in the eighteenth century grew relatively slowly and modestly in terms of economy and population. Nevertheless, at least until the railway was constructed in the mid-nineteenth century, King's Lynn maintained its importance as a regional centre. In respect to its relationship with the nation, King's Lynn had been incorporated and granted several privileges by royal charter since the eleventh century. King's Lynn was also one of the parliamentary boroughs and had two members of Parliament who

---

[7]   This interpretive framework was developed by the Webbs in the early 1900s. See S. and B. Webb, *English Local Government*, 5 vols. (London 1908). Recent urban historians, however, have presented more flexible interpretations of this matter. See R. Sweet, *The English Town, 1680–1840: Government, Society and Culture* (London 1999).

[8]   As there are no formal records for the population of King's Lynn before 1789, earlier figures are only estimates. The population of 1789 was assessed by the Guardians of the Poor. King's Lynn Borough Archive (KLA), KL/C7/15 Hall Book, 14 Feb. 1789.

[9]   Commission for inquiring into the state of the several municipal corporation in England and Wales, *Report on the Borough of King's Lynn* (London 1835), 2423.

were able to reflect the town's local interests at the level of national politics. The MPs for King's Lynn during the eighteenth century included Sir Robert Walpole, a Whig and the first prime minister in England, and his son, Horace Walpole.

Figure 1.1   William Raistrick's plan of King's Lynn, 1725

Source: Norfolk Record Office, BL/4/1.

Traditionally, the urban elite were those holding political power through legally defined and institutionalised means: that is, the senior officials of town government under whatever institution, whether formally incorporated or not. In this context, the council members of King's Lynn, comprising twelve aldermen (including the mayor) and 18 common councilmen, could be classified as the elite. These members were the representatives of the freemen and the formal members of the municipal corporation. However, these 31 men represented only a small percentage of all inhabitants.[10] They were a

---

[10]   The freemen in Lynn had the vote and several kinds of economic privileges. Based on the freemen register, it is estimated that approximately 300 freemen lived in King's Lynn at the end of the eighteenth century. See Norfolk and Norwich Archaeological Society, ed., *A Calendar of Freemen of Lynn 1292–1836* (Norwich 1913). Thus the freemen made up three per cent of a total population of 9,000.

select and politically privileged body, an elite. However, in order to join the urban elite in eighteenth-century King's Lynn, it was not always necessary to be a member of a ruling political institution. This change was partly caused by the decline of the role and status of freemen in the urban community. As the field of activities of non-freemen expanded, there was a corresponding decrease in the corporation's power.[11] Consequently, there emerged a number of urban leaders who did not join the formal political organisations but who became engaged mainly in non-political fields. As urban society became diversified and more pluralistic, the elite included a wider range of people than has been traditionally assumed.

One example of this new elite was Daniel Gurney, who came from a prestigious banking family, well-known for its Quaker affiliation. The Quaker Daniel Gurney attained significant wealth through his banking business but held no political office in King's Lynn, although his bank was sometimes involved in depositing or disbursing money for local government works.[12] It is most unlikely that Daniel Gurney was excluded from holding a political post because of his religion. In fact, King's Lynn had been exceptionally generous to dissenters. Indeed, the Quaker Joseph Taylor became the Mayor of King's Lynn in 1800. Instead of political offices, Daniel Gurney was deeply involved in several important voluntary associations. He devoted his energy to the foundation and management of the first medical hospital in the area, the West Norfolk and Lynn Hospital. In 1835, with medical specialists playing a central role, a voluntary association consisting of many influential people in King's Lynn was organised for the purpose of founding a new hospital. Gurney was clearly one of the most committed people in the association. A local historian J. D. Thew remembered in the later nineteenth century that

> The West Norfolk and Lynn Hospital is a standing monument to the memory of Daniel Gurney, who through many years of his life not only contributed to its resources, but, as chairman of its governing committee, took an active part in its financial and general management.[13]

As Thew wrote, it was natural for people of that time to regard him as a member of the elite:

---

[11]   E. Konishi, 'Change and Continuity of Local Administrative Bodies: Special Reference to King's Lynn in the Long Eighteenth Century', *The Comparative Urban History Review*, 22, no. 2, 2003, 41–58 (in Japanese); E. Konishi, 'Local Administration and Community in Long-Eighteenth-Century England: Special Reference to the King's Lynn Paving Commission', in Study Group of British Urban and Rural Communities and Tohoku University Economics and Business History Group, eds, *The Studies of British Urban History* (in Japanese) (Tokyo 2004), 193–220.

[12]   Daniel Gurney served in the office of the County High Sheriff.

[13]   J. D. Thew, *Personal Recollections* (King's Lynn 1891), 145.

> It was as a philanthropist that Mr. Gurney was best known to the inhabitants of Lynn. Foremost either in starting or aiding every good work for the benefit of his fellows, whether rich or poor, Mr. Gurney set a munificent example.[14]

Another example was the non-freeman attorney, Harvey Goodwin, who was likewise not a central member of the political organisation. Neither an alderman nor a common councilman, Goodwin participated only in the Paving Commission, which was a statutory commission established by an act of Parliament in 1803. This commission was a new political organisation and not a traditional organ of the corporation. As a commission member, he became one of the biggest purchasers of bonds issued by the commission in order to raise money for its projects.[15] It seems that Goodwin's main concerns were social and cultural rather than political, and he was known foremost as a philanthropist. When he died in 1819, he received the following tributes from local newspapers:

> The inhabitants appreciating the excellency of his character, manifested on the day of his funeral such marked respect for a private individual, as rarely witnessed. The shop windows throughout the day were closed, and numbers of every class in Society went on the London Road to meet the gloomy funeral procession.[16]

Sermons of tribute were held in both the Anglican Church and the Dissenters' chapels, which was very unusual.[17] Clearly, Goodwin held his elite position irrespective of any religious boundaries. In addition, through voluntary subscriptions by King's Lynn residents, a monument to the memory of Harvey Goodwin was erected in the church at the cost of £180.[18] It seems that, despite his political career, he was recognised by the people more for his social awareness and charitable works.

It has been observed that there was a geographical expansion of the eighteenth century urban elite. As people living in the country began to share experiences with urban dwellers, a new type of urban elite living in the countryside began to emerge. Some country gentry living near King's Lynn illustrate the phenomenon of elites who did not hold urban political power but had social and cultural power in Lynn. Anthony Hamond, for example,

---

[14] Ibid.

[15] The largest purchaser of bonds was another commissioner, George Hogg, merchant and esquire, freeman, and bought £1,000 worth of bonds. The second largest amount was Harvey Goodwin's £900. KLA, KL/PC/2/1-4 Paving Commissioners' Minutes, 1803–1830; KL/PC/4/1-2 Paving Commissioners' Securities Register, 1803–1865. See Konishi, 'Change and Continuity', 50–51 and 54–5. For further discussion see the next section.

[16] *Norwich, Yarmouth, and Lynn Courier*, 1 May 1819.

[17] Ibid.

[18] *Norwich Mercury*, 29 May 1819; *Norwich, Yarmouth, and Lynn Courier*, 5 June 1819.

was a traditional member of the lesser gentry residing in a country house near King's Lynn. He had connections through marriage with members of the Bagge family, which sent several family members to the King's Lynn council. It was part of Hamond's routine to visit King's Lynn every Tuesday for meetings with his attorney regarding land management or for shopping at the weekly market and other activities.[19] Hamond was not a member of the council or any commission in King's Lynn and was not involved in the town's political affairs.[20] However, he was occasionally called to formal meetings concerning the administrative matters of King's Lynn and asked for his comments.[21] For example, he attended the Turnpike Meeting in 1815.[22] On another occasion, he was called to a meeting of the Paving Committee of the corporation in order to discuss how to obtain the approval of the Paving Commission, although he was not a committee member.[23] Moreover, he purchased £600 worth of the Paving Commission's bonds collected for promoting the activities of the commission, the eighth largest amount of 86 investors.[24] In addition, Hamond attended every important social and cultural event in King's Lynn. He was an active member of the main voluntary associations, including the benevolent societies and the charity school.[25] He also made public appearances in cultural events such as concerts, assemblies and balls.[26] Country gentry though he was, his lifestyle was identical to those of the members of the elite living inside the town. In this sense, he should be regarded as part of the urban elite.

With the expansion of urban sociability and public arenas, women acquired greater opportunities to play important roles in these social and cultural spheres. In recent studies, women's roles in the public sphere, especially in the cultural sphere such as assemblies and theatres, have been positively re-evaluated, although it has also been argued that toward the end of eighteenth century women increasingly withdrew from the 'public' to the domestic sphere.[27] Some scholars have stressed women's important position

---

[19]   Norfolk Record Office (NRO), HMN 4/37/21, Hamond's Diary.

[20]   In 1812, W. Richards wrote that the low rate of attendance for the council meetings was caused by the fact that the many council members were not residents of the town proper. As council members were not restricted to the urban residents of King's Lynn, Hamond could have become a political member. W. Richards, *History of Lynn* (King's Lynn 1812), 1156.

[21]   Several cases have appeared in his diary. NRO, HMN 4/37/21.

[22]   Ibid., 23 Nov. 1815.

[23]   KLA, KL/PC1/1, Paving Committee Minutes, 18 March 1791.

[24]   KLA, KL/PC4/1-2.

[25]   His name sometimes appeared in local newspapers such as *The Norwich Mercury*, *The Norfolk Chronicle*, *The Lynn and Wisbech Packet*, or *The Norwich, Yarmouth and Lynn Courier*.

[26]   NRO, HMN 4/37/21.

[27]   L. Davidoff and C. Hall presented this thesis in *Family Fortunes: Men and Women of the English Middle Class, 1780–1850* (London 1987). However, this has been challenged by others, for example, M. C. Martin, 'Women and Philanthropy in

in terms of social display, which was most characteristic of urban society. However, others maintain that women were not independent agents but merely the means for indicating the status of men, whom they served as assistants. Consider the case of Pleasance Bagge, a clergyman's daughter who married into one of the most prominent merchant families in King's Lynn.[28] According to her diary, Pleasance participated in many cultural events in fashionable society, as did many other women of similarly high social standing.[29] She no doubt attended such events wearing the expensive accessories mentioned in the Bagges' inventories.[30] She was also active in the social sphere; she was a principal member of the Visiting Society, a group that visited and attended to the needs of the sick and the poor.[31] Formed in 1826, the society was organised and managed by women for the purposes of charity, and, as every newspaper understood, was one of the most active and important voluntary associations in King's Lynn.[32] Thus elite women were not always known by their association with their husbands or as 'decoration' for social organisations.

There is no doubt that the people mentioned above were regarded as members of the elite of King's Lynn. The examples of these individuals show that the eighteenth century was a period in which power in King's Lynn was recognised for its social and cultural as well as political and economic influences. The urban elite were able to take leadership roles in one or more arenas and were not restricted only to the political sphere. In other words, a pluralistic elite existed.

Walthamstow and Leyton, 1740–1870', *London Journal,* 19, 1995, 119–50; A. Vickery, 'Golden Age to Separate Sphere? A Review of the Categories and Chronology of English Women's History', *Historical Journal,* 36, 1993, 383–414.

[28]   Pleasance Bagge's father was the Rev. Hulton, who was from one of the oldest families of the gentry in west Norfolk. The head branch of the family was awarded the title of Baronet due to the great effort of the Bagge family.

[29]   NRO, BL Vla (XII) Pleasance Bagge's Diary.

[30]   NRO, BL XII d Grace Bagge's Holdings of Diamond and Jewels; Bagge Family's Private Collection, Bagge Family's Holdings of Jewels.

[31]   KLA, KL/TC2/2/1, Public Meetings and Voluntary Committee Minutes. It is not quite certain that Pleasance Bagge joined the society as a committee member. Nevertheless, she described attending the 'Ladies Visiting Society'. See NRO, BL Vla (XII), 12 Jan. 1837. From this entry, it is clear that Pleasance Bagge was not just an ordinary member but had a responsible position in the society. Although the Visiting Society was initially organised only by women, male organisers appeared in the 1830s. This was likely due to a change in the policy.

[32]   The other associations where women took the initiative but did not directly manage were the Soup Charity Society and the Child Bed Linen Society in King's Lynn.

The relationship among the elites: conflict or co-operation?

This essay has demonstrated the emergence of new types of elites in eighteenth century King's Lynn. An additional question is if there were power struggles or antagonisms between the old and the new and between the different types of elites? It is generally assumed that there were severe conflicts in many towns between various kinds of urban elites, including political and the other types of leaders. Several studies have shown that there were large oppositions even within the political elite – between leaders of traditional political organisations and those of new ones. This was not the case in King's Lynn, however, and such confrontations were relatively rare. Far from antagonism, one is struck by the harmony and co-operation among different types of elites in public activities and in the private sphere. In this section, we will first consider the relationship between the Paving Commission and the corporation, since historians have considered these two organisations to have been bitter political rivals.

The Paving Commission was the sixth and the largest statutory commission in King's Lynn. With the approval of Parliament, it was established in 1803 for the purpose of improving the town's infrastructure.[33] The commission was concerned with constructing and paving new roads, streets and walks, maintaining and mending existing streets, buildings and the market, providing streetlights, and naming new streets as well as erecting street signs in every street.[34] At the same time, the commission considered matters concerning policing and sanitation, and problems such as foul air and other annoyances.

Responsibility for most of these services had previously been taken by the corporation. It should be noted, however, that in King's Lynn the Paving Commission did not deprive the corporation of a role. In fact, the statutory commission was a useful ally for the corporation, which was facing growing financial and administrative burdens in coping with residents' increasing demands. In other words, the corporation entrusted some of the works that it could no longer properly handle within its own existing financial and institutional capacity to the commission, which was organised for the purpose of dealing specifically with such problems. Therefore, although the activities of the Paving Commission and the Corporation partly overlapped, they did not compete. Rather, they had a complementary relationship and sometimes even co-operated together. A project concerning the improvement of the market is a good example of their collaboration.

---

[33] The Act of Parliament, 43 Geo. 3. for Paving & c. the Borough of King's Lynn (1803). It was amended in 1806. 46 Geo. 3. for Amending, Altering, and Enlarging the Power of the said Act (1806).

[34] KLA, KL/PC2/1–4.

Table 1.1 Members of Paving Commission and Council, 1803–1810

a) Members of the Paving Commission and Council

Name	Occupation*		
Allen, Maxey	merchant/distiller	CA	F
Allen, Thomas	gentleman	C	F
Bagge, Thomas Philip	merchant	CA	F
Bagge, William jun.	esquire	C	F
Blencowe, John Prescott	merchant	C	F
Edwards, George	merchant	CA	F
Edwards, John	esquire	CA	F
Elsden, Charles	merchant	C	F
Everard, Edward	merchant	A	F
Everard, Scarlet	merchant	CA	F
Green, Robert	merchant	C	F
Hadley, Samuel jun.	merchant	C	F
Hogg, George jun.	gentleman	CA	F
Lawrence, Joseph	gentleman	CA	F
Self, Lionel jur	merchant	A	F
Stockdale, John Bailey	merchant	C	F
Swatman, William	merchant	C	F
Toosey, James Bramall	merchant	C	F
Whincop, Robert	attorney	C	F

b) Members of the Council

Name	Occupation		
Bagge, Henry Lee	merchant/banker	C	F
Bagge, Thomas	merchant	A	F
Bagge, William	merchant	A	F
Bagge, William Wilson	banker	C	F
Bell, Henry	esquire	A	F
Bonner, Gamble Yates	merchant	C	F
Bowker, Alexander	merchant	A	F
Cary, John	merchant	A	F
Case, William	gentleman	A	F
Dixon, Johnson	merchant	C	F
Elsden, Edmund	esquire	C	F
Elsden, Edmund Rolfe	merchant	A	F
Everard, Edward jun.	merchant	A	F
Freeman, Robert	merchant	A	F
Hemington, John	gentleman	A	F
Hogg, Fountaine	merchant	C	F

Hogg, William	merchant	C	F
Lane, Frederic	solicitor	C	F
Taylor, Joseph	merchant	A	F
Wardell, John	grocer	C	F

c) Members of the Paving Commission

Allen, Stephen	Rev., clerk	F
Audley, Thomas	merchant	F
Bailey, George	gentleman	NF
Bailey, Thomas	tallowchandler/grocer	F
Baker, Samuel	merchant	F
Birkbeck, John	banker	NF
Blackburne, Thomas	merchant	F
Brame, Thomas	merchant	F
Cooper, Thomas	upholster	F
Dixon, John	grocer	F
Gales, Thomas	druggist	NF
Goodwin, Harvey	gentleman	NF
Hankinson, Robert	Rev., clerk	NF
Hankinson, Thomas	gentleman	NF
Hawkins, George	n. a.	NF
Hedley, Isaguey	n. a.	NF
Hogg, George**	merchant	F
Lake, William	mariner	F
Lane, Samuel	esquire	F
Lee, Johnson	n. a.	NF
Newham, Samuel	surveyor/builder	NF
Newman, Charle	n. a.	NF
Oxley, Thomas	merchant	F
Peek, George	grocer	NF

Note: F (Freeman), NF (Non Freeman), n. a. (not available), A (Alderman), C (Councilman), CA (Alderman promoted from councilman during the period)

* Occupations are based on the information of the Freemen Register. However, the ones for the people who did not mention their occupations or non-freemen are from the Paving Commission's and so on.

Source: KLA, KL/C7/15-16, KL/PC4/1-2, KL/PC2/1-4, and *A Calendar of Freemen of Lynn*.

As for funding, the statutory commission was permitted to levy a local rate for its activities. But the financial base was initially extremely weak. In order to raise money, the Paving Commission had to issue and sell bonds.[35] Between 1803 and 1810, there were 86 investors, including the corporation itself, who paid from £100 to £1,000.[36] The larger the sum of bonds one person purchased, the greater his say or influence. For example, a freeman merchant, Thomas Bagge was the third largest purchaser of bonds (£800), and a freeman merchant, Edward Everard, was the tenth largest (£500). Both were council members but not members of the Paving Commission. The Rev. Edward Edwards, a freeman and the third largest purchaser of bonds, was the clerk of the corporation but neither a member of the council nor a member of the commission. The previously mentioned Anthony Hamond, a member of the country gentry and non-freeman, was the eighth largest (£600), and bankers Henry Birkbeck and John Gurney, and surgeon Thomas Dixon, all non-freemen, purchased £400 worth of bonds each.

Apart from these investors, there were 40 commission members who took responsibility for the commission. They were selected from wider social groups than the council members of the corporation; it did not matter whether they were freemen or non-freemen. As some historians have claimed, the commission members included newcomers who did not have any experience in the old political sphere. However, it should be stressed that there were council members among the commission members as well. The total number of commission and council members in the period 1803–1810 was 63. Among these, 20 participated only in the council, 24 were only in the commission, and the remaining 19 (30 per cent) were in both (see Table 1.1). In short, almost a third was involved in both new and old political organisations. Thus for the overlapping membership there was clearly no competition.[37]

Against this background of harmony among the elite, there was a change in the nature and the composition of the corporation and the urban community. Although the council remained the supreme institution in the corporation, it needed to conform to a changing situation in urban society by

---

[35]   There were two other ways to collect money: to ask for donations and to issue annuity bonds. There were only a few people who made donations for the commission such as the MPs in King's Lynn, Horatio Walpole and Martin Browne Folkes, and the Gurney, Birkbeck and Taylor Bank. The latter method was not initially popular, but it became important in the 1830s. See KLA, KL/PC4/4, Copies of Grants of Annuity.

[36]   KLA, KL/PC2/1–4; KL/PC/4/1–2. See the table 3 in Konishi, 'Change and Continuity', 54–5.

[37]   Unlike King's Lynn, where the new and old elites had similar trade interests, in some towns, there was antagonism, since the interests of the new elite, in manufacturing for example, clashed with those of the old elite.

setting up relatively independent committees,[38] and by holding public meetings under the council's control. The important point is that not only the council members but also other freemen and non-freemen were now permitted to attend public meetings and given an equal opportunity to comment on public matters.[39] This was partly because the council needed professional knowledge to deal with problems such as medical matters, but also because it could no longer ignore the interests of non-freemen, for example in trading matters related to the new rich. Non-freemen were not formal members of the corporation, and previously their requests had not been considered seriously at council meetings. Even ordinary freemen did not have chances to interact with council members. Including people from outside the council in the council's public meetings meant that a wider

Figure 1.2 A charity dinner to celebrate the return of peace in 1814

The dinner for 6,000 citizens was given in the Tuesday Market Place to celebrate the return of peace in 1814 after the long war against France.

Source: King's Lynn and West Norfolk Borough Council.

---

[38] Initially, the committees had quite close ties to the corporation. However, in the second half of the eighteenth century, the committees' independence from the council became stronger.

[39] For example, there were public meetings dealing with the outbreak of cholera, the poor, river management, a petition to the Parliament, etc. See KLA, KL/TC2/2/1.

stratum of urban society became *de facto* participants in the traditional political sphere.

A public charity dinner in 1814 offers one example of this policy of inclusion. The dinner was held in celebration of the end of the Napoleonic wars. Some 6,500 poor people, more than half of the population, were invited to the dinner, which was one of the largest events in King's Lynn in this period.[40] Public meetings were held to discuss preparations for the dinner: how to collect money; how to organise; how to choose the poor to be invited; and who should provide the food and drink for the dinner.[41] Despite the fact that the dinner was formally organised by the corporation, not only the leaders in the political sphere but also a large number of non-political social leaders played an important role, regardless of their political influence or office.

Outside the political sphere, we also see complementary or collaborative relationships. One example of co-operation between the corporation and a voluntary association, the New Theatre Society, was the construction of a new theatre in 1813. In the English 'Urban Renaissance', there was a distinct trend of building an impressive theatre to compete with other towns. The theatre was not just a central place of entertainment but also a symbol of a town's wealth, pride and identity. As a result, many prominent people in King's Lynn from different spheres became members of the New Theatre Society. On the other hand, the corporation also provided considerable assistance, although the initiative for the project was taken by the society. Another organisation, the Theatre Committee, which was different from the New Theatre Society, was created under the auspices of the council and had several meetings to discuss the new theatre with the members of the association.[42] The amount of money necessary for building a new facility was so high that the committee had to open a subscription. Nearly 40 people, from various urban elites in Norfolk – political and economic as well as cultural and social – contributed sums ranging from £25 to £200. Reflecting the cultural aspect of this project, it is natural that besides the political or social elites many members of the cultural elite, including aristocrats and the country gentry, were involved. The consensus of the Theatre Committee seems to have been one of support for the Theatre Society, and, as a result, the corporation became the largest subscriber.

Another example of the co-operation of voluntary associations and the corporation was the Visiting Society established in 1826. Mentioned in the previous section, this association was managed by women whose purposes

---

[40]   The figure of 6,500 poor people (more than half of the whole population) is quite big, but the council was still worried that the uninvited might become angry and thwart the party. At the meeting, this and other issues were discussed to ensure that the event went smoothly. Ibid.

[41]   Ibid, July 1816.

[42]   KLA, KL/C8/41, Theatre Committee's Minutes.

were 'the encouragement of industry and frugality, amongst the poor, by visits at their own habitations; the relief of real distress, whether arising from sickness or other causes; and the prevention of mendacity and imposture'.[43] The objectives for the new organisation were actually decided at a public meeting in December 1826 before the association was formally founded.[44]

In many other cases, the apparently disparate elites were united. In the cultural sphere, for example, the stewards of the Lynn Subscription Assemblies illustrated the unity of the King's Lynn elite.[45] The assemblies were held every month in the winter social season, always organised by different 'respectable' people. Some of these were central figures in the town and worked as members of the municipal government as well as serving on the committees of voluntary associations. Besides traditional merchant families and country gentry, these assemblies included successful new men from the business world. On the other hand, some people, both town and country dwellers, were less active in political and social affairs, participating in these matters only by making contributions to public subscriptions. In the assemblies, these pluralistic elites worked in co-operation to create a lively urban scene.

Thus, the various public spheres were neither completely separated nor opposed to each other. At least in King's Lynn, despite several small conflicts, a united public sphere could be observed. Therefore, the urban elite could be active in multifarious spheres and could perform their role as leaders without confrontation.

Reappraisal of the Municipal Corporation Act

This portrayal of the elite in the long eighteenth-century of King's Lynn casts a different light on the accepted interpretation of the 1835 Municipal Corporation Act, which has maintained that the 1835 reform finally brought power to a new group of men and hence a sudden change in the structure of local government. The historian M. L. Bradfer-Lawrence wrote that 'the death knell of the autocratic merchant community of Lynn' was sounded by the 1835 Act.[46] Indeed, many council members changed, and the new political leaders were drawn not only from among the merchants but also from a wider field of occupations, especially the professions.

---

[43] KLA, KL/TC2/2/1, 18 Dec. 1826.

[44] Ibid.

[45] Subscription assemblies were announced and advertised in the local newspapers, from which the information here is mainly drawn. For the name of the newspaper, see footnote 25.

[46] H. L. Bradfer-Lawrence, 'The Merchants of Lynn', in C. Ingleby, ed., *A Supplement to Blomfield's Norfolk* (Norwich 1929), 145–203, esp. 203.

But as suggested in the previous section, these claims are exaggerated. In fact, ten older town council members in 1834–1835 were re-elected as members of the new council in 1835, and all of them, except the merchant Oxley English were from traditional elite families.[47] The other 14 members were new recruits. They did not have any prior experience in the council, and were from outside the old political sphere. Additionally, some new members had connections with families, such as the Bagges, Hoggs, or Everards, who were at the centre of the old political elite. For example, the new councillor James Dillingham had presided over the business of the Hogg family for a long time.[48] Another was William Bonner, who had been apprenticed to 'Everard, Bagge and Hogg, Merchants and Co-partner'; and William Clifton had been apprenticed to Edmund Rolfe Elsden, another traditional elite family related to the Everards.[49]

As many new council men did not seem to have special connections to the traditional elite families, it appeared that the 1835 Act gave huge power to a new set of political leaders. However, it is not true that the new political leaders appeared suddenly on the public scene of King's Lynn after 1835. In fact, prior to that date they had already been active in the public sphere as social and cultural leaders.

An example to illustrate this can be found in the person of the banker Francis Cresswell, who was described in Thew's *Personal Recollection* in 1891 as

> an active man in the public life of Lynn'. He was a member of the Corporation, and also of the Paving Commission; was of for several years churchwarden of St. Margaret's; and took an active part in the founding and supporting of schools in the town, and all its charitable organisations. He filled the office of Mayor in 1845.[50]

According to this description, Francis Cresswell appears equally influential in both the political and social spheres. His appearance, though, in the political sphere was not until 1835. Subsequently he became a central political figure in the corporation, the Paving Commission and the parish vestry. He therefore worked like a 'new man'. Prior to 1835, Cresswell had been recognised as part of the social elite, involved with charitable organisations, and at the centre of the cultural elite. Furthermore, Cresswell had close connections with one of the most traditional families, the Bagges; he was involved in the banking business with William and Thomas Philip Bagge in the early nineteenth century.[51] Such common economic interests sometimes

---

[47]   Concerning the council members in the long eighteenth century, see KLA, KL/C7/14-16, Hall Books.
[48]   Thew, *Recollections*, 146.
[49]   *A Calendar*.
[50]   Ibid. 146.
[51]   'The Bagge Dynasty at Stradsett', *The Field*, 17 May 1986, 60–62.

contributed to the uniting of the urban elite. Similarly, the names of other 'new political leaders' such as J. Platten, Dr. Wayte and J. B. Stockdale had already been seen on the list of the committees of major voluntary associations in Lynn or subscription balls alongside those of many traditional political leaders. This interaction assisted in creating harmonious relationships between various elites in the town before the 'new political leaders' appeared in and after 1835.

Thus, through common experiences, such as participation in committees on the same voluntary associations and serving as stewards in the subscription assemblies, the new political leaders had already worked together harmoniously with the old political leaders in the social and cultural spheres of King's Lynn. They had long shared the roles of the urban elite in different capacities. Therefore, it is understandable that rather than confusion, there was continuity before and after the reform of the corporation in King's Lynn. There is no doubt that the reform in 1835 brought the political system into line with social reality – an important change, indeed – but this does not mean that it created an entirely new elite. The urbanisation of long eighteenth-century England was a multi-faceted process and differed from one place to another, from one type of town to another. King's Lynn, a traditional provincial centre supported by commerce and agriculture, was not like the rapidly growing industrial towns in the north where discord and confrontation were apt to come to the fore. But the case study of this provincial town could apply to many other middle-rank towns, especially the urban settlements in agricultural eastern and southern England. Long before 1835, the urban elite in King's Lynn extended to many occupations, including professionals and manufacturers as well as merchants; it also crossed the geographical boundaries of town and country, the religious division between Anglicans and dissenters, and even gender differences.

CHAPTER TWO

Urban Power, Industrialisation and Political Reform: Swansea Elites in the Town and Region, 1780–1850

Louise Miskell

Introduction

Recent research on the history of British urban elites has produced some important studies of the character, activities and connections of urban, social and cultural actors.[1] The geographical spread of these studies has been uneven, however, with the midlands, the north of England and Scotland providing the primary focus for this scholarship.[2] Wales has fared less well. On the face of it Welsh towns, with their relatively small populations and their apparently minute middle-class presence, have little to offer the historian of elites and urban power structures in the nineteenth century. From a wider, British perspective, urbanisation in Wales has been seen as lagging behind developments in other parts of the country.[3] Despite some pioneering studies in the 1960s and 1970s, Welsh urban history has also, to some extent, fallen behind.[4]

There are of course some notable exceptions to this picture. Cardiff, which became Wales' most populous town by 1881, achieved city status in

---

[1]   See for example, W. D. Rubinstein, *Elites and the Wealthy in Modern British History. Essays in Social and Economic History* (Brighton 1987); J. Smith, 'Urban elites c.1830–1930 and urban history', *Urban History*, 27, 2000, 255–75; R. J. Morris, 'Voluntary societies and British urban elites, 1780–1850: an analysis', *Historical Journal*, 26, 1983, 95–118.

[2]   N. Morgan and R. H. Trainor, 'The dominant classes', in W. H. Fraser and R. J. Morris, eds, *People and Society in Scotland*, vol. 2: *1830–1914* (Edinburgh 1990), 103–37; R. H. Trainor, *Black Country Elites. The Exercise of Authority in and Industrial Area, 1830–1900* (Oxford 1993); R. H. Trainor, 'The elite', in W. H. Fraser and I. Maver, eds, *Glasgow*, vol. 2: 1830–1912 (Manchester 1997), 227–64.

[3]   P. Clark and R. Houston, 'Culture and leisure, 1700–1840', in P. Clark, ed., *The Cambridge Urban History of Britain, vol. 2: 1540–1840* (Cambridge 2000), 577–8.

[4]   See for example, H. Carter, *The Towns of Wales. A Study in Urban Geography* (Cardiff 1965), and E. G. Bowen, 'Carmarthen: an urban study', *Archaeologia Cambrensis*, 17, 1968, 1–7.

1905 and became the principality's official capital city in 1955, has rightly attracted attention from historians interested in the study of urban elites and their power base.[5] Prior to Cardiff's growth in the second half of the nineteenth century, however, the town of Swansea, located further west along the south Wales coast, had arguably the best claim to being Wales's premier urban centre. From the early decades of the eighteenth century, Swansea emerged as an important industrial location, with coal and copper forming its two main economic pillars. In addition, from the 1780s onwards, the town also developed into a fashionable sea-bathing resort with a range of tourist amenities that no other town in the region could offer. This combination of industrial wealth and well-developed urban facilities enabled Swansea to establish itself as the principal urban centre within an important industrial region. Moreover the regional dimension provided an important sphere for elite activity beyond the confines of the town. This was particularly important for the new crop of industrialists, who were among Swansea's wealthiest and most important employers, but who found themselves largely excluded from the key posts in the town's local government institutions through the first three decades of the nineteenth century. These people were able to by-pass the restrictions that operated within the town and find an outlet for their ambitions within institutions that had a wider, regional and even national focus.

Swansea's rise to prominence

The 'Swansea region' with which this chapter is concerned extended along the south Wales coast as far west as the town of Llanelli in Carmarthenshire, as far east as Taibach, and inland along the river valleys of the Tawe, Nedd and Afan, all within a twenty-mile radius of the town of Swansea. At the root of the region's industrial growth was its location at the western end of the south Wales coalfield where abundant seams of bituminous coal lay very close to the coast. Although the region's coal reserves provided the foundation for its economic growth, it was as a copper smelting centre that it really earned its industrial reputation. Two factors influenced developments in this sector. Firstly, the coal found in this section of the coalfield was particularly well suited for use in ore smelting furnaces. Secondly, the coast of south Wales was just a short sea passage away from Cornwall, where Europe's most important copper ore field was located. This favourable location ensured that for much of this period, the Swansea region was the undisputed world centre for the production of refined copper. According to

---

[5]   J. Davies, *Cardiff and the Marquesses of Bute* (Cardiff 1981); M. J. Daunton, *Coal Metropolis. Cardiff 1870–1914* (Leicester 1977); N. Evans, 'Urbanisation, elite attitudes and philanthropy: Cardiff, 1850–1914', *International Review of Social History*, 27, 1982, 290–323.

one recent business historian it was also 'the most highly concentrated major British industry in the eighteenth and nineteenth centuries'.[6]

Swansea had emerged as the industrial centre of this region by the 1720s, when the banks of its river became the favoured location for the establishment of new copper smelting works. Improvements in transportation infrastructure, especially the development of the Swansea valley canal from the 1790s and the establishment of a harbour trust in the town in 1791 brought further advantages, and by the beginning of the nineteenth century there were some seven copper smelting works located in the vicinity of the town. Swansea was also the region's dominant coal port. It was blessed with a wide and sheltered natural harbour which by the end of the eighteenth century was shipping an annual total of 244,976 tons of coal from its shores.[7] In addition pottery production was carried on successfully within the town, with two rival earthenware manufactories operating there by 1814.[8] These industrial developments also stimulated population growth. The town's inhabitants had numbered around 1,000 in the last quarter of the sixteenth century. Even by 1750 there were still fewer than 2,000.[9] The demographic momentum increased in the second half of the eighteenth century, however, and a population of over 6,000 was recorded in the 1801 census, making Swansea Wales' second most populous town.

But industrial growth was only part of the story of Swansea's increasing importance. From the late eighteenth century it also achieved considerable success as a fashionable bathing resort. The decline in continental travel during the Napoleonic war years stimulated increasing demand for domestic leisure facilities in Britain. Towns like Swansea with an attractive coastline suitable for sea bathing were becoming favoured destinations, and from the 1780s onwards Swansea developed a range of facilities for these seasonal visitors. The latest bathing machines were acquired, a new theatre was built, libraries and reading rooms were expanded, and work also commenced on the building of new public assembly rooms complete with spaces for reading, billiards and cards, drinking, dining and dancing.[10] By 1804 a new provincial newspaper, the *Cambrian*, was being printed in the town. There was a well-respected grammar school, to which middle-class merchants and industria-

---

[6]   E. Newell, '"Copperopolis": the rise and fall of the copper industry in the Swansea district, 1826–1921', *Business History*, 32, 1990, 75–97, esp. 77.

[7]   Figures abstracted from J. Williams, *Digest of Welsh Historical Statistics*, vol. 1 (Cardiff 1985), 318–31.

[8]   H. L. Hallesy, *The Glamorgan Pottery Swansea, 1814–38* (Llandysul 1995).

[9]   W. S. K. Thomas, 'Municipal government in Swansea, 1485–1640', in S. Williams, ed., *Glamorgan Historian*, vol. 1 (Cowbridge 1963), 27–36, esp. 27–8, and A. H. John, 'Introduction. Glamorgan, 1700–1750', in G. Williams and A. H. John, eds, *Glamorgan County History*, vol. 5: Industrial Glamorgan (Cardiff 1980), 1–46, esp. 5.

[10]   D. Boorman, *The Brighton of Wales. Swansea as a Fashionable Seaside Resort, c. 1780–1830* (Swansea 1986).

lists from elsewhere in south Wales sent their sons.[11] Nowhere else in Wales
was there a town with such a well-developed range of urban facilities in the
early years of the nineteenth century. The iron town of Merthyr Tydfil, which
had a larger population than Swansea, had a far less mature urban
infrastructure. According to one historian, by 1800 Swansea was 'clearly the
nearest Wales had to a capital.'[12]

The parallel growth of industry and leisure not only gave Swansea a lead
over other Welsh towns as a centre for commerce and recreation, but also
brought an element of diversity into the make-up and character of the town's
elites. The area's principal landowner, the Duke of Beaufort, was an absentee
landlord, but a more visible gentry presence was maintained by the visits of
other landowners, resident in the vicinity, who frequented Swansea's
fashionable recreational facilities. The town consequently developed a
reputation as 'a winter residence of the neighbouring gentry'.[13] Landowners
from throughout south Wales, including Thomas Mansel Talbot of Margam,
Lord Vernon of Briton Ferry and William Rees of Aberpergwm, Thomas
Wyndham of Dunraven Castle and Samuel Homfray of Merthyr were all
subscribers to the Swansea theatre and assembly rooms.[14] Swansea's long-
established trading functions also meant that it had developed a commercial
middle class of bankers, shipowners and merchants whose business activities
brought wealth and prestige to the town. The existence of a Mercantile Society
since at least the 1780s and a Commercial Society from the 1820s testified to
the organization and strength of this middle-class contingent.[15] Their wealth
was also evident in the development of a new, distinctively middle-class
residential quarter with prestigious town houses designed and built by architect
William Jernegan in the early decades of the nineteenth century.[16]

Also contributing to Swansea's wealth and influence were the
entrepreneurs who established copper works and collieries in Swansea's
vicinity beginning in the 1720s. These industrialists were almost entirely men
of established wealth from outside the region who brought the high levels of
capital required to establish copper works. In the mid-nineteenth century even

---

[11]   For example, Charles William Nevill of Llanelli. See H. M. Jones, *Llanelli
Lives* (Llandybie 2000), 105.
[12]   P. Jenkins, 'Tory industrialism and town politics: Swansea in the eighteenth
century', *Historical Journal*, 28, 1985, 102–23, esp. 104.
[13]   G. Nicholson, *The Cambrian Traveller's Guide* (Stourport 1808), 602.
[14]   West Glamorgan Archive Service (WGAS), Swansea Library collection (SL)
WM1/6, Swansea Tontine Society Account Book.
[15]   University of Wales Swansea Archive (UWSA), Collins Box 10. Collins
records dining with the members of the Swansea Mercantile Society on 1 September
1783 at the Fountain, and his subscription payments are recorded in his accounts. See
also WGAS, Grant Francis Collection (GGF), B7, Swansea Commercial Society
minutes, 2 March 1824.
[16]   J. C. M. Rees, 'Evolving patterns of residence in a nineteenth century city:
Swansea 1851–1871', University of Wales Swansea Ph.D. thesis, 1983, 160–61.

the smallest works was said to require £45,000 in order to be viable, compared to just £10,000 for a small colliery.[17] Early investors included Bristol physician Dr John Lane and businessman Thomas Coster.[18] Robert Morris, who took over the Landore works from John Lane in 1726, hailed from Shropshire on the mid-Wales border.[19] A later influx included men with family backgrounds in the Cornish copper mining industry, most notably the Vivians and Grenfells. John Vivian, who established one of Swansea's largest and most successful copper smelting works in 1809, was a member of the Cornish Metal Company, founded in 1785 to represent the Cornish mines at the ore markets,[20] and also a partner in the Cornish Bank at Truro, which helped him with the finance for his entry into the smelting industry in south Wales.[21] Towards the end of the nineteenth century the prominent copper mine owner and solicitor from Anglesey, in north Wales, Thomas Williams, also entered the Swansea smelting industry.[22] The town's main pottery manufactory, the Cambrian, was taken over in 1802 by Lewis Weston Dillwyn, son of an Ipswich-based Quaker family. With their established commercial backgrounds, these men were broadly typical of the 'business middle class', which formed the backbone of Britain's industrial entrepreneurship in the early nineteenth century.[23]

The impact of these industrialists upon local government in Swansea, however, was minimal. Throughout the late eighteenth and early nineteenth-centuries the main feature of urban governance in the town was its growing exclusivity. This was typical of local government in Britain during this period.[24] Swansea's main institution of urban government, the corporation, was dominated by the Duke of Beaufort. His steward effectively controlled the appointment of burgesses and the selection of the twelve senior corporation members, the aldermen, who acted as a kind of executive council and held office for life. Under this system, participation in public life was restricted to members of a small circle of families, principally from the town's merchant and trading sectors. This was particularly true of the upper

---

[17] P. R. Reynolds, 'Industrial development', in G. Williams, ed., *Swansea. An Illustrated History* (Swansea 1990), 29–55, esp. 33.

[18] R. O. Roberts, 'The White Rock copper and brass works near Swansea, 1736–1806', in *Glamorgan Historian,* vol. 12 (Barry 1981), 136–51, esp. 137.

[19] W. Jones, 'Robert Morris, the Swansea friend of John Wilkes', in *Glamorgan Historian,* vol. 11 (Barry 1975), 126–36, esp. 126.

[20] UWSA, Yorkshire Imperial Metals (YIM), Vivian Papers, A1, Abstract of agreement for establishing the Cornish Metal Company, 1 Sept. 1785.

[21] R. R. Toomey, *Vivian and Sons, 1809–1924. A Study of the Firm in the Copper and Related Industries* (London 1985), 196.

[22] J. R. Harris, *The Copper King. A Biography of Thomas Williams of Llanidan* (Liverpool 1964).

[23] F. Crouzet, *The First Industrialists. The Problem of Origins* (Cambridge 1985), 99.

[24] See for example, P. Cadogan, *Early Radical Newcastle* (Consett 1975), 10.

echelons of local government where access to principal posts was restricted to a few key individuals. In Swansea the position of portreeve, the head of the corporation, was held by a few select men. For example, from 1782 to 1805, Rowland Pritchard and Thomas Maddocks, the latter a banker and prosperous shipwright,[25] each held the post of portreeve three times. Other key families such as the Powells and Jeffreys also regularly took their turn.[26] The forging of useful connections with the established order helped these men rise to the top of Swansea's local government circles. Rowland Pritchard, for example, was married to Sarah Bassett, sister of the Reverend Miles Bassett, who was vicar of Swansea for almost fifty-seven years.[27] Various members of the Powell family held the post of steward to the Duke of Beaufort in the eighteenth and early nineteenth centuries, providing them with a direct avenue to corporation activity.[28]

The incoming industrialists had little hope of breaking into this restricted circle, especially not while Gabriel Powell, the man known as 'the uncrowned king of Swansea', held the post of steward to the Duke of Beaufort.[29] Powell was particularly resistant to the introduction of new faces and new ideas into local government. He strongly opposed the attempts made in 1787 to set up new bodies to look after the management of the town's harbour and the paving of the streets, both of which required urgent attention as the volume of commercial traffic through the port and the town increased. He declared the plans to be 'prejudicial to our ancient customs, rights and privileges'.[30] He also exercised tight control over burgess appointments, both in terms of the number and character of recipients. This was significant because candidates for corporation membership could only come from within the burgess body. Between 1760 and 1789, only fifty-five men were granted burgess membership in Swansea.[31] And as table 2.1 illustrates industrialists were not represented amongst them.

Of course the large number of unknown occupations makes a precise analysis difficult, as does the high proportion described simply as 'gentleman' in the freemen's roll. Nevertheless, it appears from the figures that very few came from the ranks of high status middle-class occupations

---

[25]   UWSA, Miscellaneous 3, 'File of notes by H. M. Stevens on banking in Swansea', December 1791.

[26]   J. R. Alban, *Portreeves and Mayors of Swansea* (Swansea 1982), 8–11.

[27]   WGAS, D/D W. C. Rogers Collection (WCR), biographical notes, vol. 129.

[28]   WGAS, D/D WCR, 122.

[29]   T. Ridd, 'Gabriel Powell: the uncrowned king of Swansea', in *Glamorgan Historian*, vol. 5 (Cowbridge 1968), 152–60.

[30]   WGAS, B/S Corp B7, Hall Day Minute Book 1783–1821, 5 February 1787; T. Ridd, 'The development of municipal government in Swansea in the nineteenth century', University of Wales Swansea M. A. thesis, 1955, 15–16.

[31]   J. R. Alban, *Calendar of Swansea's Freemen's Records from 1760* (Swansea 1982), 3.

Table 2.1   Occupational profile of Swansea burgesses, 1760–1789

Occupational category

Construction	5
Craft	8
Gentleman	15
Merchant	2
Professional	3
Retail / Processing	2
Transport	7
Clerk	1
Unknown	12

Source: J. R. Alban, *Calendar of Swansea's Freemen's Records from 1760* (Swansea 1982), 15–31.

such as merchants, professionals or industrialists. Instead craftsmen, including shipwrights, cabinetmakers, shoemakers and coopers, and those engaged in transport, particularly mariners, contributed greater numbers. There is a sense here that Swansea's ruling elite was anxious not to advance the interests of those industrialists who might have posed a threat to their own established order.

The picture was not one of total exclusion, however. After Gabriel Powell's death in 1789 there was a flurry of new burgess appointments, among them John Morris. Present in the town since the 1720s, the Morris family had recognised from an early stage the need to align themselves with the Powell-Beaufort interest. For example, Robert Morris went to considerable lengths during his time at the Landore copper works to develop good relations with the Duke of Beaufort through his steward, presenting him with gifts of oysters and butter and urging his partner Robert Lockwood to 'rivet a lasting friendship with him as he may on many occasions be very serviceable to your interests'.[32] Others found a voice in local government through the separate administrative bodies set up, again after Powell's death, to look after the interests of the harbour and the town's streets. The Harbour Trust, established in 1791, included twelve 'proprietary trustees' made up of representatives of the district's collieries and manufactories. This brought for the first time a number of key figures from business and industry into the public life of the town. George Haynes (banker and pottery manufacturer), John Smith (a colliery proprietor), Richard Phillips (a barrister whose father was agent for White Rock Copper Works), and Calvert Richard Jones (prominent townsman and commercial booster) were all among the trustees appointed to represent the interests of Swansea's business and industrial

---

[32]   UWSA, Morris 1, 'History of the Copper Concern, 1717–1730' (1774), 105.

groups.[33] Likewise the act establishing the Paving Commission in 1809 named pottery manufacturers Lewis Weston Dillwyn and George Haynes, and coal proprietors John Morris and Charles Smith amongst its commissioners, along with the portreeve and prominent corporation members.[34] At least here there were signs of participation in the institutions of Swansea's urban administration by a widening range of interest groups.

Swansea elites in the town and region

Principally, though, it was to the wider region rather than to the town that Swansea's elites looked for opportunities to enter public life in this period. Lewis Weston Dillwyn, who owned the Cambrian Pottery in Swansea, was a good example of this. He developed a range of county contacts during his time as a magistrate and was appointed high sheriff of Glamorgan in 1818. This was an important office which charged its holder with the responsibility of acting as the King's representative in the county. Duties included holding county courts, empanelling juries, accompanying visiting justices who officiate at the great sessions and acting as returning officer at elections.[35] The post was traditionally restricted to a very small number of county families but from the early nineteenth century industrialists began to make their mark upon it. In some ways Dillwyn's appointment epitomised this gradual transition. As well as his manufacturing interests, he had recently inherited the estate of Penllergare, just outside Swansea, and so fitted the typical profile of the office holder as landed proprietor. The appointment significantly raised his profile within the region. His inauguration was attended by 'nearly all the principal gentlemen of the county' and during his tenure he frequently attended magistrates' and county meetings as well as the assize courts with fellow legal officials from Swansea, Cardiff and all of the principal towns in between.[36]

County posts, it seems, provided an important source of public honours for some of the Swansea industrialists in a period when access to the highest municipal honours was closed to them. John Morris and John Henry Vivian both followed in Dillwyn's footsteps to become high sheriff of the county in 1822 and 1827 respectively.[37] Some of the principal copper smelters,

---

[33]   W. H. Jones, *History of the Port of Swansea* (Carmarthen 1922), 67.
[34]   WGAS, Acts of Parliament relating to Swansea, 1791–1822 (D/Dxjk), An Act for the better Paving, Repairing, Cleansing, Lighting and Watching of the several streets. ... (1809).
[35]   *A List of the Names and Residences of the High Sheriffs of Glamorgan from 1541–1966* (Cardiff 1966), 11–16.
[36]   H. J. Randall and W. Rees, eds, 'Diary of Lewis Weston Dillwyn', in *South Wales and Monmouth Record Society*, vol. 5 (Newport 1963), 15–98, esp. 19.
[37]   *List of the Names*, 30.

including Vivian and Pascoe St. Leger Grenfell also served as justices of the peace and deputy lieutenants of the county. It is not difficult to see why the Swansea men were favoured with these honours. Within the wider industrial district there were few residents with the kind of wealth and status to rival the Swansea industrialists. An assessment of the neighbouring town of Neath identified only around twenty resident burgesses and a population of labourers from the local works. It was also noted that 'the proportion of poor houses to good ones is very high'.[38] Further east, Aberavon's urban growth had also been limited. In the early 1830s the parish of Aberavon had only 125 houses, of which only eleven had a rateable value of £10 or above, and its offices of portreeve, aldermen and sergeant at mace were said to be 'at present filled by mechanics and publicans who can hardly read or write and who do not appear themselves to know the limits of the borough'.[39] In contrast Swansea, with its grammar school, its public buildings, leisure facilities and its growing contingent of commercial and professional inhabitants, was an altogether more likely breeding ground for ambitious elites.

Official recognition of Swansea's dominance over this wider region was expressed most clearly in 1832 with the passing of the new Reform Act, which redrew the lines of parliamentary representation in Britain. Before 1832, Swansea had formed part of the old political unit of Cardiff Boroughs. In this large and unwieldy seat, in existence since the Acts of Union between England and Wales (1536–1542), Swansea was one of seven contributory boroughs, all combining to return one member to parliament. Under the 1832 Reform Act, however, this constituency was broken up. A new Swansea District was created, comprising Swansea town, Aberavon, Kenfig, Neath and Loughor.[40] This new seat had twice the electorate of the remainder, which formed a modified Cardiff division. The reform was an important recognition of the extent to which Swansea's wealth and status as an urban centre had grown over the previous half century. The new parliamentary seat closely mirrored the industrial region that had developed during this period and confirmed Swansea's place as its administrative and urban centre. The boundaries of the town itself were also redrawn to take account of the industrial developments that had re-shaped it over the first three decades of the nineteenth century. The new parliamentary borough, created in 1832, included the expanding industrial areas to the north and east of the town, along the banks of the river Tawe. The worker settlements at Trevivian and Morriston, along with other outlying industrial districts were all included, so that the extent of the town was expanded from just 230 acres to 5,400 acres.[41]

---

[38] WGAS, GGF, F32, Neath.
[39] WGAS, GGF, F28, W. Wylde, 'Notes on Aberavon'.
[40] R. Grant, *The Parliamentary History of Glamorgan, 1542–1976* (Swansea 1978), 45–6.
[41] Jones, 'The city and its villages', 80–81.

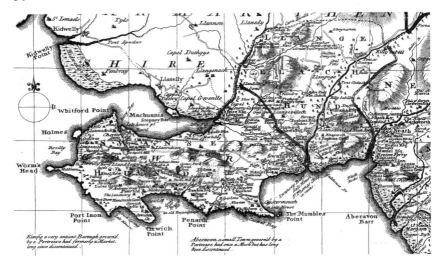

Figure 2.1   Thomas Kitchin's map of Glamorgan, around 1750

Source: West Glamorgan Archives Service

Most importantly, for the purposes of this analysis, the new constituency also
provided politically ambitious Swansea men with an opportunity for access
into parliamentary life for the first time. Since 1734 the boroughs seat had
been controlled by Cardiff's principal landowning family, the Butes. Apart
from a brief interlude in 1818 when Lewis Weston Dillwyn had threatened to
oppose them, the Bute family's dominance of the constituency had gone
uncontested. With the creation of a new Swansea Boroughs seat there was
now an opportunity for the western boroughs to send a representative of their
own choosing to parliament. Added to this, the Reform Act also granted the
county seat of Glamorgan a second representative. Previously this single-
member constituency had been dominated by the Margam estate, with a
member of the Talbot family at the helm. However, the creation of a second
member in 1832 meant another potential opening at Westminster for
someone from outside the traditional circle of landed representation.

Swansea industrialists were the immediate front runners for these new
openings. John Henry Vivian, head of the Hafod copper works, had been one
of the leading campaigners for the creation of an additional boroughs seat in
Glamorgan.[42] When the plans were confirmed he wasted no time in putting
himself forward as a candidate and was returned to parliament unopposed
from 1832 until his death in 1855. In his position as parliamentary

---

[42]   National Library of Wales (NLW), Vivian L24, extracts from the *Cambrian*
regarding John Henry Vivian's views on the Reform Bill.

representative for Swansea Boroughs the *Times* described Vivian as 'all powerful, his native business-like habits and great interest rendering him a fitting – perhaps the only fitting representative (…) it appears to us absolutely futile to attempt to oust Mr. Vivian'.[43] Although the electorate of the new seat numbered only around 1,500, Vivian's representation received much wider endorsement from the public at large at the traditional chairing ceremonies that accompanied each of his election successes, when he was carried in triumph through the streets of Swansea on a golden chair to the delight of cheering crowds.[44] This ritual 'chairing' of the victorious candidate was the main opportunity for popular participation in elections at a time when the parliamentary franchise was very limited.[45] In Swansea it gave the inhabitants of the town and the other contributory boroughs a chance to show their approval of Vivian's success.

As with Vivian, the re-organisation of parliamentary representation in the region also propelled Lewis Weston Dillwyn into public life at the highest level. Already a prominent figure in county circles, Dillwyn was encouraged by many, including the Talbots of Margam, to put himself forward as a candidate for the newly-created second county seat. The two families were closely allied in this period and Dillwyn had actively supported Christopher Talbot's election as the single county member in previous years. Dillwyn had often been a guest at the Margam estate and he declared himself to have 'never felt happier' than when the two families were united by the marriage of his son John to Emma Talbot in 1833. With their support behind him, his success was virtually assured, but he left nothing to chance and conducted a rigorous canvass of the county during September and October of 1832. His efforts were rewarded on 17 December when he and Talbot were returned unopposed to represent Glamorgan in parliament.[46]

Dillwyn's parliamentary career was not as long-lived as that of his friend and fellow townsman Vivian, and he retired from his seat in 1837. But his position as an MP during these years undoubtedly had a galvanising affect upon the members of the Swansea Corporation. In August 1834 they took the belated step of conferring burgess membership upon John Henry Vivian and Lewis Weston Dillwyn in recognition of their 'great and important services' to the borough and the 'great personal respect' with which they were regarded in the town.[47] Burgess membership had broadened considerably

---

[43] *Times*, 10 May 1847.

[44] W. W. Price, *Biographical Index of W. W. Price* (Aberystwyth 1981), vol. 28, reel 10, 15.

[45] F. O'Gorman, 'Campaign rituals and ceremonies: the social meaning of elections in England 1780–1860', *Past and Present*, 135, 1992, 79–115.

[46] Details of Dillwyn's canvassing activities and the election can be found in Randall and Rees, 'Dillwyn's Diary', 72.

[47] WGAS, B/S Corp B9, Hall Day Minute Book, 1821–1835, 8 August 1834. See also Ridd, 'development', 96–7.

since the days when Gabriel Powell had kept appointments to a bare
minimum. The number of individuals admitted as burgesses had increased
from just thirty-five in 1789 to fifty-three in 1802 and 104 by 1833.[48] As the
number of burgesses increased, their occupational profile broadened
correspondingly to reflect the widening range of economic activities of
Swansea's middle classes. An illustration of this trend can be seen in table
2.2. By 1835 the ranks of burgesses in Swansea were dominated by
professionals who accounted for almost 18 per cent of the total. The number
of 'gentlemen' had diminished considerably while industrialists had just
begun to make their appearance. In both periods representatives were drawn
in similar numbers from the craft and retail sectors as well as the transport
and construction trades.

Table 2.2   Occupations of Swansea burgesses, 1760–1792 and 1835

	1760–1792		1835	
Occupational category	Number	Percentage	Number	Percentage
Construction	7	7.8	4	4.7
Craft	17	19.0	7	7.8
Gentleman	22	24.7	7	7.8
Industrial	0	0.0	2	2.3
Merchant	6	6.7	7	7.8
Military	0	0.0	4	4.7
Professional	4	4.5	15	17.8
Public Service	0	0.0	2	2.3
Retail	6	6.7	4	4.7
Transport	10	11.2	11	13.0
White Collar	2	2.2	2	2.3
Unknown	14	15.7	19	22.6

Source: Alban, Calendar, pp. 15–57.

This widening burgess membership by the 1830s went some way towards
preparing the path for municipal reform, which altered not only Swansea's
local government but that of other British towns. The Municipal Reform Act
of 1835 brought an end to the reign of the old, self-elected corporations with
their narrowly defined mandate of managing borough revenues and defending
their own rights and privileges. In their place a new household franchise gave
the towns elected councillors with a much wider range of potential powers. In
Swansea the first local elections since the passage of the Act took place in

---

[48]   Alban, *Calendar*, 3.

Table 2.3   Swansea's first Town Council, 1836

Upper Ward

Name	Votes	Occupation
Thomas Walters	241	Grocer / tea dealer
J. H. Vivian*	231	Copper smelter
N. Cameron*	219	Coal proprietor
M. J. Michael	218	Corn and flour merchant
M. Williams	215	Gentleman
Samuel Jenkins	211	Ironmonger and bar iron warehouse
David Sanders	205	Military rank: captain
John Grove	192	Merchant
Richard Aubrey	168	Merchant

Lower Ward

Name	Votes	Occupation
Lewis W. Dillwyn*	199	Landowner / manufacturer
R. M. Phillips*	179	Military rank: major
S. Benson*	156	Copper smelter
D. Edwards*	154	Unknown
Sir J. Morris	139	Industrialist
William Martin	123	Unknown
John Davies	122	Unknown
J. Richardson	119	Shipowner
William Moyse	116	Unknown

* signifies alderman
Source: Cambrian, 2 January 1836.

January 1836, and a new eighteen-member town council was elected with nine members representing each of the town's two new upper and lower wards. At the time, contemporaries were keen to emphasise the elements of continuity between the old and new regimes. Paving commissioner Henry Sockett, for example, pointed out that the eighteen newly elected council members included four men who had previously served on the old corporation. He also expressed his hope that the new body would continue the work of the old corporation which 'had contributed largely towards the improvement of the public edifices of the town'.[49]

---

[49]   *Cambrian*, 2 January 1836.

Within the ranks of the new councillors, however, there were signs that a significant shift had taken place in the make-up of local government (see table 2.3). Some of the more prominent names from industrial and commercial life in the town were immediately elected to the new town council, including John Henry Vivian of the Hafod copper smelting works and Lewis Weston Dillwyn of the Penllegare estate and the Cambrian Pottery. Another prominent copper smelter, Starling Benson, also took his place in the new body as did John Richardson, whose family had moved from Northumberland to Swansea in the 1820s and entered the town's expanding shipping trade. The professions, merchants and gentlemen who had held sway over the old corporation had thus given way to an influx of commercial and industrial interest groups. This transition had occurred, according to the *Cambrian*, as a result of popular will rather than aggressive campaigning. Several of the new body, including Lewis Weston Dillwyn and Colonel Cameron, claimed not to have known that they had been nominated until after the candidates for each ward had been announced.[50] The implication was that they were responding to the public will rather than actively seeking their own advancement.

Municipal reform thus brought with it a clear shift in the balance of power among Swansea's local elites. Prominent industrialists were no longer obliged to look to county posts for an opportunity to enter public life. Election to the town council was now a possibility and the high number of votes cast for Vivian and Dillwyn in particular, suggests that the electorate craved representation by the highest profile figures from business and industry. This personnel change did not necessarily alter the character of local government, however, and it is important not to overstate the 'watershed' brought about by 1835 reform. Studies of several towns have shown that the reforms rarely effected abrupt transformations.[51] In practice the reformed town councils could only extend their activities into new areas of local government, like street improvement, harbour management and policing, for example, where the various commissioners and trustees previously responsible for these matters were willing to surrender their powers and where they had access to sufficient resources. As a result the new councils were often seen as being little different from the old corporations.[52]

Although the new faces in Swansea seemed to herald a new era, the scope of their activities was restricted, almost from the outset, by a severe lack of funds. A lengthy memorial to the Treasury in 1841 outlined the stark fact that, with an income of just £1,700 from its property, and recent expenditure

---

[50]   Ibid.

[51]   See for example, G. Bush, *Bristol and its Municipal Government, 1820–1851* (Bristol 1976), 210; A. Temple Patterson, *A History of Southampton, 1700–1914*, vol. 1: *An Oligarchy in Decline, 1700–1835* (Southampton 1966), 161.

[52]   J. Prest, *Liberty and Locality. Parliament, Permissive Legislation and Ratepayers' Democracies in the Nineteenth Century* (London 1990), 18–19.

of £20,000 on a new market, guildhall and public rooms, the town was left with a debt of £24,095.[53] The mayor and his council requested permission from the treasury lords to sell off parts of the town lands as a means of raising money for further improvements, but their plea was turned down. Advised instead to seek a reduction of the interest rate on its current debt, the new council found itself working within the same financial constraints as the old corporation and thus prevented from taking a radically different approach to urban governance. This situation made for much frustration and delay as agreement could not be reached on how to fund important initiatives such as the improvement of the harbour.

For some of Swansea's successful industrialists who had become accustomed to office-holding at a regional and even national level, the frustrations of operating within a cash-strapped local municipal body occasionally showed through. In a letter to Swansea's harbour trustees in 1839, John Henry Vivian revealed a measure of his exasperation at the slowness of progress, lamenting that the proposed improvements had 'been so long under discussion that it has become a subject on which it is impossible to enter without a considerable degree of reluctance (...) I almost despair of offering to your notice any remarks.'[54] Given the difficulties and limitations of local urban administration in the period after municipal reform, it is not surprising that men such as Vivian continued to look to beyond the town to the regional and national arena as more fruitful outlets for their talents. Institutions with more outward-looking agendas continued to be important to Swansea's elites, especially the town's scientific society, established in 1835, which later evolved into the Royal Institution of South Wales. This was the Wales' premier learned institution with a national reputation for scientific endeavour, and a wide membership base which extended through south Wales and the west-country.[55] County posts such as that of high sheriff also continued to attract Swansea's leading industrialists. Lewis Weston Dillwyn's son, John Dillwyn Llewellyn, held the sheriff's office in 1835 and Swansea coal owner Charles Smith followed in 1839.[56] Likewise, parliamentary honours attracted the next generation. Dillwyn's second son gained election to the parliamentary seat vacated with Vivian's death.

To some extent the existence of these other outlets for elite office-holding activity compensated for the frustrations of municipal government in the period. The outward-looking perspective that had helped the town's industrialists to gain public honours on a regional and national level in the

---

[53]   WGAS, B/S Corp, B10, Council Minute Book, 1835–1844, 8 January 1841.

[54]   WGAS, Volume of reports and correspondence regarding the harbour (D/DZ207), letter dated 1839.

[55]   L. Miskell, 'The making of a new "welsh metropolis": science, leisure and industry in early nineteenth-century Swansea', *History*, 88, 2003, 32–52.

[56]   *List of the names*, 30–31.

early decades of the nineteenth century remained something of a tradition amongst the upper echelons of Swansea's elites, even after the political reforms of the 1830s had opened up local positions to them. Parliamentary representation, county office and membership of learned institutions all provided opportunities for status and achievement beyond the confines of the town. These positions took on even greater significance for Swansea's elites as the town began to feel the pressure of urban growth elsewhere. Urban Wales was being re-shaped in this period. The 1840s saw the beginnings of a new phase in Cardiff's growth as new dock and rail links facilitated its emergence as the main shipping port for the mineral wealth of south Wales. Further east, Newport was also emerging as a serious commercial rival. Swansea's days as the dominant urban power in south Wales appeared to be numbered. In these changing circumstances, the status to be derived from regional honours assumed an even greater significance for the town's most ambitious elites. Moreover, in aspiring to succeed outside their immediate locality they displayed much in common with their counterparts in other British towns, where ambitious, non-parochial and outward-looking perspectives were equally evident in the upper echelons of urban society.[57] That Swansea's elites shared these characteristics is perhaps not surprising, but it adds an important new Welsh dimension to the growing body of evidence relating to the activities of Britain's urban elites, as well as a useful reminder that the power structures within which they operated extended well beyond their immediate town boundaries.

---

[57] L. Miskell, 'Civic leadership and the manufacturing elite: Dundee, c.1820–1850', in L. Miskell, C. A. Whatley and B. Harris, eds, *Victorian Dundee. Image and Realities* (East Linton 2000), 51–69, esp. 68–9.

CHAPTER THREE

Who Really Ran the Cities? Municipal Knowledge and Policy Networks in British Local Government, 1832–1914

James Moore and Richard Rodger

'Pax Britannica' and 'Workshop of the World' are just two epithets associated with nineteenth-century British power and dominion. The British Empire, coloured red in the atlases of generations of British schoolchildren, was at its zenith in the nineteenth century. Together trade and empire might have been expected to figure prominently in the daily work of the British people. They did, of course. In the commercial and financial sector of the British economy the rate of growth of male employment rose more than in any other of sector between 1841 and 1921, yet it only just outstripped the expansion of public administration workers and the difference was probably within the margins of statistical error in the census takers' data.[1]

The nineteenth century was the age of Britain's bureaucratic revolution. Although public administrative employment remained modest compared to some other sectors in absolute terms, for example, being only about one-third the size of transport or agriculture, the rate of growth was rapid. As the sanitary strategy developed from mid-century into areas of one municipal trading in gas, water and tramway operation, as well as into the cultural agenda associated with libraries, galleries and museums, and ultimately into housing and town planning the municipal payroll expanded accordingly.[2]

Paid as these local government workers were by a single employer, their presence in the town and city was also highly visible, congregating around

---

[1] B. R. Mitchell and P. Deane, *Abstract of British Historical Statistics* (Cambridge 1971), 60–61.

[2] For rising burdens of local taxation see Mitchell and Deane, *Abstract*, 416–21; for London, see A. Offer, *Property and Politics 1870–1914: Landownership, Law, Ideology and Urban Development in England* (Cambridge 1981), 284–5. For a discussion of the national public finances see M. J. Daunton, *Trusting Leviathan: The Politics of Taxation in Britain 1799–1914* (Cambridge 2001).

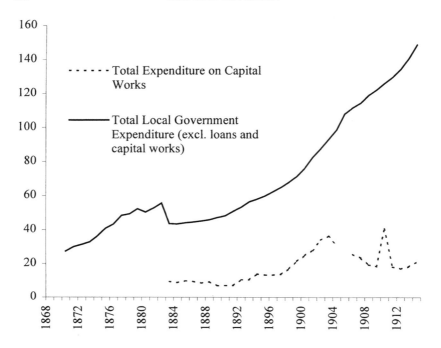

**Figure 3.1 Local government expenditure in England and Wales,
1870–1914**

Source: Mitchell and Deane, *Abstract*, 416–21.

the premises from which the municipalities functioned. Glasgow City
Council, that paragon of municipal socialism, itself employed over 14,000
men in 1911 – 4,400 of them in the Tramways Department under the
supervision of James Dalrymple in the 1890s. No other employer in the city
approached such a scale and even the largest categories of employment –
iron-manufacturing, the diverse building trades, and food processing were
fragmented in a multiplicity of associated firms scattered throughout the
city.[3] Not long after London County Council (LCC) was formed in 1888 it
assumed responsibility for 1,000 schools, 115 parks, 66 fire stations, 160
miles of tramways, administered cross-river traffic on ten bridges and four
tunnels.[4] The LCC needed armies of employees to operate this municipal
infrastructure, managers to manage them, and experts to advise according to
benchmarks adopted by professional organisations. The LCC acquired three

---

[3]   British Parliamentary Papers, *PP 1913, LXXX,* Census of Scotland, vol. 2,
446, table XXXIV.
[4]   R. J. Dennis, 'Modern London', in M. J. Daunton, ed., *The Cambridge Urban
History of Britain,* vol. 3: *1840–1950* (Cambridge 2000), 101–105, here 103.

plots of land by Westminster Bridge in 1906 to accommodate its burgeoning bureaucracy and elsewhere, as in Edinburgh for example in 1872, the City Council discovered it was already the second largest landowner in the city with control over more urban space than all of the railway companies combined.

These municipal tentacles affected the management of urban space, and amenities both cultural and physical. In some instances municipal management was strongly associated with the very ethos of the city. Birmingham's claim to be the 'best-governed city' in the Empire positioned it at the epicentre of civic improvement. The claim, more imagined than real, nonetheless was, and perhaps still is, the driving force of modernity as the city centre experiences its third reincarnation in a century. Behind the municipal management in Birmingham, as elsewhere, were powerful individuals – experts in their fields of civil engineering, medical science, and materials. These were the city surveyors, medical officers of health, borough engineers, sanitary scientists and analysts, building control officers, police superintendents and chief fire officers with a legion of inspectors to support them. This was the executive branch of city government. Theirs was specialist knowledge, an increasingly specialist knowledge as the nineteenth century entered its final quarter, managed by the city czar, the 'omnipotent' Town Clerk.[5] They might not actually make policy in the council chamber, but they certainly worked closely with the committee chairmen to do so. Men like Alfred Tozer, the Birmingham Chief Fire Officer (1879–1906) and Henry Duncan Littlejohn, the Edinburgh Medical Officer of Health (MOH) (1862–1908) dominated their fields of expertise for decades.[6] They even secured their professional dynasty. Littlejohn's son Harvey followed his father as MOH, and Tozer's sons Alfred and Charles were both Second Officers in Birmingham for over 30 years, as was his grandson, and Alfred Tozer's third and fourth sons, William and Fredrick, who were respectively Chief Fire Officer for nearby West Bromwich and station officer for Manchester for lengthy periods.

The expansion of municipal functions during the second half of the nineteenth century required ever greater expertise to manage the cities. The generalist roles of the executive town clerk and city treasurer went into decline, and the participation of the elected business class also went into decline as demands on their time became more pressing. The ascent of the expert with his professional qualifications was consequently assured.

---

[5]   T. E. Headrick, *The Town Clerk in English Local Government* (London 1962). For a hierarchy of positions amongst Town Clerks, see B. Doyle, 'The changing functions of urban government', in Daunton, *Cambridge Urban History*, vol. 3, 287–313, esp. 296.

[6]   S. D. Ewen, 'Power and administration in two Midland cities c.1870–1938', unpublished University of Leicester Ph.D. thesis, 2003, 120; Obituary by T. S. C., 'Sir Henry Littlejohn', *Edinburgh Medical Journal*, 13, 1914, 404–7.

Between these two phases, at a differing pace according to place and not
without resistance, committee chairmen retained important powers as the city
'boss' within their particular committee remit. Ultimately, their position, too,
was challenged as the combined forces of labour emerged from the 1880s, as
municipal expenditure continued to rise and put civic officials under extreme
political pressure, and as instances of municipal corruption undermined the
integrity of municipal management to a degree. In addition, standards of
technical knowledge continued to advance across the wide front of civic
activities, and the national and international transfer of expert knowledge
ensured that an audit culture ultimately constrained the powers of the town
clerk and committee chairmen. This chapter explores these themes, beginning
with an overview of the administrative and political reforms that facilitated
these managerial shifts.

Administrative and political reforms in the nineteenth century

The history of the political reform movements of the nineteenth century has
often been written from a Westminster perspective.[7] The great reform bills of
1832, 1867 and 1885, which extended the parliamentary franchise, are
frequently viewed as landmarks in the processes of democratisation and
political liberalisation, even though the basic structures of parliamentary
administration were little changed. In contrast the organs of local government
– the organs of government that most citizens experienced in the course of
daily life – underwent a revolution.[8] Beginning in 1835, local administration
was restructured and reorganised, new corporate bodies were created, powers
and responsibilities were redefined, and political participation was gradually
widened.[9]

These municipal reforms were important not simply because they
redefined the structure of local authority, although this was clearly
significant.[10] Nor were they important merely because they altered the
structure of power between parliament and the locality, although again this

---

[7]   M. Bentley, *Politics without Democracy, 1815–1914* (Oxford 1985); J. Parry,
The Rise and Fall of Liberal Government in Victorian England (Yale 1993); M. Pugh,
The Making of Modern British Politics, 1867–1939 (Oxford 1993), and M. J. Turner,
British Politics in an Age of Reform (Manchester 1999).
[8]   The most comprehensive account of the process is still K. B. Smellie, *A
History of Local Government* (London 1969). See also, J. A. Phillips, *The Great
Reform Bill in the Boroughs: English Electoral Behaviour 1818–1841* (Oxford 1992).
[9]   This process began in Scotland in 1833. For an overview of Scottish
administration see G. S. Pryde, *Central and Local Government in Scotland since 1707*
(London 1960).
[10]   J. Garrard, *Democratisation in Britain* (Basingstoke 2002), esp. 63–8, and J.
Davis, 'Central government and the towns', in Daunton, *Cambridge Urban History*,
vol. 3, 261–72.

had profound consequences for the operation of British government. The reforms were of crucial importance because municipal government was the agency through which nineteenth-century social and infrastructural improvement was made possible. Local government administered poor relief, built sewers, formed streets, provided new housing, regulated development, promoted libraries and museums, licensed the drink trade, supervised the police and oversaw much of the criminal justice system. Mayors of Leeds, Nottingham, Liverpool and other leading cities were major political figures. Reform initiated by local government could have a profound effect on national government policy. Indeed, municipal government 'possessed imagination and technical ability not at all inferior to Westminster departments'.[11] In short, local government mattered.

How, then, did municipal government obtain and exercise its authority? This chapter will provide an overview of the policy and information networks that existed within and between the units of nineteenth-century urban government. While many have seen the growth in authority of the central state as the key influence in policy development, we argue that the policy communities and professional bodies that had emerged by 1900, provided a brake on the growth of government control, while developing their own agendas and standards. It will also be suggested that although local government units were seen increasingly as unitary bodies, they were often very fragmented, not merely in policy or ideological terms, but due also to local government structures that encouraged personal ambition through processes of individual initiative. The committee system and decentralised structure of administration relied on access to specialist knowledge and often cutting-edge technologies. Local government developed its own information networks. Both pragmatically and through recognised channels, administrative procedures developed to produce a measure of convergence in municipal policies. However, since policy experts were initially councillors and not civil servants and were rarely constrained by institutional structures or professional standards, then considerable scope was retained for 'local solutions to local problems, locally identified'.[12]

The nature of nineteenth-century local government

To discuss a local government system in Britain before 1835 is something of a misnomer. Local administration was characterised by a lack of both systematic regulation and an effective statutory framework. The primary unit of local government in 178 towns was the corporation. These administrative

---

[11] P. J. Waller, *Town, City and Nation: England 1850–1914* (Oxford 1983), 281.
[12] E. P. Hennock, 'Central/local government relations', *Urban History Yearbook*, 1982, 38–49.

units were established by power of royal charter and the largest number had been created between the reign of Henry VIII (1509–47) and the 'Glorious Revolution' of 1688. Almost all of these corporations were established on the principle of self-election and were designed to render the governing class independent of the main body of the urban citizenry.[13] Thus these corporations were not public bodies in any real sense. They were merely groups of unelected burghers acting primarily in their own private interest, which might incidentally coincide with that of the town more generally. The rights of the corporation were an extension of their own private property rights. Fraser has argued that in practice 'most corporations were corrupt, inefficient, and insensitive to real local needs'.[14] Yet it should be stressed that not all fitted this characterisation. Some, as in Oxford, introduced important sanitary improvements and were relatively 'open' in political terms. Many were concerned primarily with the administration of local justice, the operation of charities and, notoriously, the management of parliamentary elections. Yet they were all undeniably different, exercising different powers and each governed by its own charter. In unincorporated boroughs the ancient unit of local administration was the court leet, a feudal legacy and convened by the lord of manor or his officers. These operated in a similar way to corporations but had more limited powers that were frequently disputed, particularly their rights to levy taxation.[15]

Beyond the borough boundaries, the parish vestry was the primary unit of administration. Operating largely under the aegis of the Church of England, vestries had no statutory foundation but were instead a product of the common law. In some cases the approval of the parish vestry was required before a court leet could levy a manorial rate or duty, but their main and most controversial function was that associated with the administration of poor relief. The composition and governance of the parish vestry varied considerably. In principle it was constituted as a result of an open meeting of (usually male) parishioners, but in practice strategies were adopted to limit

---

[13] See First General Report of the Commission appointed to Inquire into the Municipal Corporations in England and Wales, PP (1835), vol. XXIII, pp. 17, 34 and 49. There is a copy in W. Thornhill, ed., *The Growth and Reform of English Local Government* (London 1971), 31–3. For an assessment of the 1835 Act see G. B. M. A. Finlayson, 'The Municipal Corporation Commission and Report 1833–1835', *Bulletin of the Institute of Historical Research*, 36, 1963, 36–52. For an overview of urban administration see R. Sweet, *The English Town 1680–1840* (Harlow 1999), 75–109, 141–52, and J. Innes and N. Rogers, 'Politics and government 1700–1840', in P. Clark, ed., *The Cambridge Urban History of Britain,* vol 2: *1540–1840* (Cambridge 2000), 529–74.

[14] D. Fraser, ed., *Municipal Reform and the Industrial City* (Leicester 1982), 4, and E. P. Hennock, *Fit and Proper Persons – Ideal and Reality in Nineteenth Century Urban Government* (London, 1973).

[15] See the example of Manchester in A. Redford, *The History of Local Government in Manchester*, vol. 2 (London 1939) 3–6.

participation to wealthier householders, especially in expanding industrial towns such as Bolton, where the operation of parochial authority was particularly controversial.[16] The powers and functions of the vestry also depended on convention and common law rather than statutory authority. While some parishes did obtain parliamentary Acts for the regulation of poor relief, others merely interpreted the Elizabethan Poor Law legislation as they saw fit.[17] Finally, the Justices of the Quarter Sessions wielded the overarching power within the parishes. Unlike other units of local government that were almost entirely free from central government direction or even contact, the Quarter Sessions did receive limited instructions from the Home Office, usually through the monarch's legal representative in the counties, the Lord Lieutenant. This contact was not, however, designed to regulate the everyday judicial role of the Quarter Sessions, but rather so that adequate provision could be made to quell revolts or civil unrest.[18]

Fragmentation of local government made policy co-ordination very difficult. It inhibited the development of integrated information networks and the sharing of administrative knowledge. There were few formal channels of information between the different units of local governement and almost none between local government and the central state. This patchwork of governance, described by a contemporary authority as 'a striking and almost obtrusive lack of unity' was seen primarily as a network of local administration rather than a system of local government.[19] As Loughlin observed, when the processes of urbanisation began to transform the physical environment and threw up new challenges to policy makers, political elites did not look to the old units of local government to foster solutions, but instead created new statutory institutions and instruments to deal with specific policy areas.[20] The result was a network of Turnpike Trusts and Improvement Commissions, established almost always by local initiative and each authorised by their own Act of Parliament. Consequently each had its own rules, regulations, powers and geographical orbit. Aside from these private Acts there were very few general Acts relating to the operation of local government – and when they were introduced they were often ignored.[21] The Sturges-Bourne Act 1819, for example, introduced plural voting to vestries but was widely ignored and parliament lacked any agency to enforce its provisions. Other legislation, such as the Prisons Act 1791 and the County Asylums Act 1808, was

---

[16] P. Taylor, *Popular Politics in Early Industrial Britain: Bolton 1825–50* (Keele 1995).
[17] B. Keith-Lucas, *The Unreformed Local Government System* (London 1980), 154.
[18] Ibid. 150.
[19] G. C. Brodrick, 'Local government in England', in J. W. Probyn, ed., *Local Government and Taxation* (London 1875), 6.
[20] M. Loughlin, *Legality and Locality* (Oxford 1996), 28–9.
[21] Keith-Lucas, *Local Government*, 149.

generally ignored by the magistrates and county authorities responsible for their implementation.

The reasons for this independence of local government from central direction were complex. Poor internal communications with many regions before the coming of the railways made supervision physically difficult, though this proved less of a hindrance in France, for example, where a centralised system of local government supervision developed. The British system was complicated and thus difficult to reform. Indeed, this was why discrete corporate bodies were established to deal with specific policy problems. It was politically much easier to create new statutory bodies than to interfere with the authority of existing corporations and manorial courts. Many also opposed reform since they believed that the very foundation of English liberty relied on the fragmentation of political authority and that local self-government represented a powerful counterweight to the power of an autocratic centralised state.[22]

Reform of local administration was eventually precipitated by two crises, one associated with taxation and the other associated with parliamentary franchise reform. Rising poor law costs, particularly in the south of England were the stimulus for change. The Speenhamland system, a form of poor relief based on a supplement to wages when agricultural incomes were low, had been widely adopted in this region, resulting in rapid increases in relief and thus in taxation. It was a practice that was offensive to the proponents of a free labour market and it resulted in the establishment of a Poor Law Commission in 1832 to investigate the system of poor relief.[23] Most of the members of the Commission were disciples of Jeremy Bentham and advocates of a utilitarian political theory that promoted the view that 'all government is a great evil'.[24] Though Bentham also acknowledged that intervention was warranted where 'action takes the name and character of good', later a stronger case for the legitimacy of government intervention in individual lives was made by John Stuart Mill who argued that public services provided out of general taxation were legitimate where general utility was advanced or private provision was incompetent.[25] Thus, in the 1830s, the prevailing reform ideology focused on the evident inefficiencies and inconsistent policies that operated in relation to Poor Law administration. Parochial authorities were condemned for failing to share information with their neighbours, being ignorant of more efficient practices of administration,

---

[22]   Loughlin, *Legality*, 36.
[23]   For the most authoritative account of the Poor Law see K. D. M. Snell, *Annals of the Labouring Poor* (Cambridge 1985).
[24]   B. Webb and S. Webb, *English Local Government – English Poor Law History,* part II, vol. 1 (London 1929 private edition), 26–7. See also J. Bentham, *Introduction to the Principles and Morals of Legislation* (1789).
[25]   See Daunton, *Trusting Leviathan*, 8–9.

and of not educating new Poor Law administrators in the operation of the system:

> At present, the experience which guides the administration of relief is limited to the narrow bounds of a parish and to a year of compulsory service. The common administration is founded on blind impulse or on impressions derived from a few individual cases; when the only safe action must be regulated by extensive induction or general rules derived from large classes of cases, which the annual officer has no means of observing (…). In petty and obscure districts, good measures rarely excite imitation, and bad measures seldom yield warning (…).[26]

What was being condemned was not so much a failure of policy as a failure of information exchange. Knowledge was lost through frequent changes in personnel, lack of an information network between authorities, and an ignorance of good practice. Insularity exacerbated maladministration. Nor was there a hierarchy of authority in administration – no system of 'line management', to use current parlance.[27] The solution adopted was a radical one that would set a precedent for the future relationship between local government units and the centre.[28] The Commission encouraged the establishment of a central board to control the administration of the Poor Law, with the power to frame uniform regulations and remove officers thought to be inefficient. These officials were to be civil servants rather than MPs with the power to issue mandatory rules for poor law authorities.[29] The subsequent act of 1834 did not abolish the existing local authorities and local civil servants were appointed to assist the Poor Law Guardians with administration. However these local civil servants, although in the service of local administration, were subordinated to the power and supervision of a central board. It was an administrative model imprinted with Edwin Chadwick's fingerprints. As a civil servant involved in major enquiries into poverty and public health in the 1830s and 1840s, Chadwick's predilection for local accountability to centralised agencies reflected his strong belief in collecting and processing information, followed by the dissemination of best practice as defined by a central board. Regulations and monitoring emerged, as for example, through the General Board of Health in 1848, though Chadwick's insensitivity to local priorities irritated local interests and undermined this standardising initiative, not only in the arena of public health.[30] The centralising tendency was not without its successes, however.

---

[26] Report of the Poor Law Inquiry Commissioners, 1834, 280–87, 301 in Webb, *Local Government*, 76–7.

[27] F. Redlich and F. W. Hirst, *Local Government in England*, 2 vols. (London 1903).

[28] C. Bellamy, *Administering Central-Local Relations 1871–1919* (Manchester 1988).

[29] Smellie, *Local Government*, 26–9.

[30] The standard studies include S. E. Finer, *The Life and Times of Edwin Chadwick* (London 1952), and R. Lambert, *Sir John Simon 1816–1904 and English*

For example, when central government agreed to assist in the foundation of art schools in the 1840s, it did so by setting up a central board and providing the salaries for local headmasters who were employed by and responsible to the central agency and not local committees.[31]

Pressure for the reform of municipal corporations also came as a by-product of parliamentary reform.[32] Before 1832 corporations played a key role in controlling the election of MPs. It was logical following the electoral reforms initiated at the national level that municipal voting should also be subject to review. But there was an additional concern that prompted municipal reform. It was the anxiety that incorporated boroughs witnessed the worst scenes of public disorder in the 1831 agitation for voting reform.[33] The incorporated boroughs of Bristol and Nottingham were particularly affected. In such an environment a review of municipal corporations was inevitable. Significantly parliament adopted the same method of investigation for municipal corporations as for the Poor Law – the establishment of a Commission of Enquiry.

In many respects the 1835 Commission established the modern form of English local government, although initially it provided for elected authorities only in the 178 existing incorporated towns. London was excluded. The Municipal Corporations Act 1835 left major industrial centres, such as Manchester and Birmingham, untouched. Only by the costly process of drawing up a charter and applying to Parliament for approval could urban areas eventually join the original list of 178 places and participate in the new forms of urban administration that it permitted. The significance of the Municipal Corporations Act 1835 lay in the fact that it imposed a uniform principle of government, namely, that an overall authority should assume responsibility for local government.[34] The new municipal corporations, or town councils as they were also known, were to be elected by a common system based on property qualifications, though a quarter of their number were still nominated by the Corporation.[35]

Administration (London 1963). Central-local tensions were very durable and widespread. *The New Annals of Rochdale* reported in 1856 that a series of Sunday concerts were set up as a protest against undue influence exercised in London.

[31] Q. Bell, *The Schools of Design* (London 1963); S. MacDonald, *The History and Philosophy of Art Education* (London 1970).

[32] A. Briggs, 'The background to the English parliamentary reform movement in three English cities', *Cambridge Historical Journal*, 10, 1952, 293–317.

[33] Fraser, *Municipal Reform*, 5.

[34] Loughlin, *Legality*, 33.

[35] Rates were the name for local taxes payable to the municipality, and were levied on the basis of property values. Ratepayers, therefore, were local taxpayers, and were generally resistant to the escalation of municipal expenditures. See Daunton, *Leviathan*, chapter 9, entitled 'Athenian democracy: the fiscal system and the local state 1835–1914'.

Political radicals, urged on by Richard Cobden's *Incorporate Your Borough,* saw municipal reform as the opportunity to throw off aristocratic patronage and Anglican control.[36] It is unsurprising, therefore, that those towns with large middle-class nonconformist populations were often the first to secure incorporation. No less surprisingly, they had to face the ire of Tory and Anglican opposition.[37] Leaders of the old corporations saw the imposition of a new pattern as an infringement of their ancient rights and an attack on their property. Opponents of municipal reform battled through the courts and it was not until the case of *Rutter v Chapman* in the mid-1840s that the authority of the newly reformed corporations was legally undisputed.[38] Even then Tories in some towns refused to regard the new corporations as legitimate governing bodies and boycotted municipal elections.[39] Thus battles for incorporation became a regular and ritualised feature or urban politics.

Initially the costs of promoting a parliamentary bill for incorporation had to be borne by promoters, limiting incorporation to larger urban boroughs. But after 1877 costs could be met out of the local taxation, encouraging many smaller towns to press for corporate status. Smaller towns and villages, however, had to wait until the late-1880s before their system of local government was overhauled, and it was only from 1889 in county councils and from 1894 in district and parish councils that plural voting was abolished and popularly elected administrative units introduced. London, excluded by the municipal reforms of 1835, was a mosaic of separate bodies and private provisions. Along a 100 metre stretch of street, vestries, improvement commissions and corporations were responsible for the pavement, the road, cleansing, police and lighting, with gas and water that were supplied by private companies. Some consolidation of these responsibilities was achieved under the Metropolitan Local Management Act 1858 and the formation of the Metropolitan Board of Works that resulted in 1871.[40] Only with formation of the London County Council in 1888 was there a unified authority, in stark contrast to the position in other European capital cities.[41] It took half a

---

[36] D. Fraser, *Urban Politics in Victorian England* (Leicester 1976), 119–20.

[37] See, for example, anti-incorporationist handbills in Redford, *History*, vol. 2, 16–17.

[38] D. Fraser, *Power and Authority in the Victorian City* (Oxford 1979), 157–8; Fraser, *Municipal Reform*, 6–7.

[39] P. Whitaker, The growth of Liberal organisation in Manchester from the 1860s to 1903, unpublished University of Manchester Ph.D. thesis, 1956, 211–12.

[40] D. Owen, *The Government of Victorian London 1855–1889: The Metropolitan Board of Works, the Vestries and the City Corporation* (Cambridge, MA 1992), and J. Roebuck, *Urban Development in Nineteenth Century London: Lambeth, Battersea and Wandsworth 1838–1888* (Chichester 1979).

[41] Dennis, 'Modern London', 101–4.

century, therefore, from 1833 in Scotland and 1835 in England and Wales, to achieve the reform of the local government system in Britain.[42]

The new corporations were the most politically powerful units of local government, yet the precise powers they could exercise were influenced by a number of factors. Firstly, there was the question of the power of the *ancien regime*. In some urban areas the authority and power base of former manorial and landed interests was such that neither parliamentary nor municipal reform could make much impression. For example, the second Marquis of Bute's economic and political penetration of Cardiff society, the influence of the Dudleys in the Black Country and the role of the Dartmouth family in West Bromwich are all instances where administrative reform produced little political change.[43] Secondly, there was the question of whether a new group or network of citizens was adequately united to form a political faction with a common agenda.[44] Party labels were not themselves a sufficient force. Indeed, those towns that underwent the most rapid political transformation may have been those where nonconformists provided a distinctive policy community for the new corporation. For example, a small knot of Unitarian families led two of the most radical cities, Manchester and Leicester, initially.[45] Thirdly, there is the question of how the new political leaderships obtained sufficient knowledge and relevant information to govern their towns.

Networks of knowledge and the development of local power after 1835

In most cases the new regimes acquired boroughs with limited social infrastructure. The fragmented provision of services before 1835 was associated with disjointed administration, limited knowledge, overlapping jurisdictions, and a mixture of provision by different bodies, public and private. The first task of the new authorities was to explore their areas of competence. Many of the legal powers were untested and thus uncertain. Under the previous system the courts had primary responsibility for regulating the conduct of local authorities and local public bodies operated almost unchecked by central government. The new corporations had powers

---

[42] For details see Smellie, *Local Government*, 39–49; *An outline of the Parish and District Councils Bill* (London 1893).

[43] See examples in D. Cannadine, ed., *Patricians, Power and Politics in Nineteenth Century Towns* (Leicester 1982), and R. Trainor, *Black Country Elites: the Exercise of Authority in an Industrial Area 1830–1900* (Oxford 1993).

[44] For another west midlands example where party politics was slow to gain a foothold, see J. B. Smith, The governance of Wolverhampton elite c.1840–1880, unpublished University of Leicester Ph.D. thesis, 2001.

[45] M. J. Turner, *Reform and Respectability* (Manchester 1995), and W. Lancaster, *Radicalism, Co-operation and Socialism: Leicester Working-Class Politics 1860–1906* (Leicester 1987).

defined by statute, though in practice these definitions were somewhat vague. Powers were often permissive; in many policy areas councils were enabled but not compelled to act. For example, the reformed corporations that had the powers to organise police forces were only required to do so in 1856. As the new corporations were legitimised through a mandate from taxpayers there was a natural concern that they might interpret their powers too broadly, develop a monopoly over particular trades, and thus injure private interests. Elected corporations, acutely sensitive to this charge, were often very cautious as a result and so injured the public interest by their restraint. The leading civil servant of the corporation, the town clerk, was the council's chief legal officer and the primary source of legal opinion for the ordinary corporation member. In many authorities the town clerk held office not merely for several years but for several decades, often obtaining a position of social prestige at least as great as the mayor.[46] The caution of the town clerk was often the key restraining influence on the council, warning councillors when they were in danger of proposing actions that were outside their powers. It was the town clerks, therefore, who as the repository of local knowledge not uncommonly defined the rate of innovation and policy initiatives in relation to municipal intervention.

When corporations wanted to pursue activities that were deemed to go beyond the scope of their statutory powers, they could appeal to parliament for a private act to extend their authority in a specific area. Major infrastructural projects such as water and sewerage systems usually required private acts of parliament as they affected the property rights of individuals or other corporations and often required loans for these large-scale capital projects. However, by petitioning to adopt the framework of national 'permissive' legislation private acts became less common with the passing of successive decades in the second half of the nineteenth century. Perhaps, inevitably, some authorities exercised powers without promoting specific private legislation or adopting existing Acts. For example Salford, never adopted the Public Libraries Act 1850 that empowered corporations to establish municipal libraries, but this did not prevent the corporation from establishing free libraries or levying a free library rate. Indeed, as Mullen points out, when the Public Libraries Act was passed on 14 August 1850, the Salford public library had already been open for seven months![47] This was particularly remarkable as one the promoters of the Act of 1850 was the local MP, Joseph Brotherton, and it was almost half a century later that the corporation's actions were legitimated when Salford gained powers to levy library rates through a local improvement Act.

---

[46] Headrick, *The Town Clerk*, 24. Manchester, for example, was served by just two town clerks for the first eighty years of its existence. Sir Joseph Heron was town clerk of Manchester from 1838–1889; his successor, Sir William H. Talbot was in office from 1890 to 1910.

[47] B. Mullen, *The Royal Museum and Libraries, Salford* (Salford 1899), 15.

Local government initiatives were rarely experimental and the Chadwickian condemnation of the old poor law for its failure to share knowledge of policy developments continued to reverberate around the town halls of mid-Victorian Britain. Not surprisingly, therefore, municipal initiatives developed within an atmosphere of utilitarian political ideas and narratives of scientific rationalism. In practice, however, the power that corporations enjoyed depended to a considerable degree on their own efforts and local political leadership.[48] Networks of knowledge conditioned the character of towns as they responded to public policy opportunities in the second half of the nineteenth century. Some of these knowledge networks were initiated by central government, some were created by local government, and others by external agencies.

In keeping with these divisions, historians have traditionally identified three phases in municipal policy development: (i) the sanitary, (ii) the cultural and (iii) the discretionary.[49] Although this characterisation may be broadly accurate, phases of municipal intervention overlapped and there were many local differences. For example, in Leicester, where death rates were significantly above the national average throughout the nineteenth century, the cultural initiatives preceded the sanitary ones by several decades. By contrast, in Birmingham large-scale improvement plans associated with Joseph Chamberlain's initiatives did not begin until the late-1860s, corresponding roughly with the cultural agenda. The rhythm of municipal policy developed at different rates because the nature of local problems, the application of national legislation, the interpretation of public expectations, and the power of particular policy networks differed from place to place. In short, the way in which municipal knowledge was acquired was fundamental to roles corporations adopted as they sought to resolve their urban problems.

The administrative shape of councils was an important influence on the dissemination of information and thus the ability to develop policy. Unlike national government, the doctrine of the separation of powers had only a limited influence over municipal administration. Aldermen and councillors were often magistrates in the local courts, while at the same time they chaired law-making council meetings and held executive posts in council committees. In many cases the same men made by-laws, prosecuted offenders and passed judgement. However councils themselves were functionally divided in as far as full council meetings framed regulations, by-laws and proposed legislation, while individual committees were the main executive authorities. Indeed it was the functional fragmentation of the committee system that prevented mayors and finance committees from

---

[48] J. Garrard, *Leadership and Power in Victorian Industrial Towns, 1830–1880* (Manchester 1983).

[49] Typically associated with J. R. Kellett, 'Municipal socialism, enterprise and trading in the Victorian city', *Urban History Yearbook*, 1978, 36–45, and Hennock, 'government relations', 38–49.

exercising despotic authority. Each committee took responsibility for a particular policy area and had considerable discretion within that area, subject to the constraints of an annual budget voted to it by the full council. Committees varied, but typically consisted of one each for finance, policing (the Watch Committee), health, markets, public improvements and nuisances. Later, as local government expanded, committees for parks, libraries, gas supply, transport, as well as housing and planning were often added to the list. Although these committees were sometimes very large, often only the committee chairman, vice-chairman and committee clerk were involved in the everyday execution of council business. Moreover committees often divided their functions to smaller sub-committees for the management of specific projects, especially where these required more specialist knowledge or oversight. Though there was a greater degree of accountability and auditing, a few elected officials could promote public policies in a manner not unlike that of the unreformed corporations in the era before 1835.

Committees often adopted the character of semi-autonomous fiefdoms ruled by their chairman. Each committee tended to be composed of members who in their private or commercial life were functionally associated with specialist responsibilities of that committee. Predictably, this produced conflicts of interest. Engineers and coal merchants dominated the gas committee; the housing or planning committees were associated with the construction and building trades. In an acrimonious ethical battle in 1880 Councillor William Watherstone declined the chairmanship of the Edinburgh committee responsible for authorising new building permits on the grounds that such a position should not be occupied by 'a builder or one connected with the building trades'.[50] Though businessmen claimed that their specialist knowledge brought expertise to bear on municipal policies at no cost to the council, there can be little doubt that many aldermen and councillors sought such positions to benefit their business interests. Strictly speaking, this was illegal. The Municipal Corporations Act 1835 maintained the restriction imposed by previous anti-corruption legislation by disqualifying those who held

> any Office or Place of Profit, other than that of Mayor, in the Gift or Disposal of the Council of such Borough, or during such time as he shall have directly or indirectly, by himself or his Partner, any Share or Interest in any contract or Employment with, by, or on behalf of such Council.[51]

---

[50] *The Edinburgh Courant*, 29 October 1880. The intractability of vested interests can be seen from the fact that Watherstone was still campaigning for impartiality in 1890. *The Scotsman*, 4 July 1890.

[51] Quoted in A. Doig, *Corruption and Misconduct in Contemporary British Politics* (Harmondsworth 1984), 65.

Occasionally councillors did fall foul of the legislation. The well-known social reformer Councillor Charles Rowley of Manchester used his position on the art galleries committee to give his picture framing business a council contract, was exposed, and subsequently declined to stand for re-election.[52] Though many councillors successfully concealed the range of their business interests, towards the end of the nineteenth century the increasing complexity and frequency of municipal committees imposed such demands on councillors' time that businessmen had already begun to retreat from involvement in local government.[53] For those who continued to serve the restrictions proved unworkable and the law was relaxed in the course of early twentieth century reforms.[54]

Strong bonds of mutual self-interest that provided a vital local policy information network cemented the composition of committees. Committee members provided crucial information on local market conditions, entrepreneurial opportunities and private development plans.[55] As most met in private, they were the conduits in which confidential information could be exchanged and political deals could be struck. Although the party politicisation of local government caused intense rivalry in full council meeting, in private differences could be reconciled. Such were the business ties and homosocial bonds associated with committee activity that many council members saw loyalty to committee as important as loyalty to party; it was often the unwritten law of municipal business.[56] Only latterly, from the 1880s did women play a significant part in committee business and conventionally they were involved in those 'caring' and 'cultural' committees – education, libraries and museums – and on the Boards of Guardians concerned with the administration of the Poor Law.[57]

Age mattered, too, and the principle of seniority governed most committee appointments. Consequently long serving aldermen usually had the first choice of committee places and junior members were left to occupy places on less prestigious committees, such as the Nuisance Committee. The principle of seniority applied to aldermen and, predictably, to committee chairmen too. This convention had no legal basis, but it was the accepted

---

[52] *Manchester City News*, 18 October and 25–27 October 1884, and J. Scott, *Leaves from the Diary of a Citizens Auditor* (Manchester 1884), 30.

[53] Hennock, *Proper Persons*, and D. McCrone and B. Elliott, *Property and Power in a City: the Sociological Significance of Landlordism* (London 1989), table 4.2, 80–81.

[54] B. Keith-Lucas and P. G. Richards, *A History of Local Government in the Twentieth Century* (London 1978), 95–6.

[55] For the importance of social, business and religious networks see R. J. Morris, *Class, Party and Sect: the Making of the British Middle Class: Leeds, 1820–1850* (Manchester 1990).

[56] *The City Ledger*, February 1888.

[57] P. Hollis, *Ladies Elect: Women in English Local Government, 1865–1914* (Oxford 1987).

norm in many councils.[58] Chairmen were rarely appointed without a long record of committee service and when they were installed they usually held office for very long periods. The custom of Manchester City Council was to appoint committee chairmen for what amounted to life, reappointing them every year until they died. Up and down the land, the town council roll of honour provided similar evidence of long-service amongst chairmen aged over fifty, with some well into their seventies.[59] The result was that senior committeemen were the repositories of collective memory and precedent; it proved difficult for inexperienced committee members to counter such a weight of accumulated municipal knowledge. Scope for radical policy options was circumscribed by this inherent conservatism in appointments and the sense of continuity with the past invoked to justify the *status quo.*

As the most important figure guiding the policy of the committee, chairmen were responsible for service delivery. They often assumed a position akin to that of a commercial managing director. The committee system, however, was much more than a method of conflict resolution and policy exchange. For the executive authority of committees to function specialist knowledge and expertise was necessary. One place the committee could turn was, of course, its own membership. This was particularly important in an era before the salaried appointment of professionals in engineering, public health and transport. As the complexity and scale of local government expanded, sometimes exponentially from the 1870s, then reliance on business experience and social networks were insufficient as the basis of policy formation. Though in county and market towns[60] the town clerk retained what seemed like absolute power, increasingly in the larger urban areas a body of permanent officials – local civil servants – supported committee chairmen and were responsible for both the management of the department and policy advice. For example, the construction and delivery of water systems from the 1860s and the municipalisation of the gas supply and tramway operation were areas in which a high degree of specialist knowledge was essential for the effective operation of the service.

Much depended on the relationship between the committee chairmen and his permanent officials. Some chairmen clearly supervised the management of their committees very closely; others left day-to-day management in the hands of their civil servants. Such a strategy could prove disastrous. Large contracts associated with local government made for potential corruption, and since accounting practices were often rudimentary, it was possible for dishonest officials to demand commissions and bribes in awarding of council contracts. The Salford gas scandal of 1887 illustrated just how easy it was for

---

[58] J. Moore, The transformation of urban Liberalism, unpublished University of Manchester Ph.D. thesis, 1999, 176–7.

[59] E. D. Simon, *A City Council From Within* (London 1926), 93.

[60] For further information on this point see the chapter by D. McHugh in this volume: 'The Unregulated Town', (71–91).

officials to conceal secret commissions and how petty corruption had become systemic in some areas of council business.[61] Before 1889 bribe-taking and secret commissions for corporation contracts were not illegal, and though the law was tightened at the end of the decade, it did not prevent a major fraud within Wolverhampton council during the Edwardian period.[62] While malpractices have been revealed it is arguably surprising that more evidence of corruption has not been forthcoming.

Experts and the sources of municipal knowledge

By the end of the nineteenth century councils were able to access an extensive network of municipal knowledge. One of the earliest sources of information was the 'official' information provided by local government. Following the special commissions in the 1830s on the poor laws and on the reform of municipal government, commissions of enquiry and select committees became a favoured device by which parliament and central government could both de-fuse controversial issues and also influence the stance of other agencies, including local government.

In 1839 the Poor Law Commissioners were ordered to extend their sanitary investigations in London to the rest of the country. As a result of this enquiry Edwin Chadwick produced his path-breaking *Report on the Sanitary Condition of the Labouring Population of Great Britain* (1842) that illustrated the scale of the sanitary problems, which confronted large cities throughout Britain. While these investigations were being conducted a Select Committee on the Health of Large Towns reported, in 1840, calling for sweeping legislation with specific instructions to local authorities on the maintenance of water supplies, sewerage, open spaces and slums. Not surprisingly this call went unheeded but it led indirectly to the Royal Commission on the State of Large Towns and Populous Districts, which reported in 1844 and 1845. This Royal Commission recommended that public health should 'rest with single local authorities directly under the crown', a conclusion that reasserted the centralizing principle in relation to local government initiatives.[63] In fact the eventual legislation, the Public Health Act 1848, was mainly permissive although it required sewer connections, for example, where urban death rates were exceptionally high.[64]

---

[61]   J. Garrard, 'The Salford Gas Scandal of 1887', *Manchester Region History Review*, 2, 1988–9, 2–6.

[62]   J. B. Smith, 'Certified correct: the great Wolverhampton Council fraud 1900–1918', in J. Moore and J. B. Smith, eds, *Corruption in Urban Politics and Society, Britain 1780–1950* (Aldershot forthcoming 2007).

[63]   Redford, *History*, vol. 2, 136.

[64]   D. Eastwood, *Government and the Community in the English Provinces* (Basingstoke 1997), 161–2.

Such major commissions of enquiry were influential. Firstly, they provided local councillors with a quasi-scientific analysis of specific social problems. Secondly, they offered specific courses of action, with the implication that local authorities neglecting such issues would be failing in their duties to local citizens.

Before 1900 most major parliamentary legislation relating to local government was concerned with the protection of a minimum level of service provision. Most of the controls that were established did so in a way that seemed to respect the autonomy of local government. The County and Borough Police Act 1856 required the Home Secretary's consent in the appointment of chief constables and gave him authority to make orders in areas of basic management. He did not, however, have the direct power of compulsion. If police authorities fell below a minimum standard of efficiency all that the Home Secretary could do was to withdraw the central grant.[65] Yet the mere presence of a statutory minimum standard clearly did have an influence on the operation of local authority. Again a scientific narrative of efficiency provided a gold standard against which citizens could measure the performance of their local government. Although not compelled to accept these standards, no proud new corporation was prepared to be nationally graded as offering substandard service. Thus the practice of establishing officially recognised standards helped to spread new techniques of efficient governance and foster competition between local authorities. Death rates, tax levels, overcrowded housing, the ratio of WCs and baths per resident and a multiplicity of other measures were adopted in the name of scientific local government.

Despite the acknowledged need for technical information council committees rarely co-opted outside specialists as full members of a committee. In principle, burgesses were eligible for co-option as aldermen to serve in a specific management or advisory role, though before 1914 few were appointed in this way. In practice, almost all aldermen were appointed on the basis of an existing long-service record as a councillor in the municipality.[66] The only exceptions were the public library, museums and art gallery committees to which book collectors, art patrons and artists were often added. Such appointments were partly for practical reasons since it was a way in which art patrons could be encouraged to donate works of art to the municipality and to supply paintings for annual exhibitions. Appointments could, however, also have a ceremonial role. In a tone of indictment concerning the cultural knowledge of his fellow councillors, E. D. Simon, Lord Mayor of Manchester, noted that the presence of art patrons 'clearly

---

[65] Loughlin, *Legality*, 40–42.

[66] The only exception to this rule was when a municipality extended its boundaries to take in new suburbs. In these cases, local worthies from the suburb were often appointed directly as aldermen in order that the area was seen to be represented in the new authority.

raises the prestige of the committee in the art world to a much higher level than would be possible if it consisted only of city councillors'.[67]

Though initially legislation from Westminster was permissive rather than mandatory, it was not toothless as has sometimes been claimed.[68] Consistent with the prevailing Benthamite approach, the establishment of minimum standards necessitated a system of central inspection that cast a lengthening shadow that affected factories, mines, railways, the poor law and education in the 1830s and 1840s and by the last quarter of the nineteenth century left few areas of policy untouched.[69] Accidents, mileages, output data and the number of inmates were recorded and returned to headquarters in London. Police authorities were obliged under the terms of the County and Borough Police Act 1856 to issue annual reports and submit to inspection from the Home Office. Public health inspectors were permitted by the Public Health Act 1875 to attend all meetings of local authorities. As the tentacles of municipal activity extended into new areas of responsibility in mid-Victorian Britain, so the Local Government Act 1858 provided a standardised form of building byelaws and provided the precedent for the formation of a Local Government Board in 1871.[70] This Board offered a measure of specialist advice and control to towns and cities of all sizes and was itself, therefore, an agent of standardization in the process.[71] With local circumstances varying considerably, no simple chronology can be established to convey the pace of inspection and the availability of centralised knowledge that affected towns and cities in Britain. Taylor, Hobsbawm and others argue that the Benthamite approach of minimalist government intervention had by 1870 lost its former dominance as the principle of a mixed government and state interventionism became accepted.[72] The inspectorates were not necessarily confrontational bodies, designed to intimidate local authorities, but they were important conduits of knowledge, committed to the sharing of policy and the promotion of specific governmental agendas of efficiency.

Towns and cities were themselves often willing accomplices in this process. Leeds, Liverpool and Newcastle were amongst the first cities to obtain Private Acts to address their environmental health concerns in the

---

[67]   Simon, *City Council*, 88.

[68]   Eastwood, *Government*, 161–5.

[69]   For an account of the creeping intervention in mid-nineteenth century see J. B. Brebner, 'Laissez-faire and state intervention in nineteenth century Britain', *Journal of Economic History*, 8, 1948, 59–73; W. Holdsworth., *A History of English Law*, vol. 15 (London 1965), and G. Kitson-Clark, *An Expanding Society: Britain 1830–1900* (Cambridge 1967).

[70]   S. M. Gaskell, *Building Control: National Legislation and the Introduction of Local Byelaws in Victorian England* (London 1986).

[71]   Loughlin, *Legality*, 40–44.

[72]   A. J. Taylor, *Laissez-faire and State Intervention in Nineteenth Century Britain* (Basingstoke 1972), 50. See also E. J. Hobsbawm, *Industry and Empire* (Harmondsworth 1968), chapter 12.

1830s and 1840s, and between 1847 and 1857 over 3,000 towns and cities presented private Acts to Parliament as they, too, sought similar powers to contain the contamination associated with rapid urbanisation. With over 130,000 pages for MPs to consider in these bills brought before parliament it was inevitable that these local initiatives would prompt some codification and centralised control in housing and environmental policy. The Local Government Act 1858 and the Local Government Board Act 1871 were the logical development of the diverse nature of local government in nineteenth-century Britain. To complicate matters further, these two acts were shown to be inapplicable in Scots law and so the Burgh Police (Scotland) Acts of 1862 and 1892 were required to provide a framework for the adoption of local byelaws and municipal regulation north of the border.[73] On both sides of the border, therefore, there was a recognition that economies of scale existed where administrative knowledge could be pooled. The passage of these acts of parliament, therefore, recognised that towns and cities benefitted individually by developing national networks of administrative knowledge.

To ignore official channels of advice was to court public embarrassment. It would be a mistake, however, to view the encroaching power of inspectors as simply a growth in central government power. It was, in reality a by-product of both the increasing scrutiny of local government affairs and the rise of the doctrines of scientific efficiency. Interestingly, some of the most formidable inspectors came not from central government but from the locality itself. Some corporations had elected 'citizen's auditors'. Traditionally these figures were important local individuals who provided a cursory audit of corporation accounts. However, they could be sometimes used to highlight crucial weaknesses in council administration. In 1884 Joseph Scott published a damning report on the inefficiencies of Manchester City Council. Some parts were mildly satirical. Council members had run up bills of over £500 on deputations and 'Pic-nics', £875 had been spent on wine, and one committee alone had managed to consume 3,500 cigars during the year, all at public expense.[74] Other parts of the report, however, revealed a catalogue of commission-taking, bribery and mismanagement.[75] The incidents caused public outrage, with Scott's report being widely circulated by pamphlet and through a weekly column in the local press.[76]

Perhaps what was most revealing was that many councillors who were not on the committees accused of excess seemed genuinely shocked and surprised at the revelations about their colleagues. Many were entirely ignorant about the activities of other committees. The decentralised nature of

---

[73] For a brief overview see G. F. A. Best, 'Another part of the island', in H. J. Dyos and M. Wolff, eds, *The Victorian City: Images and Realities*, 2 vols. (London 1978), vol. 2, 389–411.

[74] Scott, *Leaves*. 5, 17–18.

[75] Ibid. 9, 43–45.

[76] *Manchester City News*, 18–27 October 1884.

committee government discouraged members from asking questions about those committees on which they did not sit. Gradually from the 1870s, full council meetings began to scrutinise sub-committees much more closely and thus councillors obtained vital information about the wider operations of the council and took an active interest in policy areas outside the immediate committee interests.

Formal processes of audit, inspection and report were by no means the only way in which municipal knowledge could be acquired. The statistical revolution of the early nineteenth century was not limited to central and local government departments, although the development of the national census from 1801 and the system of registration of births, marriages and deaths were very influential.[77] So, too, were the annual returns to parliament from railways, companies, friendly societies, trade unions, overseas trade and a multitude of organisations, though there is scant evidence in municipal committee minutes that local government administrations systematically quarried this mine of information in determining levels of service provision required.[78]

Composed of a town's leading citizens and patronised by leading municipal figures, local statistical societies also played a vital role in the distribution of data about the rapidly developing nineteenth-century city. The papers and surveys associated with the work of these societies were often on a larger scale than that conducted by municipal authorities themselves and therefore could represent the most important single body of knowledge on a particular problem. Moreover the scientific method associated with the statistical societies was often copied by pressure groups seeking to influence municipal leaders.[79] Saturated by ratios and numerical evidence, Edwin Chadwick's *Report* in 1842 and Charles Booth's surveys of the London poor, published in 1903, are well known, but similar surveys of poverty and deprivation were conducted in other major cities.[80] Temperance campaigners kept detailed records outlining the growth of drunkenness and public houses.

---

[77] For a general account see M. J. Cullen, *The Statistical Movement in Early Victorian Britain: the Foundations of Empirical Research* (New York 1975); R. Woods and N. Shelton, *An Atlas of Victorian Mortality* (Liverpool 1997).

[78] For an accessible compendium of this information see Mitchell and Deane, *Abstract*.

[79] See, for example A. J. Kidd, '"Outcast Manchester": voluntary charity, poor relief and the casual poor 1860–1905', in A. J. Kidd and A. W. Nicholls, eds, *City, Class and Culture* (Manchester 1985), 48–73.

[80] T. S. Simey, *Charles Booth Social Scientist* (Westport 1980); B. N. Butler, *Victorian Aspirations: the Life and Labour of Charles and Mary Booth* (London 1972); T. S. Ashton, *Economic and Social Investigations in Manchester, 1833–1933* (London 1934); H. Bosanquet, *The Poor Law Report of 1909* (London 1909); Glasgow Municipal Commission on the Housing of the Poor, *Report and Evidence* (Glasgow 1904), and *Annual Reports of the Leicester Domestic Mission* (Dare Reports) 1846–1877.

Smoke abatement groups and chemical trade organisations alike presented their arguments through statistical survey and analysis. Religious organisations were alert to the use of statistical techniques in their struggles against urban social problems. The Manchester Unitarian Domestic Mission, for example, encouraged its officers and volunteers to keep detailed records of the successes amongst the poor and in its educational activities and the Edinburgh Society for the Relief of Indigent Old Men kept annotated accounts of disbursements to those who received relief.[81] Gazetteers, Municipal Yearbooks, Post Office and Kelly's *Directories* were a universal source of statistical information about times, distances, and municipal amenities.

In short, the late nineteenth century was an age of statistics. Councillors, like other citizens, were selective about their usage, but there can be little doubt that surveys played a key role in providing material for political debate and an important focus for policy development. They also offered the prospect of an objective understanding of social and economic problems and attracted considerable contemporary interest in newspapers and meetings.

Generally, it was rare for councils in Britain to commission large-scale statistical surveys. Indeed unless surveys were specially authorised by act of parliament in an improvement scheme, such action would probably have been contrary to the uses to which local taxation could be put. Councils did have other methods for obtaining specialist policy information without having to rely on either central government or politically motivated local agencies. The most obvious was through their links with other councils. Local authorities were generally very enthusiastic about sharing information about their own policy successes. Corporations that pioneered large-scale improvement schemes were usually willing to show these off to nearby authorities and visitors were welcome. Such schemes usually involved large-scale capital expenditure and could be politically controversial. If admirers and copyists could be attracted from other corporations, local leaders could promote these visits as a form of external validation. Deputations were the usual way in which information was shared. A small group from a specialist committee, usually the chairman, vice-chairman and clerk, would meet with their counterparts in a nearby town and then tour the facility or building to be studied. The deputations were usually conducted amid much formality and ceremony, but there can be little doubt that they did represent an effective way of sharing information. Town planning deputations, often to Germany as the perceived leader in this arena, were not uncommon as a result.[82]

---

[81] See Manchester Domestic Mission proceedings [microfilm], Manchester Metropolitan University library; Edinburgh City Archives, ACC 237, Minute Book of the Society for the Relief of Indigent Old Men, 1832; Report Book 1856.

[82] H. Meller, 'Philanthropy and public enterprise: international exhibitions and the modern town planning movement, 1889–1913', *Planning Perspectives*, 10, 1995, 295–310.

Figure 3.2 Henley on Thames Town Hall

Local government existed prior to the Norman Conquest, 1066, and was confirmed in charters of 1526, 1571 and 1772. In 1883 the unreformed corporation was abolished and borough status with a town council of 16 elected representatives established. Borough status was lost in the local government reforms of 1974, at which point the new Town Council paid for a Coat of arms, displayed on the front of the building, with the motto 'Semper Communitas' meaning 'A borough for a long time in Community for ever.'

Source: Courtesy of Richard Rodger.

Often deputations would return home and write up detailed reports of their findings, present them to committee, and then make the findings the centrepiece of future policy. Edinburgh hosted many such national and international delegations with the express intent of promoting the city as a centre of excellence. Municipal engineers, for example, were entertained as part of the cultural and scientific agendas that the city of Edinburgh wished to promote; the visits of municipal engineers placed Edinburgh in centre stage in this arena; and the postmaster-general and government representatives from London were invited so that the city could present itself favourably in national circles of opinion.[83]

Aside from deputations, public ceremonies often provided opportunities for sharing information about new initiatives. Municipalities were keen to mark the inauguration of new town halls, libraries and even sewerage works with lavish opening ceremonies and demonstrations, to which neighbouring municipal leaders were invited. In part these ceremonies were expressions of civic pride, municipal power and political legitimacy.[84] However they also provided opportunities for councillors to inspect new facilities and to discuss practical municipal problems with their near neighbours. Again, although these activities were highly formalised occasions, they were usually followed by lavish dinners and entertainment in which municipal leaders could engage in informal social discourse. Civic and local pride encouraged emulation. In some cases committees tried to simply duplicate the work of their neighbours. For example, Stockport Corporation modelled their new municipal park and art galley, Vernon Park, almost directly on that in nearby Salford. The municipal pride and local jealousies that generated town hall testosterone as one municipality sought to outdo its neighbour in the scale and grandeur of its public buildings did not discourage the sharing of specialist information or attempts to copy best practice.

The growth of exhibitions and conferences provided other opportunities for municipal leaders to access information about new technologies and share information with other authorities. The Great Exhibition of 1851 in London inspired many imitators, some general and some concentrating on specific technologies.[85] Many were organised by local mechanics institutes and specialist traders. Yet not all were modest affairs; the Manchester Art Treasures Exhibition of 1857 was probably the most important art exhibition every held in Britain and the Edinburgh International Exhibition of 1886 put the city on the world trade maps.[86] Specialist conferences also grew in popularity and, as seen in table 3.1, covered a wide range of interests.

---

[83] R. Rodger, 'The Common Good and civic promotion: Edinburgh, 1860–1914', in R. Colls and R. Rodger, eds, *Cities of Ideas: Civil Society and Urban Governance in Britain 1800–2000* (Aldershot 2004), 144–77.

[84] For a recent discussion see S. Gunn, *The Public Culture of the Victorian Middle Class* (Manchester 2000), and Rodger, 'Common Good', 158–63.

[85] L. Purbrick, ed., *The Great Exhibition of 1851* (Manchester 2001).

[86] For outline of significance see F. Haskell, *The Ephemeral Museum* (New Haven 2000), 82–9.

Table 3.1   Edinburgh City Council and the sponsorship of conference delegations, 1879–1913

Year	Conference hosted	cost £
1879	International Telegraph Conference	37
1882	International Fisheries Exhibition	291
1887	Institution of Mechanical Engineers	191
1888	Iron and Steel Institute	211
1889	National Association for the Advancement of Art and its Application to Industry	227
1892	YMCA Annual Conference	168
1892	British Association for Advancement of Science	256
1892	Institute of Journalists	172
1893	British Institute of Public Health	226
1894	Congress of the Educational Institute of Scotland	180
1894	Society of Chemical Industry	185
1894	Opthalmological Society	115
1894	Young Men's Guild	19
1895	British Dental Association	111
1895	Registered Plumbers Congress	68
1896	Incorporated Society of Musicians	242
1896	Trade Union Congress	245
1897	Franco Scottish Society	480
1897	United Presbyterian Church	405
1897	Independent Order of Rechabites	227
1898	British Medical Association	586
1898	Free Gardeners' Society	18
1899	UK Commercial Travellers Association	455
1899	Independent Order of Good Templars	233
1900	World Women's Christian Temperance Union	283
1901	Baptist Union of Great Britain	231
1902	Charities Association Organisation	18
1903	National Independent Order of Oddfellows	18
1904	Church of Scotland Congress	34
1904	Institute of International Law	167
1904	International Home Relief Congress	211
1905	American Members of the Society of Chemical Industry	45
1905	Canadian Manufacturers' Association	48
1905	International Conference on the Blind	38
1905	Municipal Electrical Association	56
1907	Council of the Boys' Brigade	14
1907	Esperanto Congress	49
1907	Incorporated Phonographic Society	6
1907	International Conference of Teachers of the Deaf	42
1907	Pan Celtic Congress	49
1907	Royal Institute of British Architects	59
1908	Council of the Tonic Sol-fa College	32
1908	British Order of Free Gardeners	10
1908	Pan Congregational Church	57

1908	Prussian Botanical Society	5
1909	British Women's Temperance Association	117
1910	National Association of Consumption and Tuberculosis	180
1910	World's Missionary Conference	323
1911	National Conference of Friendly Societies	39
1911	Tercentenary of the Society of High Constables	153
1911	Triennial Conference of the Reformatory and Refuge Union	113
1912	Federation of Master Printers of the UK	37
1912	National Federation of Meat Traders	51
1912	Scottish Association of Master Bakers	120
1913	British Carriage Manufacturers	48
1913	British National Conference of YWCA	147
1913	World Conference of YMCA	204

Sources: Edinburgh City Archives, Abstract of Accounts, Statements of Casual Expenditure, SL35/1 (1869), SL35/7 (1875), SL35/17 (1885), SL35/27 (1895), SL35/30 (1898), and SL35/46 (1914); City of Edinburgh, *Report on the Common Good* (Edinburgh 1905).

Corporations were particularly keen to host the conferences of high profile national organisations and learned societies. The British Association for the Advancement of Science and the British Medical Association annual meetings were amongst the most important of these, with municipalities competing to attract prestigious conferences and their influential organising committees. Councils often greeted such conferences with mayoral receptions and grand dinners for delegates and neighbouring corporations. These events presented great opportunities for municipalities to promote themselves as centres of learning and culture, but at the same time brought together local municipal leaders, helping foster a culture of co-operation and emulation.

As time passed, municipal corporations, if anything, became more willing to cooperate in areas of mutual advantage. This was partly because of central government's decision to establish the Local Government Board in 1871. This new central government body was given various supervisory functions, including a number previously exercised by the Secretary of State or Privy Council, and most of those of the former Poor Law Board. The centralisation of supervisory power into own body naturally attracted suspicion, but what was most resented was the Board's power, under a new Borough Funds Act, to veto draft legislation presented by local authorities, before it was presented to Parliament. Manchester's town clerk, Sir Joseph Heron, condemned it as 'subversive of the principles of local self-government, and calculated to paralyse all efforts on the part of governing bodies to carry out necessary local and sanitary improvements'.[87] The Act generated large-scale opposition, particularly from the larger municipal corporations such as Liverpool, Manchester, Sheffield, Birmingham and Nottingham who organised a

---

[87] Sir Joseph Heron quoted in Redford, *History*, vol. 2, 297.

conference to petition parliament in opposition to the new legislation. Their petition was not successful but the meeting did lead to the creation of the Association of Municipal Corporations, a body committed to defend their 'interest, rights and privileges'. This Association became the mouthpiece of local government over the next decades and of crucial importance as a conduit of municipal information and expertise.

The Association of Municipal Authorities was, however, only one of many voluntary bodies established in the second half of the nineteenth century, committed to the sharing of municipal expertise and technocratic policy support. Most did not grow out of conflict between local and national government, but simply out of the professionalisation of many local government functions and a recognition that economies of scale could be achieved by sharing administrative information. Changes in the law encouraged many smaller towns to petition for incorporation. Many of these new corporations had such small departments and a more limited internal network of specialist knowledge to rely upon. For these corporations municipal professional organisations were of vital importance. The British Association of Gas Managers (founded 1864) and the Municipal and Sanitary Engineers and Surveyors Association (1873) were the oldest and most important groups.[88] Over the next thirty years more specialist groups developed, such as the Libraries Association, the Museums Association and, with the development of electric tramways, the Municipal Passenger Transport Association. Alongside these new associations came professional journals, dedicated to the distribution of information about new products and new policy initiatives. Some, such as the *Gas Journal*, were aimed more at professional contractors than municipal policy makers, but others, such as the *Municipal Sanitary Engineers' Journal*, were specifically aimed at municipal professionals.[89] In the early twentieth century more general journals appeared, including the *Municipal Journal* in 1902 and the *Local Government Chronicle* in 1907 and both were aimed at both councillors and municipal civil servants, reporting on activities of general interest to municipalities and relationships with national government. Crucially they were non-partisan journals reporting on innovative policy development at a time when political partisanship was increasingly coming to dominate local government affairs.

Perhaps, predictably, the strongest professional network was a medical one. A tight fraternity of Medical Officers of Health existed. They were, for most of the nineteenth century, trained at one of the three great medical

---

[88]   J. Garrard and V. Parrott, 'Craft, professional and middle-class identity', in A. Kidd and D. Nicholls, eds, *The Making of the British Middle Class? Studies of Regional and Cultural Diversity since the Eighteenth Century* (Stroud 1998), 148–68.

[89]   Founded in 1875, this also provided a register of members and associations in the field.

schools in Britain – Edinburgh, Glasgow or London. Locally and nationally the MOH had a formidable reputation and the names of Baker in Leeds, Duncan in Liverpool, Russell in Glasgow and Littlejohn in Edinburgh still possess local resonances more than a century after their deaths. Russell published over 100 scientific papers, Littlejohn's *Report* of (1865) was widely quoted, and the first MOH of all, W. H. Duncan, influenced many of the early sanitary decisions in Liverpool.[90] As knowledge concerning public health established its central place in municipal administrations, the agenda switched from sewer connections and clean water supplies to slum clearance and town planning initiatives.[91] Sanitary engineers, city surveyors and by the 1880s and 1890s, town planning officials became established in many cities. In the 1860s and 1870s urban redevelopment projects limited to a few streets were completed. Then, instead of demolition, new construction of municipal housing followed, with more ambitious Garden Suburbs and fully integrated town planning schemes involving transport, housing and landscaping proposed from the 1890s, though mostly concentrated in the years immediately preceding World War One.[92] There were many influential town planners – Ebenezer Howard, Raymond Unwin and Patrick Geddes are internationally renowned for their pioneering town planning proposals – but there were important clusters of municipal expertise, too, with T. C. Horsfall, and W. Thomson, for example, rallying interest in the Town Planning Association and related organisations.

Party politics and the convergence of municipal policy

The emergence of political parties in local government provided new conduits of administrative knowledge. Political parties drew on their own

---

[90] H. D. Littlejohn, *Report on the Sanitary Condition of the City of Edinburgh* (London 1865); E. Robertson, *Glasgow's doctor: James Burn Russell, MOH* (East Linton 1997), and P. Laxton, 'Fighting for public health: Dr Duncan and his adversaries 1846–1863', in S. Sheard and H. Power, eds, *Body and City: Histories of Urban Public Health* (Aldershot 2000), 59–88.

[91] J. A. Yelling, *Slums and Slum Clearance in Victorian London* (London 1986); C. M. Allan, 'The Genesis of British Urban Redevelopment with Special Reference to Glasgow', *Economic History Review*, 17, 1965, 598–613, and R. V. Steffel, 'The Boundary Street Estate: An Example of the Urban Redevelopment by the London County Council, 1890–1914', *Town Planning Review*, 47, 1976, 161–73.

[92] See for example, G. Cherry, *Pioneers in British Planning* (London 1981); A. Sutcliffe, *Toward the Planned City: Germany, Britain, the United States and France, 1780–1914* (Oxford 1981); H. Meller, *Patrick Geddes. Social Evolutionist and City Planner* (London 1990); H. Meller, *Towns, Plans and Society in Modern Britain* (Cambridge 1997); M. Miller, *Raymond Unwin. Garden Cities and Town Planning* (Leicester 1992), and W. R. F. Phillips, 'The "German example" and the professionalization of American and British city planning at the turn of the century', *Planning Perspectives*, 11, 1996, 167–83.

sophisticated information networks, including ward parties, local MPs, party publications and national political leaderships. Political manifestos provided prescriptive solutions to local problems, often promoting administrative reform, scrutiny of office holders and closer financial audit.

The development of political partisanship in local government coincided with the rapid growth of municipal expenditure from the 1860s. The growth of public services and investment in infrastructure projects brought about a rapid rise in local taxation (rates).[93] This in turn provoked increasing scrutiny of council expenditure and passionate crusades against waste and extravagance and in 1889 a revision to municipal government funding was introduced.[94] A stronger central government component in municipal funding was the result. The inflexible and regressive nature of the rating system meant that the lower middle class was particularly hard-hit.[95] Many organised themselves into Ratepayers Associations to investigate excesses and lobby against tax rises. Such was the power of these groups that some have seen the division between economists and spenders as one of the key cleavages of local urban politics in the nineteenth century.[96]

This was a cleavage that often cut across party lines and inhibited the growth of party politics within local authorities. However, by the 1870s most of the large municipal authorities were divided into conflicting Liberal and Conservative camps. In some cases this division concealed a high degree of consensus on most issues, so much so that often there were no contested elections for long periods of time. Even late in the century uncontested elections were common; Leicester had no contested elections for three years between 1887 and 1889. In many local elections, voters were influenced as much by loyalty to their local employers as by political issues.[97] One important influence on the growth of party organisation and local politics was the extension of the parliamentary franchise in 1867 to include most urban males – universal suffrage was only achieved in 1885 for men and in 1928 for women. By the early 1880s most large towns had developed representative political associations with each ward responsible for nominating local candidates and the reorganisation of London government in 1888 injected a further degree of party political activism there, which was

---

[93]   R. Millward, 'The political economy of urban utilities', in Daunton, *Cambridge Urban History*, vol. 3, 315–49. For background see Waller, *City and Nation*, 298–316.

[94]   G. R. Baugh, 'Government Grants in Aid of the Rates in England and Wales 1889–1950', *Bulletin of the Institute of Historical Research*, 1992, 215–37.

[95]   B. M. Doyle, 'The changing function of urban government: councillors, officials and pressure groups', in Daunton, *Cambridge Urban History*, vol. 3, 287–313, esp. 290–94.

[96]   Hennock, *Proper Person*; E. P. Hennock, 'Finance and politics', *Historical Journal*, 6, 1963, 212–15.

[97]   P. Joyce, 'The factory politics of Lancashire in the later nineteenth century', *Historical Journal*, 18, 1975, 525–53.

issue-driven.[98] The new associations increasingly chose candidates for their political beliefs rather than simply for their social status. Elected representatives were frequently expected to advocate specific policies.[99] The socialist Independent Labour Party (ILP) viewed its representatives as delegates and required them to vote as instructed, or face de-selection. Not only was policy guidance and knowledge thus generated from outside the council, council policy itself was actually being made outside the council.

Programmatic manifestos that had only really emerged at parliamentary elections in 1885 soon found their way into municipal politics. The decision of the ILP to develop specific policy programmes for local government encouraged the Liberal Party to follow suit and by the early months of Gladstone's fourth ministry in 1892, Asquith began to actively encourage local Liberal groups to adopt a model municipal programme, a suggestion that cities like Manchester and Leicester took up with great enthusiasm. Although each municipality continued to have a great deal of independence, the policy goals adopted were often very similar. While political parties did not seek to impose specific proposals on municipal leaders, the adoption of what amounted to national local government manifestos had huge influence. In many respects the programmes reflected genuine change in grass-roots Liberal opinion.[100] Even so, there can be little doubt that some Liberal councils did feel compelled to adopt the left-wing programmes recommended by the National Liberal Association. To reject them would be to face censure from their own radicals and possible political defeat at the hands of socialists.[101] Thus party programmes provided increasingly important sources for administrative and policy innovation.

The growth of social science and scientific approaches to government did not necessarily lead to greater uniformity of policy or increasing central control. The fragmentation of British local government and a powerful localist tradition meant that growth in the central authority of the state was gradual and incremental. Indeed those who did advocate centralisation, like Matthew Arnold, felt greater centralisation could be achieved without the fear that it would become despotic, precisely because the British commitment to

---

[98] S. Pennybacker, *A Vision for London 1889–1914: Labour, Everyday Life and the LCC Experiment* (London 1995), and D. Feldman and G. S. Jones, eds, *Metropolis – London. Histories and Representation since 1800* (London 1989).

[99] For the classic description of the methods of the party machine see M. Ostrogorski, *Democracy and the Organisation of Political Parties*, vol. 1 (London 1902), esp. 371–493.

[100] J. Moore, 'Progressive pioneers: Manchester Liberalism, the Independent Labour Party, and local politics in the 1890s', *Historical Journal*, 44, 2001, 989–1013.

[101] P. F. Clarke, *Lancashire* (Cambridge 1971), 162, and J. Hill, 'Manchester and Salford politics and the early development of the Independent Labour Party', *International Review of Social History*, 26, 1981, 171–201.

local self-government was so strong.[102] This fragmentation of local government did make it difficult at local level to co-ordinate policy development to tackle social problems; even the most powerful nineteenth century corporation had no power over public education, which was in the hands, after 1870 of separately elected school boards, or the poor law, which was still administered by poor law unions.

If there was an increasing uniformity in local authority policy development, it was because local authorities were developing information networks which drew on the expertise of those outside their own immediate ranks. Specialised standing committees drew on a diverse pool of business and commercial knowledge, whilst supported by an increasingly professionalised local civil service. The doctrines of municipal pride encouraged rather than inhibited the sharing of information about the development of new public facilities. Systems of deputation and ceremonial opening enhanced information exchange and helped maintain mutually beneficial municipal networks. External contractors, aware of the growing market power of municipalities reoriented their activities to cater for public needs, initiating trade fairs and specialist conferences. Specialist policy communities inside municipalities developed their informal networks into formal professional associations. When central government threatened to take away local government functions, municipalities responded by creating a federation of municipal authorities not just to oppose the plans but also to establish a common platform of resistance.

Paradoxically, the development of these voluntary networks and their role as agents of standardisation accelerated the national influence on local government. Sanitary engineers developed common standards for construction work. Library associations developed common methodologies to classify subjects. Art galleries developed common practices of picture hanging. Museums adopted similar systems of classification for their artefacts. Policy formation was often emulative and frequently followed fashions.[103] There was a compulsive shared interest in technical standards in all areas connected with municipal engineering. During the 1860s corporations competed to build the most prestigious town hall. In the 1870s almost every major corporation developed branch public libraries and had the rudiments of a tramway system. Thirty years later, public gymnasiums were the order of the day. Newspapers of course, partly due to the external pressure of public opinion, influenced these policy fashions with an increasingly regional perspective on urban social questions. In reality, much of the detail of development could only be worked out through local government's own policy networks on which central government was an important influence, both through its statutory role and as provider of

---

[102] Eastwood, *Government*, 157.
[103] A. Briggs, *Victorian Cities* (Harmondsworth 1990, orig. London 1963), 150–53.

'official' information. But central government was not invariably the most important influence on municipal knowledge since in many instances specialist information could be readily acquired from neighbouring authorities, professional organisations, national and international bodies, and the municipal corporations associations. Municipal knowledge was not bounded by physical boundaries; it had assumed international currency.[104]

By the beginning of the twentieth century, the growth of political parties within local government had already influenced the way policy was formulated. Many in local government who would never have accepted Benthamite centralisation voluntarily adopted national policy programmes. In some respects the growth of these programmes was merely a logical development of scientific approaches to government advocated by Chadwick. Once local government entered into networks in order to emulate today what would be called 'best practice', they subscribed to the view that universal principles could be applied to measure performance. The leaderships of the Liberal and Independent Labour Parties who used them to justify the development of local government manifestos willingly accepted these notions. If, even at the end of the nineteenth century local government had preserved much of its autonomy, the national nature of information and policy networks meant that policy variations were more limited than before. Whatever their ideological make up, corporations rather than the private sector were the main service providers by 1900. All had accepted large debts to fund improvement programmes.[105] Most had 'municipalised' key industries, such as energy supply and public transport. Ideological and local differences were still important and local government did retain a great deal of independence. Yet the nationalisation of municipal knowledge and information networks, assisted by the rise of social sciences, helped create growing consensus and policy convergence.[106]

By 1914 the main conduits of municipal knowledge led to a national network of information and policy exchange incorporating professional organisations, interest groups, political parties and central government. Although encouraged by doctrines of scientific efficiency and the advantages of economies of scale, the development of this network was not the product of central government imposition. Rather it developed as local government sought to find solutions to the policy challenges of a diverse and maturing urban society.

---

[104] See, for example, M. Hietala, *Services and Urbanization at the Turn of the Century* (Helsinki 1987).

[105] Offer, *Property*.

[106] G. Kearns, 'Town Hall and Whitehall: Sanitary Intelligence in Liverpool, 1840–63', in Sheard and Power, eds, *Body and City*, 89–108.

CHAPTER FOUR

Running an Unregulated Town: Strategies of Lincoln's Municipal Elite, 1860–1910

Denise McHugh

This study considers the composition and urban management policy of a municipal elite in a medium sized English provincial centre in the period between 1860 and 1910. While the broad historiography of British towns and cities in this period is that of hard-fought 'progress' and of increasing intervention and regulation, this study offers an alternative analysis of improvement resisted or delayed and local independence asserted in the face of statutory authority and central government control.[1]

In the period between 1835 and 1870 the management of British towns and cities was formalised by extensive parliamentary legislation which created institutions for handling the problems of the growing towns and cities at a local level. For many industrial towns these bodies were new creations. In the traditional urban centres however, the reformation of long-standing governing bodies frequently lead to upheavals in the urban social structure.[2] In all towns, new and reformed institutions, including town corporations and sanitary boards, provided the vehicles for the urban elites to pursue programmes of urban regulation. The most significant of these was the municipal corporation.

The municipal corporations created by the 1835 Act were regarded by central government as a cheap and efficient way of administering the expanding towns. They provided a pragmatic response to the increasing urban problems without centralising responsibility.[3] Devolved power enabled the newly enfranchised urban middle class to develop hegemony over the

---

[1]   This article forms part of a chapter in D. McHugh, 'Remaking the Victorian County Town 1860–1910' unpublished University of Leicester Ph.D. thesis, 2002.

[2]   See J. Moore and R. Rodger, 'Who Really Ran the Cities? Municipal knowledge and policy networks in British Local Government, 1832–1914', in this volume 37–69. See also A. Briggs, *Victorian Cities* (London 1963). For a general explanation of the changing structure of local government see R. Sweet, *The English Town 1680–1840: Government, Society and Culture* (Oxford 1999).

[3]   Briggs, *Victorian Cities*, 370.

town environment and economy.[4] In the industrial cities the middle class embraced this opportunity enthusiastically, frequently promoting urban improvement, often developing unique forms of civic identity and sometimes even remodelling town centres and raising the national profiles of their cities. In doing so, they consolidated the authority of the municipal elite and of local government and strengthened the identity of the broader middle class whom they represented.[5] In some expanding manufacturing centres of Victorian England the absence of an established social hierarchy or a formal system of town administration could create a power vacuum in which the middle class established themselves as princes in charge of city states. Established historic towns were in a different position; reform of the municipal corporation often overthrew decades, if not centuries, of established social and political leadership. Patricians, often Anglican and Tory, were usurped by a more commercial, Liberal and often non-conformist middle-class elite. Lincoln provides a good case study of an established urban centre where municipal reform created a newly ascendant commercial elite after 1835. What characterised this municipal elite and how did they run the town?

The town and its economy

Lincoln was an ancient ecclesiastical settlement and a county town; it had been an important town in Roman Britain and remained substantial in the medieval period. From the early modern period county administrative centres like Lincoln provided professional and market functions for a defined hinterland and this status allowed Lincoln to enjoy a brief renaissance in the eighteenth century. By the industrial age, however, Lincoln was a town in slow and steady decline. The major factor in this decline was its geographical location; like many cathedral cities[6] Lincoln stood at the heart of a large and

---

[4]   D. Fraser, *Urban Politics in Victorian England: The Structure of Politics in Victorian Cities* (Leicester 1976), 14; D. Cannadine, ed., *Patricians, Power and Politics in Nineteenth-Century Towns* (Leicester 1982); D. Smith, *Conflict and Compromise, Class Formation in English Society 1830–1914: A Comparative Study of Birmingham and Sheffield* (London 1982), and R. J. Morris, *Class, Sect and Party: The Making of the British Middle Class, Leeds 1820–1850* (Manchester 1990).

[5]   Briggs, *Victorian Cities*; E. P. Hennock, *Fit and Proper Persons: Ideal and Reality in Nineteenth-Century Urban Government* (London 1973), and Smith, *Conflict and Compromise*. Morris, *Class, Sect and Party*. For a discussion of the debate on the urban elite see J. Smith, 'Urban elites c. 1830–1930 and urban history' *Urban History*, 27, 2000, 255–75, esp. 255–7.

[6]   In Britain, towns containing a cathedral and the see of a bishop are accorded the status of 'city' regardless of size. In this paper the term 'town' has been used for Lincoln in recognition of its relatively small scale and its position in the urban hierarchy.

predominantly rural region at the edge of the East Midlands. The town was not part of an urban network and possessed only the most basic of communication systems. The industrial and urban growth of the midlands region further disadvantaged Lincoln as the focus of innovation and investment shifted from the traditional towns to rising industrial centres. Lincoln was too far east from the dynamic centre of England and too isolated; its communications centred on traditional waterways, wharves and turnpike roads and impeded competition and expansion. The railways did not reach Lincoln until 1846, when a branch line arrived from Manchester and

Figure 4.1 'Uphill Lincoln' showing the Cathedral and castle, 1947

Source: Photograph courtesy of Simmons Aerofilms Limited.

Sheffield, cities with which Lincoln had little or no previous contact. Lincoln's position remained peripheral.

The internal topography of Lincoln's townscape was also problematic. The cathedral was positioned on an extensive plateau above a sharp incline. Around the cathedral were clustered the castle, the institutions and the 'better' properties. These were substantial eighteenth century townhouses and were mainly inhabited by clergy and urban professionals.

The high street and main thoroughfare ran down the incline from the cathedral and the commercial areas and the working class population were clustered around the waterways and marshland of the lower town at the base of the hill. This lower area was divided both by a canalised river which ran at a right angle to the high street and by a railway line. 'Uphill' and 'downhill' Lincoln, as they were known, presented two very different faces; 'uphill' was sleepy, respectable, historic and picturesque, 'downhill' was bustling, dirty, cramped and disordered. Socially, they were two different worlds with separate value systems and minimal interaction. Social status and success was inextricably linked to being and living 'uphill'.[7] In Victorian Lincoln these enduring divisions were at once real and symbolic with important consequences for economic development, for the urban elite, and for the wider middle class.

Geographical disadvantage influenced the development and the nature of industry in Victorian Lincoln. The resultant structural difficulties ensured that keeping the town running and economically viable was a complex operation. Despite external isolation and internal fragmentation, manufacturing became a significant activity in the town. By the mid-nineteenth century 39 per cent of employed men and 43 per cent of working women were engaged in manufacturing. Many of these occupations remained traditional with the majority of workers engaged in producing hats, shoes and clothes and smaller numbers engaged in boat building and luxury goods. From the traditional town foundries which had produced diverse items such as agricultural implements, mills, winches and stoves emerged a modern engineering industry. Railway transport overcame locational disadvantage to an extent and brought pig iron and cheaper coal from surrounding regions. Iron foundries flourished and by the 1860s there were five major engineering firms established in the town, mainly producing agricultural machinery.[8] Several large-scale engineering plants, producing similar products and each employing up to a thousand men, occupied an extensive area downhill and fundamentally re-orientated the structure and social tone of Lincoln between 1860 and 1910.

This iron industry was thriving but vulnerable; there were limitations to the industrial process and problems in the market. Lincoln foundries mainly cast pig iron and were too isolated from the raw materials and technological innovation to develop a steel industry. This dependence on pig iron production meant that Lincoln firms were restricted in the range of products that they could offer. Diversification compensated to some extent as production moved from agricultural equipment to steam engines, boilers and

---

[7]   J. F. H. Brabner, ed., *The Comprehensive Gazetteer of England and Wales* (London 1894), 15, and J. B. Priestley, *English Journey* (London 1934), 367.

[8]   Lincolnshire Archives (LA) Book Collection, author unknown, *Forgotten Lincoln* (Lincoln 1898).

electrical lighting equipment.[9] Lincoln foundries looked for new products suited to their skills and processes in a changing global market.

In 1870, Britain dominated the world iron and steel market and was the world's leading supplier of engineering products.[10] However, there was a serious slowing in the growth of the market and industry during the last quarter of the nineteenth century.[11] In Lincoln the impact of cyclical industrial depressions was compounded by structural decline as pig iron based engineering was superseded, first by wrought iron and then by steel. The product range of local firms compounded this market vulnerability as all the foundries had specialised in agricultural engineering products and found themselves driven out of export markets by both tariff barriers and American and German competition.[12] This slump in international demand was compounded regionally by the onset of the agricultural depression after 1873 which was particularly severe in eastern England.[13]

The vulnerable character of the iron industry led to significant structural weakness in Lincoln's economy. By the 1870s, the town was already overly reliant upon a single industry; by the 1880s over five thousand working men in Lincoln were employed in the five major foundries and a single employer, Robeys, supported up to ten per cent of the town's population.[14] Crises in the Lincoln iron foundries were more likely to mean short-time working, or lay-offs, rather than company failure, but demand problems in the industry were felt across the whole community. After manufacturing, 'dealing' was the second largest male occupational sector in Lincoln and all forms of trading, factoring, shops and shopping formed a central part of the traditional county town economy. The wages of the workers, particularly the higher disposable incomes of the skilled workers such as the town's boilermakers, had become essential to the urban economy in little over two decades. In 1875, for example, during a depression in iron exports, local businesses began to fail and economic depression deepened.[15] Despite the structural problems in this industry it had created a great expansion in the town population; between

---

[9]   W. White, *White's History, Gazetteer and Directory of Lincolnshire 1882* (Sheffield 1882), 498.

[10]   S. Pollard, *Britain's Prime and Britain's Decline: The British Economy 1870–1914* (London 1989), 22, and P. L. Payne, 'Iron and steel manufactures', in D. H. Aldcroft, ed., *The Development of British Industry and Foreign Competition 1875–1914: Studies in Industrial Enterprise* (London 1968), 71–100, esp. 71.

[11]   F. Crouzet, *The Victorian Economy* (London 1982), 240, and Payne, 'Iron and steel manufactures', 75.

[12]   Parliamentary Papers (PP), *Royal Commission on Depression in Trade and Industry, First Report 1886*, vol. XXI; Irish University Press (IUP) Trade and Industrial Depression I, Session 1884–1886, 318–20. Pollard, *Britain's Prime*, 21, and S. B. Saul, 'The engineering industry', in Aldcroft, *The Development of British Industry*, 186–238, esp. 235.

[13]   Saul, 'The engineering industry', 211.

[14]   White, *White's History*, 498.

[15]   F. Hill, *Victorian Lincoln* (Cambridge 1974), 203.

1861 and 1911, Lincoln's population increased from 21,000 to 57,000 an increase of 273 per cent.[16] The most significant population increase occurred in the 1870s which was also one of the most economically problematic decades in the town.

From 1870 Lincoln's municipal elite developed an urban policy primarily designed to stabilise the local economy. Strategies were aimed at safeguarding the development and profitability of the town's vulnerable industry while maintaining urban growth and the diversity of the traditional economic sectors. The obvious and growing divergence between the uphill and downhill communities was mirrored in the conflicting agendas within the urban elite. The major manufacturers argued that Lincoln must remain a low cost environment claiming this compensated for the inconvenience of their relative isolation and kept production costs competitive. At the same time the manufacturers required a healthy and mobile workforce. The gentry and professional elements, concentrated 'uphill' around the Cathedral, wanted a healthy, clean and improved town in both environment and morals.[17] In between these interests were the merchants and traders who wished to attract and maintain middle-class and agrarian custom to the town but without increasing their overheads. In the second half of the nineteenth century the various networks of economic, social and political power in Lincoln converged upon the council chamber where local interests came into conflict with agendas imposed by central government. From the mid-century onwards the municipal elite, as represented in the town's corporation and sanitary authority, found themselves subject to increasing statutory obligations emanating from national government, all of which were expensive. In Lincoln, urban management policy arose directly from the composition of the municipal elite. Those who managed the town were also those who profited from it.

The composition of Lincoln's municipal elite

Victorian Lincoln contained two powerful elite bodies; the cathedral with its body of Anglican clergy and the Municipal Corporation.[18] Only the corporation had control over the urban environment and a direct connection to the economy. The church authority was part of a wider network, appointed independently of the town. The municipal elite was essentially a shopocracy, dominated by traders and merchants, incorporating the influential larger

---

[16]   PP, *Census of England and Wales*, 1851–1911.

[17]   D. M. Thompson, 'Historical survey 1750–1949', in D. Owen, ed., *A History of Lincoln Minster* (Cambridge 1994), 252–62.

[18]   At various times in the nineteenth century the municipal elite was called 'Lincoln Corporation', 'Lincoln Council' and 'Lincoln City Council' here, for the purpose of clarity, 'Lincoln Corporation' is used throughout.

manufacturers and a modest but stable section of professionals. As retailers, almost a quarter of the town's municipal elite was directly dependent upon the general marketing and central place functions of Lincoln. As in all towns during this period these retailers were very varied in character.[19] Chemists, drapers, grocers and wine and spirit merchants all featured strongly, but saddlers, seed merchants, confectioners and hairdressers also appeared in the municipal elite. These individuals were all dependent upon the general economic wellbeing of the county town, on its ability to compete with other urban centres to draw consumers in from the hinterland in order to maintain daily sales. The more substantial and successful retailers, with one or two premises in the High Street and city centre, served as councillors on the Lincoln Corporation. In terms of social status these retailers had a local significance, reputation and sometimes wealth which stretched beyond the lower middle-class 'shopkeeper' label. By contrast very few neighbourhood or suburban shopkeepers gained access to the municipal elite.[20]

The growing manufacturing industry was also well represented in Lincoln's Municipal Corporation; all the major ironmasters served on the council and the leading industrialists took turns at the mayoral office during the 1850s.[21] However, despite the fact that Lincoln became increasingly dependent upon manufacturing for urban wealth creation and employment, there was no sign that manufacturers 'packed' the council chamber. One reason for this was the large scale of the manufacturing plants; there were actually very few ironmasters and a handful of men owned the major plants in Lincoln. Continuity was important. Most of the major manufacturers represented in the municipal elite in the middle of the century were still present half a century later. There was a dynastic succession from father to son. Despite the relative scarcity of large-scale manufacturers they possessed a great deal of long-term political influence. Large manufacturers were elected to office easily and proved successful in municipal ambitions; in Lincoln 20 per cent of mayors between 1860 and 1910 were manufacturers. Once in office manufacturers had almost a 50 per cent probability of achieving mayoral status. The electorate welcomed manufacturers as council-

---

[19]   G. Crossick, 'The emergence of the lower middle class in Britain', in G. Crossick, ed., *The Lower Middle Class in Britain 1870–1914* (London 1977), 9–39, esp. 15.

[20]   LA, *Biography of Lincoln City Council Members Holding Office 1835–1914*, miscellaneous deposit 157. *Minutes and proceedings of the Common Council 1865–1877*, document L/1/1/11; *The Lincolnshire Directory, 1855;* W. White, *White's History, Gazetteer and Directory of Lincolnshire 1872* (Sheffield 1872); *Lincoln Pocket Guide* (Lincoln 1874); W. White, *White's History, Gazetteer and Directory of Lincolnshire 1882* (Sheffield 1882); *Cook's Lincoln Directory, 1885* (Lincoln 1885); *Cook's Lincoln Directory, 1897* (Lincoln 1897); *Kelly's Directory of Lincolnshire* (London 1896); *Ruddock's Lincoln Directory* (Lincoln 1903); *Kelly's Directory of Lincolnshire* (London 1906), and *Kelly's Directory of Lincolnshire* (London 1909).

[21]   LA, *Biography of Lincoln City Council.*

lors and considered the experience of large-scale business as a positive force
in local government. With their strong local power base and an active interest
in participating in urban government, manufacturers were able to mobilise
councillors from other occupational groups around their own agendas.

The shopocracy and manufacturers were joined in the municipal elite by
another identifiable occupational group, the professionals. Almost one fifth
of Lincoln's councillors were professionals of various types and they
maintained a steady presence on the Corporation over the period. There was
neither a decline in their status as numbers increased in the area, nor any
evidence of extended political influence; the professional presence remained
stable through electoral and party upsets. Their continuity of presence and
numerical strength was maintained through networks of professional
patronage and by strong linkages to councillors with different economic
interests.[22] Between 1860 and 1910 a professional elected to Lincoln
Corporation had a one in four probability of achieving mayoral office. This
suggests that the council and the rate-paying electorate valued professional
status and knowledge only to a slightly lesser degree than they valued that of
manufacturers. The presence of professionals in the municipal elite also
reflected the strength of the professional vote among the rate-paying
electorate. Certain wards in Lincoln were 'safe seats' for professionals and
they could retain their elected position in the municipal elite for as long as
they wished. Personal and occupational connections were highly influential
and the municipal electoral process was tightly controlled and orchestrated.
Overall, the professionals in the Lincoln municipal elite were more likely to
be Conservative than Liberal. They also tended to represent the Upper or
Middle wards, the Cathedral and upper town area rather than the Lower
Ward, the industrial 'downhill' part of Lincoln.

Professionals were elected by the Anglican elite and their neighbours to
represent the traditional hierarchy of the cathedral and county town. Among
the professionals in the municipal elite solicitors were particularly successful.
Lawyers had a privileged status which allowed access to, and movement
between, a number of public positions where knowledge of both national
policy and local economics was an advantage. The solicitors elected to
Lincoln Corporation were those who were closely connected to the dealing
and administrative role of the town. They were also directly involved in state
and county administration. These factors gave the solicitor councillors access
to other sources of power in the urban environment, such as the Cathedral
clergy and representatives of the state, which proved beneficial to their
municipal careers. Solicitors were also successful office holders exploiting
the pluralistic nature of the town environment. They had strong business links
in the urban community outside their own profession. Half of the solicitors
on Lincoln Corporation held directorships in local companies, they also

---

[22]   Ibid.

controlled the chairmanships of the local bank, newspaper and brick company.[23] These positions gave them a direct interest in the industrial economy and strengthened their allegiances to other councillors who were also directors of 'downhill' companies.

Professionals and manufacturers in the elite were closely allied. In a case of economic trouble, even the Official Receiver was a solicitor serving on the Corporation. Internal municipal committees also offered possibilities for the consolidation of professional linkages and common interest and could overcome political considerations.[24] Those solicitors with the densest professional networks enjoyed longer municipal careers, although those whose time on the council was very brief arguably still possessed impressive, if opaque, connections and potential influence.

The solicitor councillors demonstrated the highly networked nature of the municipal elite and the necessity for successful councillors to be well connected in addition to possessing specialist knowledge and status. Professionals in the municipal elite inhabited and represented the upper town but they were also tightly linked to the industrial and 'trade' sectors of the lower town economy. Far from being tainted by an association with 'trade' the Lincoln lawyers relied upon their links with local industry for significant portions of their income. Professionals in the elite acted both as a communications conduit and the glue which linked the upper and lower town elements in the municipal elite. Professional knowledge in the Lincoln municipal elite did not guarantee 'professional' policies or management although professionals have been thought to support urban improvement when present in corporations.[25] Professional, business, social and familial connections and networks enabled the municipal elite to exert influence and authority across the urban space but industrial conditions and economic imperatives should not be overlooked.[26] When running the town strong ties to local businesses and an intimate knowledge of the economy could inhibit the development of professional-led policies in areas such as health.

It has already been noted that in Lincoln social status was a matter of geography. Class and status influenced both access to municipal office and the subsequent success of councillors' careers. In accordance with the town's topography Lincoln's upper ward represented the Anglican, Tory and cathedral middle-class ratepayers who inhabited the area. This ward provided

---

[23]   Lincoln Central Library local collection, G. R. Riley, *The Rise of Industrial Lincoln 1800–1959* (unpublished manuscript), and LA, *Biography of Lincoln City Council members*.

[24]   LA *Minutes and proceedings of the Common Council 1865–1906*, document L/1/1/11–13.

[25]   Hennock, *Fit and Proper*, 40.

[26]   M. J. Wiener, *English Culture and the Decline of the Industrial Spirit 1850– 1980* (Cambridge 1981), 15–16, 30; H. Perkin, *The Rise of Professional Society. England Since 1880* (London 1989), and K. T. Hoppen, *The Mid-Victorian Generation 1846–1886* (Oxford 1998), 44.

a way to retain traditional values in the reformed municipal elite. The housing in Lincoln's upper ward remained socially exclusive long into the twentieth century and this was reflected by the preference of its voters to return candidates of a high social status. Electoral success in Lincoln was dependent upon a good candidate-to-ward match and borough wards were differentiated by status. Far from being open, the electoral process for the municipal elite was controlled, organised and complex, individual council seats were highly nuanced with class and cultural implications. Reformed municipal elites contained and maintained many of the traditions and tensions of the local 'ancien regime', harnessing these to new programmes or strategies of urban governance.

Coherence in the composition of the municipal elite was due to its stability. Lincoln's elite was small; in the course of half a century the list of corporation members comprised only 119 individuals. The relatively low number of council members across the fifty-year period can be explained by the longevity of service. This stability distinguished Lincoln from industrial centres or larger Victorian cities where the 'average triennial turnover of council members' was between 36 and 45 per cent in any three year period.[27] In Lincoln the average number of years served by councillors, both in their capacity as elected representatives and as aldermen, was 21. This stability in elections and in office holding was the result of a significant number of elected councillors who were almost permanent; one member served for 49 years, while two others managed 46 and 44 years in office. However, there was just enough turnover to incorporate aspirational members of the middle class and to accommodate culturally influential groups such as professionals. The stability of elite membership reflected the size and governing traditions of older settlements. Common aims in the municipal elite were reinforced by the middle-class status and shared economic interests among councillors. At the core of Lincoln Corporation there was a small group of powerful individuals able to drive policy.

This inner circle remained relatively inaccessible to newly elected councillors and gaining access to the heart of municipal power was dependent upon a web of invisible urban networks. For those who wanted to achieve mayoral office or pursue a long-term council career it was necessary to be well integrated in the local middle class and to have strong occupational, business and social connections. Two of the strongest influences operating in the municipal elite were occupational and kinship links which allowed a disproportionate level of local authority. Occupational links have already been identified but kinship remained a durable influence even after municipal reform. During the period 1860 to 1910, Lincoln Corporation contained at least six father-son pairings, although there were no examples of the two

---

[27]   J. Garrard, *Leadership and Power in the Victorian Industrial Towns 1830–1880* (Manchester 1983), 65.

generations serving concurrently. These families were high street retailers and manufacturers, other councillors were connected through the less obvious links of marriage, creating wider kin networks in the community. Families provided powerful vehicles for ideological and political continuities in the municipal elite and noted 'old' town families were perceived as intimately connected to the fortunes of the town. Councillors used this perception to their advantage; the evidence suggests that in the late Victorian period municipal government in the traditional town was often seen as a logical extension of the family business. Kinship links enabled the Corporation to pursue consistent municipal policy and management strategies over an extended period of time.

Religion was also an important unifying force in the Lincoln municipal elite and it played a significant part in town politics. Despite an Anglican cathedral and clergy, Lincoln contained large dissenting communities and these congregations were reflected in the council chamber. Although Lincoln was dominated physically, visually, socially and symbolically by the Anglican community, non-conformists played a central part in urban management after 1835. During the period 1860–1910 over a fifth of Lincoln Corporation councillors were Methodists and active non-conformists; 16 per cent of councillors were Wesleyan Methodists as were seven out of ten mayors. Non-conformity and, particularly, Methodism shaped the civic vision of Lincoln as a liberal hard-working town based on independent trading. During this time non-conformists remade old rituals such as the corporation's annual church procession and reformed urban institutions such as the schools and infirmaries. Non-conformity was acceptable among the wider voting middle class and among the business community but, while Liberal Methodists and other non-conformists could hold the balance of power on the council and achieve the office of Mayor with relative ease, the social elite representing the Upper Ward and its Cathedral remained an impenetrable bastion. Lincoln was a town polarised by social class and religion and to achieve long term municipal success often required the work, or networking, of a lifetime.

Lincoln Corporation demonstrated the representative nature of reformed municipal elites; it reflected the broad nature of the town's urban middle class whilst being skewered towards the lower end of the scale. There is very little evidence of any direct aristocratic or gentry influence in this period, although many councillors had business links with local gentry and some had kin or marriage connections to landowners outside the town. The municipal elite was urban and industrialised and represented both the diversity and the differences within the local middle class. Local interests and property united the councillors; very few had any personal economic interests, except some transport investment and agricultural land, outside of Lincoln. Municipal policy and relations with central government were conditioned by consideration of the weekly profit generated by all forms of town business. The personal investments of councillors made Lincoln's municipal elite resistant to environmental improvement and regulation and hostile to outside interference in urban governance.

Elite management and an unsanitary town

There is no doubt that Victorian Lincoln was in desperate need of environmental management; it was both dirty and dangerous. As early as 1849 a local report presented to Lincoln Corporation highlighted the sanitary defects in the town infrastructure, commenting that there was 'no system of connected underground drainage in Lincoln (only) surface or street drainage'.[28] The report argued that if, following the recent railway development, the population should continue to grow 'the evils resulting from a total absence of combined sewerage will be daily augmented, and diseases which are consequent thereon, must prove more fatal in their effects'.[29] By 1850, Lincoln Corporation were legally obliged to undertake sanitary improvements under the Health of Towns Act because of the high level of urban mortality which stood at 24 in 1,000. However neither this fact nor the report had any impact on the behaviour of the municipal authority; no improvements were undertaken in the mid-century period.

Over the four decades from 1850 the Lincoln urban elite achieved very little in the field of environmental health improvement. Municipal strategies widely adopted elsewhere to improve urban welfare including the supply of pure water, thorough drainage, slum clearance and efficient sewerage were not addressed until the 1890s in Lincoln. By the end of the nineteenth century the management of sewerage and the provision of water in Lincoln remained primitive while slum clearance was non-existent.[30] The urban infrastructure had changed little since the 1850s, yet industrial expansion in Lincoln had created a high concentration of working-class inhabitants 'downhill' in housing conditions which were 'regarded with apathy for years by the city councillors'.[31] The lower town, was a spectacularly unhealthy urban environment; 'as late as 1886 the infant mortality rate for Lincoln was three times the national average' and most of the water supply was 'liable to contamination of a dangerous character'.[32] The town corporation acted as the sanitary authority for Lincoln and 'Administration by Sanitary Authority

---

[28]   G. Giles, *Report made to the Sanitary Committee of the Corporation of Lincoln* (Lincoln 1849), 7.

[29]   Ibid. 35.

[30]   PP, *Report on the Inland Sanitary Survey of England and Wales 1893–95*, IUP, Health 17, 152–153.

[31]   Riley, *Rise of Industrial Lincoln,* 132.

[32]   I. Beckwith, *The Book of Lincoln* (Buckingham 1990), 98, and PP, *Report on the Inland Sanitary Survey,* 52.

(was) very defective as a rule.'[33] By the time the sanitary authority was created in 1866, what little piped water Lincoln had was of debatable quality since there was no underground drainage and few municipal facilities generally.[34]

Lincoln in the 1890s presented the ideal conditions for the outbreak of an epidemic disease. However, it was a decade later before the full impact of sanitary neglect led to the appearance of a water-borne disease. Typhoid broke out in Lincoln at the end of 1904; it spread rapidly, peaked in 1905, and was not eradicated until 1907.[35] Over a thousand people in the town were recorded as suffering from the disease during 1905 and 1906 and when the outbreak was over 131 people had died.[36] It was one of the last significant epidemics of typhoid in Britain, a disease that had appeared in most urban areas in the 1860s and 1870s.[37]

Subsequent reports and investigations blamed the municipal elite for the epidemic. During a period when most urban authorities began to control their environments to improve urban health Lincoln's municipal authority took little action. It was within their powers to implement adequate health and sanitary improvements yet they failed to do so. Why was this so? Resistance to intervention in Lincoln was usually articulated in terms of cost and this was a central concern in all municipalities contemplating improvements to the urban fabric. However, Lincoln Corporation was no worse off, financially, than many others; indeed as an ancient corporation it had many assets and sources of income including farmland and so was able to avoid raising a borough tax until 1874.[38] It has been argued that the lack of improvement in Lincoln in the mid-nineteenth century was due to this lack of income.[39] Local resistance to taxation was often articulated as a cost objection but formed part of a broader ideological concept of Lincoln's urban function. Rather than an improved town the municipal elite focused on creating a specialist economic environment in Lincoln, a free trade, low tax area.

The retardation of Lincoln's environmental and sanitary development was unusual, but it was not unique. The historiography of the Victorian city has largely focused on the cities' experiencing dynamic growth or pioneering eye-catching or progressive municipal strategies, as yet we know little of the urban elites who resisted change or simply failed to manage it. It can be

[33] PP, *Report on the Inland Sanitary Survey*, 52.

[34] LA, *Lincoln City Council, Notice of Motions 1860s*, document L/1/1/7.

[35] R. Briscoe, J. S. English and E. A. Melrose, *The Typhoid in Lincoln* (Lincoln 1980); Hill, *Victorian Lincoln*, 234–6.

[36] N. R. Wright, *Lincolnshire Towns and Industry, 1700–1914* (Lincoln 1982), 233; Briscoe, English and Melrose, *Typhoid in Lincoln*.

[37] P. J. Waller, *Town, City and Nation, England 1850–1914* (Oxford 1983), 303.

[38] LA, *Minutes and proceedings*; *White's Directory of Lincolnshire 1882*, 501.

[39] Wright, *Lincolnshire Towns and Industry*; Hill, *Victorian Lincoln*, 167.

argued that an established tradition of urban government may well have made older cities more conservative in their actions.[40] What made Lincoln Corporation's lack of civic improvement notable was that the absence of environmental regulation did not arise from apathy or lack of funds but rather formed a pillar of a coherent, ideological programme of urban management. The municipal elite prioritised economic growth and the promotion of trade, two aspects of town life which were not strictly within the remit of municipal corporations, over public health and civic regulation, responsibilities which they held by law. In Lincoln the ideological concepts of free trade and liberalism took the form of providing a low-cost unregulated urban setting within which businesses could thrive. 'Free trade' measures taken by the

Table 4.1   Sources of urban instability and elite responses, 1860–1910

Sources of instability in Lincoln's urban economy	Action taken by the urban elite to promote stability
New young industries	Spread risk through elite-directorships / no regulation
Uncertain demand (tariff barriers, depression)	Diversify product range / seek wider market
Remoteness from centre	Improve local mobility
High local costs	Keep rates low and retain labour
Rapidly growing population	Control urban mobility and activities of working class
Competition	Specialise
Competing elite interests	Exploit professional, kinship and religious networks

council in Lincoln were concerned with modifying the environment to ensure the free-flow of goods and labour in order to foster industrial and economic growth (see Table 4.1). In Victorian Lincoln, the costs of industry or the external diseconomies were not charged to the public purse but were absorbed by individuals in terms of health risks.[41]

Lincoln Corporation took an active part in urban management or in supporting individual actions only where they were related directly to trade and urban income. The development of the waterside and wharf area (Brayford Pool) provides a good illustration of elite priorities. The municipal authority owned and regulated this port in 'downhill' Lincoln. Although waterways were well-known risks to health, the elite did little to improve the pollution of the pool and river but instead focused on improving wharf access

---

[40]   B. M. Doyle, 'The changing functions of urban government: Councillors, officials and pressure groups', in M. J. Daunton, ed., *The Cambridge Urban History of Britain*, vol. 3: *1840–1950* (Cambridge 2001), 287–313, esp. 294.
[41]   LA, L/1/1/11, *Minutes and proceedings.*

and ensuring the free flow of goods.[42] The waterside area in Lincoln remained dedicated to trade and commerce throughout the late nineteenth century but received little regulation or reconstruction.

Alongside trade, the expansion of local industry was encouraged by the elite. The largest manufacturers had established their premises along the waterfront from the mid-century and industry expanded to infill this marshy area between river and railway, until the 1890s. There is no evidence to suggest that this development was regulated in any way, which was hardly surprising given the leading roles played by manufacturers in civic government. Lincoln's industrial development was assisted by the refusal of the municipal government to regulate the locations of factories or railway lines, to levy a borough rate, to control the pollution of the local watercourse or in any way to incur expense which would fall upon property owners.

Lincoln Corporation also tried to aid employers by controlling the growing manufacturing workforce in relation to the availability and mobility of labour in the borough. The elite achieved both through the speculative development of unregulated housing for the working classes and by providing corporation footbridges across the watercourse to enable easy access to workplaces.[43] Early leisure provision for the working classes aimed to retain labour within the town as a Corporation motion proposing the development of a park indicated:

> The increased and increasing population of the city of Lincoln especially amongst the Artisans and the Working Classes whose occupations confine them to the workshop and place of business during the hours of labour, render it essential for the maintenance of health and the present facilities afforded by the railway system to townships and others make it desirable that some attractive place of public outdoor recreation should be provided to which the population of the city could be admitted either free of at a trifling cost. (...) no such place for public recreation now exists within the city.[44]

The industrial working class was encouraged to settle and to remain in Lincoln, moving efficiently between home and workplace and spending both their leisure time and earnings within the borough. It was widely understood that the various economic functions of the town were interdependent, so while the rhetorical emphasis was placed upon the iron industry and wharf-side activities, much of the support for these municipal policies came from the shopocracy.

The influential nature of shop owners has been recognised in other studies of local government during this period and they have been described as

---

[42] Ibid.

[43] Wright, *Lincolnshire Towns*, 226–7.

[44] LA, *Lincoln City Council, Notice of Motions, 26th October 1870,* document L/1/1/7.

initially radical supporters of municipal reform.[45] The conservatism and thrift of the shopocracy has been stressed in the later Victorian period.[46] In Lincoln there was a direct and clear correlation between the industrial fortunes of the town and the prosperity of the retailers. In terms of capital improvements to the urban fabric, the shopocracy have been described as the 'group most actively antagonistic to proposals of increased expenditure'.[47] This was because of the retailer's intimate daily knowledge of the uncertain flow of urban income and expenditure. Shopkeepers brought this retail-based concept of urban economics into the Lincoln council chamber and influenced municipal policy in relation to civic expenditure.

The urban elite and, to an extent, the town economy was stabilised through the town Corporation. Improvements to the urban fabric, which incurred high capital costs, were regarded as a threat to this stability and, while the debate focused on water supply and drains, the issue in question was a more fundamental one of autonomy. Lincoln's municipal elite were not concerned with establishing the limitations of municipal power or its use but with the right of the municipality and locality to be in charge of its own affairs and spending. In Lincoln, resistance to outside interference (expense) from central government and statutory obligation coalesced over the issue of sanitary improvement.

Local government and central government

From the 1860s, local elites were beginning to find their earlier independence eroded and the Sanitary Act of 1866 marked a decisive shift in the central government stance towards local government. The permissive was replaced by compulsion.[48] From 1870, the Local Government Board (LGB) was instituted by Parliament to ensure that corporations carried out their new responsibilities, with particular attention paid to environmental issues. Yet still no significant improvements had yet been undertaken in Lincoln where urban resistance to central government regulation and communication developed into opposition to national legislation. Practical issues of sanitary improvements were married to questions of legislative expansion and legal obligation. In 1865, the corporation recorded:

---

[45] See V. A. C. Gatrell, 'Incorporation and the pursuit of Liberal hegemony in Manchester 1790–1839', in D. Fraser, ed., *Municipal Reform and the Industrial City* (Leicester 1982), 15–55, esp. 36–7.

[46] H. Fraser, 'Municipal socialism and social policy', in R. J. Morris and R. Rodger, eds, *The Victorian City, A Reader in British Urban History 1820–1914* (London 1993), 258–81, esp. 261; Crossick, 'The emergence of the lower middle class', 39.

[47] B. Barber, 'Municipal Government in Leeds', in Fraser, *Municipal Reform*, 61–108, esp. 104.

[48] J. Prest, *Liberty and Locality: Parliament, Permissive Legislation and Ratepayers' Democracies in the Nineteenth Century* (Oxford 1990), 209.

The mayor and fourteen councillors and the surveyor have visited Worthing and Croydon for the purpose of enquiring into the practical working of drainage and sewerage utilisation adopted in those towns.[49]

While they were there 'enquiries were made by several of the deputation as to the working of the Local Government Act. Croydon has been held up as a total failure of all that was sought for (from the act)'.[50] Lincoln Corporation was obliged to adopt the Act in 1866 but had not done so willingly. The resultant election produced a Conservative withdrawal and twenty years of Liberal party control in Lincoln.[51]

In many British towns and cities during this period the domination of the Liberal party resulted in programmes of urban improvements and the fostering of civic pride. However local politics in Lincoln had revolved around an easy alliance of Tories and old-fashioned Whigs (Liberals) based on social equality and status connections.[52] Local contemporaries had interpreted this situation in terms of occupations, perceiving politics in the mid-century as divided into two camps: those who made their money in trade and commerce facing an educated professional group which included the Cathedral authorities and clergy.[53] Party politics followed an 'uphill' and 'downhill' divide and the social fracture within the Liberal party- 'respectable' uphill Liberals v. 'noisy' downhill ones continued long after the Liberal-Tory alliance dissolved in the late 1860s. The alliance was typical of the lack of effective party organisation in county towns beyond the brief intervals of parliamentary elections. In the last three decades of the century the party machines became more organised and Lincoln liberals unified, only to split again over Ireland and the Home Rule bill in 1886.[54] Other fault-lines were created by religious distinctions within the liberals and by new occupational differences.[55] In late Victorian Lincoln party politics came second to the ideological commitment to low rates and elections were lost rather than won over the previous term's rate increases.

Throughout this period the lack of urban improvement and the emphasis on constraining expenditure, combined with the complete absence of a tradition of civic intervention, resulted in a deficit of capital investment in the urban fabric of Lincoln. Objections to this state of affairs, from whatever quarter, were met with hostility or derision at corporation meetings. Internal objections and external pressures combined to further delay improvement. Municipal government was characterised by resistance to, and resentment of,

---

[49] *Minutes and Proceedings of the Common Council*, 19th December 1865.
[50] Ibid.
[51] Hill, *Victorian Lincoln*, 45.
[52] Ibid. 44.
[53] R. J. Olney, *Rural Society and County Government in Nineteenth Century Lincolnshire* (Lincoln 1979), 87.
[54] Hill, *Victorian Lincoln*, 195.
[55] LA, *Biography of Lincoln City Council Members Holding Office*.

central 'interference' and statutory authority.[56] There was little sympathy with modern ideas or with demands issuing from parliament or the LGB in London. This resistance became a central characteristic of Lincoln Corporation between 1860 and the 1890s, defining its municipal power.

In the middle decades of the century Lincoln's municipal elite resisted external controls or demands for expenditure by simply ignoring them. However from the 1870s the complexity of municipal business was utilised by the Corporation for their own ends. This strategy was generally adopted in the pursuit of a liberal business environment and in deflecting the requirements of central government. The corporation conducted a type of guerrilla resistance to central authority, manipulating the procedures of formal meetings, reports and committee work. The Corporation, acting as the Urban Sanitary Authority, took a number of environmental actions in the late Victorian period, including the purchase of the gasworks and waterworks and the beginnings of sewerage and electricity provision in the town. These developments were regarded as sound business investments, yet, despite the legal obligations imposed on all urban sanitary authorities there remained in Lincoln strong opposition to investment in large-scale projects. Infrastructure improvements such as drainage produced urban disruption and required high levels of capital expense. It is significant that the gas and water plants were purchased after they had proved their commercial viability, while the development of anything resembling effective sewerage occurred much later.[57]

In 1870, the Home Secretary investigated the provision of sewerage in Lincoln and, following constant political pressure, drainage was laid at the end of the 1870s, twenty years later than in most other towns. Not that the comparison was considered to be important. Lincoln Corporation believed that they understood local conditions best and invitations to visit other town councils or to join them in campaigns were generally refused. Government enquiries were derided and reports from medical officers were refuted aggressively.[58] Where the municipal elite was legally obliged to make provision, particularly in the field of health, it was possible for them to pass an issue back and forward between different, essentially internal, authorities, boards or committees. These were delaying tactics to avoid expensive municipal action. In 1891, the council sitting in committee resolved:

> That it is inexpedient to adopt the provision of the Infectious Diseases (Notification) Act, 1889 unless and until the Urban Sanitary Authority are prepared to provide a reasonable amount of hospital accommodation to provide for cases requiring compulsory isolation, and that the Council be

---

56 LA, *Correspondence of Lincoln Local Board 1866–91.*
57 Hill, *Victorian Lincoln*, 220.
58 LA, *Correspondence of Lincoln Local Board 1866–91.*

recommended to provide for such accommodation at a cost not exceeding £ 4,000.[59]

Between the two authorities composed of the same elite individuals the hospital provision was delayed and, when provided, inadequate. This particular delay was not simply a cost-related objection to the hospital, but also a moral one, as many of the councillors objected to the idea of isolation involving the separation of families, or of mother and child. This delaying strategy was also used to avoid other forms of intervention, and, in this manner, problems with the water supply were allowed to continue for more than thirty years until the typhoid epidemic of 1905.

Compared to other municipal authorities Lincoln passed little local regulatory legislation. In 1880, byelaws relating to new streets and buildings were brought into force and regulations on common lodgings houses introduced in 1882. Despite this apparent progress, however, enforcement was another matter. By the 1890s, the Inland Sanitary Survey found that the common lodging houses were in a 'very bad' state and the slaughter houses 'generally dirty and dilapidated'.[60] While the council had adopted regulations on dairies, cowsheds and milk shops, these were also found to be in a poor state, particularly those owned by the Municipal Corporation itself.[61]

The lack of improvements even under statutory obligation and the failure to enforce existing regulations soon drew the attention of the LGB, a government agency established in 1871 to monitor the working of environmental legislation.[62] Lincoln Corporation was brought to the notice of the LGB for their prevarication in various areas of provision. The habitual response of the council to ignore all new statutory requirements or responsibilities for as long as possible was antithetical to the operation of the Board which sought effective local implementation of national legislation. In Lincoln, the permissive Public Health Act of 1848 was ignored successfully for some time and so later compulsory statutes met the same initial response.[63] This behaviour and the presence of another elite powerful body within the borough raised the negative profile of Lincoln in London. When the Dean and Chapter of the Cathedral were unhappy with a corporation service they complained directly to the LGB.[64] In 1891 the Board wrote to the Lincoln Sanitary Authority forcing the authority to 'consider' a letter 'containing a complaint from the Precentor (cathedral clergy) of Lincoln'. However, the LGB could complain, cajole, pressurise and demand, but,

[59]   LA, *City of Lincoln Epitomes, Urban Sanitary Authority Meetings, 1891–94*, 15/12/1891' document L. Lin 614.

[60]   PP, *Report on the Inland Sanitary Survey of England and Wales 1895–99*, 152–3.

[61]   Ibid.

[62]   C. Bellamy, *Administering Central-Local Relations, 1871–1919: The Local Government Board in its Fiscal and Cultural Context* (Manchester 1988), 112.

[63]   Hill, *Victorian Lincoln*, 166–7.

[64]   *City of Lincoln Epitomes*, 27/2/1891.

ultimately, they could not force change in the provinces, since they had little financial or political power to exert.[65]

In Lincoln it was rare to find any elite acceptance or validation of external criticism; there was only resentment. The Corporation, acting as the Urban Sanitary Authority, received continual complaints about environmental issues, particularly with regard to water supply, but rejected criticism. When the council received:

> A letter from the Army Service Corps, at Sheffield, complaining about the quality of water supplied at the Barracks, Lincoln (...) the clerk was directed to reply that the Corporation take all possible precautions to render the supply of water to the city pure and fit for domestic purposes.[66]

The complaints and personnel emanating from the LGB in London only hardened the conviction of the municipal elite as to their right to run the town as they saw fit.

Religious and cultural influences were also strong local factors in the elite's rejection of outside evaluation as the example of hospital provision demonstrated. W. B. Maltby a chemist, councillor and Methodist attributed the city's health problems 'to the mysterious workings of a Superior Power' at a council meeting in 1864 and called for 'temperance, proper food, ventilation and better houses'.[67] All measures which were the responsibility of the individual or the open market rather than the elite. As seven Lincoln mayors during this period were Wesleyan Methodists and several were also lay preachers, 'moral' explanations for social and economic problems remained popular in Lincoln long after they had become discredited in other areas. There was also a strong local scepticism about the developments in sanitary science and technology, which was surprising given the uptake of new forms of industrial technologies in late Victorian Lincoln.[68]

Eventual environmental improvements in the town were neither internally generated nor innovative responses to local urban issues but largely a result of external pressures – obligations finally acceded to after a long period of procrastination.[69] All municipal improvements carried out by the elite before the 1880s were undertaken with reluctance. Lincoln remained at least two decades behind many Victorian cities in environmental control although the Corporation had no intention of admitting this. The lack of intervention and regulation by the municipal elite that resulted in an unhealthy environment, high mortality, and general squalor also failed to produce any external manifestations of civic pride in late Victorian Lincoln. The wave of

[65]   Bellamy, *Administering Central-Local Relations*, 111.
[66]   *City of Lincoln Epitomes*, 20 & 27/2/1891.
[67]   Hill, *Victorian Lincoln*, 116.
[68]   C. H. J. Anderson, *The Lincoln Pocket Guide* (London 1880), 172.
[69]   Fraser, *Power and Authority*, 151.

municipal building that occurred in towns and cities across Britain after 1860 bypassed Lincoln. The town had no purpose built town hall, no municipal offices or fire station, no museum or library building. The municipal elite did their utmost to avoid capital projects which would incur high levels of investment. The occupational and economic structure of the town produced very little support or, apparently, demand for cultural amenities. In late Victorian Lincoln ideals of civic consciousness and public health were sacrificed to the elite's requirements for an unregulated cheap manufacturing and trading environment.

Conclusions

The municipal elite of Lincoln pursued three major strategies between 1860 and 1900. Firstly, the Corporation was concerned to maintain a low cost, low tax business environment. Secondly, councillors exhibited a strong local resistance to central government 'interference' and statutory authority; and finally, they established high levels of elite cohesion and advantage. This last was achieved through strong and active personal, professional, political, business and religious networks which operated both within and outside the corporation chamber. Cohesion was further cemented by the avoidance of expenditure and antipathy to outside interference which could temporarily unite factions within the corporation and assist in the construction of a local identity. While the Municipal Corporations Act of 1835 and subsequent legislation can be considered as primarily concerned with managing the new urban pressures, the Lincoln elite hijacked these institutions to create conditions for profit and urban stability. While the physical environment could be dangerous to health and life, the municipal elite in Lincoln feared the slumps created by trade cycles or the loss of skilled men or retail profits more. The elite was formed from the intense network of social, familial, business and occupational connections operating within the county town. These networks enabled the elite to overcome the 'uphill'-'downhill' social divide and to maintain stability and resist national government intervention. It is also probable that elite business linkages inhibited the development of party politics or a party programme of urban management. For the municipal elite, local identity, social connection and economic interest were all more powerful foci of individual loyalties in late Victorian Lincoln than professional or party ideologies. Running the town was simply a matter of keeping business running well.

CHAPTER FIVE

The Challenge of Urban Democracy: Municipal Elites in Edinburgh and Leipzig, 1890–1930

Michael Schäfer

The emergence of the nineteenth-century urban bourgeoisie in Britain as well as in Germany has been widely researched by historians. We now know quite a lot about the social composition of urban elites, as well as the strategies, discourses and languages that enabled them to exert local hegemony. As a result we can assess the accomplishments and failures of the *Bürgertum* in responding to the challenges of industrialisation and urbanisation.[1] But these rather clear cut images of the urban bourgeoisie as a class in action seem to get blurred by the late nineteenth century. In historical studies on urban governance after 1900, and even more so after 1914, the dealings of bourgeois civic elites appear to be of little interest. Local politics in early twentieth-century British as well as German cities now seems to be primarily a matter of political parties, social, religious or ethnic movements and economic pressure groups.[2] On the other hand, German urban historians have long been fascinated by the rise of professional municipal administration, which by the turn of the century seemed to have taken urban governance out of the hands of middle-class notables.[3] Thus the urban bourgeoisie, the *Bürgertum*, loses historiographic attention at the very moment when its alleged hegemony is seriously challenged.

---

[1] L. Gall, ed., *Stadt und Bürgertum im 19. Jahrhundert* (Munich 1990); L. Gall, ed., *Stadt und Bürgertum im Übergang von der traditionalen zur modernen Gesellschaft* (Munich 1993); H.-W. Schmuhl, 'Bürgertum und Stadt', in P. Lundgreen, ed., *Sozial- und Kulturgeschichte des Bürgertums* (Göttingen 2000), 224–48; R. Trainor, 'Urban elites in Victorian England', *Urban History Yearbook*, 1985, 1–17; E. P. Hennock, *Fit and Proper Persons. Ideal and Reality in Nineteenth Century Urban Government* (London 1973), and R. J. Morris, *Class, Sect and Party: The Making of the British Middle Classes: Leeds, 1820–1850* (Manchester 1990).

[2] But see B. M. Doyle, 'The structure of elite power in early twentieth century Norwich, 1900–1935', *Urban History*, 24, 1999, 179–99.

[3] See for example J. Reulecke, *Geschichte der Urbanisierung in Deutschland* (Frankfurt am Main 1985), 120–22.

Bringing the urban bourgeoisie back into focus is a general aim of this essay, which draws on a comparative local case study of the cities of Leipzig and Edinburgh.[4] What happened to the cities' bourgeois elites after the late nineteenth century? Did they just quietly retire, leaving the field to the anonymous forces of bureaucratic rule and democratic mass politics? Or did they manage to stay in control behind the scenes or even on the scene? Can we still outline the contours of a civic elite in terms of a body of upper middle-class notabilities after 1900 or even after 1918? How did bourgeois elites in both cities cope with the emergence of urban democracy? First, I consider the constitutional framework of local government in both cities and their respective countries. Then I deal with the interdependence of municipal constitutions and local socio-political power constellations. Thirdly, I discuss the respective role of municipal bureaucracies in local government. Lastly, I compare municipal housing policies in both cites to examine the impact of democratisation and professionalisation on urban governance.

The frameworks of urban democracy

The frameworks of urban governance in Britain and Germany share a set of similar basic features. In the first decades of the nineteenth century local government reforms handed over town administration to local citizens and their freely elected representatives and gave them the right and the duty to run local affairs – with a certain measure of central government supervision. In the British case, the crown's failure to impose an absolutist regime in the seventeenth century had left local affairs almost exclusively to local elites. Municipal reform acts in 1833 (Scotland) and 1835 (England and Wales) abolished non-representative, co-opted town councils, handing the running of incorporated cities over to bodies elected by and responsible to local ratepayers. Municipal reform in pre-unified Germany in the first decades of the nineteenth century lacked the basic uniformity of the British reform acts. In some areas new urban government legislation curbed the autonomy of virtually independent cities, whereas in Prussia the tight control of the absolutist state over the municipalities was loosened, giving citizens a measure of local self-government. Even after unification in 1871, German municipal law resembled an irregular patchwork of local and regional rules and regulations, with local government legislation remaining a prerogative of the formerly independent states.[5]

---

[4]   M. Schäfer, *Bürgertum in der Krise. Städtische Mittelklassen in Edinburgh und Leipzig von 1890 bis 1930* (Göttingen 2003).

[5]   K. B. Smellie, *A History of Local Government* (London 1968), 9–33; D. Fraser, ed., *Municipal Reform and the Industrial City* (Leicester and New York 1982), 1–14, and W. R. Krabbe, *Die deutsche Stadt im 19. und 20. Jahrhundert* (Göttingen 1989), 10–14 and 24–7.

Nonetheless, there are certain specific features of German urban governance that differ significantly from British municipal government. The relationships of central to local government in Germany and Britain rested on fundamentally different principles. German state governments were legally endowed with a broad range of powers, which enabled them to exert a tight control on the municipalities and to interfere deeply in urban administration – if they wanted to. Local government boards in England and Scotland had comparatively few means of direct intervention into the workings of urban governance. In practice, however, German city governments often enjoyed a greater measure of autonomy from the central state than their British counterparts. Urban governance in Germany rested on the principle of 'universal competence'. That means, municipalities could take over any function or spend local taxpayers' money on any purpose not expressly forbidden by law or government ordinance. In Britain local government agencies had to be empowered by law for virtually every single administrative act. Thus the very core of Britain's constitutional tradition, Parliament's supreme legislation and taxation prerogatives, restricted the scope and the autonomy of local government.

Basic features of the two countries' political constitutions also left their marks on the internal structure of municipal government. Local government in nineteenth-century German cities mirrored in many ways the bureaucratic constitutionalism of state and national governments. The Leipzig system can be regarded as fairly typical for German urban governance: a 'parliament' of directly elected Citizens' Representatives (*Stadtverordnete*) levied rates and acted primarily as a supervisory body for the city 'government' or council (*Stadtrat*). The Leipzig City Council, where professional, remunerated mayors and councillors played a leading role, was elected by the Assembly of Citizens' Representatives. But once in office, City Councillors were not responsible to their electors and could not be removed by them. In English and Scottish cities parliamentary rule prevailed: town councils as well as local school and poor law boards acted as sole decision-making agencies in the respective areas of responsibility assigned to them. The emerging professional municipal bureaucracy was clearly subordinated to representative bodies elected directly by the ratepayers.[6]

German and British municipal reforms in the early decades of the nineteenth century restricted the rights of participation in local government to a rather small section of the urban population. In Britain we can easily identify a pattern of piecemeal extension of the municipal franchise in the course of the late nineteenth and the first half of the twentieth centuries. In 1868 all male householders were included in the urban electorate, and up to

---

[6] Krabbe, *Stadt*, 35–7, 42–7; H. Goetz, 'Die ausländischen Gemeinden im Vergleich zu den deutschen, in H. Peters, ed., *Handbuch der kommunalen Wissenschaft und Praxis*, 3 vols. (Berlin 1956–1959), vol. 1, 597–603, and W. H. Dawson, *Municipal Life and Government in Germany* (London 1914), 29–57.

the turn of the century women gradually gained formally the same active and passive voting rights as men. In practice, however, relatively few women qualified for the local vote as householders, house owners or shopkeepers. Municipal franchise rested basically on the payment of local rates levied on residents and (in Scotland) on owners of houses and business premises. In effect, the householders' families and lodgers as well as all those who had not paid their rates or received poor relief were excluded from voting.

A closer look at Edinburgh's franchise regulations reveals that the working classes were in many ways discriminated against by this system. Firstly, many more potential working-class than middle-class voters were excluded from the voters' rolls, because they could not afford a directly taxed house or flat, evaded the paying of local rates or had been on public relief. Secondly, though no single person could cast more than one vote, middle-class *families* were in effect favoured, because house-owners and occupiers or owners of business premises were granted the local vote. In Scotland lodgers could qualify for voting if they paid a rent of more than £10 per annum. Thus in Edinburgh a considerable number of the more affluent householders' wives qualified for the house-owner vote, whereas many of their adult sons and daughters living at home were admitted to the voters' rolls on a specific reading of the lodger clauses of the Scottish Burgh Acts. British local government franchise was extended again in 1918, when the wives of male householders were enfranchised, and people who had failed to pay their rates or received poor relief were no longer disqualified from voting. But in principle the ratepayer franchise remained in force until 1944.[7]

The development of local government franchise in Germany in the nineteenth and early twentieth centuries is marked by a much greater degree of discontinuity. Before 1918 the great majority of adult inhabitants of most German cities were either wholly excluded from participation in municipal government or their rights were severely restricted. Leipzig's local franchise system featured most of the common devices of exclusion and discrimination found in German municipalities: the right to vote in local elections was restricted to adult male 'freemen' (*Bürger*) of the city. The granting of freemanship depended on certain income qualifications and the payment of a fee. Thus paying rates in Leipzig, as well as in other Saxon and Bavarian cities, did not automatically include the right to vote. Throughout Germany women were excluded from the municipal vote, although in Leipzig they could obtain freemanship. In 1894 the city of Leipzig supplemented these

---

[7]   M. G. Sheppard, 'The effects of franchise provisions on the social and sex compositions of the municipal electorate, 1882–1914', *Bulletin of the Society for the Study of Labour History*, 14, 1982, 19–23; A. Midwinter, 'A return to ratepayer democracy? The reform of local government finance in historical perspective', *Scottish Economic and Social History*, 10, 1990, 61–68, esp. 64–5; B. Keith-Lucas and P. G. Richards, *A History of Local Government in the Twentieth Century* (London 1978), 18–20; Schäfer, *Bürgertum*, 40–41.

restrictions with the introduction of a three-class franchise, the system in force in most of the Prussian provinces, in Baden and in other German federal states where freemanship was not a precondition to vote. Thus in 1910 only about six per cent of Leipzig's inhabitants had the right to vote (in Edinburgh it was approximately 22 per cent), and four fifths of those who were enfranchised elected only one third of the Citizens' Representatives. In the course of the revolution of November 1918 all franchise restrictions in German cities were at once abolished, and the local vote was given to every adult inhabitant of German nationality.[8]

Urban elites and local government

It is quite evident that local government franchises should have had profound effects on the social profiles of municipal bodies. However, if we compare the composition of the Edinburgh Town Council and Leipzig's Assembly of Citizens' Representatives on the eve of the First World War, the differences appear to be remarkably small, at least after taking into account the two cities' vastly different franchise systems. Indeed, both city parliaments were dominated by businessmen, house-owners and master artisans, and to a lesser extent by upper middle-class professionals like lawyers or doctors. With more careful investigation differences in the social (and political) backgrounds of Edinburgh Town Councillors and Leipzig Citizens' Representatives become clearer, but they seem even more remarkable than the similarities. In spite of Leipzig's freeman's and three-class franchise, the share of the city's working class representatives in the municipal parliament amounted to almost one third of the total, and most of these were former or even active blue collar workers. In the Scottish capital less than one eighth of the councillors were representatives of organised labour and even fewer Town Councillors were active or former workers.

Nevertheless, the specific impact of the franchise system on the composition of Leipzig's Assembly of Citizens' Representatives is clear. In 1894 Leipzig's local election byelaws transferred the right to select one third of the Citizens' Representatives to the top five per cent of the local ratepayers. Because in Leipzig and in most other German cities local taxes were paid mainly on income and only to a limited extent on ownership of houses and land, many of the 2,000 first-class voters in 1910 belonged to the city's commercial and industrial elite. This elite selected their representatives to sit in the town hall mostly among themselves. Thus the first-class section

---

    [8]   W. Hofmann, 'Aufgaben und Strukturen der kommunalen Selbstverwaltung in der Zeit der Hochindustrialisierung', in K. G. A. Jeserich et al., ed., *Deutsche Verwaltungsgeschichte*, 6 vols. (Stuttgart 1983–88), vol. 3, 606–12; L. Ludwig-Wolf, 'Leipzig', in *Verfassung und Verwaltungsorganisation der Städte*, 7 vols. (Leipzig 1909), vol. 4/1, 136–9, and Schäfer, *Bürgertum*, 39–43.

of the Citizens' Representatives Assembly consisted mainly of merchants, publishers, industrialists or upper-class lawyers, many of them millionaires. The next third of the Citizens' Representatives were elected by a middle range of 6,000 ratepayers, among them many who qualified by paying rates on houses and land situated within the city boundaries. This second-class section was filled primarily by the representatives of the house owners', master artisans' and shop keepers' associations. Roughly half of the 32,000 third-class voters in 1910 were blue collar workers, and the other half consisted mostly of middle and lower rank civil servants and clerks, smaller artisans and shopkeepers. At the beginning of the new century almost all candidates elected Citizens' Representatives' from the third class had been nominated by the socialist working class movement, most of them paid functionaries of the Social Democratic Party and the socialist unions or employees of the co-operative societies.[9]

In many respects the 1894 introduction of a class-stratified franchise reflected a crisis of legitimacy for Leipzig's bourgeois civic elites. When the city incorporated its large industrial suburbs after 1889 and thereby more than doubled its population within three years, the urban establishment had to face the challenge of a highly organised working class movement. Since the 1860s, Leipzig had been a stronghold of the German Social Democratic Party and the socialist unions. After the repeal of Bismarck's Anti-Socialist Law in 1890, labour candidates soon drew enough support in Leipzig's Citizens' Representatives elections to seriously challenge the established political forces. In practice voters chose between lists of candidates for the whole of the city, a relative majority of votes being sufficient to gain all contested seats in the annual elections. In 1894, when a Socialist landslide victory seemed only a matter of time, Leipzig City Councillors and Citizens' Representatives changed the rules by switching from an equal to a three-class franchise system.[10]

This *coup d'etat* safeguarded the power of the urban bourgeoisie for the next 25 years, but the legitimacy of their municipal hegemony steadily eroded. After 1894 and up until 1918 Leipzig experienced growing protests against oligarchic rule in local government. The most obvious political effect of the introduction of class franchise was the mobilisation of the working class and even part of the lower middle-class vote for Social Democracy.

---

[9]   Schäfer, *Bürgertum*, 51–62; M. Schäfer, 'Bürgertum, Arbeiterschaft und städtische Selbstverwaltung zwischen Jahrhundertwende und 1920er Jahren im deutsch-britischen Vergleich', *Mitteilungsblatt des Instituts zur Erforschung der europäischen Arbeiterbewegung*, 20, 1998, 192–5.

[10]   F. Seger, *Dringliche Reformen. Einige Kapitel Leipziger Kommunalpolitik* (Leipzig 1912), 10–14; Ludwig-Wolf, 'Leipzig', 131–7; M. Schäfer, 'Die Burg und die Bürger. Stadtbürgerliche Herrschaft und kommunale Selbstverwaltung in Leipzig 1889–1929', in W. Bramke and U. Hess, eds, *Wirtschaft und Staat in Sachsen im 20. Jahrhundert* (Leipzig 1998), 275–9.

When it became evident after the turn of the century that the Social Democrats would win all the seats in the third voters' class, the Leipzig election system came under pressure from non-socialist forces as well. Especially the associations of teachers, clerks and civil servants, the so-called 'new middle class', complained about their virtual exclusion from representation in municipal affairs. In the years before the First World War there were several attempts in Leipzig to reform the local franchise. The Social Democrats took the most radical stand, calling not only for the restoration of an equal franchise but also for the abolition of the freemanship, as well as gender and ratepayer qualifications, in order to extend the local vote to every adult inhabitant. The proposals of the non-socialist critics of the existing local election system were mostly content with certain modifications to class franchise.

In 1906 the Leipzig City Council brought forward a plan to substitute the three-class franchise with a system that had been introduced by the neighbouring cities of Dresden and Chemnitz in the preceding years: voters would be assigned to six classes according to their professional and social status. The local press, non-socialist politicians and bourgeois notables all did their best to isolate the labour movement in their public discourse. Thus discussions of local franchise reform focused very much on the question of which share each urban group or 'estate' (*Stand*) ought to have in local government and what system might ensure this outcome. But even more important seemed to be which franchise system would most effectively keep political extremism, namely Social Democracy, out of municipal affairs.[11]

The discussions about local franchise in the pre-war years indicate that the citizens of Leipzig had completely lost a basic consensus on the rules of the game. Once the principle of one-man-one-vote was abandoned and the debate was opened on how to apportion votes to house-owners, civil servants, workers or businessmen in local elections, it became almost impossible to find a mode of voting that every affected group was ready to accept. The opponents of the three-class franchise were deeply split between socialist and anti-socialist factions, into workers and non-workers. This constellation helped the ruling majority in the Assembly of Citizens' Representatives to block any reform before the eve of the November Revolution in 1918. The deep socio-political cleavage of local politics in Leipzig (and in many other German cities) and the dynamics of confrontation between the liberal-conservative *Bürgertum* and organised socialist Labour also left their marks on the composition of the Leipzig City Council. Unlike the Assembly of Citizens' Representatives, the City Council up to 1914 was manned exclusively by members of the traditional municipal elite. The city parliament's non-socialist two-thirds majority ensured by the three-class franchise made it possible to block any socialist candidate for City Council.

---

[11]   Schäfer, 'Burg', 271–6, and Schäfer, *Bürgertum*, 46–9.

Only in 1916 under the auspices of national solidarity during wartime, was the first Social Democrat appointed to the *Stadtrat*.[12]

In Edinburgh local franchise was never a major issue in public debates in the pre-war decades. The householder vote, the principle of one-man-one-vote, and the simple rule that paying local rates entitled one to a say in the spending of public money were widely regarded as fair and just. Labour occasionally criticised minor issues in the working of the system. For example, one point was the exclusion from the voters' lists for not paying rates or having received poor relief. Women's rights activists maintained that married women should get the householder vote, but at the same time local suffragettes praised the local government franchise as a model for national elections. Despite a comparatively open and equal local franchise system the city of Edinburgh was governed by a clear majority of 'bourgeois' Town Councillors, and the labour movement made only slow progress up to 1914. A closer look, however, reveals that only a handful of Edinburgh Town Councillors may be regarded as representatives of the Scottish capital's merchant and professional elite. Most city parliamentarians were businessmen and professionals belonging to an upper middle strata of urban society.[13]

But how did Edinburgh's civic elite manage to cope with the challenge of urban democracy in a comparatively egalitarian constitutional framework? One explanation for the stability of bourgeois hegemony in the Scottish capital may be found if we consider the mode of local elections in British cities. Whereas local voters in Leipzig chose primarily between lists of candidates, in Edinburgh a much more personal style prevailed in municipal elections. Edinburgh ratepayers were assigned to one of the city's 16 voting districts. Voters in each of these 'wards' were entitled to send three representatives to Town Council, one each year. Thus a body of only 4,000–6,000 voters annually elected a single representative from among candidates who were often known to them personally. When a councillor stood for re-election, in many wards there was no contest at all. Town Councillors were regarded primarily as safeguards of the interests of their wards, and a candidate who stood against a 'sitting councillor' could easily find himself charged by public opinion for provoking an unnecessary contest and thereby

---

[12] Schäfer, *Bürgertum*, 48–9 and 59–60, and M. Atkinson, *Local Government in Scotland* (Edinburgh 1904), 33.

[13] D. McCrone and B. Elliott, *Property and Power in a City. The Sociological Significance of Landlordism* (Basingstoke and London 1989), 88–9, and E. Knox, 'Between Capital and Labour: The petite bourgeoisie in Victorian Edinburgh', University of Edinburgh Ph.D. thesis, 1986, 337 and 539–40, and Schäfer, *Bürgertum*, 49–51 and 60–62.

wasting the ratepayers' money. Therefore, it is not very surprising that the Edinburgh Town Council resembled an assembly of parochial notables.[14]

The culture of parochialism made it difficult for the labour movement to make headway even in working class wards. It was rather significant that among the few Town Councillors who sat for Labour in Edinburgh City Chambers in 1913–1914 we find a dentist, a civil engineer, a grocer and a city missionary, exactly the kind of men of personal standing and parochial prominence usually elected to city parliament. But if we compare the Edinburgh Labour Party's relatively modest success in municipal elections to the role of Leipzig Social Democracy, we must take into account the more general – national – socio-political constellations. In many respects, the city of Leipzig can be called the birth place of the German Social Democratic workers' movement, the proving ground of the SPD's founding fathers Ferdinand Lassalle, August Bebel and Wilhelm Liebknecht, who laid the foundation of an independent workers' party in the 1860s, cutting the labour movement's ties to liberalism. Since then and up to 1914 the German Social Democratic Party and its allies, the Free Trade Unions, operated in a highly adverse political and social environment, ostracised by the established parties, temporarily outlawed, discriminated against and constantly harassed by the police and other state agencies. By 1900 Social Democracy in urban Germany and especially in Leipzig had become – at least in the eyes of their *bürgerlich* opponents – a militant mass movement with a revolutionary programme and anti-patriotic attitudes. At the turn of the century the British Labour movement had only just started to loosen its political alliance with liberalism taking the first steps towards an independent political party.

Looking at Edinburgh, we see that even in 1914 this process had not been finished. The Edinburgh Labour Party was still more a loose alliance of trade unions and small 'socialist' groups than a political party, lacking the organisational network at ward level that the Edinburgh Liberals and Unionists could depend on. The dynamics of political confrontation between a 'proletarian' and a 'bourgeois' camp, so typical for Leipzig and other German cities, were developing comparatively slowly, if at all, in pre-1914 British cities. In Edinburgh many working-class voters still entrusted their national representation, as in local affairs, to Liberal and sometimes even Unionist notables.[15]

---

[14] Schäfer, *Bürgertum*, 51–4; Atkinson, *Local Government*, 42–4, and D. D. Buchan, *Edinburgh in its Administrative Aspect* (Edinburgh 1908), 30–32.

[15] M. Rudloff and T. Adam, *Leipzig – Wiege der deutschen Sozialdemokratie* (Berlin 1996), 29–101; T. Adam, *Arbeiterbewegung und Arbeitermilieu in Leipzig 1871–1933* (Cologne 1999), 258–71; R. Q. Gray, *The Labour Aristocracy in Victorian Edinburgh* (Oxford 1986), 180–82, J. Holford, *Reshaping Labour. Organisation, Work, and Politics – Edinburgh in the Great War and after* (London 1988), 148–50; Schäfer, *Bürgertum*, 61–9, and Schäfer, 'Bürgertum, Arbeiterschaft', 198–204.

In this respect there seems to have been remarkably little change in the Scottish capital during the First World War and the post-war years. The Edinburgh Town Council in the mid 1920s was still dominated by the same kind of parochially based businessmen, shopkeepers and professionals, and Labour managed to exceed its pre-war level of representation in the local parliament only after 1926. The aftermath of the British General Strike in that year brought at least a minor breakthrough for the Edinburgh Labour movement in municipal elections. During the strike the Town Council had taken active measures against the striking workers. A few months later 'sitting councillors' standing for re-election in working-class wards had to face their constituents' critical questions. Quite a number of them were not returned, and Labour more than doubled its seats in the Edinburgh Town Council. But even after 1926 Labour was far from winning a majority in the Council, holding just 17 of 69 elected councillors' seats in 1929. Considering that Labour won half of the city's six seats in that year's national election, the continuous hegemony of Edinburgh's urban bourgeoisie in local government seems to be quite remarkable.[16]

In Leipzig the 1918 Revolution brought a virtual breakdown of the rule of the traditional urban elites. After the first local election under a democratic franchise in January 1919, only a handful of the representatives of the first and second class kept their seats, and the socialists gained a majority in the Assembly of Citizens' Representatives. Majorities alternated during the 1920s, but even when Social Democrats and Communists were in the minority, the old merchant, industrial and house owner elites were far from regaining the position they enjoyed under the three-class franchise. The non-socialist – bürgerlich – groups and parties in the local government bodies were composed much more heterogeneously than before 1918, and now included teachers, civil servants, clerks and even workers or their union representatives. On the other hand, the Leipzig Labour movement did not manage to take over the central agency of municipal governance, the City Council. In December 1919 all non-salaried City Councillors were newly elected by the Citizens' Representatives. The new system of proportional representation prevented a socialist majority in the city's executive body, because the salaried City Councillors stayed in office for the time being. When the Citizens' Representatives received the legal right to dismiss the old professional Stadträte in 1923, the Social Democrats and Communists had already lost their majority in the Representatives' Assembly.[17]

---

[16]   Holford, *Reshaping Labour*, 253–6; R. A. Fox, *Members of the Labour Party Elected to Edinburgh Town Council 1909–1917* (Edinburgh 1971), 1–5; Schäfer, *Bürgertum*, 239–42 and 247–9, and Schäfer, 'Bürgertum, Arbeiterschaft', 220–27.
[17]   Schäfer, *Bürgertum*, 251–4 and 264–5.

Municipal bureaucracy and urban democracy

One of the most characteristic features of urban governance in Germany before 1945 as compared to Britain was the statutory power of salaried city officers. Though still consisting of a majority of honorary members in the 1920s, the key positions of the Leipzig City Council, the Lord Mayor, the second and third mayors and almost all heads of departments and chairmen of committees were filled by professional officers with a status similar to higher civil servants. In British cities the professional heads of municipal administration departments were clearly subordinated to the honorary and directly elected Town Councillors. They possessed no voting rights in the Town Council or its committees. In practice however, leading city officers, like town clerks, city chamberlains or medical health officers, could exert – by virtue of long and continuous terms of service, personal standing and professional expertise – a great measure of influence on urban decision-making under certain circumstances. But their position was by no means comparable to the legally based power of salaried mayors and councillors in German cities.[18]

The salaried City Councillors' claim to leadership in urban government and the primacy of professional expertise over honorary office were widely accepted by Leipzig citizens and their directly elected representatives. When Johannes Junck, chairman of the Assembly of Citizens' Representatives, lauded the importance of honorary office at the opening of the new Leipzig town hall in 1905, he was quick to assure that 'the corporation virtually could not do without the higher skills of the professional city officer'. The mayors and salaried City Councillors were 'the men we trust in, and they shall have the lead'.[19] Statements like this would have been unthinkable in turn-of-the-century Edinburgh. Although experienced and ambitious town clerks and other leading city officers could de facto exert major influence on municipal decision-making in their respective fields, Town Councillors meticulously insisted on their statutory prerogatives. In 1911, for example, the Burgh Engineer remarked on the height of a parapet on one of Edinburgh's main bridges: 'that should there be any reduction below that measurement he thought it would be fraught with such results that he personally should not care to be responsible for'. When this was read in the Town Council a heated debate arose whether a city officer could deliver such a statement on his own account. The honorary treasurer declared that the councillors 'were all willing to take responsibility' and that there 'was no one going to make the Burgh Engineer responsible'. One of his fellow Town Councillors exclaimed: 'We

---

[18] Krabbe, *Stadt*, 44–6; G. Häpe, 'Königreich Sachsen', in *Verfassung und Verwaltungsorganisation der Städte*, 7 vols. (Leipzig 1905–1908), vol. 4/1, 41–5; Keith-Lucas and Richards, *History*, 24–8, and Atkinson, *Local Government*, 51–3.

[19] Cited in *Leipziger Tageblatt*, 7 October 1905, supplement, 6.

are not going to have dictation from any official'.[20] A comparative view on such discourses, therefore, indicates the deeply entrenched character of political mentalities of urban elites in Germany and Britain, diverging on the very principles of political order, namely the relationship between state and civil society.

One can even sometimes detect traces of such mentalities in the recent writings of German urban historians. In their version, professional mayors and councillors since the late nineteenth century were wresting local government out of the hands of the old notables and taking over the administration of German cities in a spirit of enlightened reform, and thus becoming the *Kaiserreich*'s alternative governing elite, more liberal and *bürgerlich* in outlook than the conservative state bureaucracy.[21] But a closer look at the Leipzig case casts certain doubts on the validity of this interpretation. The rise of municipal bureaucracy did not necessarily go hand in hand with the growth in power of lord mayors and professional city officers, and the general decline of honorary office in local government. Johannes Junck in his speech at the town hall opening in 1905 even claimed: 'Today we see honorary office spread to all branches of urban administration, a process which surely will go on.'[22] An analysis of the workings of municipal governance in Leipzig reveals that after 1900 the Assembly of Citizens' Representatives took over a more active and direct part in the city's administration. The City Council's committees were increasingly substituted by so-called mixed committees of City Councillors, Citizens' Representatives and expert citizens. This was in part a pragmatic response to the steadily growing number of decisions upon which both municipal bodies had to find consensus. Moreover, the political mobilisation of lower middle and working-class voters by the franchise debates and the increasing role of political parties, voters' associations and special interest groups in local elections and in city parliament itself had far-reaching effects on urban governance. Citizens' Representatives had to look after the wishes and interests of their voters in a more active way than by just controlling the City Council's work and approving local rates. This in turn provided an incentive for city parliament to take the initiative in urban government. In this sense local government in pre-war Leipzig was characterised not only by a rapid

---

[20]   Cited in *The Scotsman*, 6 December 1911, 13.
[21]   See, e. g., J. Reulecke, 'Bildungsbürgertum und Kommunalpolitik', in J. Kocka, ed., *Bildungsbürgertum im 19. Jahrhundert*, 4 vols. (Stuttgart 1985–1993), vol. 4, 122–45, esp. 141; W. Hoffmann, *Zwischen Rathaus und Reichskanzlei. Die Oberbürgermeister in der Kommunal- und Staatspolitik des Deutschen Reiches von 1890 bis 1933* (Stuttgart 1974), 26–35, and W. R. Krabbe, *Kommunalpolitik und Industrialisierung: Die Entfaltung der städtischen Leistungsverwaltung im 19. und frühen 20. Jahrhundert* (Stuttgart 1985), 182–6.
[22]   Cited in *Leipziger Tageblatt* 7 October 1905, supplement, 6.

growth of professional municipal administration but also by the development of parliamentarian rule.[23]

Urban historians have stressed the fact that many professional (lord) mayors and other leading municipal officers appointed under the rule of class franchise before 1918 were still in office in the 1920s.[24] But this continuity of professional elites in German cities has rarely been dealt with in connection with another issue that is commonly regarded as a heavy burden on Weimar democracy: namely, the problem of an antidemocratic bureaucratic elite running a democratic state. At least in the case of Leipzig's city politics between 1918 and 1930/33, it is problematic not to discuss the role of a pre-democratic municipal elite in urban democracy. After 1918 the legal status of salaried mayors and councillors made it difficult to dismiss them, especially when they had been elected for life. Even to many Leipzig Social Democrats it did not seem advisable to replace the professional experts in the City Council with their own men. Instead they advocated a reform of local government along lines that were similar to the British model of urban governance. Powers of decision-making should entirely rest with the Assembly of Citizens' Representatives, whereas the City Council was to be restricted to purely executive functions, subject to the city parliament's instructions. The leftist Saxon state government pushed through a local government reform that followed these principles in 1923. This reform was harshly criticised by professional councillors and bourgeois opinion leaders alike. They portrayed Leipzig's post-war Citizens' Representatives' Assembly as a body dominated by group interests and party politics, by insufficient expertise and irrational moods. In their perception, the democratisation of local government had paved the way for political parties that could try to install their programmes and supporters without regard to public welfare. They called instead for a municipal administration run along 'rational' lines by 'impartial', 'non-political' professional experts.

Parliamentary rule in the Leipzig town hall did not last. In 1925, only two years after its passing, the Saxon municipalities act was revised by a liberal-conservative government, and the dualism of City Councils and Representatives' Assemblies was more or less restored. In the following years the Leipzig socialists attempted to install their own men as salaried councillors, but they did not achieve a majority in the City Council before 1933. The confrontation of two bodies of local government with equal rights of decision resulted in partial deadlock, especially in periods of socialist majorities, with many decisions transferred to state arbitration. After 1930 urban governance in Leipzig and many other German cities took the shape more and more of an

---

[23]   Schäfer, *Bürgertum*, 79–82.

[24]   Krabbe, *Stadt*, 141–4, and C. Engeli, 'Städte und Stadt in der Weimarer Republik', in B. Kirchgässner and J. Schadt, eds, *Kommunale Selbstverwaltung – Idee und Wirklichkeit* (Sigmaringen 1983), 163–81, esp. 165–6.

authoritarian regime ruled by the Lord Mayor and the professional councillors and sanctioned by central government emergency orders. Thus urban democracy had already been suspended before the Nazis virtually abolished independent local government.[25]

There is no sign that the authority of the directly-elected ratepayers' representatives in Edinburgh was challenged by municipal officers or bourgeois elites in any comparable way after 1918. Considering their relatively stable hegemony, the traditional urban elite hardly perceived a deepening crisis of local government. Moreover, in a deeply rooted parliamentary culture claims of bureaucratic supremacy would have been a rather unsuitable argument to justify oligarchic rule. There was, however, as in Leipzig, a widespread rhetoric against the role of political parties in local government. This criticism was mainly directed against the Labour movement's style of pursuing local politics, including the nomination of candidates by a central party agency and the forced commitment of Town Councillors to a municipal party programme and to party discipline in city parliament. But in the later 1920s criticism was also voiced against non-socialist parties by independent candidates and local press columnists, reflecting a growing tendency, especially by the Unionist party organisation, to intervene in local elections. Critics of party politics in local government called for a return to the ideals of urban civil society, an imagined community of citizens choosing among themselves the most capable and competent men and women, who would devote their work in Town Council to do the best for their city, independent of political programmes, party machines or special interest groups.[26]

Municipal housing in Edinburgh and Leipzig

In this last section I focus on the question of how different power constellations in the two cities, before and after 1918, left their marks on decision-making about the provision of housing for the working classes, one of the most important issues of urban government since the turn of the century. Local government agencies in Leipzig and Edinburgh had to meet a similar challenge. By 1900 the acceleration of urbanisation had caused a marked shortage of housing. Before 1914 municipal elites in both cities

---

[25] Schäfer, *Bürgertum*, 261–8; R. Siegert, *Das Verhältnis der Gemeindeverordneten zum Gemeinderat nach der Sächsischen Gemeindeordnung* (Leipzig 1927), 16–28; B. Lapp, *Revolution from the Right: Politics, Class and the Rise of Nazism in Saxony, 1919–1933* (Atlantic Heights 1997), 111–19 and 132–5, and J. Paulus, *Kommunale Wohlfahrtspolitik in Leipzig 1930 bis 1945. Autoritäres Krisenmanagement zwischen Selbstbehauptung und Vereinnahmung* (Cologne 1998), 32–45.

[26] Schäfer, *Bürgertum*, 249–51.

shared a deep scepticism about municipal building programmes. This attitude can be explained at least in part by the social composition of local government bodies, namely the strong presence of building and house-owning interests and of many businessmen who distrusted municipal enterprise, at least when there was a strong possibility that the returns would not cover the outlays. Barring the temptation of outright economic interest, notions of self help and voluntary philanthropic effort were considered the best remedies to solve the housing question, and were still strong in the bourgeois public opinion of both cities on the eve of the First World War.[27]

The city of Leipzig abstained wholly from building houses for the working classes before 1914. The City Council concentrated its efforts on supportive measures for self-help associations, for example the sale or long-term lease of municipal land or the provision of loans on favourable conditions for co-operative building societies. There were a few supporters of a more active housing policy among the city officers, but the same could be said of some of the National Liberal Party notables among the first-class Citizens' Representatives. After the turn of the century the Leipzig National Liberals, the city's leading non-socialist party, having lost its long-held inner-city *Reichstag* seat to a Social Democrat in 1903, was attempting to develop a more popular profile. In a move intended to attract the city's commercial clerks and lower grade civil servants, a rapidly growing pool of voters, the party called for a moderate local franchise reform and supported measures to enhance the provision of affordable housing for the salaried lower middle classes. Thus one of the Liberal first-class Representatives complained in early 1914 that 'in Leipzig there has not been much done to tackle the problem of housing. (...) And the little that has been done did not derive from City Council's initiative but from our suggestions.'[28] On the whole there seemed to be a fundamental agreement between professional and bourgeois elites. In practice, there was a kind of minimal consent of salaried council-lors, Liberal Citizens' Representatives and the Social Democrats that helped to forge majorities for the Council's supportive measures overruling the house-owners' faction of the three-class parliament.[29]

Edinburgh Town Council had been engaged since the 1860s in the re-development of the city's historical Old Town, which had become a slum

[27] C. Zimmermann, *Von der Wohnungsfrage zur Wohnungspolitik* (Göttingen 1991), 128–30, and 170–89; M. J. Daunton, *Home and House in the Victorian City: Working-Class Housing 1850–1914* (London 1983), 190–304; R. G. Rodger, 'Crisis and confrontation in Scottish housing, 1880–1914', in R. G. Rodger, ed., *Scottish Housing in the Twentieth Century* (Leicester 1989), 25–46, and Schäfer, *Bürgertum*, 97–103.

[28] 'Citizens' Representative Tscharmann, 18 February 1914', in *Verhandlungen der Stadtverordneten zu Leipzig* 1913/14 (Leipzig 1914), 91.

[29] Schäfer, *Bürgertum*, 98–100.

Figure 5.1   Municipal tenement houses in Leipzig-Wahren, around 1930

Source: City Archive of Leipzig, BA 1987/24260.

area during the nineteenth century. As the renovated or newly built houses proved to be too expensive for the former inhabitants, overcrowding and unsanitary conditions just moved on to the neighbouring areas. To solve this problem the corporation since the 1890s built subsidised houses for former inhabitants of redeveloped areas. But apart from Old Town improvement schemes, the Edinburgh Town Council before 1914 was as reluctant as their Leipzig counterparts to provide houses for the lower classes. In both cities municipal elites agreed that the housing of the poor should be left as far as possible to market forces, to the self-help of the people affected or to voluntary philanthropic effort.[30]

During World War One, the cessation of new construction coupled with rent control measures aggravated the housing shortages in big cities dramatically. On the other hand, political leaders, especially the British, fostered the expectation of soldiers and munitions workers that the state would take care of the provision of 'Homes Fit for Heroes' after the war. Beginning in

---

[30]   P. J. Smith, 'Planning as environmental improvement: Slum clearance in Victorian Edinburgh', in A. Sutcliffe, ed., *The Rise of Modern Urban Planning* (London 1980), 99–133, and G. Gordon, 'Working class housing in Edinburgh, 1837–1974', *Wirtschaftsgeographische Studien*, 3, 1979, 75–8.

**Figure 5.2   Construction of municipal tenement houses in Leipzig-
Reudnitz, 1926**

Source: City Archive of Leipzig, BA 1988/26633.

**Figure 5.3   Newly erected tenement houses in Leipzig-Eutritzsch, around
1925**

Source: City Archive of Leipzig, BA 1988/26626.

the last year of the war, in both Britain and Germany central governments obliged municipalities to provide sufficient housing and subsidised municipal construction with treasury grants and the allocation of tax revenues. But the way in which those obligations were implemented at the local level was left more or less to the municipalities.

Thus municipal housing policies reflected to a certain extent local power constellations. In Leipzig the old bourgeois elite's loss of power paved the way for a radical turn of the city's housing policy. In the 1920s the corporation not only committed itself to a huge housing programme but also created a newly formed municipal building company with exclusive rights to build council houses, which excluded the private building industry. Leipzig's post-war housing policy was supported by rather stable majorities in the Assembly of Citizens' Representatives including not only the socialist factions but also the representatives of the white collar section of the lower middle classes, especially within the left-liberal Democratic Party. The implementation of the housing programme was made considerably easier by a difference of opinion among the salaried City Councillors. Whereas a number of city officers, led by the head of the Housing Department, considered municipal housing schemes as the only way to solve the city's housing problem, some of their colleagues, including the Lord Mayor, remained sceptical and opposed, especially, to the exclusion of private builders. Thus housing schemes drafted by the Housing Department not only complied with the wishes and demands of the socialist parties but also found an overall majority in the City Council.[31]

Considering the composition of Edinburgh Town Council, it seems rather surprising that under the corporation's housing schemes during the 1920s even more houses were built per capita than in Leipzig. Once started, it proved to be difficult even for a body dominated by businessmen and house-owners to terminate the public provision of housing. Since not only blue collar but also white collar workers moved into the newly erected council houses, many local government voters profited from such schemes, and during local election campaigns even prominent house owners felt obliged to declare their support for the continuation of the corporation's building programme. As in Leipzig, the professional city officers disagreed on the issue. The Director of Housing promoted the continuation of local government house building, the City Chamberlain called for an early stop to costly housing schemes, and the Medical Officer of Health proposed to adapt the municipal housing policy to the needs of the city's sanitary improvement schemes. The most striking difference of post-war housing policy in Leipzig and Edinburgh was the way in which the municipal housing schemes were

---

[31] Schäfer, *Bürgertum*, 269–74; H. Liebmann, *Zweieinhalb Jahre Stadtverordnetentätigkeit der USP in Leipzig* (Leipzig 1921), 101–10, and H.-U. Thamer and J. C. Kaiser, 'Kommunale Wohlfahrtspolitik zwischen 1918 und 1933 im Vergleich (Frankfurt/Leipzig/Nürnberg)', in J. Reulecke, ed., *Die Stadt als Dienstleistungszentrum* (St. Katharinen 1995), 325–70, esp. 360–61.

implemented. Like the Leipzig Social Democrats, the Edinburgh Labour Party demanded that council houses be erected by 'direct labour' (namely by a municipal work department), but their councillors were almost totally isolated on this issue. Thus all municipal housing schemes were carried out by the local building industry. Moreover, Edinburgh Town Council subsidised the building of owner-occupied houses and even offered council flats for sale. From the mid-1920s onwards the city of Edinburgh used government housing subsidies increasingly for more traditional slum clearance projects. There was even a revival of housing philanthropy in the Scottish capital around 1930, when the Edinburgh Welfare Housing Trust was formed to accommodate those people for whom council flat rents had proved too expensive. In this respect the lasting municipal hegemony of Edinburgh's urban bourgeoisie clearly left its mark on housing policy in the city.

But in this case we should be careful not to generalise when we draw conclusions about German and British cities. If we look at Glasgow, for example, where Labour was a major force in the Town Council since the 1919 local elections, the political constellation that supported municipal housing policy resembled the Leipzig more than the Edinburgh case. On the other hand, few German cities in the 1920s resorted to radical measures like directly managing the construction of council houses.[32]

Conclusion

What happened to the old civic elites in German and British cities by the early twentieth century? Can we still outline the contours of a bourgeois civic elite at all after 1900? The pre-1918 Leipzig urban bourgeoisie as a socially cohesive and interconnected body of leading citizens took a relatively clear-cut shape. The three-class franchise helped to preserve the key position of the city's upper-class bourgeoisie in local government and helped to shape a second middle-class civic elite of well-to-do shop-keepers, master artisans and house-owners. We can still discern the contours of this second group in municipal representative bodies during the Weimar period. However, the period when a representative sample of Leipzig's eminent merchants, publishers, industrialists and professionals would take their seats in town hall ended in 1918–1919. It is more difficult to describe Edinburgh's civic elite in the first decades of the twentieth century in terms of an interconnected social entity. Edinburgh City Chambers were surely not the meeting place of the city's commercial and professional elites. However, it would also be

---

[32] Schäfer, *Bürgertum*, 274–7 and 309–10, and A. O'Carroll, 'The influence of local authorities on the growth of owner occupation before the Second World War', *Urban History*, 24, 1997, 221–41.

misleading to suggest that the Scottish capital was governed by a petty bourgeois 'shopocracy'.[33] Edinburgh Town Council was basically an assembly of parochial notables of mostly upper middle-class background.

Evidence from the local case studies of Leipzig and Edinburgh clearly suggests that up to 1930 bourgeois civic elites did not retire, at least not voluntarily. The Leipzig urban bourgeoisie defended its positions of power with ferocity and force up to the last, surrendering only to Revolution in November 1918. As the institutional foundation of their local power – the class franchise – dissolved, a majority of Leipzig's traditional 'city fathers' were forced almost immediately out of local government bodies; still they certainly exerted influence on municipal politics behind the scenes. Edinburgh's urban bourgeoisie remained active urban political actors until 1930 and beyond. One major factor for this remarkable persistence of the Edinburgh municipal elite, on one hand, and the early loss of the legitimacy of bourgeois rule in Leipzig, on the other, can be found in the degree of anti-bourgeois political mobilisation among the lower classes of urban society. Whereas Leipzig's urban *Bürgertum* had to deal by 1890 with a militant socialist party, which could mobilise a mass following for national and local elections, their Edinburgh counterparts met the challenge of a working-class movement rather easily until well into the 1920s, and only slowly loosened ties with the Liberal Party and local notables.

If civic notables did not retire from city parliaments, did they leave the field of local governance to the emerging municipal bureaucracy? Considering the rapid growth of urban administration after 1890 there can be no doubt that the Town Councillors, Citizens' Representatives and non-salaried City Councillors did not manage the bulk of day-to-day business – if they ever did before. In Edinburgh leading city officers, by virtue of their expert knowledge and professional standing, may have had a decisive share in shaping policies. But decision-making rested with the ratepayers' representatives alone and they seem to have jealously guarded this right. In Leipzig the professional heads of municipal administration had the statutory right and duty to take initiative in all matters of local government, as did members of City Council at least before 1923. In most matters, however, they had to seek the consent of their non-salaried colleagues in City Council as well as that of the Representatives' Assembly. After the turn of the century city parliament played an increasingly active role in urban governance and in many respects became a moving force of municipal politics after 1918. One should be careful, moreover, not to overstate the cleavage between professional city officers and bourgeois notables before World War One. On most issues salaried and non-salaried City Councillors and first class Citizens Representatives shared a basic consensus. After 1918 Mayors and professional Councillors, most of whom had been chosen by the old three-

---

[33]   McCrone and Elliott, *Property*, 79.

class parliament, turned out to be the strongest pillar of what was left of the rule of the urban bourgeoisie.

How did middle-class elites cope with the emergence of urban democracy? The case of Edinburgh represents in many ways a British pattern of piece-meal reform and gradual expansion of participation rights, leaving urban elites ample time to adapt to democratic change. Town Councillors could count on resources of personal prestige as community leaders of their neighbourhoods and wards, claiming to promote the 'practical' interests of their constituents. The Edinburgh Labour Party found it difficult to challenge the credibility of this claim, even in working class wards. Leipzig's civic elite had lost much of its credibility long before the 1918 revolution. In many respects the Leipzig urban bourgeoisie tried to meet the challenge of urban democracy by authoritarian measures: by the ruthless imposition of a local class franchise in 1894 and by the suspension of democratic government after 1930.

PART II

Diversity – Formal and Informal Structures of Continental Europe's City Elites

Governing Trondheim in the Eighteenth Century: Formal Structures and Everyday Life

Steinar Supphellen

Trondheim – a brief introduction

The Norwegian town of Trondheim was and is a small town in a small country. This presents both handicaps and advantages when trying to understand how towns were generally governed in the eighteenth century. The mechanisms of government may be more transparent and easier to trace in a small town, but they are also formed by local and often unique conditions and therefore of less general interest. In the case of eighteenth-century Trondheim local conditions may have been important, but the promulgation of both uniform and individual decrees to all towns in the country by the absolutist king in Copenhagen provided a framework that shaped powerfully urban political life.

With a population of 8,800 inhabitants in 1800, Trondheim was the third largest Norwegian town, far smaller than Bergen but almost the same size as Christiania (Oslo), and the only town in the northern half of the country throughout most of the eighteenth century.[1] Without question, Trondheim was a town of merchants, who can be divided into three groups.

The leading group, called the merchants or the 'real merchants', dominated export and import trade. Thus when I refer to the merchants of Trondheim it is generally with this dominant group in mind. The second group lived part of the year outside of town, mostly in the north where they traded with fishermen, supplying grain and equipment and buying fish. These itinerant traders would return to town periodically with products from the

---

[1] In 1997 Trondheim celebrated its millennium with a six-volume history written in the Norwegian Tradition: J. Sandnes, ed., *Trondheims historie 1977–1997*, 6 vols. (Trondheim 1997). See S. Supphellen, ed., *Urban history. The Norwegian Tradition in a European Context*, Trondheim Studies in History, No. 25 (Trondheim 1998).

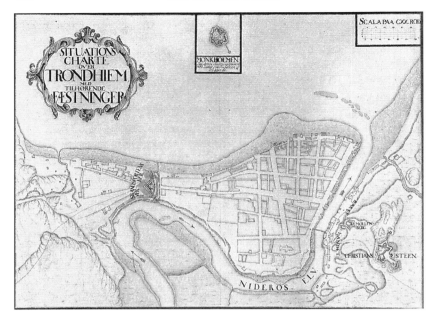

Figure 6.1 Map of Trondheim, drawn in 1733

All Trondheim burnt down in 1681 and the king ordered the town rebuilt according to a new plan. There were few protests and this plan has since dominated the structure of the town centre.

Source: *300 years with Cicignon* (Trondheim 1981), 90. Orig. in The Royal
              Library, Copenhagen.

fisheries and to outfit themselves for a new season. Some of them also visited local markets closer to town. Members of the third group were 'small-retailers' in town.

The real merchants were the town's 'economic' elite, and they operated a vast network of trade. From the northern half of Norway they distributed three main products: fish from the long coastline, timber and other products from the woods in Trøndelag, and copper ore from the mountains south of the town. Destined for a European market, these products were exported to towns like Dublin, London, Amsterdam, Hamburg, Königsberg and Riga. Dried fish was purveyed as far away as the Mediterranean. From these same towns the merchants imported goods needed in Trondheim and in the northern part of Norway – grain and textiles, sugar and salt, coffee and tobacco, and all sorts of equipment for the fisheries, the mines, and the sawmills. Via Trondheim these goods were supplied to a vast district.

The prosperity and growth of the city depended on this trade and on the functioning of this commercial network. The leading merchants formed both the economic and 'social' elite of the town. They were mostly immigrants or descendants of immigrants. As this trade had developed in the seventeenth century, merchants from the Netherlands and especially from the German town Flensburg on the Danish border had moved to Trondheim and formed the core of the merchant group. They brought with them some capital and knowledge, married into the local elite, and soon came to dominate both the economic and the social life of the town.[2] The social elite also included the bishop and a few other prelates, the leading civil administrators, and a few officers. Craftsmen and artisans had little chance of entering this social stratum dominated by the merchants.

Formal structure of government – the political elite

When the Danish King in Copenhagen gained absolute power in 1660–1661, the union of Denmark and Norway became the most 'legitimate' absolutist state in Europe. In the period up to 1814 the king formally appointed all persons who exercised official power in the country. All persons in civil, military and church administration acted with the authority conferred by a written appointment from the king. Officeholders of all kinds required confirmation for their positions from the king, even those appointed or chosen to perform minor functions in the town.

After 1660–1661, the absolutist king worked out plans for a new structure of municipal administration. In Trondheim as in other Norwegian towns the citizens' council (*byråd*), mostly elected in some way or other by their fellow citizens and only formally confirmed by the highest local state official, was replaced by a new council called the *magistrat*, which was now appointed directly by the king. This magistracy was to be headed by a president and included one or two mayors and a number of so-called councillors (*rådmenn*).

This model was used consistently, but the number of municipal officials declined throughout the period. Only four Norwegian towns had a president, and only the largest town Bergen had two mayors. According to instructions given by the king in 1666 the magistracy of Trondheim consisted of a

---

[2]   I. Bull, *De trondhjemske handelshusene på 1700-tallet: slekt, hushold og forretning* (Trondheim Merchant Houses in the Eighteenth Century: Family, Household and Business), Trondheim Studies in History, No. 26 (Trondheim 1998). See also by the same author 'Merchant households and their networks in eighteenth-century Trondheim', *Continuity and Change*, 17, 2002, 213–31; and 'City merchants as structuring element in the Norwegian region Trøndelag', in H. Th. Gräf and K. Keller, eds, *Städtelandschaft – Réseau Urbain – Urban Network* (Vienna 2004), 171–84.

president, a mayor, and six councillors. During most of the eighteenth century five persons, the president, the mayor and only three councillors formed the *magistrat*. After 1774 there were only two councillors.[3] In 1814, at the time when the Norwegian constitution was written and implemented, the entire magistracy of Trondheim consisted of just three persons; from 1818 it was reduced to one person alone, the president, whose title was changed to mayor in 1829. After 1837 a new form of administration was introduced: members of new administrative boards in local communities and towns were to be 'elected', thus ending the residual absolutist practice of royal appointment. This transition went smoothly due to more or less informal practices that had developed already under the old regime.

Throughout the eighteenth century, however, the town magistracy executed the will of the king. This absolutist authority was reinforced by the head of the regional administration that resided in the town, which was instructed to keep an eye on the magistracy. Who were the members of the magistracies and what were their functions? The presidents were often recruited from outside, including from other towns in the kingdom. Local citizens usually filled the remaining positions in the magistracy, and here the merchants were heavily represented. Serving as a mayor or a councillor conferred a certain prestige and some persons were eager to obtain a position. This was not always an easy task, and one of Trondheim's most prominent merchants in the mid eighteenth century did not succeed in becoming mayor as he wished. A position in the magistracy required some work but did not provide a solid income. Hence councillors were often men of significant financial means. One of the reasons why the number of councillors prescribed by the king in 1666 was later reduced was the expense. Salaries were stipulated by the king, but had to be paid with special taxes imposed on certain products brought into town from the countryside. By order of the king, the president received the largest share of the stipulated sum, which secured him a comfortable salary. The mayor got less but still enough to make a decent living. In contrast, the councillors could not live as members of the upper social stratum from their salaries and complained about their economic conditions. They were paid extra, however, for some of their official functions. Since the councillors shared a fixed sum from the designated tax revenues for performing these official duties, the fewer councillors there were to share this income, the better the conditions for each of them.

The magistracy also functioned as a court, meeting one day a week in the town hall, where cases were discussed and judgements passed. Some of the cases were appealed from the first court level in town, the king's bailiff

---

[3]   S. Supphellen, 'Byadministrasjon I Noreg på 17.h.' (The Administration of Towns in Norway in the Eighteenth Century), in B. Ericsson, ed., *Stadsadministrasjon i Norden på 1700-talet* (The Administration of Towns in the Nordic Countries in the Eighteenth Century) (Trondheim 1982), 115–72.

(*byfogd*). From the court of the magistracy (*rådstueretten*), appeal could be made to a centralised Norwegian court and in some cases to the Supreme Court in Copenhagen.

The magistracy's function as an ordinary court was not as important for town government as resolving various disputes and discussions. When the magistracy met in the town hall all kinds of matters could be addressed, including applications for citizenship, for permissions to start businesses, and for statements of economic status. The municipal court also established prices, settled complaints, read official letters and decrees, and discussed plans and proposals on how to make the town prosper. The magistracy also appointed subaltern officials to perform the smaller public functions. Several persons were needed at the town hall, at the town prison and as guards on the streets both day and night, especially to prevent disastrous fires. Most of these persons were to be paid by the town, and their salaries accounted for a considerable part of the budget.

Holding a seat in the magistracy obviously provided many opportunities to exercise real power. Direct orders from the king had to be followed, but these were rather few; they were also frequently founded on information that the magistracy provided the king, or they were answers to the magistracy's direct questions to the king. Thus the magistracy was able to influence royal policy and therefore relatively free to set its own agenda. The members of the magistracy were in a solid position and possessed the best opportunities to govern the town. Formally they must be considered the political elite in the town.

But not all magistracy members belonged to the core of the economic and social elite, which limited the merchants' direct control. At the same time the magistracy had little chance of opposing the leading merchants who had several ways of exercising a decisive influence. Some merchants had contacts in high places in Copenhagen on whom they could call if necessary. The magistracy also financed new municipal projects by borrowing from the merchants, who offered loans on the surety of long-term tax revenues. Naturally money could not be borrowed for activities of which the merchants did not approve. The municipal budget is thus a crucial document for analysing the real day-to-day governing of the town.

The budget – a test case

The people of eighteenth-century Trondheim did not pay ordinary taxes to the central government. Extra and special taxes were levied frequently, but no regular, annual tax was paid. The town budgets show only the expenses for administration, of which salaries took a good part. The town had to pay a physician, the king's bailiff, secretaries and servants at the town hall, policemen and their chief, a teacher, a musician, an administrator of poor relief, a chief and more than one hundred members of a fire brigade, as well as several others appointed to provide small community services. All of these petty officials argued relentlessly for higher salaries. At the same time, the need for new services – along with eager applicants who sought paid appointments to provide them – developed almost constantly.

Another significant share of the budget satisfied military obligations. After a garrison was placed in Trondheim, the town was then required to quarter soldiers or pay them each a fixed sum. The magistracy was responsible for this obligation, and town residents naturally wanted to reduce the burden as much as possible. The Trondheim Magistracy also faced financial burdens for maintaining and improving infrastructure: streets

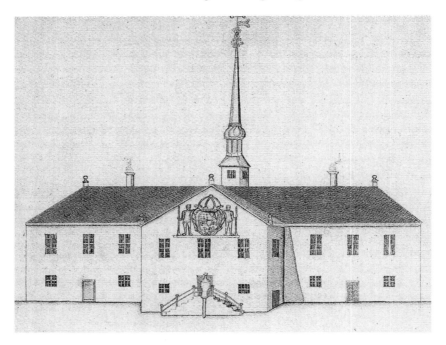

Figure 6.2 Town Hall of Trondheim. Drawing by G. Schøning in the 1770s

Formally the town was governed from the town hall. It was built in 1702 and was used for more than two centuries. Today it is still in use as part of a library.

Source: *The History of Trondheim 997–1997*, vol. 2 (Trondheim 1997), 127.
              Orig. in The Royal Library, Copenhagen.

required maintenance, the harbour necessitated looking after, the bridge needed inspection and repair, the town hall required some new equipment as did the fire brigade. The list was in fact endless, and the problem was – as ever – limited funds. Priorities had to be made, since everything could not be done. Those forced to pay usually wanted to minimise the burden, to postpone expenses as long as possible, and to avoid adopting new obligations.

If we take a closer look at the process of setting up a budget and the conflicts this entailed, we can illustrate some of the differences between formal structures and everyday life. Establishing the budget was an expected function of the magistracy. This occurred in January when the magistracy summoned the citizens to meet in the town hall. The townspeople did not assemble to discuss the budget but to be informed of its content and especially the total sum to be collected. The magistracy then asked the assembled burghers to name members of a committee with the unpleasant job of collecting the taxes from their fellow citizens. Traditionally four merchants were appointed and four persons from the group of craftsmen, half from each of the town's two parishes. This appointment had to be accepted by turn, as did the duty of tax collection, according to the committee's instructions.

Naturally the inhabitants had their opinions, and they commented on the budget, especially those required to pay the largest sums. The magistracy depended on the co-operation of the leading group of citizens to accept the budget, to collect the taxes, and to send the register to Copenhagen. From this arrangement of more or less formal co-operation evolved a new, initially informal institution that came to be called 'the twelve elected men'. Its origin remains partly unclear, though such a group had formed shortly after 1660. By around 1720 the twelve men was an accepted and working institution. In principle the twelve members were 'elected', but it was seldom that exactly twelve served nor was the group elected exactly.

There were three methods of maintaining this institution, and during the eighteenth century all three were used. If the magistracy approved an election, the citizens elected the twelve men in the town hall. Sometimes designated groups of citizens made a selection, from which the magistracy made official appointments. The third method involved self-recruitment where the remaining twelve men themselves appointed new colleagues. The twelve men did not have to be twelve for the institution to function, however, and for long periods they were fewer.

Who were the twelve men? As one would suspect, they were merchants, and they kept their position throughout the eighteenth century. In this particular council, the town merchants were always eager to occupy all the seats. In the beginning it was a more informal group, but it soon was formalised and increasingly so during the eighteenth century. Throughout eighteenth-century Denmark-Norway all the largest towns developed similar institutions. In Bergen the king authorised the institution of the '16 elected men' of the town in 1680. However, the king did not order the establishment of such institutions in the towns directly; rather he just registered their existence and, as several documents show, counted on their co-operation. His local representative – the *stiftamtmann* – usually played a role in appointing the members, thus formalising the institution. Before the middle of the eighteenth century, we find the function of the council mentioned, for example in the privileges of the town of Oslo in 1735 and 1749. The 1735 document stated that the elected men might discuss important matters and consult the magistracy on interesting projects. In 1749 it was emphasised that the magistracy ought not to introduce new expenses and decide on important economic matters without the consent of the elected men. In reality the elected men had obtained the power of a sort of veto.

The significance of this development in Trondheim is evident. At the beginning of the century the magistracy formed a budget, presented it to the citizens – especially their leading representatives, the twelve elected men – in the town hall, and had the tax collectors appointed. In the 1730s the elected were more actively involved. Money was needed to equip and strengthen the fire brigade, and a special tax on houses was introduced. This caused some problems, and in 1738 a confrontation between the magistracy and the twelve men took place. When the magistracy presented the budget, the twelve men demanded to have it handed over so they could take it home, study it and then respond. They wanted to see the books from the previous year to study several dispositions made by the magistracy. The magistracy refused and the twelve men left; the conflict lasted for many years. The magistracy felt that its authority was under attack, and the elected men refused to co-operate if they were not given the opportunity to deliberate and influence decisions.

In the long run the twelve men had their way, not by royal decree, however, but through the step-by-step development of a new practice. The power of the magistracy was reduced, and the influence of the twelve elected men grew. For the first time in 1787 the king introduced common instructions for the elected men and regulated their co-operation with the magistracy. The main trend was to make the magistracy a more purely administrative institution and accept the elected men as more of a 'political' board. In this regard, there are two important points. First, both the king and the magistracy intended that the board of twelve elected men represent all citizens. This was stated in documents from the king, and most clearly at the end of the century. This order was not followed, however, at least not in Trondheim. The magistracy had been ordered to see to it that the board contained competent persons from all groups of the burghers. This directive was also ignored. In Trondheim, until 1837, all the elected men were merchants, who managed – despite the king's instructions – to reserve these positions for themselves. Second, the group of merchants was not always firmly united. As we have seen most of the members of the magistracy were merchants themselves, usually among the most affluent. The conflict between the magistracy and the twelve men was partly a conflict between those few merchants who had built careers on a magistracy position and the others. There were also some strong personal conflicts, but basically the merchant group managed to maintain its position and thus dominate the town.

As the magistracy gradually became less important, especially in the last part of the century, the twelve men gained more direct and decisive influence on the budget and on other issues critical for governing the town. At the same time leading persons in the merchant group tended to withdraw from official positions, as members both of the magistracy and of the twelve men, and they sought to avoid taking their turns in the different official functions. In this period, these persons also formed a more evident cultural elite in the town. The rest of the merchants, and in fact the entire society, depended upon them, giving them power to influence indirectly where they wanted.

Trends of development – self-government in an absolutist state?

The absolutist king formed a new system for governing towns like Trondheim in 1660. The system was not fully implemented, but in principle all authority emanated from the king, and his officials were installed as town executives. In practice these representatives depended on a certain amount of co-operation from the burghers. The merchants sought positions as representatives of the king. At the same time they acted as representatives of the burghers in accordance with older traditions. Due to their economic and social positions in the town, they managed to gain solid control, and they kept this control within their group, despite inner conflicts and directives from the king. The absolutist regime did not fully support the formal system, but did in fact encourage the development of a representative institution and tried, unsuccessfully, to make it an instrument of its own.

This representative institution, the twelve elected men, must not be thought of as a democratic one. Throughout the eighteenth century it was an instrument for the merchant group. Because of their economic and social positions in Trondheim, they were able to develop and use this institution as one means to control both town budgets and the activity of the formal authorities.

Throughout the century the magistracy was reduced in number and importance. When the formal system ended in 1814 and definitively in 1837, the new and more democratic system could be implemented without many problems. From 1837 on the town was to be governed by a new elected board together with representatives from the new democratic government. There is an obvious line of continuity between the elected twelve men and this new governing board; nevertheless, the total control of the merchants, both in town government and in general, was over. Times had changed and

Trondheim was no longer dominated economically and socially by the merchants.

Who governed the town of Trondheim in the eighteenth century? The answer must be: the merchants. They formed the economic and social elite and in practice they were the political elite, directly and indirectly. In regard to indirect and informal influence, it must be mentioned that there were individuals besides the merchants themselves who played important roles, for example their wives. The face of the town centre was formed architecturally in the 1770s, when three leading ladies competed to build the most imposing residence near the marketplace – the winning project is today the royal residence in Trondheim.

CHAPTER SEVEN

German Urban Elites in the Eighteenth and Nineteenth Centuries

Ralf Roth

Introduction: problems of defining an elite

In the eighteenth century Frankfurt citizens would observe and comment on a doctor, Johann Christian Senckenberg, who walked absentmindedly in a zig-zag line in the street. The explanation for Senckenberg's strange behaviour was interesting: it was believed that he was attempting to avoid colliding with the invisible souls of his former patients. Senckenberg was a quiet and diffident person in unfamiliar surroundings. Despite this, he, and not his brother Johann Erasmus, a Frankfurt senator, shaped significantly the character of Frankfurt. Johann Christian Senckenberg did this by setting up a foundation in 1763 to create a hospital and a centre for the study of natural sciences to provide medical knowledge and poor relief. Additionally, the foundation later created a natural history museum and research institute. One hundred and fifty years later, the medical department of the University of Frankfurt was erected thanks to Senckenberg's foundation. Although this famous civic philanthropist never held a single political position in Frankfurt in his entire life, he was regarded as a member of the elite class.[1] This is an excellent example which aptly illustrates many of the inherent problems in defining an elite.

What qualified someone in the eighteenth and nineteenth centuries as a member of the elite in a German city? This is not only a hotly debated question in the social sciences; there is also an ongoing discussion about the social constitution of Germany's burgher classes. It is apparent that an urban

---

[1] On the role of Senckenberg see R. Roth, '"Der Toten Nachruhm". Aspekte des Mäzenatentums in Frankfurt am Main (1750–1914)', in J. Kocka and M. Frey, eds, *Bürgerkultur und Mäzenatentum im 19. Jahrhundert* (Berlin 1998), 99–127, and R. Roth, 'Von Wilhelm Meister zu Hans Castorp. Der Bildungsgedanke und das bürgerliche Assoziationswesen im 18. und 19. Jahrhundert', in D. Hein and A. Schulz, eds, *Bürgerkultur im 19. Jahrhundert. Bildung, Kunst und Lebenswelt* (Munich 1996), 121–39, here 127–9.

elite ruled and dominated the development of a city.[2] But who belonged to this group? The immediate answer that comes to mind is the 'burghers'. But what exactly was a 'burgher'? There were patricians, wealthy merchants, the educated middle-class, retailers and craftsmen, all of whom together constituted the group known as 'burghers'. But can we characterise them as an elite? Certainly, we have an easier task assessing wealthy merchants and the educated middle-class. But what about poor retailers, craftsmen, or members of the state-government? It clearly comes as no surprise that members of the lower classes as well as women did not belong to the elite. Access to political rule was sharply limited to male burghers. There is no evidence that the lower classes entered the elite in the eighteenth century. In the middle of the nineteenth century the restricted suffrage created by the census or three-class franchises restricted drastically the participation of workers and sub-proletarian groups.[3] The implication here of a kind of homogeneity among the elite at that time necessitates further discussion of whether this was actually the case. The political structure of German cities

---

[2]   For this discussion see H.-U. Wehler, 'Die Geburtsstunde des deutschen Kleinbürgertums', in H.-J. Puhle, ed., *Bürger in der Gesellschaft der Neuzeit. Wirtschaft – Politik – Kultur* (Göttingen 1991), 199–209; H.-U. Wehler, *Deutsche Gesellschaftsgeschichte*, 4 vols. (Frankfurt am Main 1987–2003), 1:203; 2:175–8, 183–4; 3:13, 119, 132, 191, 450, 536, 750, and 1254–1257; H.-U. Wehler, 'Bürger, Arbeiter und das Problem der Klassenbildung 1800–1870. Deutschland im internationalen Vergleich', in J. Kocka, ed., *Arbeiter und Bürger im 19. Jahrhundert. Varianten ihres Verhältnisses im europäischen Vergleich* (Munich 1986), 1–28, esp. 3, and D. Rüschemeyer, 'Bourgeoisie, Staat und Bildungsbürgertum. Idealtypische Modelle für die vergleichende Erforschung von Bürgertum und Bürgerlichkeit', in J. Kocka, ed., *Bürger und Bürgerlichkeit im 19. Jahrhundert* (Göttingen 1987), 101–20. On the educated middle class see H. Siegrist, ed., *Bürgerliche Berufe. Zur Sozialgeschichte der freien und akademischen Berufe* (Göttingen 1988); U. Engelhardt, *Bildungsbürgertum. Begriffs- und Dogmengeschichte eines Etiketts* (Stuttgart 1986), and W. Conze and J. Kocka, eds, *Bildungsbürgertum im 19. Jahrhundert*, 2 vols. (Stuttgart 1979). For *Bürgertum* research at the University of Bielefeld see U. Frevert, 'Bürgertumsforschung. Ein Projekt am Zentrum für interdisziplinäre Forschung (ZiF) der Universität Bielefeld', *Jahrbuch der Historischen Forschung*, 1986, 36–40. For a discussion of this model see D. Blackbourn, 'The German bourgeoisie: An introduction', in D. Blackbourn and R. J. Evans, eds, *The German Bourgeoisie. Essays on the social history of the German middle class from the late eighteenth to the early twentieth century* (London and New York 1991), 1–45, esp. 2–4, and K. Tenfelde, 'Stadt und Bürgertum im 20. Jahrhundert', in K. Tenfelde and H.-U. Wehler, eds, *Wege zur Geschichte des Bürgertums* (Göttingen 1994), 317–53, esp. 317–18. For a critique of this debate see R. Roth, *Stadt und Bürgertum in Frankfurt am Main. Ein besonderer Weg von der ständischen zur modernen Bürgergesellschaft 1760 bis 1914* (Munich 1996), 16–19.

[3]   For the Frankfurt example see Roth, *Stadt*, 81–8, and 481–9, and R. Roth, *Gewerkschaftskartell und Sozialpolitik in Frankfurt am Main. Arbeiterbewegung vor dem Ersten Weltkrieg zwischen Restauration und liberaler Erneuerung* (Frankfurt am Main 1991), 74–9, and 198–210.

would counter the idea of homogeneity among elite groups. German city societies in the eighteenth and nineteenth centuries were in many ways fragmented. There were not only distinctions between patricians, educated middle class, merchants and craftsmen, but also between burghers and different groups of non-burghers. Moreover, the fragmentation was complex and reflected the legal rights and access to political participation that distinguished these groups, including members of different religious communities such as Lutherans, Calvinists (*Reformierte*), Catholics and Jews. Each group had particular as well as common burgher privileges, and each participated in the political sphere in specific ways. In other words, the political institutions mirrored this social fragmentation, and there was no general exclusion of the main groups from the upper level of political positions in the nineteenth century.

It is apparent, however, that not every member of these groups was a political actor or 'decision-maker'. One traditional approach for addressing this complication was and still is to consider as 'elite' only those higher position-holders in the political regime.[4] Of course, the example of Senckenberg stands in direct contradiction to this traditional solution and illustrates perfectly its limitations. It should also be noted that it was these non position-holders who had tremendous influence on urban political, economic and cultural developments in these centuries.[5]

---

[4] For a long time social historical elite theories were not very specific and of a hypothetical nature. For the discussion on different models see D. Herzog, *Politische Führungsgruppen. Probleme und Ergebnisse der modernen Elitenforschung* (Darmstadt 1982), and H.-G. Schumann, 'Die soziale und politische Funktion lokaler Eliten', in B. Kirchgässner and J. Schadt, eds, *Kommunale Selbstverwaltung – Idee und Wirklichkeit* (Sigmaringen 1983), 30–38.

[5] Critical social sciences and cultural history created a new focus on institutions of local power such as city governments. Especially influential for the new emphasis on cultural forces, including the mass media, was Antonio Gramsci, who elaborated much of his theory in his prison writings from the 1920s. See A. Gramsci, *Philosophie der Praxis. Eine Auswahl* (Frankfurt am Main 1967), 412. Gramsci also played an important role in the critique of German social history developed by David Blackbourn and Geoff Eley in the last decades. See D. Blackbourn and G. Eley, *The Peculiarities of German History. Bourgeois Society and Politics in Nineteenth-Century Germany* (Oxford and New York 1984), 87–90, 129, 135, 174 and 290. In the 1990s the German historical professional was influenced by and restructured following this critique. See A. Söllner, *Geschichte und Herrschaft. Studien zur materialistischen Sozialwissenschaft* (Frankfurt am Main 1979), 208–10; C. Ginzburg, 'Der Inquisitor als Anthropologe', in Ch. Conrad and M. Kessel, eds, *Geschichte schreiben in der Postmoderne. Beiträge zur aktuellen Diskussion* (Stuttgart 1994), 203–18; P. Bourdieu, 'Structure, Habitus, Power: Basis for a Theory of Symbolic Power', in N. B. Dirks, et. al., eds, *A Reader in Contemporary Social Theory* (Princeton 1994), 155–99, and G. Eley, 'Nations, Publics, and Political Cultures: Placing Habermas in the Nineteenth Century', in ibid., 297–335. For a general overview on the subject see U. Daniel, 'Kulturgeschichte – und was sie nicht ist', in

Indeed, many aspects of city life were self-regulated by special institutions which were not closely connected to the political sphere. Economic relationships were dominated by guilds or special boards of trade. Social problems were eased by independent philanthropic foundations. Since the Middle Ages the churches were the primary caretakers of cultural life and educational institutions. They later shared this role at the beginning of the nineteenth century with a broad associational movement with its hundreds of societies and clubs.[6] This would lead us to assume that in most German cities, the elite were not only composed of different social groups, but also included many who were not formally political leaders.

Because of the many contradictions that have arisen in our brief attempt to define a city elite, it appears necessary to make additional distinctions. I therefore propose a new definition that broadens our traditional perspective. Instead of focusing just on politicians, one solution could be to distinguish those 'burghers' who were regarded as honourable citizens and therefore elected as leaders of economic, political, social or cultural organisations and institutions within the complex machinery of German cities.[7] This would allow us to distinguish between a group of political leaders, often the most influential economically, and those who shaped opinion in the public sphere. In German cities of the eighteenth and nineteenth centuries many of these

---

U. Daniel, *Kompendium Kulturgeschichte. Theorien, Praxis, Schlüsselwörter* (Frankfurt am Main 2001), 7–25.

[6]   See O. Dann, 'Die bürgerliche Vereinsbildung in Deutschland und ihre Erforschung', in É. François, ed., *Sociabilité et société bourgeoise en France, en Allemagne et en Suisse* (Paris 1986), 43–52. For the Frankfurt example see Roth, *Stadt*, 173–9, 248–60, and 309–51.

[7]   For discussions of elites in Kitzingen, Reutlingen, Cologne, Luzern, Frankfurt, Basel, Nuremberg and Braunschweig see E. Weyrauch, 'Zur sozialen und wirtschaftlichen Situation Kitzingens im 16. Jahrhundert', in I. Bátori and E. Weyrauch, eds, *Die bürgerliche Elite der Stadt Kitzingen. Studien zur Sozial- und Wirtschaftsgeschichte einer landesherrlichen Stadt im 16. Jahrhundert* (Stuttgart 1982), 27–90; H.-J. Siewert, *Lokale Elitensysteme. Ein Beitrag zur Theoriediskussion in der Community-Power-Forschung und ein Versuch zur empirischen Überprüfung* (Tübingen 1979); C. von Looz-Corswarem, 'Die politische Elite Kölns im Übergang vom 18. zum 19. Jahrhundert', in H. Schilling and H. Diederiks, eds, *Bürgerliche Eliten in den Niederlanden und in Nordwestdeutschland. Studien zur Sozialgeschichte des europäischen Bürgertums im Mittelalter und in der Neuzeit* (Cologne 1985), 421–44; P. Hoppe, 'Zum Luzerner Patriziat im 17. Jahrhundert', in K. Messmer and P. Hoppe, eds, *Luzerner Patriziat. Sozial- und wirtschaftsgeschichtliche Studien zur Entstehung und Entwicklung im 16. und 17. Jahrhundert* (Luzern 1976), 217–416; R. Koch, *Grundlagen bürgerlicher Herrschaft. Studien zur bürgerlichen Gesellschaft in Frankfurt am Main 1612–1866* (Wiesbaden 1983); Ph. Sarasin, *Stadt der Bürger. Bürgerliche Macht und städtische Gesellschaft Basel 1846–1914*, 2nd edn. (Göttingen 1997), and H. W. Schmuhl, *Die Herren der Stadt. Bürgerliche Eliten und städtische Selbstverwaltung in Nürnberg und Braunschweig vom 18. Jahrhundert bis 1918* (Gießen 1998).

functions depended on burgher law (*Bürgerrecht*). For this reason it is essential that we take a closer look at the specific characteristics of municipal legal codes.

The relationship between burgher law and burgher community

In the period leading up to the nineteenth century, the characteristics of burgher law changed, as did the descriptions of those who qualified as a burgher. In relation to the non-burgher inhabitants of German cities, burghers held superior political, economic and social privileges. The number of citizens who benefited from burgher law varied from city to city. But in direct contradiction to general opinion, the number of burghers as a proportion of urban population was bigger at the beginning than at the end of the nineteenth century.

It was the introduction of modern city constitutions that dramatically limited the size of the community of privileged burghers.[8] Over centuries, self-governing structures had developed in all cities. This included the city government (*Rat*) and administrative control institutions (*Bürgerausschüsse*), which later became the magistrate and the city assemblies. Some German cities were free republics that deferred only to the imperial rule of the German emperor. Most territorial cities were also organised as republics, but followed the princely rule of the many and variegated German territorial states. This should be kept in mind when considering the regional particularities and the wide differences in law between the various states of Germany. In many of these territories the negative impact of state administrations on urban self-government was very dramatic. In keeping with its absolutist and authoritarian reputation, Prussia in particular restricted these self-governing urban structures.[9] In areas west of the Rhein River burgher status during the Napoleonic era had been reduced to a meaningless note in the state registers. All economically independent men received the right to vote, but it was only those notables with higher incomes who could be elected.[10]

---

[8] See D. Reuter, 'Der Bürgeranteil und seine Bedeutung', in L. Gall, ed., *Stadt und Bürgertum im Übergang von der traditionalen zur modernen Gesellschaft* (Munich 1993), 75–92, esp. 79.

[9] See A. Nachama, *Ersatzbürgertum und Staatsbildung. Zur Zerstörung des Bürgertums in Brandenburg-Preußen* (Frankfurt am Main 1984), 134–6.

[10] In Aachen not more than 15 per cent of all heads of household (*Haushaltungsvorstände*) possesed the burgher right in 1846. In Cologne it was 25 per cent. On Cologne see G. Mettele, *Bürgertum in Köln 1775–1870. Gemeinsinn und freie Assoziation* (Munich 1998), 28–30. Other Rhenish cities had maximum participation rates between 18 and 36 per cent for adult males. See F. Lenger, 'Bürgertum und Stadtverwaltung in rheinischen Großstädten des 19. Jahrhunderts. Zu einem vernachlässigten Aspekt bürgerlicher Herrschaft', in L. Gall, ed., *Stadt und Bürgertum*

In other parts of Prussia the development of burgher law was different. Here the burgher law was reinstituted with the Prussian Local Governance Law of Karl vom Stein in 1812. In the years before the 1848 Revolution, Prussia restricted the local franchise and increased the voter census. At first these restrictions were relatively moderate. Due to the impact of the state legislation, however, economic privileges were increasingly excluded from the burgher law and regulated by the common law system. Despite the fact that all residents of a Prussian city now received the same economic and commercial rights, the political sphere remained the arena of a small minority of wealthy burghers. In Dortmund the burgher community declined from 54 per cent of all inhabitants at the end of the eighteenth century to only 37 per cent around 1850. In 1863 the burgher community of Dortmund was only 30 per cent of all residents. By the end of the century, however, the number increased, reaching its peak in 1895 when over 80 per cent of all adult male inhabitants qualified as burghers. But this expansion of the franchise was tied to the three-class voter system. This meant that the mass of people in the third class could elect at most one third of all members of the city parliament. For this reason the majority of voters were excluded from having any real political influence.[11]

In the former states of the Rhenish Union, which existed between 1810 and 1813, burgher law was open minimally to those burgher groups that already had access to other burgher privileges. The legal differences between merchants, craftsmen, and non-burgher residents (*Beisassen* and *Schutzverwandte*), as well as those between the different confessions, were also being abolished step by step. As a result of these developments the size of the burgher community was considerably reduced. An excellent example of this is the city of Augsburg around 1800. At that time 68 per cent of the entire population was made up of burghers. Only a few years later this number dropped to 32 per cent, and in 1869 it reached its lowest point at 27 per cent.[12] By contrast, however, in the southwestern German states of Württemberg and Baden the moderate census franchise was replaced by an even more liberal political model, and the number of burghers in most

---

im 19. Jahrhundert (Munich 1990), 97–169, esp. 114–16. In contrast to the notables model at the district level, the political system of the Rhenisch province was based on a three-class franchise and between 70 and 80 per cent of the male population took part in elections. In this respect we can speak of a certain kind of democracy. See J. Reulecke, *Geschichte der Urbanisierung in Deutschland* (Frankfurt am Main 1985), 133.

[11] For the Dortmund example see K. Schambach, *Stadtbürgertum und industrieller Umbruch. Dortmund 1780–1870* (Munich 1996), 232–5.

[12] See F. Möller, *Bürgerliche Herrschaft in Augsburg 1790–1880* (Munich 1998), 39–41, and H. W. Schmuhl, 'Bürgerliche Eliten in städtischen Repräsentativ-organen', in J. Puhle, ed., *Bürger in der Gesellschaft der Neuzeit. Wirtschaft – Politik – Kultur* (Göttingen 1991), 178–98, here 186.

communities remained a solid 50-60 per cent.[13] In these states becoming a burgher required no more than providing proof of a solid income.[14] That is why city constitutions differed so much from city to city.

During the nineteenth century the traditional characteristics of local German burgher law underwent comprehensive change. Many of the previously entrenched economic privileges were abolished, for example the requirements for setting up or conducting a business. At the same time, however, the political rights were transformed into census or three-class franchises, which reduced in many ways the circle of burghers with significant political influence.[15] The general trend of achieving more homogeneity in German burgher society should obscure neither that the process developed very differently in different regions, nor that the character of urban citizenship became distinctly local and fragmented in the last third of the nineteenth century.

How to explore the elite of German cities in the context of the burgher law?

Keeping these preliminary observations and the particularities of German burgher law in mind, we can not limit our focus to a single pre-determined social group when we analyse German city elites in the eighteenth and nineteenth centuries. First, one might consider the bourgeoisie as an elite. Second, it is impossible to limit research to a sampling of political position-holders, such as members of the city government (*Rat*) or assembly. Third,

---

[13] Indeed citizens constituted 72 per cent of the burgher community of the Württemberg city of Heilbronn in 1822 when the new city constitution was introduced. Likewise in Esslingen servants and employees were incorporated into the circle of residents with political privilege. In this early period, the ideal of liberals who envisaged a society made up of people of a moderate income had become a reality in Württemberg. See D. Reuter, 'Das Heilbronner Bürgertum und seine Führungsgruppen 1770 bis 1880', Goethe University Ph.D. thesis, 1993, 21–4, and H. Tiessen, *Industrielle Entwicklung, gesellschaftlicher Wandel und politische Bewegung in einer württembergischen Fabrikstadt des 19. Jahrhunderts. Esslingen 1848–1914* (Sigmaringen 1982), 98–9, and 288–9. The Badenese city of Mannheim is proof of the general development of the political system in this region of Germany. See D. Hein, 'Badisches Bürgertum. Soziale Struktur und kommunalpolitische Ziele im 19. Jahrhundert', in Gall, *Stadt und Bürgertum im 19. Jahrhundert*, 65–96, here 81–2. See also W. Leiser, 'Die Einwohnergemeinde im Kommunalrecht des Großherzogtums Baden', in B. Kirchgässner and J. Schadt, eds, *Kommunale Selbstverwaltung. Idee und Wirklichkeit* (Sigmaringen 1983), 39–55, here 51.

[14] See Th. Weichel, 'Die Kur- und Verwaltungsstadt Wiesbaden 1790–1822', in L. Gall, ed., *Vom alten zum neuen Bürgertum. Die mitteleuropäische Stadt im Umbruch 1780–1820* (Munich 1992), 317–56, here 323–3.

[15] See M. Sobania, 'Rechtliche Konstituierungsfaktoren des Bürgertums', in Gall, *Stadt und Bürgertum im Übergang*, 131–50.

we must also consider political as well as economic, religious and cultural criteria as determinants of elite status. And finally, we must base our analysis on a clear picture of urban society and its self-governing institutions, including its development through the eighteenth and nineteenth centuries.

These points were taken into consideration in the research project, 'City and burghers in the nineteenth century' (*Stadt und Bürgertum im 19. Jahrhundert*). This project was based on a common methodological approach and compared 14 German cities. It attempted to answer the following fundamental questions: First, which social groups existed inside the city? What were the distinctions of legal 'burgher' rights and their political influence, economic weight, and main cultural patterns? What did each group have in common with the other citizens, and what set them apart from each other? Second, how did the political regime develop over the centuries? Third, what was the role of economic institutions such as guilds, the chambers of commerce and later, the supervisory boards of big enterprises? What role did the various religious communities and the other numerous institutions of self-governing societies and foundations play in urban society?[16] On the basis of this analysis, the researchers of the different cities tried to identify those citizens who had been elected as leaders in different forms and for different purposes.

---

[16] The sample of cities included trade cities, residence or administrative cities, university cities, business cities of the eighteenth century, industrial cities of the nineteenth century and the type of city without specific improvements. See the following monographs: on Augsburg, Möller, *Herrschaft*; on Bremen, A. Schulz, *Vormundschaft und Protektion. Eliten und Bürger in Bremen 1750–1880* (Munich 2002); on Dortmund, Schambach, *Stadtbürgertum*; on Frankfurt am Main, Roth, *Stadt*; on Karlsruhe and Mannheim, D. Hein, 'Stadt und Bürgertum in Baden. Karlsruhe und Mannheim vom Ancien Régime bis zur Revolution 1848/49', unpublished Johann Wolfgang Goethe-University Habil. thesis, 1995; on Cologne, Mettele, *Bürgertum*; on Munich, R. Zerback, *München und sein Stadtbürgertum. Eine Residenzstadt als Bürgergemeinde 1780–1870* (Munich 1997); on Münster, S. Kill, *Das Bürgertum in Münster 1770–1870* (Munich 2001); on Wetzlar, H.-W. Hahn, *Altständisches Bürgertum zwischen Beharrung und Wandel. Wetzlar 1689–1870* (Munich 1991), and on Wiesbaden, Th. Weichel, *Die Bürger von Wiesbaden. Von der Landstadt zur „Weltkurstadt" 1780–1914* (Munich 1997). For the fundamental research assumptions see L. Gall, 'Stadt und Bürgertum im 19. Jahrhundert. Ein Problemaufriß', in Gall, *Stadt und Bürgertum im 19. Jahrhundert*, 1–18; L. Gall, 'Vom alten zum neuen Bürgertum. Die mitteleuropäische Stadt im Umbruch 1780–1820', in Gall, *Vom alten zum neuen Bürgertum.*, 1–18, and L. Gall, 'Stadt und Bürgertum im Übergang von der traditonalen zur modernen Gesellschaft', in Gall, *Stadt und Bürgertum im Übergang*, 1–12. For a discussion of research on German burghers see D. Langewiesche, 'Stadt, Bürgertum und "bürgerliche Gesellschaft" – Bemerkungen zur Forschungsentwicklung', *Informationen zu Modernen Stadtgeschichte*, 1, 1991, 2–5; F. Lenger, 'Bürgertum, Stadt und Gemeinde zwischen Frühneuzeit und Moderne', *Neue Politische Literatur*, 40, 1995, 14–29, and J. Sperber, 'Bürger, Bürgertum, Bürgerlichkeit, Bürgerliche Gesellschaft: Studies of the German (Upper) Middle Class and Its Sociocultural World', *Journal of Modern History*, 69, 1997, 271–97.

For this reason, a rather extensive database was compiled which included entries from address books, from tax roles, from lists of all members of all political institutions, from economic institutions and, finally, from the boards of religious communities. To these data were added the membership lists of associations and societies. Frankfurt alone includes a database of 125,000 personal entries, allowing elites to be identified and characterised according to their function within these institutions as well as in terms of how active a role they played. Collectively, the participants in the Frankfurt research program were able to distinguish between three different parts of each city's elite. The first was the group of political leaders (*politische Führungsschicht*) who were members of municipal political institutions. Second we identified those people who were the most influential economically (*wirtschaftliche Oberschicht*) and who made up the upper stratum of taxpayers. Lastly, were the opinion leaders in the public sphere (*kulturelle Elite*), defined as those elected to upper level positions of economic institutions, philanthropic foundations, prominent associations or the boards of religious communities.[17]

Using this model it was possible to reconstruct the elite of every city for specific years. In the case of Frankfurt, for example, the years 1760, 1810, 1840, 1870 and 1900 were chosen. This made it possible to describe the social composition of the elite and to answer the following questions: Which social group was represented in the elite? Who belonged to the group of political leaders, to the wealthiest citizens and to the cultural elite that dominated the associational movement for the duration of the nineteenth century? We were also able to discover the personal identity and political, economic and cultural activities of most elites. It was possible to follow the traces that each person had left, to describe how they reacted to the city's historical vicissitudes, and how they behaved in situations of political conflict caused by external powers or by various internal emancipation movements. At the same time, the result of this research could be taken as a control model for the evidence of the elite model. These were the basic methodological assumptions of our research project, 'City and burghers in the nineteenth century', whose results and conclusions I will present in this chapter using the example of the city of Frankfurt.

---

[17] For an explanation of this three-fold division see R. Jeske, 'Kommunale Amtsinhaber und Entscheidungsträger – die politische Elite', in Gall, *Stadt und Bürgertum im Übergang*, 273–94; A. Schulz, 'Wirtschaftlicher Status und Einkommensverteilung – die ökonomische Oberschicht', in ibid., 249–71, esp. 251–3, and Th. Maentel, 'Reputation und Einfluß – die gesellschaftlichen Führungsgruppen', in ibid., 295–314.

The example of the Frankfurt elite

As a German financial centre and prosperous trade city, Frankfurt already had 20,000 inhabitants in 1700. One hundred years later the city's population had increased to 40,000 and before the outbreak of World War One, it had reached 414,000.[18] I will begin with some remarks on the sociological structure of the Frankfurt elite and will continue with a short description of their political, social and cultural particularities. I will then compare the results with the elites of other German cities, and finally, I will present some observations on the role that informal networks played for such elite groups in German cities.

Frankfurt's pre-modern elite consisted of patricians, lawyers, merchants and craftsmen. Political rights were reserved for the Lutheran majority. Although some of the Catholic, Calvinist (*Reformierte*) and Jewish burghers had economic influence and belonged to the upper level of taxpayers, they did not have any political rights nor did they belong to the group of political leaders. There were also some very clear distinctions among the Lutheran political leaders. The Council or *Rat* was dominated by patricians, and the merchants were headed by the lawyers who held higher political positions. Only the Council's administrative control institutions such as the *Bürgerausschuß* were dominated by merchants. It is also remarkable that the craftsmen held such a strong position in all segments of the elite. Even in the upper strata of wealthy and successful burghers, a group of rich artisans remained prominent from the eighteenth to the middle of the nineteenth century (see fig. 7.5).[19]

Over the course of two centuries there were some remarkable changes in the composition of the elite. Within the comprehensive elite, these changes were slightly different from those of the political leaders and the upper economic class. Between 1800 and 1820 there was a decline of patricians among all members of the elite (see fig. 7.1). They lost their privileged position in the city government, while the main patrician societies lost members. Many of the patrician families left the city and later became

---

[18] The city of Frankfurt, an independent city republic (*Freie Reichsstadt*), was incorporated in 1806 into the state of Prince Karl Theodor von Dalberg (*Primatialstaat*). It was reorganised in 1810 as the Grand Duchy of Frankfurt (*Großherzogtum Frankfurt*). In 1813 the allies opposing Napoleon occupied and governed the city for two years. In 1815 the city recovered its sovereignty reflecting the decision of the Congress of Vienna. For five decades Frankfurt was an independent city and one of the four city republics inside the German Union (*Deutscher Bund*). In 1866 the city was occupied by the Prussian army and incorporated into Prussia in 1867, when it was reduced to a provincial city without any administrative functions.

[19] For a more detailed discussion on the elite of the city of Frankfurt see Roth, *Stadt*, 134–6, 308–10, 368–70, 523–5, 595, and 661.

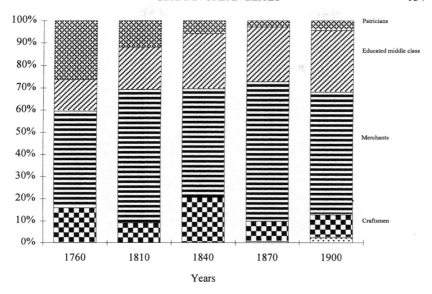

Figure 7.1   The social composition of the elite in Frankfurt, between 1760 and 1900 (in per cent)

Source: Roth, *Stadt*, 136.

involved in the princely courts of the surrounding states. The decline of the patricians was accompanied by the rise of the merchants and the educated middle class. But as we can see in figure 7.3, the newly-evolved social strength of the merchant elites was not adequately mirrored in the group of political leaders after 1816. In the long run the educated middle class became more successful than merchants and bankers in the field of politics and thus gained more political positions. In the decades between 1816 and 1900 we see a slow but steady movement of political influence from merchants and craftsmen to lawyers and other educated professionals. This movement however, cannot be observed in the social composition of the elite as a whole.

Although the merchants lost their influence in the political sphere, their position within the elite in general remained solid. The reason for this was twofold. Firstly, merchants enlarged their position among the group of the wealthiest citizens (*wirtschaftliche Oberschicht*). After 1800, more than 70 per cent and later nearly 90 per cent of the upper-class taxpayers consisted of bankers and merchants (see fig. 7.5). Secondly, they dominated the sector of independent economic institutions and cultural societies such as the Board of

Figure 7.2   The city hall of Frankfurt, called *Römer*, around 1860

Source: Institut für Stadtgeschichte, Frankfurt am Main, Foto: Rau.

the Frankfurt Stock Market (*Börsenvorsteher*) and the Chamber of Commerce (*Handelskammer*). These institutions worked as interest groups for bankers and merchants. In addition to that, and more significantly, the movement for the founding of societies was extremely important for the cultural development of the burgher society in the city. These groups were created for many cultural and social purposes and sometimes for political reasons. They also supported businesses as well. This process began with the first Freemason lodge *Zur Einigkeit* in 1740 and was followed by reading societies in the 1780s. The first society dedicated exclusively to sociability, the *Casinogesellschaft*, was founded in 1802 and admitted, with the exception of the Jews, the members of all wealthy families, regardless of their religious affiliation. These institutions and societies formed an informal network that competed with the older and more traditional political institutions. How important this network was is characterised by the fact that the burghers of the religious minorities began their struggle for emancipation as members of these societies. After reforms provided them with political

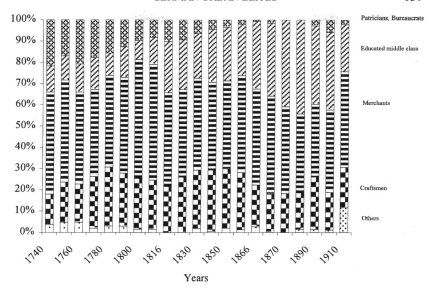

Figure 7.3 The leading political group (*Politische Führungsschicht*), between 1740 and 1914

Source: Roth, *Stadt*, 591.

rights, they later used this informal network as a platform for their rise into the group of political leaders and the elite. Because of this successful integration, the religious composition of the elite changed dramatically in the nineteenth century. There were two main processes of emancipation. The Catholics and Calvinists were granted full civil and political rights in 1806 and later the Jews in 1850 and 1864. In the second half of the nineteenth century we meet representatives of the Calvinist, Catholic and Jewish communities in all of the important institutions of the city. It is interesting to note that their participation in all political institutions and offices was almost always proportional to the size of these minority communities.

Although there were important changes in the constitution of the city and the structure of the political regime, there was a long tradition of political participation by craftsmen that lasted over two centuries. The guilds and their artisan representatives, until their abolition in 1864, enforced a closed market in the city economy. Despite this, several important manufacturers emerged from the social stratum of craftsmen.[20] The reason for the important role of

---

[20]   Roth, *Stadt*, 661.

Figure 7.4   The Frankfurt bourse, 1892

Source: Institut für Stadtgeschichte Frankfurt am Main, Foto: Mertens.

craftsmen within the Frankfurt elite and especially among the group of political leaders was because of the political rights craftsmen had acquired in the Middle Ages. Since 1816 they had succeeded in expanding the participation rights for burghers. In addition, they also profited from the extension of the power of those institutions in which they had the most influence. This is best illustrated with the creation of the city assembly (*Gesetzgebende Versammlung*). In earlier times, the assembly had full legislative powers and control over the budget of the state which most elected chambers did not have in Germany. Craftsmen were also engaged in the network of societies, forming their own relief and business societies within the broader associational movement.

To summarise these developments, we must conclude that the growing power of merchants was counterbalanced by the educated middle class and craftsmen in the political and cultural spheres of Frankfurt society. But the economic influence and cultural hegemony of Frankfurt's wealthy merchants and bankers exceeded their direct political power. One of the more far-reaching consequences of this was that there were no clear distinctions within the upper class for a long time. Indeed, the analysis of the Frankfurt elite does

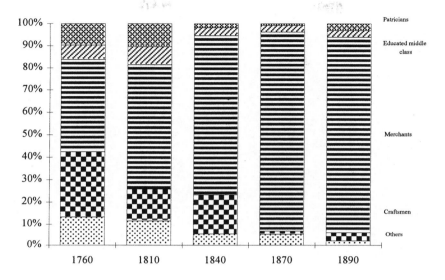

Figure 7.5 **The upper level of the taxpayers (*Wirtschaftliche Oberschicht*), between 1760 and 1900**

Source: Roth, *Stadt*, 209.

not support such a thesis, neither within the cultural elite nor within the group of political leaders. It was only among the wealthiest group of citizens that the merchants and bankers predominated.

There was a further remarkable change that took place over the course of the nineteenth century. As a consequence of the rapidly growing labour movement, which included trade unions and the Social Democratic Party, Frankfurt's city elite was forced to develop new social policies. In the 1890s, they started a highly visible program of social reforms whose aim was to reduce the social problems resulting from immigration and industrialisation. But this did not impede the rise of representatives of the working class. Between 1902 and 1914 they succeeded in changing the political composition of the city assembly (*Stadtverordnetenversammlung*), and in 1913 they also succeeded in entering the magistrate (see fig. 7.6). In the end, the Democrats and Liberals who made up the two dominant political parties of the Frankfurt burgher elite and the Social Democrats, carefully considered their strategy and formed a common network of societies and educational institutions. They

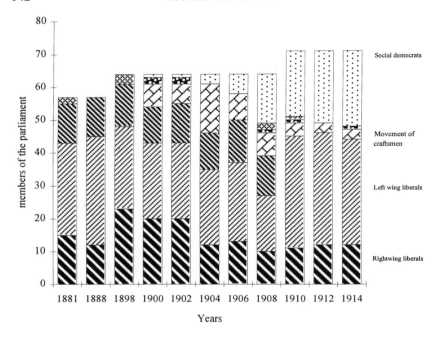

Figure 7.6 The political composition of the city assembly
(*Stadtverordnetenversammlung*), between 1898 and 1914

Source: Roth, *Stadt*, 623.

also managed to integrate a few members of the labour movement into the inner circle of political leaders.[21]

To summarise, we can consider the transition from a corporate to a modern society and the development of the burghers and their elite as parts of a combined 'longue durée'. Included in this multidimensional process was the erosion of the patrician privileges in the city administration, the gradual integration of foreigners and certain types of craftsmen, the emancipation of religious minorities long excluded from political participation and the social integration of workers into a modern civil society. As a result, we can describe the main characteristics of the Frankfurt elite as liberal and a direct counterpoint to the Prussian state. The city elite was anti-governmental, consensus-driven and integrative. However, this tendency to integrate

---

[21]   See Roth, *Gewerkschaftskartell*, 79–91, Roth, *Stadt*, 663, and R. Roth, '"Bürger" and Workers, Liberalism and the Labor Movement in Germany, 1848 to 1914', in D. E. Barclay and E. D. Weitz, eds, *Between Reform and Revolution. German Socialism and Communism from 1840 to 1990* (Oxford 1998), 113–40.

different groups had distinct limits and excluded those people who were not regarded as burghers such as journeymen and workers.[22] Frankfurt's liberal political culture was deeply rooted in the traditions of a heterogeneous elite. As we have seen in Frankfurt, we have a type of heterogeneous elite that was composed of four social groups and five religious communities. This elite structure had a profound impact upon the behaviour of the elite in times of economic, social or political crises. In the eighteenth and nineteenth centuries the elite would most often focus on unifying the civil society during critical situations thus avoiding a policy of escalation and promoting instead, the integration of burgher groups with opposing opinions. This was why the elite were receptive to longer lasting processes of emancipation. Still, this longing for a consensus policy and the integration of opponents was typical of the behaviour of the Frankfurt elite and it distinguishes the Frankfurt elite from those of other German cities in many ways.

Other elite groups in German cities

If Frankfurt was the major commercial and banking city of southern Germany, Dortmund was a small trade centre in the northwest with no more than 4.000 inhabitants, which included a few merchant families and many farming citizens. The city was incorporated into the Prussian State in 1803. In contrast to Frankfurt, the Dortmund merchants who dominated the city economy did not avoid conflicts within the leading political group, characterised by struggle between the old established families and social climbing immigrants. After the middle of the nineteenth century, the Dortmund elite developed a huge program of modernisation and industrialisation. These projects included railway construction, and the large-scale development of mining, blast furnaces for steel production and breweries. This grand push for industrialisation dramatically increased the number of inhabitants to 80,000 in 1885. It also set off a tidal wave of change in Dortmund's social structure, a process that began much earlier than in Frankfurt. In contrast to Frankfurt, the Dortmund elite attempted to bridge the gap between the different burgher groups by establishing a network of societies much later. The Dortmund elite were not as powerful as Frankfurt's and therefore less successful in integrating the new working class into civil society. As a result, Dortmund workers not only created their own network of societies, trade unions and political parties but also developed policies that harshly opposed the 'burghers world'.[23]

A social hierarchy similar to the one in Frankfurt also existed in Bremen. And just like that in Frankfurt, Bremen's social hierarchy was also based on

---

22 See Roth, *Stadt*, 658–64.
23 See Schambach, *Stadtbürgertum*, 394–9.

religion, familial connections, profession and the *Beisassen* law, a local ordinance that governed the status of non-burgher residents. The privileged community of burghers did not close its door, however, to successful social climbers as Andreas Schulz explains:

> The social acceptance of such climbers was highly evolved. Exceptional migrants such as the merchant, Diedrich Wätjen or the tobacco manufacturer, Johann E. Abegg who reached the top of urban society, were living proof that a particular kind of social openness existed at that time. This acceptance of foreigners extended to rewarding those who had followed society's code of conduct and made extraordinary efforts, with social acceptance and a prospective political career.[24]

The preconditions for their integration were formulated by a cultural hegemony of the burgher elite, which was in many ways opposite to the liberal mainstream.

> The generation of the patriarchs, which included the tradesmen, shipowners and politicians born around 1800, who had to bear responsibility during times of hardship, were provided with a full mandate for political leadership. Their social standing, economic status and positions of power and influence formed a unit. They obtained their political privileges and mandate to lead from the success they had achieved during this era. This clearly stood in direct contradiction to the idea of an open and equal society. The political system was supposed to correspond to a "natural" social order and not be dominated by the will of a majority of people chosen accidentally. (...) This autocratic regime of the burgher meritocracy (*Bürgermeritokratie*), which referred to itself as 'experts' (*Kapacitäten*), had been established under the particular circumstances of a changing society. It collided with the communal egalitarianism of the old burgher communities where political opportunities were distributed to all burghers.[25]

These changes resulted in the paradoxical situation of a free and self-governing city with traditions of collective governance, while in reality most burghers were politically disenfranchised.[26] This was not an uncommon state of affairs for many German cities during this time. In Bremen however, the reform process took considerably more time than in trade cities of similar size such as Frankfurt. It was also less influenced by state reforms in Prussian cities or the cities of the Rhenish Union.[27]

Augsburg, a business city made up of strong artisan groups and traditional merchant families, represents yet another variant. With 30,000 inhabitants in 1800, Augsburg was nearly as big as Frankfurt. Despite its size, the formerly 'Free Imperial' city was incorporated into the Bavarian State in 1803.

---

[24]   See Schulz, *Vormundschaft*, 702.
[25]   Ibid. 704.
[26]   Ibid. 705.
[27]   Ibid. 701–711.

Interestingly enough, despite a growth in population to 66,000 inhabitants at the end of the century, the situation had not really improved. Compared to the dynamic urbanisation taking place throughout Germany, Augsburg was regarded as a city with little dynamism. As in Frankfurt, the elite consisted of patricians, craftsmen, merchants and an educated middle class. In the eighteenth century Augsburg's elite was dominated by Catholic patricians, even more so than in Frankfurt, and in the nineteenth century by protestant merchants. This was particularly remarkable in a city with a majority of Catholic citizens. As in Dortmund, the city was industrialised earlier than Frankfurt and the elite did not fear riotous clashes and conflicts in the 1848 revolution. In contrast to Frankfurt, the economic rise and growing influence of merchants was not counterbalanced by craftsmen. Frank Möller, author of the Augsburg study, has drawn the following conclusion:

> Together with new constitutions and the changes in burgher rights, the burghers became more open to new groups of citizens such as bureaucrats, the salaried staff of enterprises and the educated middle class. At the same time the importance of the craftsmen decreased. Artisans with lower income were more and more excluded from the group of burghers.[28]

In Munich we experience another kind of city elite. As in Augsburg, the capital of Bavaria was dominated by Catholics. With its 40,000 inhabitants it was comparable in size to Frankfurt and Augsburg. However, Munich was a residential city (with a princely court) unlike the other two. Aside from the merchants and craftsmen living there, Munich also had powerful groups of bureaucrats, members of the military, artists and many Catholic clergy. The Munich elite had more direct contact with the state than in Frankfurt or Augsburg, and harsh conflicts as well as a groundswell of pressure resulted from this and worked to unify the burghers. Ultimately the elite included those citizens who were economically independent such as merchants, retailers and craftsmen as well as the educated middle class. It was this mixture that made it possible for the elite to reject state reforms of both the communal constitution and those proposed for the commercial world. Similarly, as in Frankfurt and Augsburg but earlier than in Dortmund, the elite established a network of societies, which strengthened the burghers' sense of unity and bridged the social differences between elite groups. After the 1848 Revolution however, the consensus decreased as a consequence of riotous conflicts and the rapid growth of the city. Although the city's inhabitants had grown to 170,000 in 1870, the Munich elite had not yet been divided into 'liberals' and 'patriots' as the more conservative faction of the burgher society called themselves.[29]

---

[28]   Möller, *Herrschaft*, 421.
[29]   See Zerback, *München*, 299.

Still another model for assessing the development of German urban elites was Cologne – similar in size to Frankfurt and Munich – which represented the most important city of Prussia's new western provinces, incorporated into the state in 1815. Like the elite groups of Frankfurt, Augsburg and Munich, the Cologne elite provided the basis of a modern civil society. Just as those of the other cities, Cologne's elite was a heterogeneous one. Unlike Augsburg and Frankfurt, however, there were no patricians, and instead this leading position was held by a group of self-confident merchants. In even sharper contrast to most other cities, the Cologne elite lacked the broad participation of educated professionals and craftsmen. This resulted in a fundamental deficiency within the leading political group, or as the author of the Cologne study, Gisela Mettele put it:

> It is often assumed that the educated middle class dominated the constitutional process of modern civil society. This cannot be confirmed however, in the case of Cologne. It was the merchants, bankers and entrepreneurs, who had the greatest influence on the most important political and cultural developments of the city in the first half of the nineteenth century. They were closely connected by the network of communication and informal organisations.[30]

Apart from their internal differences, Cologne's elites paid particular attention to burgher unity, especially in fighting the influence of the Prussian State. As in the other four cities discussed above, the Cologne burghers became involved in an extensive associational movement and formed a broad spectrum of societies for many purposes.[31] Similar to Dortmund's economic elite but unlike Frankfurt's, the Cologne merchants and bankers created the biggest industrialisation project in Germany, including the development of the Ruhr region. To that end, they succeeded in unifying the elites of many Rhenish cities in order to make gigantic investments in railway construction, mining and blast furnaces for steel production. The elite of these cities dominated the regional Prussian Parliament and strongly countered the Prussian State government. This was one reason for the outbreak of the 1848 revolution.[32]

Despite the differences in the configurations of the elites in these German cities, they all shared certain characteristics. First, they were heterogeneous and in most cases composed of different social groups. Likewise, the structures of these elite groups all changed over the 'long durée', developing

---

[30]   Mettele, *Bürgertum*, 342.

[31]   Ibid. 345–7.

[32]   See R. Boch, *Grenzenloses Wachstum? Das rheinische Wirtschaftsbürgertum und seine Industrialisierungsdebatte 1814–1857* (Göttingen 1991), and R. Roth, '"... denn die Eisenbahn war es, die nunmehr den Anlaß zu einer Kolonisation der Heide gab ...". Die Eisenbahnen und das rheinisch-westfälische Industriegebiet', in *Rheinisch-westfälische Zeitschrift für Volkskunde*, 47, 2002, 101–38.

a network of non-political societies such as the boards of foundations and religious communities, which contributed to the transition from a traditional burgher society to a modern civil society.

The role of associations for the elite in German cities

Modern associations as we know them first came into being around 1800. This clear break in the development of Frankfurt society was marked by the foundation of the Casino and Museum societies (*Casino- und Museums-gesellschaften*) or by similar organisations in numerous other German cities. After the emergence of these two, a wave of associations began to appear in all of these cities. The association movement took a different form after 1815 and established itself alongside the more traditional corporations. Permanent societies for various purposes were founded and after a while these new organisations were actively engaged in cultural, social and political activities that would have a significant social impact. Soon after the wars of liberation in 1813 and during the period of political restoration, patriotic beliefs played an important role in the foundation of new societies. It was within this context that the first confessional associations and women's societies were founded. In fact, women's associations had already been established during the French occupation around 1810 in larger cities including Bremen, Cologne, Frankfurt, and Münster. This period saw the beginning of the Frankfurt 'Society for the Foundation of an Industrial Workshop for Female Handwork' (*Industrie-Anstalt für feinere weibliche Handarbeiten*) and the Cologne 'Société Maternelle'. From these groups emerged the Fatherland Women's Societies (*Vaterländische Frauenvereine*) which developed in both cities in 1814 and 1815, whose aim was to treat wounded soldiers.[33] Not long after this, choral societies, industrial associations and the first historical societies were created in cities like Frankfurt and Augsburg. In 1816 the Frankfurt Polytechnic Society was founded on the model of the Patriotic Society of Hamburg. Its aim was to support the technical arts and sciences. The premise of this society was to combine educational training with the imperative of economic progress. To this end the society tested and

---

[33]   See Roth, *Stadt*, 188, 342–5; Mettele, *Bürgertum*, 101–102 and 120–23; Schulz, *Vormundschaft*, 333, and Kill, *Bürgertum*, 153. Some existed for only a short time but others established a tradition that reached to the twentieth century. See above all the Frankfurt and Hamburg examples and the studies of Ch. Klausmann, *Politik und Kultur der Frauenbewegung im Kaiserreich. Das Beispiel Frankfurt am Main* (Frankfurt am Main 1997), and K. Heinsohn, *Politik und Geschlecht. Zur politischen Kultur bürgerlicher Frauenvereine in Hamburg* (Hamburg 1997). See also R. Huber-Sperl, *Organisiert und engagiert. Vereinskultur bürgerlicher Frauen im 19. Jahrhundert in Westeuropa und den USA* (Königstein/Ts. 2002), and for Baden K. Lutzer, *Der Badische Frauenverein 1859–1918. Rotes Kreuz, Fürsorge und Frauenfrage* (Stuttgart 2002).

disseminated new inventions, organised lectures, and established an industrial school (*Gewerbeschule*) and a savings bank.[34] The Augsburg Polytechnic Society established itself as Bavaria's central association and focused its attention on the fight against the economic crisis of the time.[35]

The number of societies proliferated, and from these first initiatives grew 'a passion for associations', as Thomas Nipperdey wrote in his ground-breaking article: 'All of the activities of burghers were organised in associations.'[36] During the 1830s Frankfurt had more than 3,000 burghers participating in more than 30 societies. That meant that 50 per cent of all burghers belonged to this new informal network. By the 1840's there were already more than 50 societies in existence, each different from the others in purpose and function.[37]

Scarcely a year would pass without the founding of one or two new societies. The common desire for greater sociability together with an impulse for progress and social development propelled these groups forward. For this reason that there were as many types as there were motives for founding them. Some burghers used associations to represent their economic interests, while for others they served to surmount economic crisis by supporting technological innovations. And for many it was simply an enthusiasm for music, literature, science, art or physical fitness and health.[38] No matter the motive, they all flourished in a society that was becoming more complex and clearly more civic minded. As a result of this network of associations, a large group of city burghers who were once on the periphery were now integrated into a movement for change. These forms of communication and social interaction were now transformed into the framework of a modern civil

---

[34] See R. Roth, 'Das Vereinswesen in Frankfurt am Main als Beispiel einer nichtstaatlichen Bildungsstruktur', *Archiv für Frankfurts Geschichte und Kunst*, 64, 1998, 143–211, esp. 153–5, and Roth, *Stadt*, 248–58. On the foundation of the Frankfurt Society for the Support of Utilitarian arts and Sciences (*Frankfurter Gesellschaft zur Beförderung der nützlichen Künste und der sie veredelnden Wissenschaften*), see F. Lerner, *Bürgersinn und Bürgertat. Geschichte der Frankfurter Polytechnischen Gesellschaft 1816–1966* (Frankfurt am Main 1966), 27–30.

[35] See Möller, *Herrschaft*, 177–8.

[36] Th. Nipperdey, 'Verein als soziale Struktur in Deutschland im späten 18. und frühen 19. Jahrhundert', in H. Heimpel, ed., *Geschichtswissenschaft und Vereinswesen im 19. Jahrhundert* (Göttingen 1972), 1–44, here 3.

[37] In Dortmund no less than 35 societies were founded, although the associational movement there has been characterised as less developed. In the same period Münster had eleven societies. See Schambach, *Stadtbürgertum*, 201, and Kill, *Bürgertum*, 138.

[38] See D. Hein, 'Soziale Konstituierungsfaktoren des Bürgertums', in Gall, *Stadt und Bürgertum im Übergang*, 151–81, esp. 172. On Augsburg's new foundations at this time see Möller, *Herrschaft*, 185–6.

society. The growing network of societies played an important role in the development of German civic self-consciousness.[39]

Conspicuous are the numerous societies in the spheres of art and culture. It was these groups in particular that supported burghers in their search for a new identity. In this sense they played an important role in the formation process of a modern nineteenth-century civil society.[40] The art societies provide us with an example of this, and were founded, for example, in Bremen in 1824 and in Frankfurt in 1829. In their outward appearance they existed simply to support the plastic arts. But the true reason for their existence was to organise commoner burghers who could support an independent art market free from the influence of princely courts and aristocrats. At last freelance artists could receive support without the influence of the ruling class and its cultural hegemony.[41] As in Bremen and Frankfurt, similar foundations were established in Augsburg, Cologne and many other German cities in the following decade. The art societies influenced the cultural milieu of many cities by holding exhibitions and purchasing paintings and graphics using different motifs and styles.[42] The sheer number of their members together with the fact that some were often linked to the city elite illustrates the vast growing interest in art and culture.

The art societies and numerous music and choral societies were not, however, the predominant type of society in the 1830s and 1840s. Even though ten art and cultural societies had evolved in Frankfurt, there were also ten foundations established in the spheres of the humanities and the natural sciences, including the Physical Society, the Society for Geography and

---

[39] See Mettele, *Bürgertum*, 162.

[40] See D. Hein, 'Kunst und bürgerlicher Aufbruch. Das Karlsruher Vereinswesen und der Kunstverein im frühen 19. Jahrhundert', in J. Dresch and W. Rößling, eds, *175 Jahre Badischer Kunstverein. Bilder im Zirkel* (Karlsruhe 1993), 25–35, here 34.

[41] See 'Der hiesige Kunstverein', in *Frankfurter Jahrbücher*, 6, 1835, 215.

[42] The art societies supported the dissemination of private art collections. See Mettele, *Bürgertum*, 187–8; Schulz, *Vormundschaft*, 387–8; Kill, *Bürgertum*, 148–50, and Möller, *Herrschaft*, 172. Another goal of the Augsburg art society was to support craftsmen, who were forced to introduce new fashions to keep up with growing competition. See Möller, *Herrschaft*, 177. On the subject more generally see W. Grasskamp, 'Die Einbürgerung der Kunst. Korporative Kunstförderung im 19. Jahrhundert', in E. Mai and P. Paret, eds, *Sammler, Stifter und Museen. Kunstförderung in Deutschland im 19. und 20. Jahrhundert* (Cologne 1993), 104–13. The art societies were refashioined into large museum societies around 1900, demonstrating the associational movement's persistent interest in and attraction to the visual arts. On the foundation of the Städel Museum Society (Städelscher Museumsverein) in Frankfurt and the Kaiser Friedrich-Museums-Verein in Berlin see A. Hansert, *Städelscher Museums-Verein Frankfurt am Main* (Frankfurt am Main 1994), and Th. W. Gaethgens, 'Wilhelm Bode und seine Sammler', in Mai and Paret, *Sammler,* 153–72, here 169–70.

Statistics, as well as various historical societies.[43] Clearly this development supported the growing belief that the cultural advancement of a society revolved around more than just the practical application of the arts.

In the 1830s and 1840s many German cities experienced a second wave of the founding of new societies. Through these groups a large segment of the burgher community came into contact with the new communication network. First there were choral societies that opened their doors to craftsmen. Later in the 1840s, trade and industrial societies organised middle-class members from all social levels. Gymnastic societies and worker education societies further integrated the entire spectrum of the middle class as well as lower social groups.[44] In the second half of the nineteenth century, societies for nearly every purpose came into being. Citizens from every social, cultural or confessional milieu and from the business and political arenas organised themselves in a multitude of societies.[45] For this reason it would seem quite logical to ask what role exactly these societies played for the elite. To answer this we must consider two very different aspects of the situation: the first being that of certain elite societies and the second the actual activities of elite groups within the network of societies.

'From modest beginnings, a broad movement of a wide variety of societies spread throughout nearly all of the cities of Central Europe in the nineteenth century. In many of these cases one general society devoted to sociability was the starting point.'[46] This common society, frequently named *Casino*, *Museum*, *Harmonie* or *Tivoli*, has been the focus of much basic research in the last decade, and, as a result, its characteristics have become clearer. 'Whoever visited these societies regularly', as stated in one nineteenth-century Casino Society description, 'was given the feeling of being an active member of the elite.'[47] These societies increased in number around 1800. They both formed a link with the early academies (*Kollegien*), Freemason lodges and reading societies and were integrated into the developed network of societies. There are three important findings that

---

[43]   On the historical societies see W. Speitkamp, 'Geschichtsvereine – Landesge-schichte – Erinnerungskultur', *Mitteilungen des Oberhessischen Geschichtsvereins Gießen*, 88, 2003, 181–204. On the Frankfurt historical societies see R. Roth, 'Die Frankfurter Bürger auf der Suche nach ihrer Geschichte', ibid., 159–80.

[44]   See Hein, 'Konstituierungsfaktoren', 168.

[45]   The broad movement of societies with its distinctions in different parts was a new element in the city society. The societies established a new foundation for these burgher communities. In Augsburg during the 1830s, one of six principal members of a household were organised in at least one society. In Frankfurt during the same period, we find between 2,500 and 3,000 people involved in the society movement and in the 1840s there were more than 5,000 burghers organised in societies. This was more than half of the entire burgher community. See Möller, *Herrschaft*, 180, and Roth, 'Vereinswesen', 165.

[46]   M. Sobania, 'Vereinsleben. Regeln und Formen bürgerlicher Assoziationen im 19. Jahrhundert', in Hein and Schulz, eds, *Bürgerkultur*, 170–90, here 170.

[47]   Maentel, 'Reputation', 298.

should be mentioned here. First is the short period during which the foundation of these societies took place. In all of Germany's large and medium-sized cities these societies were established within just a few years. Second, detailed studies of their membership lists have demonstrated the close connection between these societies and the city elite.[48] Third, these elite societies continued to exist throughout the entire nineteenth century.

In the years after 1800 the Frankfurt *Casino* and the Frankfurt *Museum* provided the catalyst for the foundation of a multitude of societies. Similar to the reading societies, both had specially designed meeting rooms with a library for reading. In this period the terms 'educated' or 'cultivated' (*gebildet*) did not necessarily signify erudition or someone who had read much literature but rather a burgher acquainted with the various facets of economic and social life. The term 'educated burgher' encompassed a wide social spectrum that extended from wealthy merchants all the way to the academic professions. The social fabric of the *Casino* makes abundantly clear what was of greatest importance at that time. In the membership list of 1805 no less than three quarters of the total 212 members were well known Frankfurt tradesman, bankers and publishers. The next group included 30 patricians and 21 lawyers and judges, who in most cases belonged to the city administration.[49] All in all only five academics had joined the society. The fact that only twelve of these members were not listed as the highest tax payers (*Höchstbesteuertenliste*) would certainly qualify the members of the *Casino* as an integral part of the elite of the city. More than half either accepted a political office following his membership or had already been politically engaged. The *Casino* members included no less than 29 members of the *Rat*. A further 60 belonged to the city parliament which was established a few years later.[50]

Looking at the Bremer *Erholung*, the Bremer *Museum* or the Cologne *Société*, which was later called *Casino*, one finds striking similarities. The statute of the Bremer *Erholung* declared as a goal of the society 'to create a permanent union of a chosen society' and to 'inform each other'. The Bremer *Erholung* was characterised by its social gatherings and public spirit. The main purpose of these social evenings in the *Erholung* was to bring together 'like minded people from the leading groups of the Hanseatic city', in order to discuss 'patriotic affairs' and 'to enjoy the pleasant ambience'.[51] In Cologne the members of the elite met nearly every day to read the newest journals, play billiards and cards or join sociable discussions in the smoking room.

---

[48] See Maentel, 'Reputation', 295–314, and Sobania, 'Vereinsleben', 170–90.

[49] See '*Liste der 212 Mitglieder des Casino* (Frankfurt am Main 1810), and *Liste der effectiven und 10 supernumerären Mitglieder erster Klasse des Casino für das Jahr 1816/17* (Frankfurt am Main 1817).

[50] On the social structure of the Casino see Roth, *Stadt*, graphic 11 and table 21.

[51] Schulz, *Vormundschaft*, 217–18.

Half of the 57 founding members were merchants, factory owners, bankers, lawyers and doctors with city officials making up the rest. The state officials who made up ten per cent of the total were uncommonly well represented. Craftsmen did not belong to the society. Nearly three quarters of the founders were top taxpayers and listed as notables at that time. Among the members of the 'Société' were eleven members of the city parliament (*Munizipalräte*). Four of them had belonged to the Rat under the Old Régime. (...) One third was engaged in the Cologne Chamber of Commerce. Ten years previously, six of these members had founded its predecessor, the so-called *Handelsvorstand*. (...) The Société developed rapidly and soon became the central meeting point of the upper class of the city.[52]

Even in the small city of Dortmund 'newspapers and journals were deposited in reading rooms that supported the cultivation of their members, and balls or concerts were arranged for their amusement.'[53] In Munich the higher ranks of the administration together with the educated middle class and some merchants founded no less than three elite societies which they then dominated.[54] In very sharp contrast to this, neither state officials nor aristocrats played any role in the Bremer *Erholung*, the Bremer *Museum* or the Aachen and Cologne *Casino*.[55]

Throughout their existence the elite societies endured strong fluctuations in terms of their importance, and this was due to internal conflicts, breakdowns and the founding of new rival societies. In spite of these fluctuations many of these groups survived in larger cities into the twentieth century.[56] One could even speak of a renaissance after World War One. Although the Hanseatic Club in Hamburg or the Industrial Clubs in

---

[52] Mettele, *Bürgertum*, 98–101, and 163–4 for a description of the home of the society.

[53] Schambach, *Stadtbürgertum*, 186.

[54] See Zerback, *München*, 83–5, and 128–31.

[55] In Bremen there were likewise three elite societies, the *Erholung*, the *Museum* and the *Union*, and all three societies were dominated by merchants. See Schulz, *Vormundschaft*, 217–27.

[56] In Dortmund there was a quarrel about the character of this elite-organisation in 1846 and 1861. We find similar discussions in Frankfurt at the end of the 1860s. See Schambach, *Stadtbürgertum*, 199 and 361, and Roth, *Stadt*, 511–15. In Augsburg and Bremen there were also very distinct transition periods. Similar to Münster, two elite societies, *Harmonie* and *Tivoli*, had been founded, the former dominated by merchants and the latter by local state officials. Both ended in the 1830s. The gap they left, was filled by the society *Frohsinn*, which was founded by middle-income merchants, trade employees and craftsmen. But in the 1840s and even more in the 1850s a distinct strategy of social recruitment led to a change in its social composition. The portion of wealthy merchants, manufactures and bankers increased to more than 50 per cent. See Möller, *Herrschaft*, 169, 182–3, and 345–7. In Bremen *Erholung* and *Museum* found themselves in crisis in the 1860s and partially disbanded. Their role was taken over by the *Union* from 1801, which had originally been founded as a corporation for young merchants. See Schulz, *Vormundschaft*, 633–5.

Dortmund and Düsseldorf were dominated by entrepreneurs, they systematically recruited representatives from other social classes and from the main political and cultural institutions. Besides social events and informal communication they fostered an educational program that included lectures on all of the important problems of the day. These societies served in many cases as a backbone for the formation of a new elite in the Weimar period. Astonishingly enough, even to this day this group of societies has still not been fully explored.[57]

Of the elite societies and their specific characteristics examined here, we realise that a fragment of the puzzle still remains. Namely, in what other ways, aside from the economic and political institutions, did the elite make use of the network of societies? Despite the knowledge brought to light by the research of the last two decades, we still know little about the practical efficiency and effectiveness of societies as a network for the elite. Little research has focused solely on the practical interactions of society members in these informal structures. It is often forgotten that these societies not only served general communication interests but were also used for very specific and practical purposes.[58] They were, as Nipperdey often claimed, 'a medium for the formation of civil society' and they cannot be reduced to mere sociability or a vague desire for the exchange of information.[59] The claim that burghers were only looking for rules 'that middle class individuals could use to form a new society, based on the broken down framework of the Ancien Régime,' is highly questionable.[60] A definite 'no' would be our response to this. Indeed, the urban elites used networks of societies in very concrete ways and as the basis of more practical activities. The societies were instruments for 'managers'. With the skills they gained in these societies, practical trained burghers often climbed to influential political positions.[61] This is what

---

[57] As an example we can take the Frankfurt Society for Trade, Industry and Science (*Frankfurter Gesellschaft für Handel, Industrie und Wissenschaft*), founded in 1920 after the loss of World War One and the Revolution of 1918. See R. Roth, 'Die Geschichte der Frankfurter Gesellschaft für Handel, Industrie und Wissenschaft 1920 bis 1995', in L. Gall, ed., *Frankfurter Gesellschaft für Handel, Industrie und Wissenschaft – Casinogesellschaft von 1802* (Frankfurt am Main 1995), 37–82, here 41–3.

[58] J. Kocka, 'Obrigkeitsstaat und Bürgerlichkeit. Zur Geschichte des deutschen Bürgertums im 19. Jahrhundert', in W. Hardtwig and H.-H. Brandt, eds, *Deutschlands Weg in die Moderne. Politik, Gesellschaft und Kultur im 19. Jahr-hundert* (Munich 1993), 107–21, esp. 111–12.

[59] Th. Nipperdey, *Deutsche Gesellschaft 1800–1866. Bürgerwelt und starker Staat* (Munich 1983), 268.

[60] Möller, *Herrschaft*, 180.

[61] On the role of societies for the political career of the Frankfurt publisher Carl Brönner, the Bremer merchants Franz Böving and Arnold Duckwitz as well as the Karlsruhe tobacco manufacturer Christian Griesbach see R. Roth, 'Kaufleute als Werteproduzenten', in H.-W. Hahn and D. Hein, eds, *Bürgerliche Werte und Wertevermittlung um 1800* (Jena 2005), 95–118.

dramatic new research results on the middle class in Thuringian cities have brought to light. The publisher Ludwig Friedrich Froriep 'knitted a network of a multitude of relations' and from this arose positions not only in commissions and political boards but also in numerous societies.[62] This was also true for individuals such as Carl Friedrich Ernst Fromann from Jena, who like Froriep came from a publishing family, and for whom these 'societies were a natural medium of his public engagement.'[63] Without his membership in the Erfurt Industrial Society, the rifle manufacturer Johann Nicolaus Dreyse from Sömmerda could not have climbed from the position of a common craftsman to that of one of the most exciting entrepreneurs in the period of Germany's early industrialisation. We can add to this list the name Ernst Wilhelm Arnoldi from Gotha, a man engaged not only in his own society but also in numerous private societies, whom the historian Heinrich Treitschke called the most capable tradesman of Germany. The same could be said for Johann David Böhme a blacksmith, brickworks owner and citizen of Jena.[64]

It was with the help of these societies and especially shareholder societies that big projects could be realised.[65] The essential role of societies becomes abundantly clear when we take into account one of the great infrastructural projects of the nineteenth century – railway construction. The early construction of most German railways was promoted by special committees and societies, established in nearly every German city. Deeply impressed by events in England, the railway committee of Nuremberg, the standard bearer for this movement, voted enthusiastically for the building of the first German railway line. When the railway committee assembled for the first time, the board of the Chamber of Commerce as well as the Patriotic Society (*Patriotische Gesellschaft*) and the magistrate also took part. Similar railway committees were founded in Leipzig, Berlin, Frankfurt, Cologne and Aachen. In many cities burghers were united in their initiation of railway lines and organised the detailed planning of their construction. Together with these

---

[62] On the example of Froriep see W. von Häfen, 'Zwischen Fürstendienst und bürgerlicher Selbständigkeit. Der Mediziner und Verleger Ludwig Friedrich von Froriep', in H.-W. Hahn, W. Greiling and K. Ries, eds, *Bürgertum in Thüringen. Lebenswelt und Lebenswege im frühen 19. Jahrhundert* (Rudolstadt und Jena 2001), 53–80, here 76.

[63] F. Wogawa, '"Zu sehr Bürger...?" Die Jenaer Verleger- und Buchhändlerfamilie Frommann im 19. Jahrhundert', in ibid., 81–107, here 102.

[64] See F. Boblenz, '"Bete und arbeite für König und Vaterland". Zur Biographie des Industriellen Johann Nicolaus von Dreyse', in ibid., 201–29, here 221; S. Ballentin, 'Ein Gothaer Unternehmer zwischen privaten Geschäften, städtischem Engagement und nationalen Reformversuchen. Ernst Wilhelm Arnoldi', in ibid., 231–52, here 250, and F. Burkhardt, 'Zeugschmidtmeister, Ziegeleibesitzer und Stadtbürger. Zum politischen Karriereprofil des Jenaer Handwerkers Johann David Böhme', in ibid., 303–33, here 318.

[65] On the role of shareholder societies see Nipperdey, 'Verein', 2–5.

railway societies the burgher elite discussed the sense and purpose of these projects and transformed them into an experience that involved the entire community. Making use of the informal network of societies, burghers assured everyone of their full support in pamphlets, burgher meetings and public debates. It was through these activities that they paved the way for achieving a more detailed plan, procuring the necessary financial backing and fighting for state concessions. Step by step, city by city and even beyond cities they set the movement in motion.[66] When their agitation was successful and they received the concession, they then founded shareholder societies.

Later this development often repeated itself, and led from railway committees to railway societies to shareholder societies and from the shareholder societies to the industrialisation of Germany.[67] Within the structure of railway societies, burghers who were rooted in the world of relatively small cities learned how to negotiate with the state administration. This was the reason why many politicians of character and profile, for example David Hansemann or Ludolf Camphausen, began their political careers within the movement for railway construction.[68] In similar ways the societies were involved in the realisation of municipal projects of public interest, which they organised under their own leadership. Societies also organised the economic foundation of cultural institutions. We know that there were many theatre societies, zoo societies or societies for the construction of botanical gardens, which were often organised as shareholder societies. Many urban problems, such as clean water sources, were solved with the help of these types of societies. Similar societies were later founded for the construction of working-class tenement houses, and these played an important role in many German cities between 1890 and 1914.[69]

---

[66] See M. A. Lips, *Die Nürnberg-Fürther Eisenbahn in ihren nächsten Wirkungen und Resultaten* (Nuremberg 1836), 34–5, and R. Roth, *Das Jahrhundert der Eisenbahn. Die Herrschaft über Raum und Zeit 1800 – 1914* (Ostfildern 2005), 59–64.

[67] For further examples see K. Schambach, 'Geselligkeit und wirtschaftlicher Wandel. Zur Entwicklung des Vereinswesens in Dortmund im 19. Jahrhundert', *Beiträge zur Geschichte Dortmunds und der Grafschaft Mark*, 87, 1997, 117–33, here 127–30.

[68] On the Rhenish railway society and the political role of Hansemann and Camphausen see Boch, *Wachstum*, 138–148; W. Klee, *Preußische Eisenbahngeschichte* (Stuttgart 1982), 34–48, and Mettele, *Bürgertum*, 299.

[69] On the public societies for the construction of tenement houses in Frankfurt see H. Kramer, 'Die Anfänge des sozialen Wohnungsbaus in Frankfurt am Main 1860–1914', *Archiv für Frankfurts Geschichte und Kunst*, 56, 1978, 123–90. For Leipzig see Th. Adam, *Arbeitermilieu und Arbeiterbewegung in Leipzig 1871–1933. Demokratische Bewegungen in Mitteldeutschland* (Cologne et al. 1999), 205–18. The debate on a public engagement was closely tied with the social policy on the municipal level. It was discussed under the key word 'municipal socialism' (*Munizipalsozialismus*). On the problem of municipal socialism in Germany see W. Krabbe, 'Munizipalsozialismus und Interventionsstaat. Die Ausbreitung der

When we question the practical efficiency of societies there is another problem. So far we have categorised and then analysed societies according to their objective and social aspects. Interestingly enough, there has been less attention given to the impact of these groups. Although there are those rare instances where societies were insular and independent, most were part of a complex network. This of course raises the logical question of what role exactly this collection of societies played and how did this network work together with other self-governing institutions as trusts or commercial organisations? We must first consider the network of societies as a complex network of opportunities. These complex networks were used by the members of the elite who were often board members of these self-governing institutions, not only for the exchange of information and ideas but even more for the accumulation of financial resources and for the inauguration of cultural, social and political institutions. The infrastructure developed in this fashion had a more profound impact on the development of many cities because it could be used for greater projects. One could say that in a process that lasted over many decades, these networks enabled the elite to accumulate the cultural capital of German cities.

The strategic use of these networks by elites can also be observed in major social and political conflicts. This became very apparent in the 1848 revolution, when urban society was viewed as a model for a German national civil society. By forcing through a series of radical reforms during this time, the democrats broke the consensus among citizens. They were immediately confronted by a civil movement which had been initiated by the majority of the elites who made use of the non-governmental network of guilds, boards of religious communities, and societies and clubs.[70] Another example of this kind of elite activity was Frankfurt's ambitious development program of 1875. The aim was to transform the economic, social and cultural characteristics of the city. The elite successfully bridged the differences between democrats and liberals who dominated the city assembly and the magistrate. By overcoming a political stalemate, they brought together governmental boards, non-governmental institutions and associations by investing in bridges, Europe's biggest railway station, and a new harbour, as well as the regulation of the Main River. They also supported parks, a new zoo and an opera house to beautify the city, along with districts where

---

städtischen Leistungsverwaltung im Kaiserreich', *Geschichte in Wissenschaft und Unterricht*, 30, 1979, 265–83, and U. Kühl, 'Le débat sur le socialisme municipal en Allemagne avant 1914 et la municipalisation de l'électricité', in U. Kühl, ed., *Der Munizipalsozialismus in Europa* (Munich 2001), 81–100.

[70] See R. Roth, 'Die Stadt der Paulskirche als Modell einer selbstverwalteten Republik', in Bernd Heidenreich, ed., *Deutsche Hauptstädte – von Frankfurt nach Berlin* (Wiesbaden 1998), 53–68.

Figure 7.7 Lecture hall of the University of Frankfurt, 1908

Source:　　　Institut für Stadtgeschichte Frankfurt am Main.

modern industry could develop prosperous businesses. At the end of this decade, elites again overcame political differences about the kind of industry Frankfurt should attract by organising the International Electric Exhibition of 1891 (*Internationale Elektrotechnische Ausstellung*). This exhibition advertised the urban possibilities for a clean and socially harmonious industry based on electricity. Another idea on offer was constructing electric power plants outside the city so that electrical currents could be transmitted over long distances. The prime mover for this form of industry as well as new traffic systems was Jewish banker and publisher Leopold Sonnemann, a democrat, who also presided over the city assembly. He successfully incorporated all the representatives of the two liberal parties, the magistrate, the city assembly and many leaders of the non-governmental network. The latter was composed of the board of the Physical Society, which was founded by members of the Senckenberg Society for Natural Research (*Senckenbergische Naturforschende Gesellschaft*) in 1829. But this was more than just a demonstration of the prowess of the burgher sectors of society. It also layed the foundation for an industrialisation of the city that was in many aspects different from the industrialisation of other German cities.[71]

---

[71]　See Roth, *Stadt*, 566–73.

Aside from being a trade centre and banking metropolis, Frankfurt became an industrial city as well. It also established an important university and become an academic centre. How this was done was one of the most remarkable successes of the Frankfurt elite. The idea of an academy or university in Frankfurt first appeared with the establishment of the Museum Society in 1808. It then resurfaced and enjoyed a renaissance with the *Freie Deutsche Hochstift*, a society founded in the context of the anniversary of Schiller's birth in 1859.[72] Connected to this was the project of a citizen's academy, which stirred the publisher Carl Jügel into actively making moves towards establishing a university. Jügel persuaded his two sons to contribute money to the Jügel Foundation, which would support the founding of an academy. By the end of the nineteenth century the preconditions necessary to establish a university in Frankfurt finally existed. The debate on the foundation of universities was a general topic in many other cities during this time. Cologne, Leipzig and Hamburg were just a few of the cities that were also making serious plans to move forward with this idea. But the most far-reaching attempt was that of the Frankfurt elite. In 1890 the democrat Otto Kanngießer published a memorandum entitled 'Present and Nearest Future' which focused attention on the numerous local cultural institutions and societies that should be brought together in the form of a university.[73] Within only a few years this idea became reality. In 1896 the magistrate, together with the Chamber of Commerce and the Society for National Economy took the initiative in establishing a business academy for the trades (*Handelshochschule*). Not long after in 1901 the manufacturer Wilhelm Merton and his 'Institution for Public Wealth' (*Institut für Gemeinwohl*) founded the 'Academy for Social and Commercial Sciences' (*Akademie für Sozial- und Handelswissenschaften*), whose goals were to educate students in the fields of public law and national economics. But beyond this goal, the academy was to serve as a sort of nucleus for the university. As a result of these initiatives of the burgher elite, further foundations and societies were created. The members of the city assembly and even the magistrate became involved in the project. Because of the academy and the engagement of different societies and numerous foundations the groundwork for the university was being laid. The planning stages were brought to a successful conclusion by Mayor Franz Adickes between 1900 and 1913, when all of the city and state administrative preconditions were met. In the year 1909 the magistrate sent a memorandum for the foundation of a university to the Prussian Ministry of the Interior, which foresaw a university with five

---

[72] See Otto Volger, *Gründungsschrift von 1859*, quot. at F. Adler, *Freies Deutsches Hochstift. Seine Geschichte erster Teil 1859–1885* (Frankfurt am Main 1959), 34.
[73] See O. Kanngießer, *Frankfurts Gegenwart und nächste Zukunft. Eine Denkschrift* (Frankfurt am Main 1892), 56–8.

faculties that would be realised before World War One.[74] It was not the achievement of the magistrate alone but also the effort of many elites. As a result of a process which took nearly one hundred years to complete, there evolved a special kind of university in which we can clearly see the characteristics of a networking city elite. The different components of the university were created slowly and carefully and put together by the elites with great success upon its completion. However, the university itself could not have been founded without the help of the informal and self-governing networks of the burghers. In addition to the many foundations engaged in this process there is a long list of societies that should also be mentioned here including the Physical Society, the Polytechnic Society, the Geographical Society and the Senckenberg Society for Natural Sciences.[75] The foundation of the University of Frankfurt was an impressive example of the efficiency of the networks of societies and foundations. The establishment of such a noble institution sheds considerable light on the use of societies by the city elite of Frankfurt. In light of this we can therefore argue that German urban elites were groups that organised themselves into networks. And from their positions within these networks of societies, foundations, boards of religious communities and chambers of commerce, the elite acted independently of the political sphere and initiated projects which were of strategic importance for the economic, social, political or cultural development of the city.[76]

Conclusion

This commentary on the structure and development of some of the German city elites illustrates the advantages of carrying out empirical research in the context of a specific urban society. The character of the elite reflected on the

---

[74] See B. Müller, *Stiftungen für Frankfurt am Main* (Frankfurt am Main 1958), 129–30. In observing the unique attributes of the University of Frankfurt one is made acutely aware of the special role played by the Frankfurt city burghers and its network of societies. For example, because of the attention the Frankfurt burghers paid to the social question the university stressed the role of the young social sciences. It was also a new innovation to divide the natural sciences from the philosophical faculty. Physics and chemistry played an important role in the industries that had settled in the surrounding areas of Frankfurt. More evidence of the specific traditions of the Frankfurt burghers can be seen in the self government of the university by an independent board (*Großer Rat*) where the city, the Institute for Public Wealth, the Chamber of Commerce, the Polytechnical Society, the big foundations and all founders were represented. See R. Wachsmuth, *Die Gründung der Frankfurter Universität* (Frankfurt am Main 1929), 76, and P. Kluke, *Die Stiftungsuniversität Frankfurt am Main 1914–1932* (Frankfurt am Main 1972), 52.

[75] See Roth, 'Vereinswesen', 203–206, and Roth, 'Wilhelm Meister', 121–39.

[76] On the thesis that the 'formation of the elite' depended on the 'network of societies in many cities' see Zerback, *München*, 132, and Möller, *Herrschaft*, 181.

type of city, its burgher law and the city's social composition. We must take into consideration that German city elites were the elites of republics and not aristocrats. This set them apart from the elites of the different German princely states. Over the centuries, they formed a complex self-governing regime with a city government and distinct control institutions. This political machine mirrored the fragmented burgher society but bound it together in a society of burghers.

In defining the elite we have to consider guilds, boards of trade, foundations and the boards of religious communities, in addition to the city regime itself. Around 1800, sometimes earlier, sometimes later, these networks were complemented by a cultural network evolving mainly from societies, for specific economic, political and cultural purposes and interests.

In the beginning of the associational movement, the German city elites had exclusive clubs such as the 'Casino' and 'Museum' societies, but aside from that, they cannot be characterised as a separately organised group. The elite in German cities were not made up of a handful of families. It was a permanently changing group, including and excluding persons according to the roles they played in political and non-political networks. The elite often made use of these expanding networks in which they met and informally exchanged information with each other. German urban elites constituted a networking elite. Many of them were neither interested in daily policy nor engaged in the city government or city assembly. From their positions inside the network they initiated strategic stimuli for the general economic, social, political and cultural development of the city.

CHAPTER EIGHT

Voluntary Society in Mid-Nineteenth-Century Pest: Urbanisation and the Changing Distribution of Power

Árpád Tóth

Introduction

As expressions of social and political development in the modern world, voluntary societies have recently become a popular topic in historical research. A wide range of studies have explored how their activities affected or sometimes even created new fields of activity in the life of urban communities, including poor relief, medical aid, leisure pastimes, cultural life, schooling, private savings programs and political participation.[1]

Among the various interpretations for the spread of the associational institution in the late-eighteenth and nineteenth centuries, I would like to emphasise how it contributed to the bourgeois acquisition of urban power. Robert J. Morris has argued that it was voluntary societies which helped the emerging urban middle class to establish its local domination in a period of permanent social conflict after 1780. One reason why such organisations worked effectively was that their activity was more or less independent of

---

[1]   Among the most influential comprehensive or comparative works about the early and nineteenth century historical developments see R. J. Morris, 'Clubs, societies and associations', in F. M. L. Thompson, ed., *The Cambridge Social History of Britain*, vol. 3: *Social Agencies and Institutions* (Cambridge 1990), 395–443; P. Clark, *British Clubs and Societies, 1580–1800. The Origins of an Associational World* (Oxford 2000); É. François, ed., *Sociabilité et société bourgeoise en France, en Allemagne et en Suisse, 1750–1850. Geselligkeit, Vereinswesen und bürgerliche Gesellschaft in Frankreich, Deutschland und der Schweiz, 1750–1850* (Paris 1986); Th. Nipperdey, 'Verein als soziale Struktur im späten 18. und frühen 19. Jahrhundert', in Th. Nipperdey, *Geschichtswissenschaft und Vereinswesen im 19. Jahrhundert* (Göttingen 1972), 1–44.; O. Dann, ed., *Vereinswesen und bürgerliche Gesellschaft in Deutschland*. Historische Zeitschrift, Beiheft 9 (Munich 1984). Among the contributions see especially W. Hardtwig, 'Strukturmerkmale und Entwicklungstendenzen des Vereinswesens in Deutschland, 1789–1848', 11–50, and H. P. Hye, 'Vereinswesen und bürgerliche Gesellschaft in Österreich', *Beiträge zur historischen Sozialkunde*, 3, 1988, 86–96.

state aid or control. They could attract members from various ranks of the urban community, even rival factions, since what was needed was co-operation on narrow issues rather than a general consensus on political and religious questions. It is also of note that voluntary societies meant a constitutional form of legal equality for all members (eg. in voting and electing officials), while in practice the hierarchy of offices enabled those higher on the social ladder to retain their status above the 'commoner' membership.[2]

Voluntary societies, with their specific objectives, forms of recruitment and organisation, spread throughout the continent within a few decades. The sweep of this tide reached Hungary and then the Eastern part of the Habsburg Monarchy after the Napoleonic Wars. At the outset the Pest Charitable Women's Society (PCWS) was set up in 1817 in Pest, the biggest town in the country, and by the eve of the bourgeois revolution in 1848 some 500 voluntary societies were active all over the country.[3] It is the purpose of this chapter to analyse how far the activities of these clubs influenced urban life and to what extent they changed the framework of local politics. To achieve such an aim it is first necessary to examine the conditions of urban politics in Hungarian towns during that period. I then analyse several aspects of the political significance of voluntary societies, before finally drawing conclusions.

Urban politics in Hungarian towns before 1848

Political participation for town dwellers was somewhat restricted at both national and local levels on the eve of the 1848 Revolution.[4] The political framework of the urban system was still largely influenced by medieval and early modern traditions. Politics was dominated by the nobility and the gentry, and the Hungarian Parliament was still an *états généreaux* rather than a national political assembly based on the modern, liberal principle of popular representation. Some 42 free royal towns, a relatively high number compared to the 46 counties, a few other territories and the Roman Catholic chapters had the right to send MPs to the Lower House. What was new, although legal historians disagree as to the exact date of this change, was that

---

[2]   R. J. Morris, 'Voluntary societies and British urban elites 1780–1850: an analysis', in P. Borsay, ed., *The Eighteenth Century Town. A Reader in English Urban History, 1688–1820*, 2nd edn. (London 1990), 338–66.

[3]   The only overview of the history of voluntary societies in Hungary before 1848 gives G. Pajkossy, 'Egyesületek Magyarországon és Erdélyben 1848 előtt', *Korunk*, 214, issue 4, 1993, 103–109.

[4]   A good, comprehensive overview of the nineteenth century history of Hungary gives A. Gergely, ed., *19. századi magyar történelem, 1790–1918* (Budapest 1998). For one of the best general works in English on Hungarian history see L. Kontler, *Milleneum in Central Europe. A History of Hungary* (Budapest 1999).

counties had one vote *each*, whereas boroughs had only one 'altogether'.[5] In addition, invitation to the sessions of the Parliament depended on old royal privileges. Therefore populous and economically important but non-chartered urban settlements were without parliamentary representation, while a few urban constituencies had some 1,000 or 2,000 inhabitants only.[6]

This was partly because the gentry majority in the Lower House opposed an increase in the number of enfranchised towns. As a consequence, in the eighteenth century only 13 towns gained royal charters and approval by Parliament. Many of them were situated in the southern territories, which had been freed from Ottoman occupation at the end of the seventeenth century, and a few of them had been royal free towns before the Turkish period. By contrast, in the first half of the nineteenth century only one town obtained such a royal privilege.

Participation in politics was also limited within towns. By the eighteenth century civic administration in many corporate towns became the domain of narrow oligarchic groups as a result of the gradual narrowing of the electorate. After 1751, the year of unification by the national government, local elections developed a somewhat restricted meaning in royal free towns: vacancies in the twelve-member councils were elected by a wider board of senior townspeople, the 'electoral community' (*Wahlbürgerschaft*), but it was the council which had the right of nominating for all posts.[7] In addition, recruitment to the electoral community for life was solely by co-option, and freemen, who once embodied civic autonomy, even lost their restricted burgher franchise. The late eighteenth and early nineteenth centuries were also the period of bureaucratisation in Hungarian towns, supported by the enlightened efforts of the absolutist monarchs. These two processes together resulted in a sophisticated organisation and uncontrolled rule by town magistrates, who were in charge of both administration and jurisdiction. If

---

[5]   For the various views on the origin of this restriction see A. Csizmadia, *A magyar városi jog* (Kolozsvár 1941), 129–33, and S. Szőcs, *A városi kérdés az 1832–1836-os országgyűlésen* (Budapest 1996), 19–29.

[6]   This was not specific for Hungary. For comparison with England before 1832 see P. Corfield, *The Impact of English Towns, 1700–1800* (Oxford 1982), 146–7. A quantitative analysis of the urban system in Hungary in 1828 showed that among the 57 largest market centres, regarded as towns by the authors, only 22 were royal free towns, whereas many of the other chartered towns did not even have a market or other central function. See V. Bácskai and Lajos Nagy, *Piackörzetek, piacközpontok és városok Magyarországon 1828-ban* (Budapest 1984). An English summary gives V. Bácskai and L. Nagy, 'Market Areas, Market Centres and Towns in Hungary in 1828', *Acta Historica Academiae Scientiarum Hungaricae*, 26, 1990, 1–25.

[7]   For a better understanding of the names of institutions and posts, I give the German rather than the Hungarian terms. This also reflects the practice, since in many major towns (including Pest) the language of town administration was more German than Latin or Hungarian until the 1840s, and most voluntary societies usually prepared their documents in German.

the term 'urban elite' means the group of leaders in town government, in the age of the Napoleonic Wars it consisted mostly of professional officials, many with law degrees, who started careers in one of the lower posts in the clerks' office but had a good chance of eventually becoming councillors. The oligarchic nature of civic administration was one reason why the gentry opposed the increase in the importance of urban constituencies in Parliament.[8]

Such a system certainly did not allow the articulation of any efforts by popular elements. It was in 1790 that popular disturbances took place in Hungary.[9] Here the manifold impact of the French Revolution was heightened by the death of King Joseph II. His absolutist efforts to end the age-old privileges of the estates, and his neglect of national traditions and customs to integrate Hungary into his empire, had evoked the rage and resistance of the gentry. Trying to use burghers as a counter-balance to the formidable turmoil of the gentry, the new king, Leopold II, encouraged the freemen to set up militias in 1790. But after he finally compromised with the leaders of the gentry opposition on the re-establishment of constitutional order, he soon stopped supporting the burghers' demands.[10] By contrast, when in 1794–1795 a secret and almost revolutionary movement emerged to promote a more democratic political system in Hungary, the leaders were gentry landowners and non-gentry professionals, with a small number of burghers playing a minor role. Many of these leaders came from the Masonic lodges, which were the basis of this movement. In the following decades of absolutist power and conservative politics, only once did major popular rioting occur in Hungarian towns – after a great cholera epidemic in 1831 in Pest.[11] It was the Reform Age, the period of the emerging liberal and national movement from the 1830s up to the revolution of 1848, when rising public debates led to growing political activity among the town dwellers. One obvious demonstration of this was the freemen's increasing efforts to control urban mal-administration and corruption and to regain the right of the electoral community to call the council regularly to account. First in 1839,

---

[8]   D. Oszetzky, *A hazai polgárság társadalmi problémái a rendiség felbomlásakor* (Budapest 1935). Another reason was the towns' limited autonomy of government which threw doubts on whether urban MPs represented their own communities or the king, as contemporaries argued. The German character of most corporate towns was also a factor in the period of emerging Hungarian nationalism. G. Czoch, 'A városi polgárság nemzeti hovatartozásának kérdése Magyarországon a 19. század közepén', in C. Fedinec, ed., *Nemzet a társadalomban* (Budapest 2004), 51–67.

[9]   It was the same period when lower class radical riots frightened the English towns.

[10]   E. Mályusz, 'A magyarországi polgárság a francia forradalom korában', *A Bécsi Magyar Történeti Intézet Évkönyve*, 1, 1931, 225–82.

[11]   I. Barta, 'Az 1831. évi koleramozgalom', *Tanulmányok Budapest múltjából*, 13, 1961, 445–70.

under pressure from the liberal gentry, the king shifted the right of nominating urban MPs from the council to the electoral community. Then in 1843 and in 1847 the government extended the local electorate (of 100 members, in larger urban settlements) by half as many people, elected only by freemen. This measure was intended to be a significant change, but in reality it meant the inclusion of a very low proportion of the total urban population into the politically active body – in Pest there were about 95,000 permanent inhabitants in the mid-1840s, and the number of freemen exceeded 2,500. Nevertheless, when as a result of the bourgeois revolution in 1848, a considerably wider franchise based on liberal principles was introduced, according to an analysis of the voters in the Pest elections, only 70 per cent of those enfranchised voted. It is also of note that while the election created a new magistrate and outer council with a slight majority of liberal nominees, many of its members were closely related to the former, conservative, town leaders.[12]

It was not only with regard to the franchise that early nineteenth century town politics were restricted as compared to later periods. The councils themselves had relatively modest functions which included decisions about licenses for townspeople to carry out economic activities, applications for the right of freeman and the lease of certain town facilities to entrepreneurs. Examination of the annual accounts published by the Pest magistrates from the mid-1840s reveals that the greatest single cost was the town officials' and other employees' salaries. Expenditure for infrastructure did not exceed 40 per cent of the total, although this included street-lighting and street-paving, the repairing and cleaning of streets, refuse clearance, and embankment costs.[13] Many of the latter were new elements in the town budget, and they reflected the programme of the first town planning efforts in Pest (1805), implemented by the Royal Town Improvement Commission (*Königliche Verschönerungs Commission*) from 1808 onwards. Poor relief was mainly confined to the traditional alms-giving by parishes. The only development in Pest before the emergence of the voluntary societies was the setting up in 1785 of an institution (*Armen-Institut*) by the urban government to distribute small amounts of aid to the poor and destitute.[14]

---

[12] V. Bácskai, 'Pest társadalma és politikai arculata 1848-ban', *Tanulmányok Budapest múltjából*, 19, 1972, 283–326.

[13] Budget avagy sz. k. Pest v. jövedelmei és kiadásai 1845.

[14] This concerned some 250 people or households a month. See K. Tóth-Könyves, *Budapest Székesfőváros közjótékonysági, szociálpolitikai és közművelődési közigazgatásának kézikönyve* (Budapest 1930), 29.

Voluntary societies in Pest: an overview

Among all the urban settlements in Hungary, it was in Pest that the emergence of voluntary societies caused the greatest changes. This town, a part of Budapest since the Unification Act of 1873, had grown into the largest town in Hungary during the Napoleonic Wars, when its fairs had developed into major grain-trading centres of continental reputation. Its growth was remarkably rapid: by 1846 Pest's population reached 100,000, the usual threshold of cities by European standard, whereas in the 1780s with only 20,000 inhabitants it had been the fourth biggest town in the Hungarian Kingdom.[15] It also began to take on the role of a *Residenzstadt*, since the governor of Hungary as well as the major national administrative bodies and courts established their seats either there or in Buda on the opposite bank of the Danube. With the only Hungarian university, the first permanent theatre where plays were performed in Hungarian and not in German, and with a growing number of professionals and writers, Pest quickly became the cultural capital of Hungary. By contrast, the official capital with the seat of the Palatine or governor was in Buda, the king resided in Vienna, and the Parliament had its sessions in Pressburg/Pozsony, now Bratislava in Slovakia.

Among the estimated 500 voluntary societies in Hungary in 1848 some 80 were active in either Pest or in Buda.[16] A number of them were national societies attracting members from all over the country. They had their headquarters in Pest because people thought of Pest not just as an urban centre but as the capital city. Still, the creation and the existence of the majority of the associations in Pest was a direct response to the harsh social conflicts and increased social possibilities created by the rapid urban growth of the town. The first association was the PCWS, set up after the fivefold devaluation of the national currency (1816) and three consecutive years of bad harvest (1815–1817), which resulted in famine and exceptional poverty, especially among the urban population.[17] In 1827 a young aristocrat, Count István Széchenyi, established a *Casino* or debating society (*allgemeiner geselliger Verein*) as a venue for 'the intercourse of minds', that is for the discussion of public issues open in principle to every 'honorable man of

---

[15] The fourfold increase of the population in five decades exceeded that of most contemporary European capitals, second only to St. Petersburg. L. Nagy, *Budapest története a török kiűzésétől a márciusi forradalomig* (Budapest 1975), 373.

[16] G. Pajkossy, 'Egyesületek a reformkori Magyarországon', *História*, 15, issue 2, 1993, 6–8.

[17] Á. Tóth, 'A társadalmi szerveződés polgári és rendi normái. A Pesti Jótékony Nőegylet fennállásának első korszaka, 1817–1848', *FONS*, 45, 1998, 411–79, esp. 427.

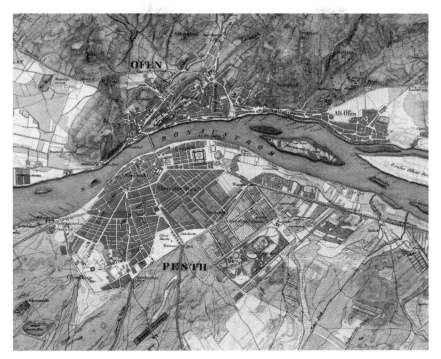

Figure 8.1   A map of Pest-Buda, around 1830

Source: Carlo Vasquez, *Buda és Pest Szabad Királyi Várossainak tájleírása* (Vienna 1837).

noble behaviour'.[18] Its library consisted of a large range of foreign and Hungarian books and newspapers, a significant resource in the period of severe censorship introduced by the absolutist government of King Francis I and the imperial chancellor Duke Metternich. In the same year a merchants' *Casino* was established to foster better relations among those interested in commerce. In 1836 a musical society was formed offering participation for both musicians and an enthusiastic audience. This was followed in 1839 by an arts society (*Kunstverein*) that organised annual exhibitions of Hungarian and foreign paintings. In addition, several societies for improving and popularising the sciences were founded, mostly by doctors and pharmacists but also with the support of a few well-to-do gentry landowners. The original idea for the setting up of an industrial society (*Gewerbeverein*) came from the British Mechanics' Institutes, but soon this association became known as the

---

[18]   *A Pesti Casino tagjainak A.B.C. szerint való feljegyzése és annak alapjai* (Pest 1828).

national organisation of the liberal opposition for the purpose of promoting economic independence from Austria. In 1835 an agricultural society developed from the annual horse-races in Pest, which had taken place since 1827. In the late 1830s further charities were founded in the form of voluntary societies, including a few nurseries (modelled on those set up by Samuel Wilderspin in Britain) and a (teaching) hospital for the treatment of poor children. In addition, several schools for training in fencing or gymnastics were set up. In the mid-1830s many of these friendly societies competed with one another, and total membership reached some eight to ten per cent of the total population of Pest by about 1840.[19] By the eve of the bourgeois revolution, a new set of voluntary societies emerged: rival political clubs (antecedents of the opposition and conservative parties), several Jewish organisations supporting Jewish emancipation, and a society to create a Hungarian national gallery.

If the number and variety of early voluntary societies in Pest has been usefully compared to their Western European counterparts, their political importance remains to be assessed. Was this a mere 'aping' of well-respected, 'civilised' Western European cities, as conservative Hungarian contemporaries argued, or was it an appropriate local response to the needs of urban society? And how far and in what way could these organisations change the rigid structure of political participation described above? The extent to which they succeeded in transforming the political framework should certainly not be overestimated. Nonetheless, in a few respects certain changes are evident, and may be regarded as antecedents of a later major metamorphosis. Below, I will analyse the legal-constitutional aspect, the social composition of the societies, the widening of public issues, and relations between voluntary associations and the state and civic boards.

The legal framework: principles and reality

The celebrated German legal historian, Otto von Gierke, analysed the appearance of voluntary societies as a sharp break with the traditional organisation of estate society based on corporate membership. These new institutions supported the liberal principle of individual and voluntary choice to join (or leave) a group of people in order to achieve common purposes. Gierke contrasted free associations with the church, estate corporations, the household and the neighbourhood, which had strictly governed individuals and allowed little room for personal freedom.[20] According to this historical tradition, voluntary societies were a radically new phenomenon in constitu-

---

[19]   This ratio was similar to that of Bristol throughout the nineteenth century. M. Gorsky, 'Mutual aid and civil society: friendly societies in nineteenth-century Bristol', *Urban History*, 5, issue 3, 1998, 302–22, esp. 311.

[20]   See Nipperdey, 'Verein als soziale Struktur', 7–8.

tional history and functioned as an 'experimental field' in the process of creating a modern, liberal democracy, where members have equal rights to speak at meetings, to hold leaders accountable and to elect them. However, recent studies have stressed that the formal legal equality of all members did not rule out the unequal distribution of leadership positions for the upper strata. In this respect, free associations contributed to the reproduction of an existing social hierarchy. In addition, the widespread use of *ballotage*, that is the voting by members on the admission of candidates, and high admission fees, often resulted in an exclusive social composition.[21]

In Pest, most voluntary societies applied the formal structures of their foreign counterparts. For example, before setting up the PCWS, its founders sent a letter to the Vienna magistrate in which they asked for a copy of the rules and the form of the subscription lists used by the Viennese counterpart.[22] The Pest benefit societies also reproduced Austrian organisational structures; an analysis of the birthplace of these club founders has revealed that most came to Pest from the Bohemian (Czech) and Austrian provinces, where the density of such societies was the greatest within the Habsburg Empire. It seems likely therefore that these immigrants, mostly master artisans, conveyed this social form to Pest.[23]

Thus it is not surprising that the rules of Pest voluntary societies usually reproduced the elaborate hierarchy and procedures of their models, such as general meetings and the election of leaders. All members had the same rights and obligations – noblemen had to pay the same fee as commoners, while in society at large one great privilege of the nobility was its exemption from most taxes and tolls. In the case of the National Casino, the rules stated expressly that 'any man of noble behaviour (can be admitted) without regard to birth or religious denomination'. The Pest Shooting Society 'was open not only to burghers but also to noblemen and non-gentry professionals'.[24]

It is difficult to judge how seriously democratic principles were taken or the extent to which they were put into practice. We know little of whether these elections were competitive since there is little documentation available about voting. It is a fact, however, that a number of office holders were dismissed on charges of fraud or favouritism, and these measures were implemented by voting rather than by the intervention of the town council as a supervisory body. Robert Zahrada, the founder of the First Pest Funeral

---

[21] M. Sobania, 'Vereinsleben. Regeln und Formen bürgerlicher Assoziationen im 19. Jahrhundert', in D. Hein and A. Schulz, eds, *Bürgerkultur im 19. Jahrhundert. Bildung, Kunst und Lebenswelt* (Munich 1996), 176–81.

[22] Magyar Országos Levéltár, Archivum Palatinale, N.22. Acta Praesidialia, 1817. III.

[23] Á. Tóth, 'Önsegélyezés és önszerveződés. Temetkezési és betegsegélyező egyletek a reformkori Pesten', *Korall*, 2, issue 5/6, 2001, 49–71, esp. 67.

[24] *A Nemzeti Casino alapszabályai* (Pest 1829), and *Scheiben-Schützen-Almanach für das Schützen-Jahr 1830* (Pest 1830) 160–66.

Society (*Erster Pesther Leichenverein*), an organisation comprising as many as 2,000 members, was replaced by a majority of the 21-member board (*Ausschuss*) of the society in 1842, even though he offered himself as a candidate again. The new vice-director was the former organiser of a smaller funeral society which later merged with the Funeral Society. He had unsuccessfully charged Zahrada many times with abuse of local council office. This incident suggests that a certain democratic practice may have existed within benefit societies, although the town magistrate certainly shunned these practices in its own governance. The first rules of this society, approved in 1834, forbade the meeting of all members (except at funerals) and authorised the board to make decisions. This was slightly eased in 1842 when the new rules allowed 'all male members to gather every three years to elect the board'. Yet, at a vote in 1845 only 28 votes were counted. There are also records of corrupt leaders being dismissed in other major benefit societies.[25]

Other types of voluntary societies experienced changes in leadership for different reasons. The rapid succession of presidents and secretaries at the Pest Arts Society was mainly due to the fierce debate within the membership and in the press about the 'national' or 'cosmopolitan' character of this association – whether or not it gave sufficient support to 'national' artists and art.[26] Although there is no evidence, it is likely that the same reason caused the resignation of several leaders of the Pest-Buda Musical Society.[27] What is clear is that the strengthening of the national opposition movement led to conflicts about symbolic issues such as the definition of 'national culture'. At a period when the public sphere was still a newly emerging phenomenon and cultural production was somewhat limited, considerable attention was paid to the activity of cultural societies and to the evaluation of their contribution to 'national culture'. Questions such as the language of the printed programme used at the concerts of the Pest-Buda Musical Society or the proportion of landscapes painted by Hungarian-born artists shown at the exhibitions of the Pest Arts Society were therefore major issues for both political newspapers and intellectuals.

By contrast, in societies of more aristocratic character there is no sign of contest between factions or viewpoints, although this might merely reflect the loss of the society minutes. In the National Casino as well as the Hungarian Agricultural Society, both dominated by great landowners, most presidents and directors belonged to the same friends' circle. Within the PCWS, changes of leadership, including the resignation of founder-president Countess Johanna Teleki (1817–1833), often occurred when these women

---

[25] Tóth, 'Önsegélyezés és önszerveződés', 58.

[26] G. Szvoboda-Dománszky, 'A Pesti Műegylet, 1839–1867', Hungarian Academy of Sciences Ph.D. thesis, 1994.

[27] K. Isoz, 'A Pest-Budai Hangászegyesület és nyilvános hangversenyei, 1836–1851', *Tanulmányok Budapest múltjából*, 3, 1934, 165–79.

moved from Pest – either to Vienna or their country estates – rather than as a result of any issues within the society.

The theoretical equality of the membership was also challenged. The transfer of the annual horse races from the Livestock Breeding Society to the Hungarian Agricultural Society between 1827 and 1835 was accompanied by a continued change in the meaning of 'membership'. In 1827 the first report listed the names of all subscribers promising to pay five *florins* for 'other purposes' than horse racing, or those who did not only bet on horses. In 1828 there was an order that meetings of the society were open only to those paying ten *florins*, then in 1830 the society declared that 'membership' was restricted to those who subscribed at a rate of ten *florins* a year for six years. Finally, according to a new rule in 1835, those considered 'real members' (*wirkliche Mitglieder*) paid ten *florins* for 'further agricultural purposes' – other than livestock breeding – while the first rows at the horse races continued to be kept for spectators contributing ten *florins* for this privilege. Throughout this period of price increases, the membership of the society changed radically, prompting a number of its earlier supporters to leave, including both gentlemen resident in Pest and Pest burghers.[28]

In other societies other forms of differentiation among 'classes' of members existed. Most associations distinguished subscribers from activists. In the PCWS the general meeting, consisting of all subscribers, elected activists and, among the activists, the board. The activists sought out 'deserving poor' living in their own district, and they recruited additional subscribers – in short it was their duty to do the bulk of the field work.[29] Yet, the published reports of this society usually listed the names of the subscribers (specifying the amount of money contributed) and the leaders only, usually omitting the activists.[30] Elsewhere the formal equality of members was undermined by special undertakings of the society. For example, the construction of a clubhouse or headquarters, usually financed through the creation of a joint stock company, created yet another hierarchy among members based on the purchase of stock.[31]

Social composition

The rules of the voluntary societies analysed here represented liberal and democratic principles, at least in theory. However, their implementation proved unclear or contradictory, and a similar picture can be drawn concerning their mixed composition. The rapid urban growth of Pest created

---

[28] Á. Tóth, *Önszervező polgárok. A pesti egyesületek társadalomtörténete a reform-korban* (Budapest 2005), 195–6.
[29] *Verfassung der wohlthätige Frauenvereine in Ofen und Pesth* (Pest 1817), rule 3.
[30] Tóth, *Önszervező polgárok*, 52 and 67.
[31] Mihály Ilk, *A Nemzeti Casinó százéves története, 1827–1926* (Budapest 1927), 14.

an unprecedented spectrum of status positions in the first half of the nineteenth century. Although no census was taken in Hungary between 1787–1851 and other statistical materials are both scarce and ill-suited for establishing Pest's social structure, some sources demonstrate the diversity of town-dwellers. Before the 1780s nearly all of Pest's inhabitants were Roman Catholics with the exception of a tiny minority of Orthodox merchants. This was why Protestants and Jews had been forbidden to reside there. But in 1847 Protestants and Jews made up five and thirteen per cent of the total population. Massive immigration increased the proportion of various social elements outside the traditional civic framework namely non-incorporated craftsmen, casual workers, professionals and rentiers.[32] In addition, the enormous flood of migrants of all sorts demanded new institutions of social integration. The 'destruction of the barriers between the estates', a leading political slogan among the liberal opposition, became an urgent necessity in Pest and it was probably in this segment of society that this process advanced more than anywhere else in Hungary.

Voluntary societies played a significant part in this development. In general, all strata of urban society who were considered 'independent' (i.e. not employed) by contemporaries, participated. The lists of subscribers included members of the Habsburg dynasty, titled magnates, gentry politicians (both conservatives and liberals), professionals, large merchants, lesser artisans and shopkeepers (whether or not freemen). In a few societies even military officers, Jews and women were admitted. It is also of importance that as time passed the published lists of the participants became more 'democratic'. The first announcement of the PCWS listed several urban social groups, rather than individuals, who supported their initiatives financially, including 'the gentry resident in Pest', 'the Pest burghers' and 'the Pest Jews', corresponding to the prevailing perception of the social hierarchy within estate society.[33] From the 1820s onwards, however, it gradually became the norm of most voluntary societies to list all subscribers (members) in alphabetic order.

Certainly, there was a great variety in the proportion of various social classes within different voluntary associations. A detailed analysis reveals that almost all of them were heterogeneous to some degree. The National Casino, regarded as an aristocrats' club by both contemporaries and later historians, was indeed organised by counts and barons in 1827. But the dominance of the higher nobility decreased after the first years, and among the 1022 members admitted before 1849 some eleven per cent gained their livelihood from 'burgher' (merchant or artisan) trades, professions or civic

---

[32] Traditional civic framework means those with the status of freeman, earning a living as a master artisan or shopkeeper and usually a house-owner as well. See Nagy, *Budapest története*, 377–405.

[33] *Hazai és Külföldi Tudósítások*, 1818, 8, 58–9.

Figure 8.2   **A view of Hotel *Europa* in Pest (left), with the seat of the National and Merchants' *Casinos* (in front), around 1850**

Source: R. Alt and X. Sandmann, Festõi Megtekintések Budára és Pestre. – Malerische Ansichten von Ofen und Pest (Vienna 1851).

office – i.e they were not rentiers. It is true that a few of these people, such as several great merchants, physicians and apothecaries, a print-owner and a carpenter, belonged to the gentry. Yet what matters is that they were admitted to an upper-class circle, and that a few of them were elected as members of the committee (*Ausschuss*), although they 'worked' for their living in a way which was considered 'inferior' by feudal standards.[34]

By contrast, the Pest Shooting Society started to admit non-burgher members in the Reform Age. This society was founded as a civic organisation in 1703, when the town regained its privilege of self-defence after its recovery from the Turks. It later lost its military function, however, and its shooting contests became social occasions. In 1840 its membership consisted of two classes: 47 'shooters' and 160 'friends of shooting', a proportion which shows that the active 'sportsmen' were an apparent minority as compared to social members. Although the comparison between the membership in different years shows that twenty members who were 'friends of shooting' in 1840 used to be 'shooters' in 1830, the analysis of the lists suggests that a number of the 'friends of shooting' were non-burgher

---

[34]   Tóth, *Önszervező polgárok*, 149.

town-dwellers, including five aristocrats, and a number of university professors, physicians, and royal and civic officials. Though the majority of the members in this society were freemen, including a few men belonging to the electoral community, they still elected an aristocrat as 'chief shooting master' (*Präsident*).[35]

The PWCS used a unique way of integrating women of different social ranks. Its committee consisted of twelve women and they divided the area of the town into six districts. In each district two committee members were in charge – one was the wife of a landowner, and the other the spouse of a burgher. Combining authority with charitable enthusiasm, this structure made it possible for women of higher social ranks to avoid being given orders by commoners. It also attracted burghers' wives who had ambitions to assume the norms and habits of the upper echelon of society. The membership of this voluntary society ranged from the Governor's wife who was also the patron to middling artisans. But its annual collection of donations for suppressing street-begging in the 1830s was supported by several thousand town-dwellers.[36]

Although benefit societies attracted members mostly from the middling strata of urban society, they were also heterogeneous in terms of the norms of estate society. The leading group consisted of guild-member artisans, but other sorts, both upper and lower, were also admitted. The First Pest Funeral Society was founded mostly by master craftsmen including twelve tailors among the 25 founders. In 1845 its committee consisted of eight guild masters as well as lawyers, a physician, a merchant, an innkeeper, a house-owner rentier, a butler and an artisan not incorporated into a guild. Another benefit society attracted 30 civic and royal officials as well as dozens of pensioned military officers into its membership which totalled 458 in 1839. The admission of maid-servants, an ennobled silk-dyer, a private teacher, a midwife, several apothecaries, the director of the civic hospital and the family of a rentier gentleman demonstrates the wide variety of the membership as well as the general demand of urban society for funeral and health 'insurance'.[37]

In 1841 one of the benefit societies decided to allow into its new 'division' 'non-Christian' town-dwellers, which was a euphemism for Jews. The great majority of the founders of this newly organised society were Jews and the membership list in 1844 indicates that half of the board, as well as a few officials as for example the doctor, the secretary and one of the cashiers, were Jews in that year. Before that time, Jews were usually not admitted into voluntary societies, although they were accepted as supporters paying for the

---

[35]   Tóth, *Önszervező polgárok*, 160–61.
[36]   Tóth, 'A társadalmi szerveződés', 443–4, 451–2.
[37]   Tóth, 'Önsegélyezés és önszerveződés', 65–8.

implementation of the various purposes set by such societies.[38] Yet, there is clear evidence available that the Merchants' Casino already admitted Jewish people in this period: among the total membership of 368 in 1840, 36 members were Jews. Moreover, in 1837 two of them were elected to the board of this society.[39] This example of the Merchants' Casino indicates that there existed a public institution for socialising between Christian and Jewish town-dwellers. Although it is not known how frequently and in what way they used this club, one might suppose that the demand for its organisation corresponded in some measure to the communication needs of both parties. By contrast, Jewish participation in cultural and charitable societies was less significant, with a couple of active members only. In addition, in the mid-1840s the Jewish community arranged its own voluntary societies, creating one association to stimulate the assimilation of the Jews by teaching Hungarian language and culture, another for the 'distribution of artisan skills among the Jews' and one Charitable Women's Society. The scarce evidence about these societies suggests that all of these were dominated by leading members of the Jewish community.

In summary, voluntary societies as organisations, recruiting members from various classes, encouraged the integration of a diverse urban society. Those people who were members or officials of several societies, or belonged to more than one estate, played a prominent role in the fostering of social relations among various communities. These 'community brokers' included Count István Széchenyi, one of the greatest landowners in Hungary, who became a freeman of Pest and later a member of its electoral community.[40] Széchenyi also initiated the setting up of the National Casino, the Hungarian Agricultural Society as well as a couple of joint stock companies; Lajos Schedius, a Lutheran professor of gentry birth at the Catholic university of Pest, was the secretary to the PCWS for 16 years and was elected the first president of the Pest-Buda Musical Society; Count György Károlyi was president of the Agricultural Society, a leader of the National Casino and a participant in the Shooting Society and the merchants' casino; his wife was elected the president of the PCWS. The remarkable overlap among the

---

[38] M. K. Silber, 'A zsidók társadalmi befogadása Magyarországon a reformkorban. A "kaszinók"', *Századok*, 126, issue 1, 1992, 113–41, esp. 118–19.

[39] When Count Széchenyi proposed a Jewish merchant as a candidate for admission to the National Casino in 1829, an aristocrat with a liberal reputation threatened to quit. Even wealthy and ennobled converted Jews could not join this upper-class club before 1841. Compare to Professor Silber's statement who argued that 'we may be sure that no Jews were allowed to join the Pest Merchants Casino before 1846'. Silber, 'A zsidók társadalmi befogadása', 119–20, and Tóth, *Önszervező polgárok*, 150.

[40] The term is developed in D'Cruze Shani, 'The middling sort in eighteenth-century Colchester: independence, social relations and the community broker', in J. Barry and Ch. Brooks, eds, *The Middling Sort of People. Culture, Society and Politics in England, 1550–1800* (Macmillan 1994), 181–207.

members of the various voluntary societies raises the question whether there existed another 'social' urban elite – profoundly different from the civic elite of the town leaders – consisting of influential men who had a considerable impact on the social institutions of Pest.

The influence of voluntary societies on urban life

But what was this 'impact' in fact? To what extent was the 'activity' of such societies something more than mere socialising for the pleasure of a few people? In what way can the 'importance' of a voluntary society be assessed? One obvious answer to these questions is that they founded several institutions which affected the life of large groups of town-dwellers. Undoubtedly, the greatest change occurred in the field of charity, after the setting up of the PWCS. In the first years, it erected a 'voluntary workhouse' (*freiwilliges Arbeitshaus*) where the poor could find work, and it established a school for poor children where they were trained in practical skills rather than in the 'useless' knowledge of the 'humanistic' schools. The setting up of these institutions can be interpreted as a clear break with the traditional perception of poor relief as alms-giving and the adoption of liberal, bourgeois social norms of 'work' and 'responsibility'. The PWCS also founded a hospital for the blind, several buildings for the care of the old and the poor and loaned money to artisans affected by the crisis in 1817. The Nursery Societies created four nurseries in Pest in the 1830s, taking care of some 600 children altogether in 1831–1832. The hospital for poor children, the fourth institution of this type in Europe, was founded by another voluntary society in 1837 and by 1844 had given medical treatment to 7,288 children.

Cultural societies were also formative in their own fields by arranging the first 'public' concerts and exhibitions. The Pest-Buda Musical Society also undertook singing lessons for children as well as arranging a 'pension fund' for old musicians. Several voluntary societies established their own libraries of books and journals, with some volumes purchased from abroad. The agricultural and the industrial societies held annual exhibitions of machines, animals and products attracting visitors from all over the country.

Thus while activist members and leaders of all voluntary societies may have amounted to no more than a few hundred people, the total number of those affected by their activities was certainly in the thousands. For instance, the subscriptions to the Arts Society reached its peak in 1842 with a membership of 1,468 people. The Art Society was the second largest society in Pest. In 1840 as many as 9,000 visitors viewed its exhibition. The first collection by the PCWS for the suppression of begging in 1831 resulted in a huge sum of money, totalling some 65 per cent of the taxes paid by the inhabitants of Pest that year. The voluntary workhouse of the society employed nearly 2,000 workers between 1817 and 1833, which is not insignificant when compared to the total town population of 40,000–50,000 people.[41]

Through their activities, voluntary societies significantly widened the concept of 'public affairs', too. Whereas civic government played a minor part in poor relief before the rise of voluntary societies, its activity grew after 1831, when the PCWS entered a financial crisis in 1831 from coping with the increased numbers of the poor, a result of massive immigration. In 1831 the town took over almost all institutions from the PCWS barring the distribution of aid to poor families. Still, this was the only field where the town government played an active part. Voluntary societies usually worked independently of the town leaders; a few did not even have a relationship with the magistrates. A new period of more intensive relations with the magistrates began only with the growth of state intervention in the 1880s.

Voluntary societies played a distinctive role in the formation of urban life in Pest in the first half of the nineteenth century. They contributed to the redefinition of social relations in this late period of estate society with their formal (legal) rules as well as their mixed social composition. It was these institutionalised societies that provided the space and occasions to meet and socialise for various ranks of society with an interest in public issues. Whereas the impact of voluntary societies can be measured both by the sum of florins gathered and spent for various causes, and by the number of people affected by their activities, one can only speculate as to how far their existence changed the character of social relations.

---

[41]   Tóth, 'A társadalmi szerveződés', 425 and 451.

CHAPTER NINE

Running 'Modern' Cities in a Patriarchal Milieu: Perspectives from the Nineteenth-Century Balkans

Dobrinka Parusheva

In a brief chapter, one can no more than identify key topics related to the larger subject of urban power in the nineteenth-century Balkans.[1] Unlike the advanced field of British urban studies, for example, there is less scholarship one could build on to discuss the urban history of the Balkans. As for the history of urban power and urban elites in this region, one might say the field is still in its fledgling stage. The nineteenth century in particular has been considered transitional, and attention has been concentrated on issues of state- and nation building. Attempting to address more than one country does not make the task easier. Despite possible limitations, this is a worthwhile challenge, and rather than an elaborate discussion, my goal is to present some ideas, illustrated by some appropriate cases. These examples should provide a comparative perspective on the Balkans and begin to answer the question whether belonging to a specific state unit matters in regard to local (urban) government. Additionally, the essay will consider whether the Balkans differ from other European countries and if so, in what respect?

Nineteenth-century Balkans: some introductory remarks

The nineteenth century was not only the period in which the political map of the modern Balkans emerged, but also a time marked by the struggle with modernisation, within both the Ottoman Empire and the newly established Balkan states. The route to modernity for all Balkan societies was emphatically difficult and explains my use of the word 'struggle'. Most of the difficulties evolved from the fact that tasks of state- and nation-building took precedence over efforts of economic modernisation. This pattern of Balkan

---

[1] I use 'Balkans' not as a geographical or political designation but as a useful term for all lands that belonged to the Ottoman Empire, regardless of their exact juridical status. For that reason I also include the two Danubian principalities which formed Romania after 1859 in this discussion.

modernisation created an imbalance between westernised institutions and ideas and traditional social structures, behaviour and mentalities. In western societies, social mobility conditions the individual who is 'distinguished by a high capacity for identification with new aspects of his environment' and able 'to incorporate new demands upon himself that arise outside of his habitual experience'. This 'mobile person' was missing in most Balkan societies and presented one of the main obstacles to modernity.[2] Balkan peoples clearly felt more comfortable interacting with acquaintances in familiar situations. In contrast, the adjustment to a new socio-cultural context and the acquiring of control over an unfamiliar environment required the abandonment of traditional customs and values.[3] Obviously, Balkan modernisation was a major transition that required significant time.

The early Balkan adoption of Western ideas and institutions is commonly described as an ineffective measure that had little impact on Balkan societies. It is this discrepancy between modern political forms and social and cultural backwardness that explains the allegedly traditional behaviour of modernising Balkan elites. Although influenced by Western ideas and in most cases educated abroad, Balkan elites adopted the functions of masters in a patriarchal society to confront the particularism of a loyalty to village, town or district. Most of the Serbian and Greek rulers of the first half of the nineteenth century behaved more like peasant leaders, either as 'fathers' of the nation like King Otto of Greece, or as national 'tutors' like Prince Mihailo Obrenovic of Serbia.[4] There was simply no other way of building modern states or creating nations out of Balkan peasant societies: techniques of state- and nation-building depended inevitably on the absence of traditional, landed elites in Serbian, Greek and Bulgarian societies and the dominating peasantry in all Balkan lands, including the ones north of the Danube River. The practice of luring and 'taming' the peasantry by observing its traditional values was institutionalised during the initial stage of state- and

---

[2]   I find the term 'mobile person' used by Daniel Lerner appropriate for analytical use with regard to some peculiarities of Balkan mentality. See D. Lerner, *The Passing of Traditional Society: Modernizing the Middle East* (Glencoe, Ill. and London 1964), 49.

[3]   A. Simic, *The peasant urbanites: a study of rural-urban mobility in Serbia* (New York 1973), 9–10.

[4]   See W. Vucinich, 'Some Aspects of the Ottoman Legacy', in Ch. and B. Jelavich, eds, *The Balkans in Transition. Essays on the Development of Balkan Life and Politics Since the Eighteenth Century* (Berkeley and Los Angeles 1963), 81–114, esp. 88. Diana Mishkova's main argument follows the same lines. See D. Mishkova, 'The nation as zadruga: Remapping nation-building in nineteenth-century Southeast Europe', in M. Dogo and G. Franzinetti, eds, *Disrupting and Reshaping. Early Stages of Nation-building in the Balkans* (Ravenna 2002), 103–16.

nation-building.[5] This forms a crucial element in any attempt to define the political and the social dimensions of the Balkan transition to modernity.

Although a huge social gap existed between the Romanian landed aristocracy and peasantry, especially in comparison with the social situation in other Balkan societies, all lacked a bourgeoisie or middle class at the beginning of the nineteenth century. It was only from the second quarter on that a thin bourgeois stratum began to emerge among the Greek, Bulgarian, Serbian and Romanian peoples. Thus, according to Robert J. Morris who argues that British towns were 'substantially the creation of their middle class, and in turn provided the theatre within which that middle class sought, extended, expressed and defended its power', one of the main actors in the creation and development of modern Balkan towns was missing.[6] Of course, I do not claim that there were no towns in the nineteenth-century Balkans. I only underscore their comparatively small number and size.

It is enough to present some numbers from the end of the nineteenth century to provide an overall picture: urban population was 14.1 per cent in Serbia (1900), 17.6 per cent in Romania (1890), 19.8 per cent in Bulgaria (1900) and 33.1 per cent in Greece (1907). At the same time in England, Germany and France, 77 per cent, 56 per cent and 41 per cent, respectively, lived in urban settlements. There was only one city of more than 100,000 inhabitants in the Balkans by 1900 – Bucharest, not counting Athens together *with* the Piraeus. In contrast, there were 33 such towns in Germany and 15 in France. The other Balkan capitals as well as three other Romanian towns had populations between 50,000 and 100,000. Serbia counted seven towns with 10,000 to 50,000 inhabitants, Bulgaria 20, Greece eleven, and Romania 23; compare these numbers to 399 similarly-sized towns in Germany and 231 in France.[7] Unfortunately, there are no reliable statistics for the early nineteenth century. Bearing in mind the situation around 1900, however, one may argue that urban life was the exception rather than the rule in the nineteenth-century Balkans.

This was clearly the case in Greece and Serbia in the early 1830s, when the former became independent *de jure* and the latter *de facto*. In addition, the

---

[5]   Just opposite of the image of the nation's establishing an independent state, typical of all romantic nationalists, in the Balkans, the state came first and then the nation. This view has already become a commonplace supported by the majority of historians and social scientists dealing with the nineteenth-century Balkans, and suggests the well known quotation of Jérôme Blanqui: 'Serbia owes to Milos the first routes penetrating its forests, order re-established in its finances, the creation of Serbian nationality.' Quoted here from M. Mazower, *The Balkans* (London 2001), 86.

[6]   R. J. Morris, 'The middle class and British towns and cities of the Industrial Revolution, 1780–1870', in D. Fraser and A. Sutcliffe, eds, *The pursuit of Urban History* (London 1983), 286–306, esp. 287.

[7]   H. Sundhaussen, *Historische Statistik Serbiens 1834–1914. Mit europäischen Vergleichsdaten* (Munich 1989), 102 and 106.

existing towns had a 'rural inclination' caused by a surrounding peasant society with dominating patriarchal values. Indeed, both Serbia and Greece were rural and impoverished countries. To quote Alphonse de Lamartine, Serbia was 'an ocean of forests', with more pigs than humans or, to use a twentieth century formulation, 'a piece of the Third World at the edge of the First one'.[8] No urban settlement in the newly established Greek Kingdom came close to the sophisticated and wealthy Ottoman cities like Smyrna, Salonika and Constantinople. Yet there were signs of revitalisation; the rapidly expanding new towns seemed to replace the old Ottoman settlements, like Athens, Patras, Tripolis, etc.

However, many cities in the Ottoman Empire underwent similar transformations. In other words, one cannot ascribe these developments to the fact that new modern states had emerged; rather, they should be considered part of one general trend towards urbanisation. The Tanzimat charter of 1839 introduced a series of initiatives to turn Constantinople into a 'European city'. Some authors have claimed that trying to order the disorder could never have succeeded because this modernisation – which is interpreted largely as 'Westernisation' – conflicted with the very texture of urban culture in such cities.[9] No matter how successful these attempts had been (if at all), they soon spread far beyond the borders of the Ottoman capital. Indisputably, they affected urban life in the whole Empire. Moreover, since Constantinople acted as a channel of Westernisation for both the Ottoman Empire and the new Balkan states (at least until the middle of the century if not longer), these changes influenced the Balkan towns and cities as well.

Change becomes visible

The government and administration of the classical Ottoman city was based on Islamic religious and political theory, which recognized the individual and the community of believers. Consequently, municipal services were not rigidly defined in terms of administrative organisation, but ultimately left to the religious, ethnic, and professional communities.[10] The real power was in

---

[8]   Quotations from Mazower, *The Balkans*, 85, and Sundhaussen, *Historische Statistik*, 21.

[9]   For instance, Kevin Robins and Asu Aksoy. See G. Mooney, 'Urban "disorders"', in St. Pile, Chr. Brook and G. Mooney, eds, *Unruly Cities? Order/Disorder* (London and New York 1999), 53–102, esp. 66–7.

[10]   The concept of the 'Islamic city' has received many definitions but most focus now on its external features: the city usually grew around important nodal points of the imperial system, expressly concerned with maintaining Ottoman power against the local population and with the protection of trade routes, characterised by its small curved streets, the impasses, the houses with inner yards, etc., where the city life did not happen on the streets but in private. For further clarifications, see St. Yerasimos, 'À propos des réformes urbaines des Tanzimat', in P. Dumont and Fr. Georgeon, eds,

the hands of *kadıs* or Islamic judges, and the *imam*, the local Muslim religious leader, who represented the *kadı's* administrative power. In non-Muslim neighbourhoods, the religious leaders of the ethnic groups and, in commercial areas, the guild leaders, assumed the *imam's* responsibilities. Therefore, in the classical Ottoman system, in contrast to modern municipal organisations, essential municipal services were provided by the people themselves and controlled by the urban administration.

This 'Ottoman model' had dominated the urban life of the Empire for centuries. From the early nineteenth century on, however, it endured some significant developments, for it had to confront another cultural model – the Occidental one. Procedures were rather different – introduced by law, peacefully or violently, and they followed different rhythms as well. But in spite of this, they were irresistible. In the years after 1830, the year of the Anglo-Ottoman commercial treaty, changes in the overall economic and commercial organisation brought an increase in the size and complexity of Ottoman and Balkan cities. The speed and fundamental nature of these changes upset many established social relationships and cast doubt upon the propriety of established values and identities. The economic change was accompanied by a demographic one: the Orthodox Christian population in the Balkan towns and cities increased, and gradually the centuries-long Muslim domination in urban life, which had persisted for mainly political and military reasons, was overcome. The relatively rapid development of handicrafts and commerce contributed remarkably to the improvement of the economic situation of the Christian population. As a result some of the local notables gained increasing influence with the representatives of Ottoman power. Simultaneously, the artisan guilds expanded their influence as well, which increased the respect they enjoyed among the population. At the same time, the instability of change fostered new conflicts.

This change deserves closer consideration. In the Bulgarian lands, for example, local government or the so called *obshtina* played a crucial role in developments that contributed to the national revival of the Bulgarian people during the nineteenth century.[11] Earlier the *obshtina* was mainly responsible

---

Villes Ottomanes à la fin de l'Empire (Paris 1992), 17–32. On transformations of traditional power distribution and changes in Constantinople see Z. Çelik, *The Remaking of Istanbul. Portrait of an Ottoman City in the Nineteenth Century* (Seattle and London 1986), 42–3.

[11]   The scholarship on this topic is very broad, of which the following represents only a very short selection: V. Paskaleva, 'Za samoupravlenieto na bulgarite prez Vazrazhdaneto' (On the self-government of the Bulgarians during the National Revival), *Izvestija na Instituta po istorija*, 14/15, 1964, 73–112; Hr. Hristov, *Bulgarskite obshtini prez Vazrazhdaneto* (Bulgarian *obshtina* during the National Revival) (Sofia 1973); Hr. Hristov, 'Obshtinite i bulgarskoto natzionalno Vazrazhdane' (*Obshtina* and the Bulgarian National Revival), in K. Kosev et al., eds, *Bulgaria 1300. Institutzii i durzhavna traditzia* (Bulgaria 1300. Institutions and state tradition), vol. 1 (Sofia 1981), 271–91.

for the collection and payment of taxes. Since the end of the eighteenth century, however, the *obshtina* began to expand its activity, becoming more and more an organ of self-government. As the *obshtina* acquired a greater function in economic and cultural life, it became the focus of sharp struggles. The power of the traditional middlemen (*chorbajiis*) between the Ottoman authorities and the population, which had been taken for granted, was challenged by the representatives of the emerging new commercial and artisan strata, the Bulgarian proto-bourgeoisie.[12] It was in this complex situation, in which an alien feudal state system dominated, that new social forces emerged and developed, and then began the transformation of power structures, including those of local government.

If we try to reconstruct the development of local urban governments in the Ottoman Empire and especially those with Orthodox Christian population, we can identify, with some generalisation, two main phases. During the first, depending on the region, it was either the church or the *kotzabasidhes, dzakis, knezes, chorbadjiis* or others who played the role of mediators between the local population and the Ottoman state system, which controlled justice and tax collection, and political representation before the Sublime Porte.[13] The second phase is characterised by the appearance of a new actor claiming power, namely the urban, commercial bourgeoisie. After establishing its economic position, this new economic elite either demanded the right to participate in the exercise of power or attempted to replace the church and other mediating actors completely.

Apart from the church and the nascent bourgeoisie, a third actor, the artisan guilds or corporations, played a greater role. The prosperity of guild members depended to a great extent on economic policy decisions made by the urban government. This explains the guilds' interest in direct participation in the political life of the city. As part of the social and state system, guilds participated in urban self-government, and their increased public role largely preceded and shaped their political activities in the second

---

[12]   Nikolaj Todorov speaks about a 'commercial and industrial bourgeoisie'. In order to avoid possible misunderstandings I should point out that due to the economic backwardness of the Balkans, one should be cautious when using the term *bourgeoisie* without some qualification. Only during the second half of the nineteenth century and its last quarter in particular could one claim the existence of a bourgeoisie in the Balkan states. See N. Todorov, *The Balkan City, 1400–1900* (Seattle and London 1983).
[13]   Ibid. 237. The church played the role of a mediator in regions with a predominantly Greek population and closer to the imperial centre Constantinople. On developments in Smyrna, for instance, see Ph. Iliou, 'Luttes sociales et mouvement de Lumières à Smyrne en 1819', in Association Internationale d'études du Sud-est européen, ed., *Structure sociale et développement culturel des villes sud-est européennes et adriatiques aux XVIIe-XVIIIe siècles: Actes du Colloque interdisciplinaire de l'Association Internationale d'études du Sud-est européen* (Bucharest 1975), 295–315.

and third quarters of the nineteenth century in Serbia and in Greek and Bulgarian lands still under Ottoman rule.[14] Although the shift in power was accompanied by social struggles in many Balkan cities, it took place with the relative non-interference of the Ottoman authorities, exactly because it was conducted in the name of, and under the banner of the guilds. That is why the role of artisan guilds did not weaken in the first half of the nineteenth century and explains why they continued to be a leading factor in economic life in the large cities in the Balkans.[15] In Serbia, because of the different socio-economic conditions and the establishment early in the nineteenth century of an autonomous and *de facto* independent Serbian principality, handicrafts and guilds had a different fate, since they were sanctioned by the Serbian national state instead of the Sublime Porte.

Although the role of the guilds differed slightly from one region to another, an obvious conclusion can be drawn: it was basically a Balkan bourgeoisie that was taking shape in these guilds. To answer the question why these people not only failed to abandon the guilds themselves but also did not want to see this old-fashioned institution die, one has to bear in mind the great obstacles that stood in the way of free economic development in the Ottoman Empire. Whereas in the West an emerging urban bourgeoisie usually enjoyed royal support for some time, in the Balkans the nascent bourgeoisie of the subjugated peoples could not rely on the support of the Ottoman government because they had outstripped the ruling nationality in their development. The situation was further complicated by the Porte's 'open door' economic policy for foreign capital in a period when, given the rapid industrial development of the West, the emerging native industry needed serious protection. Furthermore, guided by various fiscal and logistical interests (as related to the army), the government lent its support only to the guilds and the nascent bourgeoisie preferred to rely at least on this limited support. As the gap grew between the bourgeoisie's economic role and its lack of political rights, and between its cultural level and the ignorance of the Ottoman rulers, it became far more difficult to endure the Ottoman regulations.[16] Assimilation of the bourgeoisie to the guilds,

---

[14] By 1880 the Kingdom of Greece included all but a small part of the lands populated by Greeks. Bulgaria emerged on the political map of Europe in 1878.

[15] For more elaborate discussion along these lines see Todorov, *Balkan City*, 208–37. Similar views are also presented in I. Hadzhijski, *Bit i dushevnost na nashija narod* (Material and spiritual life of our people) (Sofia 1995), 240–77. Both authors contradict the opinion of St. Tsonev, who concludes that toward the end of the eighteenth century the guilds had fallen into a constant state of decay and that as early as the first half of the nineteenth century had lost their significance. See St. Tsonev, *Kum vaprosa za razlozhenieto na esnafskite organizatsii u nas prez perioda na Vazrazhdaneto* (To the question of decline of the guilds during the period of National Revival) (Sofia 1956).

[16] The constant contact with European culture and efforts to develop secular education started paying off.

however, was a useful tactic for quite a long period of time. Besides, it was not just a one-way relationship; simultaneously these people shaped some aspects of the guilds according to the needs of large-scale commerce and production.[17]

In short, change became visible but it needed time and there were many problems to take into consideration. New institutions of local government which the Sublime Porte tried to introduce were not totally successful in their attempts to bring radical changes to urban administration. New institutes appeared at first in Constantinople and later on in other cities and towns. Trying to function according to a new but not yet well-defined municipal jurisdiction, new governmental policies could not easily replace centuries-old practices based on the more personal control exercised by the local representatives of the *kadıs*. In the Balkan lands of the Empire, without significant differences in substance, this change took place with greater success. The representation of all ethnic and religious communities in the new municipal bodies should be listed as one of the main reasons. For instance, the first city council (*belediye*) in Plovdiv (Philippopoli) in accordance with the Vilayet Law (*Vilâyet Nizamnamesi*) of 1864, in which non-Muslims were present as well, was nominated in 1865.[18] Even more successful in implementing this change, which had already started during the imperial period, were the newly established Balkan states, Serbia and Greece and the two Danubian Principalities, because they felt free to 'divorce' themselves from the old rules entirely. In Serbia and Greece the absence of a native aristocracy facilitated additionally the change that occurred at the top of local governmental structures. In this respect, some peculiarities could still be observed in Romanian lands.

Modern states – modern cities?

The Danubian Principalities of Wallachia and Moldavia became Romania after 1859, and Serbia and Greece modernized rapidly after the Russian-Ottoman treaty of Adrianople from 1829. Although a latecomer that only gained its independence in 1878, Bulgaria was not excluded from the common Balkan development that followed the West European model.[19] On

---

[17] This phenomenon was clearly evident in the relationship established between various guilds and the capitalist entrepreneur Mihalaki Gümüşgerdan in the city of Philippopoli (Plovdiv). See Todorov, *Balkan City*, 230–37.

[18] St. Shishkov, Plovdiv v svoeto minalo i nastojashte. Istoriko-etnografski i politiko-ekonomicheski pregled / St. Chichcof, *Plovdiv dans son passé et son présent. Aperçu historico-ethnographique et politico-économique* (Plovdiv 1926), 372.

[19] This was a *de facto* independence; the *de jure* independence from the Ottoman Empire came in 1908.

the contrary, urban life in the Bulgarian lands showed visible similarities to neighbouring countries (as already discussed), and to Serbia and Greece in particular.

In Romania the majority of the urban elite originated from boyar or aristocratic families. The traditional governing class quickly evaluated the necessity of good education and sent their offspring to West and Central European universities to study. Education modified the social capital of wealthy Romanian landlords and allowed them to preserve and perpetuate their power positions.[20] Thus despite the fact that social structures were changing – although this process unfolded slowly – the traditional elite managed to remain in power and participate in local government as well as in national decision-making processes. It was only at the very end of the nineteenth century that representatives of the Romanian bourgeoisie found places in the municipal councils of Bucharest and other towns. One of the most important reasons for this delay was the existence of high electoral qualifications, both in terms of education and wealth, which the Romanian bourgeoisie had to overcome. It finally happened with the introduction of the new constitution of 1884 and the electoral law that followed it, whose regulations allowed more middle-class representatives to enter actively political life.

One has to reckon with a completely different situation in Bulgaria, in comparison with Romania. At the same time, processes in Bulgaria were undoubtedly very similar to those in Greece and Serbia, despite Bulgaria's somewhat later development. The lack of a traditional aristocracy and the substance of political, economic and cultural processes of the first half of the nineteenth century could explain the open political system introduced almost immediately after the establishment of national states.[21] This also explains why the main occupation of fathers of the Bulgarian political elite was either handicrafts or trade. A few were descendants of the well-known families like Moravenov, Chalakov, Chomakov and Geshov. The huge majority came

---

[20]   For a fuller discussion along these lines, see D. Parusheva, 'Political Elites in the Balkans, nineteenth and early twentieth century: Routes to Career', *Etudes balkaniques*, 4, 2001, 69–79. Additional information is in E. Siupiur, 'Les intellectuels roumains du XIXe siècle et la réorganisation de la classe politique et du système institutionnel', *Revue Roumaine d'Histoire*, 1–2, 1995, 75–95.

[21]   In Greece, a nearly universal suffrage for all men over 25 was introduced in 1844 This was because there was a requirement of possessing some property, though it did not matter what kind – a horse, even a hen was enough. In Serbia the situation was very similar. The 1869 constitution granted the right to vote to all major male citizens who were literate, if only able to write their names. In both cases, the mentioned limitations did not present serious obstacles for the enlargement of political participation. As for Bulgaria, the 1879 constitution introduced the universal (male) suffrage for all citizens over 21. See D. Djordjevic, 'Foreign Influences on Nineteenth-Century Balkan Constitutions', in K. Shangriladze and E. Townsend, eds, *Papers for the V Congress of Southeast European Studies, Belgrad, September 1984* (Columbus, Ohio 1984), 72–102.

from the small or middle scale handicrafts and trades families.[22] The distinction between Bulgaria, Greece and Serbia, on the one hand, and Romania, on the other, in terms of bourgeois background, should be pointed out here. Due to the earlier Europeanisation and bureaucratisation of the two Danubian principalities Wallachia and Moldavia *bourgeoisie* meant mostly representatives of the free professions, while in the other Balkan states the term *bourgeoisie* retained a more traditional meaning and designated mainly the small-scale producers such as artisans and merchants.

Figure 9.1 Commercial street of Sofia, 1890. Photographer Ivan Karastoyanov

Source: Photograph courtesy of Dobrinka Parusheva.

A closer look at lists of the members of the Bucharest municipal council shows considerable overlapping of the capital city with the national elite. For example, during the period from 1 September 1868 to 1 September 1869 there were two local elections; the 'Liberals' won the first and the 'Conservatives' the second one.[23] Looking at the names of both liberals and conservatives participating in the municipal council, one realises that at least one third of them belonged to the national political elite, including Constantin Rosetti, Eugeniu Carada, George Cantacuzino, Menelas Germani, and Ion

---

[22]   Parusheva, 'Political Elites', 73–4.

[23]   There were neither Liberal nor Conservative parties at the time of these elections, and both were constituted later, in the 1870s.

Florescu, to mention only the most prominent names.[24] In Sofia too, after becoming capital of the Principality of Bulgaria, real power was very often reserved for personalities who belonged to the national political elite but who were expelled temporarily from the national political scene.[25] Of course, this overlapping of urban capital with national elites comes as no surprise for the researcher of urban government.

Bourgeois interventions in the public affairs of the Bulgarian towns, which had begun already during the first half of the nineteenth century with domination of the guilds, increased over time. Still, the social dualism characteristic of all traditional societies persisted. Despite causing occasional problems, it allowed much more freedom to the family and to the local community, etc., i.e. to some, in a sense, more moderate than local government's networks and helped enormously when conflicts concerning acculturation, local politics and religious life arose.

As already mentioned, the Muslim presence was stronger in the Balkan cities south of the Danube River during the first half of the nineteenth century. Modernisation brought the emergence of a new, shared bourgeois culture, which ran across religious boundaries. Patterns of settlement changed and were now based on class rather than religion. Muslims, Christians and Jews mingled in the labour unions, guilds and bourgeois clubs.[26] Different bonds of solidarity and interest evolved, but the decline of Ottoman power re-sharpened religious boundaries between communities because a sense of defensiveness among the Muslims appeared in this newly assertive Christian world.[27]

It is interesting to observe whether or rather how nation- and state-building processes affected each other in the nineteenth-century Balkans. Plovdiv (Philippopoli) provides a perfect illustration of this dynamic. On the eve of Bulgarian liberation, Plovidiv was a typical multi-ethnic and multi-religious city, like many other commercial and military centres of the Ottoman Empire. Of the three major ethnic communities, Turks were the 'imperial' Muslim majority, Greeks represented the religious authority over

---

[24] *Rapportu din partea Consiliului Communal facut conformu art. 59 din legea communelor şi votat şi aprobat în siedintiele de la 5, 6 si 9 februariu 1870* (Bucharest 1870), 10–11.

[25] Examples include Todor Ikonomov, Nikola Suknarov, Dimitar Petkov, Ivan Slavejkov, Grigor Natchevich, and Dimitar Yablanski, all of whom occupied the post of mayor at some point in late nineteenth or early twentieth century. See *Jubilejna kniga na grad Sofia, 1878–1928* (Jubilee Book of the City of Sofia, 1878–1928) (Sofia 1928), Appendix.

[26] The example of Salonika is very appropriate here, with its multi-ethnic population of Muslims, Jews, Greeks, Bulgarians and others, and with its many clubs and circles that appeared during the second half of the nineteenth century. See M. Anastassiadou, *Salonique, 1830–1912. Une ville ottomane à l'âge des Réformes* (Leiden, New York and Cologne 1997), 359–81.

[27] See Mazower, *The Balkans*, 68–9.

all Orthodox Christians, and Bulgarians dominated the town demographically, beginning in the early nineteenth century. The other ethnic communities, like the Jewish, Armenian, or Roma, did not play important roles in the struggle for social prestige and power. In 1878 when Plovdiv became capital of Eastern Rumelia, official statistics reported a population that was about 45 per cent Bulgarian, 23 per cent Turkish and 20 per cent

Figure 9.2 Members of the city council of Plovdiv, 1891

Sitting from right to the left: Ivan Andonov (mayor), Hadji Mushon Garti (deputy mayor), Rifat Effendi, Petar Krustev (deputy mayor). Behind them other members of the city council

Source: Courtesy of the State Archives Plovdiv.

Greek.[28] Only after the region joined the Bulgarian Principality in 1885 could Plovdiv begin to turn into a modern, ethnically homogenous town: in 1900 Bulgarians were already 60 per cent of the population, while the percentage of Turks and Greeks diminished to eleven and nine per cent, respectively. One can consider this transformation completed by 1910 when Turks and

---

    [28] Eastern Rumelia was an autonomous province of the Ottoman Empire, which included a major part of today's southern Bulgaria and existed in the period 1878–1885.

Greeks together made up just ten per cent of the population and could be compared to the other small ethnic communities like Jews and Armenians. Minorities did play a role in city government, mainly by being presented in the municipal council.[29] The Serbian capital Belgrade as well as other former administrative and military centres of the Ottoman Empire underwent similar developments.[30]

Conclusion

In Bulgaria, Greece and Serbia the new, mostly bureaucratic elites were those who exerted political power, while in Romania the traditional, aristocratic elite managed to preserve its place in the political sphere. All these elites agreed on the need to modernise their countries and on the European model as one worth following. Yet, while advocating the adoption of the institutional forms of western Europe, they continued to reinforce the tradition of state paternalism and submission to the social expectations of their patriarchal societies. Apart from the national capitals and a few other towns, the population of the Balkan states, even at the end of the nineteenth century, remained overwhelmingly rural and characterised by the traditional patriarchal values that had dominated the region for centuries. In addition, a significant percentage of the urban population consisted of recent arrivals from the villages. Thus while an agent for the diffusion of modern culture, the cities were also subjected to the conservative influence of peasant culture. The consequent, long-standing instability of a tension between the modern and the traditional in all these countries was only the most visible part of the price paid by Balkan modernising elites to assert political control.

The changes in the functions of urban government went hand in hand with the developments of their economic and social structure and were accompanied by the challenges of state- and nation-building that went on simultaneously. Not surprisingly, this interweaving complicated modernisation and extended its development over a longer period of time. The list of changes addressed in this chapter is a selective rather than a comprehensive one. The attempt has been made, however, to discuss the most important ones from the point of view of the modernisation of traditional Balkan societies.

---

[29] Data about ethnic composition of Plovdiv comes from my paper 'Transformation of an Imperial City: Ethnic Communities in Plovdiv in the Nineteenth Century', presented at the conference on Ethno-religious Communities in Plovdiv, in May 2000. On Plovdiv's city government see St. Shishkov, *Plovdiv*, 371–3; V. Tankova, *Kogato Plovdiv ne e veche stolitza* (When Plovdiv was not a capital anymore) (Sofia 1994), 231–61.

[30] See, for example *Beograd u prošlosti i sadašnosti. Povodom 500–godišnjce smrti Despota Stevana, 1389–1427* (Belgrade 1927), 59–62.

First, all Balkan cities added commercial and industrial functions to their administrative and military in the course of the nineteenth century. With the emergence of the Balkan bourgeoisie and its assertion of political power, urban governments experienced a multiplication, differentiation and rationalisation of city power. Unlike the earlier periods, when Balkan towns had acknowledged the authority of only a few people like the mayor, the priest, the teacher, or the doctor, including some who had not occupied formal positions of power, by the end of the nineteenth century they already enjoyed comparatively developed and diversified local government structures. Second, since state- and nation-building proceeded simultaneously in the Balkans, one very peculiar trend of Balkan urban development in the nineteenth century was the demographic change from an imperial, multi-ethnic into an ethnically homogenous population. Third, similar to many examples from the other parts of Europe, the effectiveness of leadership in the Balkan capital cities was 'reinforced' by the considerable overlapping of leaders from different spheres (mainly national and local), especially when those higher in the social hierarchy participated in local politics and affairs. Finally, the division between the ceremonial roles reserved for the wealthiest, on the one hand, and the more energetic involvement of middle-class citizens, on the other, developed relatively late and only very slowly compared to western European models.

In short, nineteenth-century elites in all the Balkan countries, including the late Ottoman Empire, attempted to transform their societies from patriarchal into modern ones not by modernising the dominant rural sector of their economies but by focusing on urban change. Their choice explains the long-lasting conflict between national government and population (prevailingly peasant) in the modern Balkan states and is, ultimately, one of the main reasons for the numerous crises that have often shaken Balkan politics.

PART III

Democratic Metropolises – City Elites in North America

CHAPTER TEN

Class and Politics: The Case of New York's Bourgeoisie

Sven Beckert

On 7 April 1877, a crowd of New York merchants, industrialists, bankers and elite professionals marched into Chickering Hall at Fifth Avenue and Eighteenth Street in Manhattan for a meeting of 'taxpayers'. Despite their historic distaste for collective mobilisations, they assembled on this spring day to discuss a weighty issue: a proposed amendment to the constitution of the State of New York that set out to limit universal male suffrage in municipal elections. This remarkably anti-democratic amendment, unveiled only four weeks earlier, promised to consolidate significant areas of municipal government in a newly created Board of Finance. Property owners would elect the board, in effect excluding about half of the city's voters. 'The real object for which this meeting was called was to assail the principle of universal suffrage', the 'Labor Standard' commented with genuine alarm.[1]

Anti-democratic proposals were not uncommon in the polarised world of urban politics in the Gilded Age United States.[2] Yet, in an unusual show of unity and political mobilisation, upper-class New Yorkers gave this radical measure unprecedented political support: this first meeting alone, as the 'New York Times' reported, was 'a notable demonstration of the solid wealth and respectability of the Metropolis'.[3] Iron manufacturer Peter Cooper, international bankers Joseph Seligman and Levi P. Morton, merchant Royal Phelps, manufacturer and banker Josiah Macy, hotel proprietor Amos R. Eno, drygoods merchant H. B. Claflin and iron manufacturer John B. Cornell, among many others, cheered on the speakers who argued that the proposed constitutional amendment would 'separate (...) us at once from that continual change of persons which makes anything like permanent and useful administration utterly impossible'.[4] Before this warm audience, one speaker

---

[1]   *Labor Standard*, 14 April 1877, 1.

[2]   During the 1850s and 1860s, however, these proposals were usually articulated by individuals or small reform groups who failed to mobilise significant support for their ideas. They remained at the margins of bourgeois discourse.

[3]   *New York Times (NYT)*, 8 April 1877, 1.

[4]   For the names see *NYT*, 8 April 1877, 1; *Sun*, 8 April 1877, 1. The speaker was New York lawyer and Secretary of State William Evarts. For the speech see *New York Herald (NYH)*, 8 April 1877, 7.

summed up the evening's sentiment by declaring that the idea that 'a mere majority should direct how the public expenses (...) should be regulated (was) preposterous'.[5] Energised by such blunt talk, bourgeois New Yorkers seized upon this chance to increase their control over the city, a city that, in their eyes, had become dangerously unruly. They confronted, however, an equally agitated opposition of mostly working-class and lower middle-class New Yorkers who sided with labour leader Leander Thompson's judgement that the amendment represented a 'direct stab of the Institutions of free government'.[6] The battle lines were drawn.

Though the amendment eventually foundered, the effort to pass it was a crucial moment in nineteenth-century American politics. The breadth and depth of upper-class New Yorkers' hostility against popular suffrage, a central if not defining feature of democracy, was remarkable and sharply discordant with cherished notions about the rise of American democracy. It points to the limits of social and political integration in a democracy strained by spectacular social inequality and unprecedented social conflict. It demonstrates the conflicts and contradictions of bourgeois rule. And the history of the constitutional amendments shows that workers and lower middle-class New Yorkers could resist the effort by the single most powerful social group in the United States to abrogate their democratic rights.

The politics of the bourgeoisie thus matters a great deal for understanding the trajectory of nineteenth-century American history. Bourgeois politics, however, has not come under systematic scrutiny by historians. This is somewhat surprising, considering that for more than three decades, historians of the nineteenth-century United States have examined the relationship between workers and politics. In numerous community studies, in works on trade unions and in books on political parties large and small, they have explored how workers acted politically, if and how politics and political institutions reflected class identities and how workers exercised political power.[7] Labour historians had good reasons for focusing on these questions:

---

    [5]   *New-York Daily Tribune* (*NYDT*), 9 April 1877, 3.
    [6]   Miscellaneous letters, *Irish World*, 28 April 1877, 6.
    [7]   A. C. Wallace, *Rockdale: The Growth of an American Village in the Early Industrial Revolution* (New York 1972); B. Laurie, *Artisans Into Workers: Labor in Nineteenth-Century America* (New York 1989); G. Stedman Jones, *Languages of Class: Studies in English Working-Class History, 1832–1932* (Cambridge 1983); L. Cohen, *Making a New Deal: Industrial Workers in Chicago, 1919–1939* (New York 1990); L. Fink, 'The New Labor History and the Powers of Historical Pessimism: Consensus, Hegemony, and the Case of the Knights of Labor', *The Journal of American History*, 75, June 1988, 115–36; S. Wilentz, *Chants Democratic: New York City and the Rise of the American Working-Class* (New York 1984); D. Montgomery, *The Fall of the House of Labor: The Workplace, the State, and American Labor Activism, 1865–1925* (New York 1987); M. H. Frisch and D. J. Walkowitz, eds, *Working-Class America: Essays on Labor, Community, and American Society* (Urbana 1983); H. G. Gutman, *Work, Culture, and Society in Industrializing America: Essays in American Working-Class and*

For one, such approaches gave a greater sense of relevance to exploring working-class history. In effect, they made all the numerous small acts of resistance and accommodation important to understanding the sweep of American history. Moreover, *the* great issue of American history, American exceptionalism, could be explored through the lenses of the relationship between politics and class. As historians tried to explain why the United States saw neither the emergence of a powerful socialist working-class party along the lines of French, German and British organisations, nor the creation of a welfare state comparable to that of Western Europe, they tied the question of American exceptionalism directly to how class and politics related to one another.

Scholars have gone a long way to finding answers to many of these questions. Without going into the detail of their arguments, their work allows for a number of general conclusions. The most basic lesson the research of the past decades has illuminated is that there is no straightforward or 'necessary' relationship between class position, class identities and class politics. Working-class identities can express themselves in a whole range of different ways – but sharing a class culture, for example, does not mean that people will also think of themselves in terms of class, and even people who think of themselves in terms of class might not act upon these identities politically.[8] Class formation, hence, is a complicated process. Also, the literature has taught that politics needs to be broadly understood, encompassing much more than elections and parties. Power, in effect, can be exercised in many different ways. And lastly, the works of this generation of historians have shown us that while class politics emerged in the United States in many different and powerful ways, the American political system by and large did not divide along class lines. This, indeed, set the United States apart from much of Western Europe.

Historians have thus learned a great deal about the relationship between the working class and politics. Ironically, however, and despite frequent pleas for considering class as a relational category, we know much less about the bourgeoisie. The term 'bourgeoisie' was not frequently employed by capital-rich New Yorkers during the nineteenth century, who preferred to refer to themselves at first by the specific line of business they were engaged in and, later, as 'taxpayers' or 'businessmen'. Similarly, historians have employed various other terms to describe the group under review here, such as 'elites', 'aristocracy', 'plutocracy', 'ruling class' and 'middle class'. I believe, however, that the term 'bourgeoisie' grasps more precisely the historical formation with which I am concerned. 'Elite', for example, while a useful

---

Social History (New York 1976), 209–92; A. D., *Class and Community: The Industrial Revolution in Lynn* (Cambridge, Mass. 1976).

[8]   This research is best summarised and conceptualised in I. Katznelson and A. Zolberg, eds, *Working-Class Formation: Nineteenth Century Patterns in Western Europe and the United States* (Princeton 1986).

term, does not sufficiently distinguish the bourgeoisie as a fundamentally different kind of elite from other elites who have come before or after. 'Aristocracy', while used derogatorily by nineteenth-century workers and middle-class citizens resentful of the wealth and power of the bourgeoisie, is problematic because it is the distinguishing feature of United States history that no true aristocracy emerged. 'Plutocracy', in turn, insufficiently grasps the totality of the bourgeoisie, calling to mind only fat, cigar-smoking robber barons who reigned tyrannically over their enterprises. 'Ruling class' assumes the political power of the bourgeoisie instead of investigating it. The term 'middle-class' (or 'middle classes'), in contrast, by referring to a distinct elite based on the ownership of capital as opposed to heritage and birth, as the 'estate' situated between inherited aristocracy on the one side and farmers as well as workers on the other side, describes the group this book is concerned with quite well. Its usage, however, has become so overwhelmed with present day concerns that it lacks sufficient analytical clarity. Today, 'middle class' can either stand for all Americans, past and present, who are neither extremely wealthy nor homeless, or for a distinct social group that corresponds somewhat with the European notion of the 'petite bourgeoisie' – artisans, shop owners and lesser professionals. While this study is not concerned with the middle class it is in the last sense that some historians of the nineteenth century such as Stuart Blumin, Robert Johnston and Mary Ryan have begun to use the term successfully. For these reasons, the term that best fits the group of people I am looking at is 'bourgeoisie', which I use interchangeably with 'upper class' and 'economic elite'. It refers to a particular kind of elite whose power in its most fundamental sense derived from the ownership of capital rather than birth-right, status, or kinship. 'Bourgeoisie', moreover, focuses our attention squarely on the relationships between members of the city's economic elite, allowing us to place at the centre of our investigation the question of what they did and did not share. In order to come to a workable definition of the term, we have to acknowledge that its meaning will always be somewhat ambivalent, because it is the essence of modern societies that boundaries between social groups are imprecise and to a certain degree fluid. Still, for the purposes of this article the bourgeoisie most prominently and unambiguously includes the city's substantial merchants, industrialists and bankers, along with *rentiers* (people who lived from investments they did not manage themselves), real estate speculators, owners of service enterprises as well as many of its professionals. Taken together, this was the entrepreneurial or economic bourgeoisie *par excellence*. They shared a specific position in New York's social structure in that they owned and invested capital, employed wage workers (at the very least servants), did not work for wages themselves and did not work manually.[9]

---

[9]   On this question see S. Beckert, *The Monied Metropolis: New York City and*

To be sure, there have been lively debates about the European bourgeoisie (though they often also de-emphasised the importance of politics), but these debates have largely ignored the United States. Big questions thus remain unanswered: How did nineteenth-century bourgeois Americans relate to politics? And how did bourgeois politics relate to class? The lack of attention to these issues is strange and disturbing. It is strange because many labour historians implicitly, if not explicitly, link the particular political outcomes of the nineteenth century to the spoken or unspoken class interests of the bourgeoisie. It is disturbing, because the nineteenth-century bourgeoisie was the central historical actor of this most bourgeois century. Indeed, if we think about the United States in the nineteenth century in the most general terms, we almost always think about the tremendous power of the Northern bourgeoisie. It is industrialists such as Andrew Carnegie and John D. Rockefeller, not presidents such as Chester Arthur and James Garfield who come to mind. Therefore, the question of the relationship between the bourgeoisie and politics is at least as important as the one between workers and politics. If one argues that class has shaped politics, one certainly needs to focus attention also on the bourgeoisie.

Not that we are entirely in the dark about bourgeois politics in the nineteenth century. It is, for example, one of the basic truths of Gilded Age historiography (approximately 1877 to 1896) to emphasise the enormous political power of the owners of capital.[10] A second body of literature, focused largely on urban politics, talks about the retreat of bourgeois Americans from politics, about the desperate but ultimately failing efforts of reforming elites to hold on to their political influence.[11] And third, an important literature explains Progressive Era politics by referring to the particular interests and inclinations of specific segments of capital, such as merchants, corporate capitalists or railroad entrepreneurs.[12] Nevertheless,

---

the Consolidation of the American Bourgeoisie (Cambridge and New York 2001), 1–14.

[10]   Ch. A. and M. R. Beard, *The Rise of American Civilization,* vol. 2: *The Industrial Era* (New York 1937), 383–479; R. Hofstadter, *The American Political Tradition and the Men Who Made it* (New York 1948), 162–82; R. Wiebe, *The Search for Order* (New York 1967), and A. Trachtenberg, *The Incorporation of America: Culture and Society in the Gilded Age* (New York 1982). The power of business elites is also emphasised by R. Oestreicher, 'Two Souls of American Democracy', in G. R. Andrew and H. Chapman, eds, *The Social Construction of Democracy, 1870–1990* (New York 1995), 118–31, esp. 119. In the context of postwar southern policies, the power of the northern bourgeoisie is emphasised by L. Goodwyn, *The Populist Moment* (New York 1978), 6.

[11]   G. A. Almond, *Plutocracy and Politics in New York City* (Boulder, Colorado 1998); A. Bridges, 'Another Look at Plutocracy in Antebellum New York City', *Political Science Quarterly,* 97, 1982, 57–71, and J. G. Sproat, *The Best Men: Liberal Reformers in the Gilded Age* (New York 1968), 206.

[12]   Most prominently by M. J. Sklar, *The Corporate Reconstruction of American Capitalism, 1890–1916: The Market, The Law, and Politics* (New York 1989).

despite this literature's look at bourgeois politics, there are few systematic investigations into how the bourgeoisie, class identities and bourgeois politics related in nineteenth-century America. Indeed, Barrington Moore's 1966 complaint that 'an adequate study of the political attitudes of Northern industrialists remains to be written' is still valid today.[13]

I am not going to fill this gap in the next few pages. But I will explore in this essay issues of bourgeois politics by making a few general comments. I will in particular review three distinct questions: First, how did nineteenth-century bourgeois exert political power? Second, how did their politics relate to their class identities? And, third, what was the relationship between bourgeois politics and the development of bourgeois society?

In this short essay, I will speak in general terms, but root my discussions in the history of New York's bourgeoisie during the second half of the nineteenth century.[14]

The question of political power

Let me first explore the issue of how bourgeois Americans exerted political power. Obviously, in the course of the nineteenth century, tremendous change occurred in the mechanisms of bourgeois politics. Up until the middle of the century, merchants, manufacturers, bankers, and elite professionals controlled an overwhelming number of political offices on the federal, state and municipal level. Controlling these offices gave them tremendous and largely unmediated access to governmental powers. By mid-century, however, as many historians have pointed out, the share of offices controlled by the wealthy entered a long period of decline. Increasingly, politicians of lower middle-class or even working-class background entered the political fray and moved into state assemblies, Congress and the office of the mayor. The speed of this transition varied from place to place, but by the end of the century, direct bourgeois representation in political institutions had certainly declined precipitously.[15]

The shifting social origins of the holders of political offices in the city of New York demonstrate this slow but steady erosion of the once towering position of the city's economic elite.[16] One political scientist found that among 103 politically active wealthy New Yorkers only twelve ran for office in the years between 1850 and 1863, compared to thirty-two who had been

---

[13]   B. Moore, *Social Origins of Dictatorship and Democracy: Lord and Peasant in the Making of the Modern World* (Boston 1966), 125.

[14]   For a comprehensive history of New York City's bourgeoisie see Beckert, *Monied Metropolis*.

[15]   Almond, *Plutocracy*; A. B. Gronowicz, 'Revising the Concept of Jacksonian Democracy', University of Pennsylvania Ph.D. thesis, 1981, 49.

[16]   Almond, *Plutocracy*, 59–70.

candidates in the years between 1828 and 1840.[17] Historian Anthony Boleslaw Gronowicz similarly discovered that of 1,052 New York City Democratic Party activists in 1844, thirty-eight per cent were professionals or businessmen, while thirty-three per cent were skilled workers, a substantial number that was probably unprecedented in the Western world at large.[18] Increasingly, professional politicians of lower middle-class or even working-class background occupied political offices.[19]

Many historians have argued that this decline in office holding represented a decline in bourgeois political power – the onset of the age of mass politics, in effect, undermined the power of the owners of capital. This vision, however, needs correcting. For one, while bourgeois office holding declined, it did not disappear. The office of the mayor of New York City, for example, was filled more or less until the end of the nineteenth century by merchants, manufacturers and elite professionals, not workers or even modestly prosperous shop owners. As late as the 1880s, New York mayors included one of the nation's most important iron manufacturers – Abram Hewitt – and one of the city's most important merchants – William R. Grace. Moreover, bourgeois New Yorkers enjoyed numerous other ways of exerting political influence even if they did not hold office: for one, they continued to have excellent access to people in power. As they inhabited dense social networks that usually included a whole range of senior public officials, they could access these networks in order to pursue specific political goals. Social clubs, trade associations and the like usually included people in high political offices and allowed for numerous ways of projecting influence. Indeed, the venerable Union Club, testifying to its members' political involvement, counted in its ranks a former Secretary of the Navy, a United States Senator, two Governors of New York State, four mayors of New York City, as well as a Governor of Rhode Island. Incidentally, it was lawyers who in particular bridged the world of business with that of politics. Even more importantly, in this age of mass politics, political parties needed money in ever increasing amounts and it was bourgeois Americans who could provide these resources. Paying for the operations of political parties, in turn, gave them a tremendous ability to shape the parties' agenda, especially on the national level.[20] After the Civil War (1861–1865), New York merchants, especially August Belmont, became the Democratic Party's single most important source of

---

[17]   Bridges, 'Another Look', 62.

[18]   Gronowicz, 'Revising the Concept', 49.

[19]   R. Townsend, *Mother of Clubs: Being the History of the First Hundred Years of the Union Club of the City of New York, 1836–1936* (New York 1936), 136.

[20]   August Belmont bankrolled James Buchanan's presidential campaign in 1852 and supported his candidacy in 1856. See Ph. Foner, *Business and Slavery: The New York Merchants and the Irrepressible Conflict* (Chapel Hill 1941), 82; I. Katz, *August Belmont; A Political Biography* (New York 1968), 11–22. Locally as well, wealthy citizens continued to serve as chairmen of party meetings and on party committees. Bridges, 'Another Look', 63.

revenue, while the city's financiers and industrialists bankrolled the Republican Party. And, in more general but nonetheless important ways, the state itself was dependent on capital – which meant that those in control of the state had to take the interests of capital into account in shaping policies.

Thus in numerous subtle and not-so-subtle ways, bourgeois Americans could exert political power well beyond their numbers. If there was widespread agreement among the city's economic elite, these networks proved powerful mechanisms of transforming their interests into policies. While they could thus exercise enormous influence, this access to the state did not necessarily reflect bourgeois class interests nor was it always successful. Indeed, these ways of wielding power often favoured very particular interests, such as access to municipal franchises, to federal money for harbour improvements or to military protection for ventures out West. They also favoured interests sharply at odds with one another, such as demands for higher or lower tariffs, accommodation to the expansionist policies of slaveholders versus resistance against them, and demands for the regulation of railroads versus cries for market freedom. Indeed, it might be said that these ways of exerting influence largely served very particular interests and brought with them deep conflicts. Probably most characteristic of this kind of politics were debates on the guiding theme of 1880s and 1890s – the tariff.[21] Obviously, tariffs affected different segments of the bourgeoisie differently – but almost always greatly impacted the profitability of their economic undertakings. As a result, the discussions on tariffs went into minute details and tariff bills usually brought with them hundreds of amendments, favouring this or that specific industry or company.[22] The Wilson-Gorman tariff bill of 1894, for example, sported more than 600 amendments, reflecting the influence of various groups of entrepreneurs. While such bills testified to the great political influence of bourgeois Americans, they were often not the ways of bourgeois class politics.

Moreover, bourgeois political influence exerted in these ways often failed. In 1861, for example, when most bourgeois New Yorkers fought bitterly for compromise with the Southern states to prevent a break-up of the Union, using their extraordinary access to the President and high cabinet officials to pressure the administration to accept a more accommodationist policy. But their efforts came to naught. Similarly, when they called in 1865 and 1866 for a rapid readmission of the former confederate states to the union, they found insufficient support for their position in the federal government, despite extraordinary access to the President, cabinet officials and members of the House and the Senate.

---

[21]   On the importance of tariff politics for the 1880s see also M. Keller, *Affairs of State: Public Life in Late Nineteenth-Century America* (Cambridge, Mass. 1977), 376.
[22]   Ibid. 377–8.

Yet these were not the only ways in which merchants, industrialists and bankers tried to project their economic power into the political sphere. Importantly, bourgeois Americans also engaged in collective political mobilisations. This might sound strange, as we usually associate collective action with the working class, but nonetheless, capitalists as well can act collectively, though they do not do so frequently. In New York City, for example, these mobilisations occurred mostly (though not exclusively) in regard to local politics. And they occurred generally during moments of crisis, during moments in which bourgeois power seemed to be challenged. Most prominent were efforts to regain local political influence after the rise of the political machine. The machine, to elite New Yorkers, was a way to make their own resources, namely money, superfluous in local politics and thus emancipate professional politicians from their tutelage. In New York City in the 1850s, in response, they twice ran reform candidates on a bipartisan ticket, challenging machine politicians. More dramatically, in 1861, bourgeois New Yorkers mobilised behind the union war effort. In 1871, once more, they organised collectively to oust the corrupt regime of William Tweed, in 1877 they agitated for an amendment to the constitution of the state of New York, limiting suffrage rights in the state's cities and in 1896 they rallied behind hard money. In these collective mobilisations, bourgeois New Yorkers took to the streets (for example with their demand for the gold standard), organised huge assemblies and published lengthy resolutions in their newspapers of record. It was hence in moments of crisis that bourgeois class identities sharpened and translated into collective action.

These examples also show that it was exceedingly difficult for bourgeois New Yorkers to sustain such mobilisations. For one, organising on the basis of shared class backgrounds proved difficult in a democracy in which the number of voters ultimately decided political fates. Appealing to the public on the basis of class indeed invited failure. And, second, diverse interests often made these coalitions extremely fragile. The reform movements of the 1850s, for example, which represented an effort by bourgeois New Yorkers to retain their former influence in municipal politics, ultimately failed because diverse interests in national politics, namely the relationship to slavery and the future of the South, drove the bourgeois activists apart. There was only one instance, the 1871 ouster of Boss Tweed, a corrupt machine politician supported by the city's lower, middle- and working-class, in which collective action by the city's upper-class unequivocally succeeded.

Other forms of collective mobilisation, however, proved to be more successful. Employer associations, especially in the last quarter of the century, played an important role in challenging the collective power of workers. Trade organisations such as the Chamber of Commerce provided its members with sustained influence on national, state and local politics. Cultural politics, moreover, including the creation of museums, opera houses, theatres, and private welfare organisations proved to be extremely successful and influential in shaping the Gilded Age city.[23] Thus organising and mobilising on the basis of shared class identities had a substantial pay-off, especially when the task at hand was limited and the movement relied chiefly on resources under private, not public, control.

Antidemocratic tendencies

Bourgeois New Yorkers exercised political power in a wide range of different ways, most of which were not accessible to the majority of American citizens. Exceptional access to capital, social networks and information advantaged the city's economic elite. While these advantages were a constant throughout the nineteenth century, the relative degree of bourgeois political power changed significantly. It is difficult to generalise, but looking at the nineteenth century from a birds-eye perspective, it seems that in moments during which there were sharp disagreements amongst the country's economic elite, such as during the era of the Civil War and Reconstruction, considerable openings emerged for other social groups to exert influence. This was not least the case because segments of the upper class depended on these groups to effect their own goals. Southern slaves were the greatest beneficiaries of these divisions – but so were Northern workers in the wake of the Civil War. On the other hand, during moments in which bourgeois Americans agreed on the fundamental shape of the nation's political economy, it was all but impossible for other social groups to pursue alternative projects successfully. Most prominently, during the Gilded Age, with the nation's economic elite agreeing on retrenchment, the expansion of the repressive capacity of the state, hard money and the political economy of domestic industrialisations, few openings remained for workers and farmers to effect their own political goals. While workers and farmers certainly mobilised frequently, their political successes were limited. Moreover, the core of the Gilded Age bourgeois political agenda, the retrenchment of the state, transferred in itself tremendous power to the owners of capital. The more powerful markets became vis-à-vis the state, the more power accumulated in the hands of people who controlled these markets. It seems therefore fair to argue that in the course of the nineteenth century – with the national economic elite more unified and with the absence of competing elites – bourgeois political power increased substantially.

If bourgeois New Yorkers remained politically powerful throughout the nineteenth century despite the changing forms of their political activism, one last issue still awaits discussion: the relationship between the bourgeoisie and

---

[23] For a more detailed history of the cultural politics of New York's bourgeoisie see also S. Beckert, 'Die Kultur des Kapitals: Bürgerliche Kultur in New York und Hamburg im 19. Jahrhundert', *Vorträge aus dem Warburg-Haus*, 4, 2000, 139–73.

bourgeois society. There has certainly been a tendency in much of the literature on the bourgeoisie (including much of the literature on Europe) to equate bourgeois politics with liberalism and democracy, in effect making the bourgeoisie the social group that pursued the building of bourgeois society. To quote once again Barrington Moore: 'No bourgeois, no democracy.'[24] Looking at bourgeois politics during the second half of the nineteenth century, however, suggests that the relationship between bourgeoisie and democracy was considerably more complicated. Two of the complications should suffice here as examples:

For one, bourgeois New Yorkers by and large opposed the project of extending the benefits of bourgeois society to the South. Though Barrington Moore has called the American Civil War the last bourgeois revolution, it is important to note that New York's economic elite only late and reluctantly embraced this revolution – a revolution that brought the most basic and fundamental liberal rights (such as self-ownership) to slaves and freed people of the South.

Second, and most tellingly, bourgeois New Yorkers became increasingly ambivalent about central features of democracy itself. One of the most forceful expressions of this anti-democratic reorientation was their determined battle to disenfranchise the city's lower classes in municipal elections.[25] This struggle not only provides a good example for the tensions within the bourgeois political project, but also for the ways of bourgeois politics.

As we have seen at the beginning of this essay, the struggle for disen-franchisement had begun innocuously in 1875, when the Democratic Governor of New York State, Samuel Tilden, created a bipartisan commission to propose reforms in the structure of municipal government in the state.[26] When this elite commission issued its report in early 1877, it presented a strikingly anti-democratic document, asserting 'the fruitlessness of any effort for improvement through the regular instrumentality of popular election' and demanding, 'that the excesses of democracy be corrected'.[27]

---

[24]   Moore, *Social Origins*, 418.

[25]   For a detailed history of the struggle for disenfranchisement see also S. Beckert, 'Contesting Suffrage Rights in Gilded Age New York', *Past & Present*, 20, February, 2002, 116–57.

[26]   S. Tilden, '"Municipal Reform Message" Address to the Legislature, Albany, 11 May 1875', reprinted in J. Bigelow, ed., *The Writings and Speeches of Samuel J. Tilden*, vol. 2 (New York 1885), 119–37.

[27]   *Report of the Commission to Devise a Plan for the Government of Cities in the State of New York: Presented to the Legislature, March 6th, 1877* (New York 1877), 3. The language of the report reminds readers eerily of a similar language used by twentieth century elites in their challenges to 'populist' regimes. See for example M. L. Conniff, *Latin American Populism in Comparative Perspective* (Albuquerque 1982); T. Di Tella, 'Populism and Reform in Latin America', in C. Veliz, ed., *Obstacles to*

In the lengthy document the members of the commission produced, they expressed dissatisfaction with the traditional system of urban rule. More specifically, they located the problems of urban rule in high debts, excessive expenditures and high taxes.[28] The origins of these ills lay in the election of 'incompetent and unfaithful' municipal officials and the prevalence of parties in municipal politics.[29] But how to improve municipal rule? After dismissing a whole range of reform ideas that had been traditionally articulated, the Commission concluded that only an attack on the roots of the problem would do.[30] The work, they asserted, 'must begin at the very foundation of the structure'.[31] The question was 'whether the election by universal suffrage of the local guardians of the financial concerns of cities can be safely retained'.[32] The Commission resolved that such was not the case and therefore advised that 'the choice of the local guardians and trustees of the financial concerns of cities should be lodged with taxpayers'.[33]

In order to secure such an outcome, the Commission recommended the passage of a constitutional amendment.[34] At the heart of this proposed constitutional amendment was the creation of a Board of Finance, its members elected by those residents of the city who 'have paid annual tax on property owned by them, and officially assessed for taxation in such city, of the assessed value of not less than 500 dollars' or those who paid yearly rent of at least $250. These were substantial sums in a city in which workers, including skilled workers, could hope to take home between 400 and 600 dollars annually, of which they would not spend more than 20 per cent on rent.[35] The Board of Finance was to be endowed with all powers regarding taxation, expenditures and debt – including the allocation of city expenditures to specific projects.[36] As a result, the mayor as well as the Board of Aldermen, though still elected by popular suffrage, would have lost most of

---

Change in Latin America (London 1965), 47–74, and G. Ionescu and E. Gellner, *Populism: Its Meaning and National Characteristics* (London 1969).

[28] 'Report of the Commission to Devise a Plan', 4–10.

[29] Ibid. 10, 13, 15.

[30] Ibid. 21–7.

[31] Ibid. 27.

[32] Ibid. 28.

[33] Ibid. Since there was no income tax of any kind in 1877, all 'taxpayers' owned real property – a small segment of the urban population.

[34] The commission favoured a constitutional change, because, as they argued, only such an amendment would guarantee 'stability'. Ibid. 43.

[35] Ibid. 48. The wage data is from C. D. Long, *Wages and Earnings in the United States, 1860–1890* (Princeton 1960), esp. 27–8, 41 and 150, and on rents as a percentage of income, see 51–9. These are very rough estimates, and their only purpose here is to allow us to see that the property qualification was a significant hurdle that few, if any, New York workers could have passed.

[36] 'Report of the Commission to Devise a Plan', 42.

their powers.[37] An estimate by the *New York Times* found that of a total electorate of about 140,000 New Yorkers, 60,000 to 65,000 would retain the right to vote as taxpayers, with another 35,000 to 40,000 as rent-payers.[38] These numbers suggest that about 29 per cent of the city's voters would have lost their right to participate in the choosing of the 'financial guardians of the city'. This is a conservative estimate, however, since the 100,000 New Yorkers who would have still been allowed to vote constituted only 31 per cent of the total number of men 21 years or older who lived in Manhattan in 1880.[39] As many as 69 per cent of all potential voters might have lost their right to vote, gained more than half a century earlier, in 1821.[40] Among those to be disenfranchised, according to *The Sun*, were

> ten thousand clerks and salesmen of the city who live in boarding houses; (...) thousands of professional men who are neither property owners nor rent payers; (...) thousands of small shopkeepers; (...) tens of thousands of honest, industrious and patriotic mechanics and labouring men; (...) the thousands of voters who live in hotels; (...) the sons of wealthy citizens who live with their parents at home; and (...) many of the talented young men whose minds give life to the newspapers.[41]

The commission's plan was nothing less than a fundamental, even revolutionary reconceptualisation of how New York City should be ruled, albeit one that harked back to the venerable ideas of propertied republicanism. Nevertheless, it received broad support from the city's merchants, industrialists, bankers and elite professionals who were struggling to retain their control and influence over a rapidly growing city.[42] The *Commercial and Financial Chronicle*, a prominent voice of the city's merchants and bankers, editorialised, 'If we really want relief, we must bestir ourselves vigorously and at once'.[43] And indeed, they did. In public meetings, through editorials and in numerous resolutions, upper-class New Yorkers, both Democrats and Republicans, lobbied for the adoption of the amendment. The Chamber of Commerce, which, among its more than 700 members counted

---

[37]   *NYT*, 1 November 1877, 4.

[38]   *NYT*, 21 October 1877, 7.

[39]   For the number of males age 21 or older see Department of the Interior, Census Office, *Statistics of the Population of the United States at the Tenth Census, June 1, 1880* (Washington 1883).

[40]   There were also other estimates about the percentage of voters who would be disenfranchised. The *Sun* estimated that 50,000 voters would lose their suffrage, or about one–third of the total number of voters as estimated by the *NYT*. See *The Sun*, 22 October 1877, 2. At another occasion, *The Sun* estimated that 92,000 out of 190,000 voters would be disenfranchised, slightly less than 50 per cent. See *The Sun*, 14 April 1877, 3.

[41]   *The Sun*, 22 October 1877, 2.

[42]   For the characterisation of the amendment as 'revolutionary' see *The Sun*, 21 April 1877, 2.

[43]   *Commercial and Financial Chronicle* (*CFC*), 31 March 1877, 285.

virtually all of the city's important merchants and bankers, went as far as to call a special meeting in March 1877 (with an 'unusually large number of members assembled') to consider the issue and unanimously expressed its backing.[44] One of the chamber's members, the lawyer William Allen Butler, praised the plan because it excluded 'the irresponsible, floating and shiftless vote, which never has any but a mischievous and indefensible relation to the exercise of the right of suffrage'.[45] Joining him at the podium, Simon Sterne, predicted that as a result of the reforms, '(m)erchants will no longer find themselves in contest with the loafer element, which would eventually outnumber and beat them'.[46] More control, the merchant George T. Hope argued at the same meeting, would mean lower taxes.[47] Not only the Chamber of Commerce, but also the New York Stock Exchange, the Produce Exchange, the Importers' and Grocers' Board of Trade, the Council of Reform, the Union League Club, the Municipal Society, the New-York Board of Trade and the Cotton Exchange passed resolutions in support of the amendment.[48] Indeed, all major business groups of New York City endorsed the constitutional change and mobilised in support of it, the NYT noting that it 'is warmly supported by the entire commercial and tax-paying interests of the City'.[49] When it came to the constitutional amendment, New York's economic elite spoke with one voice.[50] If there was discord, it arose only because some upper-class New Yorkers embraced even more radical measures: the city's Taxpayers' Association, for example, went even further and demanded that large rent-payers also be excluded from the electorate for the Board of Finance.[51] Indeed, so united were bourgeois New Yorkers and so vigorously did they work for the amendment that when former Governor of New York State John Thompson Hoffman spoke out against the suffrage restrictions at the Annual Banquet of the Chamber of Commerce, he ended his defence with the words, 'Now, gentlemen, I did not expect that that sentiment would receive much applause here (...)'.[52] And it did not.

---

[44] *NYT*, 30 March 1877, 2.
[45] *Nineteenth Annual Report of the Corporation of the Chamber of Commerce of the State of New York For the Year 1876–1877* (New York 1877), 99.
[46] Ibid. 100.
[47] Ibid. 104.
[48] *NYDT*, 5 April 1877, 2; *NYDT*, 13 April 1877, 8; *NYT*, 25 April 1877, 8; *NYT*, 30 November 1876, 7; *NYT*, 25 April 1877, 8; *NYT*, 30 March 1877, 2.
[49] The quote is from *NYT*, 17 April 1877, 10. On the widespread endorsement of the amendment by New York's economic elites see also S. J. Mandelbaum, *Boss Tweed's New York* (New York 1965), 171.
[50] There is no evidence of any opposition to the amendment from New York's economic elite.
[51] *NYH*, 28 March 1877, 4.
[52] *Twentieth Annual Report of the Corporation of the Chamber of Commerce of the State of New–York for the Year 1877 – 1878* (New York 1878), 9–10.

The support for the amendment represented a collective and bipartisan mobilisation of bourgeois New Yorkers that had not been seen since the demonstrations in April of 1861 at the outset of the Civil War and the meetings during September 1871 when they had rebelled against the corrupt urban politics of Tammany Hall's William Tweed. Indeed, it was one of the very few collective mobilisations of property owning New Yorkers during the nineteenth century. By the late 1870s, therefore, elite New Yorkers engaged in a concerted and aggressively managed campaign to limit popular suffrage.

While the amendment itself failed, the increasing ambivalence about democracy had drastic implications for the freed people of the South, with New York's economic elite increasingly tolerating the reign of terror and disenfranchisement unleashed by the white elites of the South. This is not the place to review the strategies that Southern elites employed in this campaign, except to note that they, like elite Northerners, employed the language of taxpayers' rights to successfully advocate the disenfranchisement of the poor.[53] This was much easier as Southerners could formulate their program of disenfranchisement in terms of race, and not of class.[54] In addition, they were more successful because they stepped outside the constitutional political process by resorting to extralegal violence and because they encountered opponents who did not enjoy access to many of the usual prerequisites of successful collective action. Southern elites, in effect, not only attacked the participatory axis of democracy, namely universal male suffrage (as their counterparts did in the North), but also the procedural axis of democracy, such as the rule of law, the functional separation of the state from civil society and citizenship rights such as the freedom of speech and assembly. Despite these differences, however, it is noteworthy that elite Southerners' destruction of democracy encountered very little opposition from upper-class New Yorkers. Northern tolerance for Southern disenfranchisement, hence, speaks directly to the disenchantment with democracy among bourgeois New Yorkers, illuminating the tensions between the political projects of the bourgeoisie and the project of bourgeois society.

---

[53]   See e.g. [Charleston] *News and Courier*, 21 April 1877, 2.

[54]   Though it is important to note that even in the South appeals for disenfranchisement were at times formulated in terms of class. In Texas, for example, a group of urban business people advocated ever since the 1870s limiting suffrage rights to property owners, arguing explicitly that white workers should be deprived of political influence just as much as their African-American counterparts. For an incisive discussion of this moment in Texas politics see P. Williams, '"The Horrors of the Commune": Urban Politics and Suffrage Restriction in Post-Reconstruction Texas' (unpublished manuscript, 2001, in author's possession).

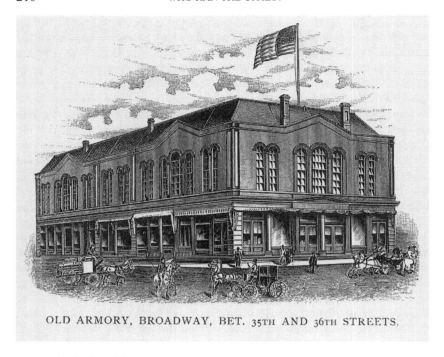

OLD ARMORY, BROADWAY, BET. 35TH AND 36TH STREETS.

Figure 10.1 The old armory of the 71st Regiment, 1850s

Source: Official Souvenir, Celebration of the Opening of the New Armory, 71st
                Regiment (New York 1894), 53. Reproduction courtesy of Harvard
                University.

Indeed, the experience of Reconstruction itself had helped fuel the
growing ambivalence among bourgeois New Yorkers about an activist state
legitimised and controlled by non-propertied voters. Though during the war
and immediately afterwards they had mostly supported federal intervention in
the South, even black enfranchisement, they had demanded an end to
Reconstruction much earlier than most Northerners. They believed that
political uncertainty along with social upheaval interfered with their
economic interests in cotton production and a climate suitable to investments
in railroads and extractive industries.[55] Reconstruction governments, in their
eyes, proved especially unable to create a stable system of labour relations so
crucial to the production of agricultural commodities for world markets. By
the early 1870s, New York's economic elite responded to this continued

---

[55] For a detailed account of the shifting attitudes towards Reconstruction see
Beckert, *The Monied Metropolis*, 157–71.

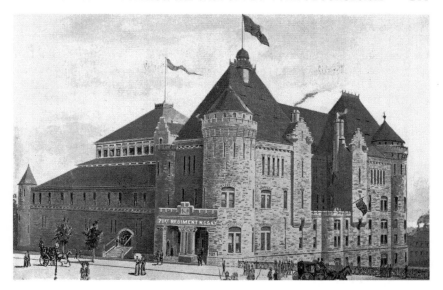

Figure 10.2 'Defensible from All Points', the armory of the 71st Regiment, 1880s

Source: Official Souvenir, Celebration of the Opening of the New Armory, 71st Regiment (New York 1894), 17. Reproduction courtesy of Harvard University.

uncertainty in the South by formulating an ever more aggressive critique of Reconstruction. Republican lawyer George T. Strong angrily noted in his diary in September 1874 that 'The governments of South Carolina and Louisiana are, I fear, mere nests of corrupt carpet-baggers upheld by a brute nigger constituency'.[56] A year later, the 'Commercial and Financial Chronicle' explained to its well-heeled readers that 'Southern States have been fearfully robbed by their ruler'.[57] So dismal was the record of Reconstruction in the eyes of the city's economic elite that by 1877 the *Commercial and Financial Chronicle* concluded that it had 'totally failed' and that it was best 'to leave every Southern State to its own people'.[58]

The disenchantment of upper-class New Yorkers with Reconstruction, then, helps account for their ever louder critique of an activist and democratically legitimised state, which, in turn, helps to explain the destruction of democracy in the states of the former Confederacy. New York

---

[56] A. Nevins and M. H. Thomas, eds, *The Diary of George Templeton Strong*, vol. 4 (New York 1974), 538, entry of 16 September 1874.

[57] *CFC*, 2 January 1875, 3.

[58] *CFC*, 18 April 1877, 383.

drug manufacturer and merchant Samuel B. Schieffelin made this point explicit when he warned of the dangerous connection between democracy in the North and the rights of freedmen in the South.[59] He advised southern states to write constitutions that would limit suffrage rights, thus saving themselves from 'future danger and evil'.[60] Universal suffrage, he bluntly asserted, 'is a curse to any community, whether white or black, until fitted for it'.[61] Views like these eased the acceptance of the eventual destruction of democracy in the South.[62]

The ambivalent relationship of the city's economic elite to the revolutionary implications of the Civil War and Reconstruction, along with its support for the proposed constitutional amendment limiting suffrage rights in New York City, suggests that the bourgeoisie at times resisted the most fundamental aspects of bourgeois society. It was instead citizens of working- and middle-class background who defended an expansive democracy.

These short excursions into the political activities of bourgeois New Yorkers in the nineteenth century suggest, among many other things, that we need to think about the relationship between class and politics in fundamentally different ways for the bourgeoisie then for the working class. Most importantly, bourgeois Americans were able to exert considerable political power without articulating collective identities. Their power rested to a very large degree on the control of capital, networks and information, not on class identities, class organisations and class mobilisations. That set the economic elite clearly apart from workers. Maybe even more importantly, the case of New York in the nineteenth century shows that class politics is difficult to sustain for the bourgeoisie, since it frightens away most voters. For workers, in contrast, meaningful power can only be exerted through collective mobilisations and these collective mobilisations had to be fuelled by often unstable collective identities. It is thus 'easier' for bourgeois to exert power than for workers, which helps to explain the fundamental unevenness of the distribution of power in nineteenth-century American society. It is also for these reasons that bourgeois collective mobilisations represented often, though not always, moments of relative political weakness – and thus the exact opposite of what they represented for workers.

---

[59]   *NYT*, 14 November 1866, 2.
[60]   *NYT*, 25 January 1867, 2.
[61]   *NYT*, 25 January 1867, 2.
[62]   Working-class political power, they believed, threatened their property rights. In this they agreed with Southern elites. One modern observer indeed argued persuasively, that 'it is probably best for analytical purposes to treat the South not as a deviant case, but as an extreme example of more general tendencies (...)'. W. D. Burnham, 'The System of 1896: An Analysis', in P. Kleppner et al., eds, *The Evolution of American Electoral Systems*, (Westport 1981), 147–202, esp. 164.

CHAPTER ELEVEN

A 'Jeffersonian Skepticism of Urban Democracy'? The Educated Middle Class and the Problem of Political Power in Chicago, 1880–1940

Marcus Gräser

Any reasonable attempt to analyse the relationship between social class and political power will question a monolithic idea of power and will recognise that different classes had different ways of accessing or exerting political power.[1] This chapter will try to avoid giving a clear-cut answer to the question 'Who ran Chicago?' It may be quite possible, however, to find an answer to another question: 'Who did not run Chicago?' and such an answer may help clarify the city's power structure. But how does 'power' need to be conceptualised if the focus is not on the proximity to, but on the distance from power? It seems that a slightly modified version of Max Weber's famous definition may be useful for this purpose: not 'the chance of a man or of a number of men to realise their own will in a communal action even against the resistance of others',[2] but instead, the chance of men and women

---

[1]   A previous version of this work was delivered at the Sixth International Conference on Urban History, Edinburgh, September 2002 (Main Session: Who Was Running the Cities? Elites and Urban Power Structures, 1700–2000), and as a lecture at the David Bruce Centre for American Studies at Keele University, Staffordshire, in the same year. It is a somewhat sketchy by-product of a larger comparative study of middle class(es) and welfare state building in Germany and in the United States, 1880–1940 – a study in which both the incapacity and the unwillingness of the American urban educated middle class to transform the political cities and its administrations into proactive agents for social reform is a key, especially when compared with the powerful German middle class (*Bürgertum*) and its civic hegemony. My research, which has a special focus on Chicago and Frankfurt am Main (as two intellectual centres of middle-class social reform), has been generously sponsored over the years by the *Deutsche Forschungsgemeinschaft*. I would like to thank the colleagues who read, heard, critiqued and improved the original version of this work: Sven Beckert, Axel Jansen, Hans-Jürgen Puhle, Ralf Roth and Axel R. Schäfer.

[2]   M. Weber, *Wirtschaft und Gesellschaft* (Tübingen 1985), 28. (For the English translation see D. C. Hammack, 'Problems in the Historical Study of Power in the

to avoid disadvantages for their own social group should serve as measure for the amount of political power successfully claimed by a social class. And any attempt to analyse a supposedly uneven distribution of power will have to consider the reasons for the powerlessness of classes or groups of actors: 'A (...) class (...) may possess wealth, ability, and high social standing, but it cannot be said to be powerful unless it successfully employs its resources in an effort to secure the policies or nominations it prefers.'[3] In the case of Chicago, which actors were too remote from political power to secure such preferential policies and to avoid disadvantages arising in the general process of urbanisation and from the political conduct of others?

Robert Ezra Park, one of the founders of the Chicago School of Sociology, argued in 1925 that

> recent local studies in Chicago seem to show that the number of competent persons in the community is frequently no real measure of the competency – if one may use that expression in this connection – of the community itself. A high communal intelligence quotient does not always, it seems, insure communal efficiency.[4]

In this somewhat ironic comment Park pointed to an obvious gap between education and politics, between intellect and communal efficiency. He suggested that there was not much of a bond between the City's political leaders and sociologists at the University of Chicago, who already saw their city as a great laboratory of urban modernism and had embarked on groundbreaking research strategies. City Hall had little interest in studies on Chicago and its problems and ignored the work of the university's Department of Sociology and the university-based Local Community Research Committee.[5] Park wanted to explain why Chicago-based Sociology was of such high quality – pointing to its enormous impact on the development of American Sociology in general – and why municipal politics and administration were of such low quality, i.e. hampered by corruption and constitutional restrictions.

But Park's statement had wider implications: He articulated a discomfort which had plagued intellectuals for some time. Not only the small group of university-trained sociologists and political scientists, but a large part of that segment of the urban population which can be considered (and which

---

Cities and Towns of the United States, 1800–1960', *American Historical Review*, 83, 1978, 323–49, esp. 323.

[3] D. C. Hammack, *Power and Society: Greater New York at the Turn of the Century* (New York 1982), 5.

[4] R. E. Park, 'Community Organization and the Romantic Temper', in R. E. Park et al., eds, *The City* (Chicago 1925), 113–25, here 113.

[5] For the complicated story of the relations between the University of Chicago and the political city see S. J. Diner, *A City and Its Universities: Public Policy in Chicago, 1892–1919* (Chapel Hill 1980).

considered itself) to be an 'educated middle class' – professionals, employees, even *rentiers* or medium-sized property holders whose 'capital' was education and a common commitment to cultural high-brow standards – felt alienated from municipal politics.[6] To them the term 'politician' had negative connotations: public office seemed synonymous with corruption. Accordingly, their fight for municipal reform was part of a culture of scepticism between this class and local politicians (and the educated middle class was the most articulate urban branch, the 'informal brain trust', of the wider reform movement known as 'progressivism'[7]). In fact, Chicago progressivism reacted to a political situation in which its supporters had been excluded from municipal politics in City Hall. They articulated more than just contempt for local politicos when they argued that universal (male) suffrage was an obstacle to 'communal intelligence' – 'an immoderate fancy', as Franklin McVeagh, president of the middle-class based 'Citizen's Association' put it.[8] In his seminal study on Chicago politics in the 1930s, Harold F. Gosnell, a political scientist at the University of Chicago, called this middle-class sentiment a 'Jeffersonian skepticism of urban democracy'.[9]

---

[6]   The historians' assessment of an American urban educated middle class counts most of those groups whose German counterparts formed the *Bildungsbürgertum*: professionals and employees whose 'capital' was college or university education. But it is doubtful that the 'educated middle class' can really be seen as a functional equivalent for the German *Bildungsbürgertum*, whose social cohesion derived not only from the social prestige of *Bildung* but also from state sanctioned education certificates and closely connected career paths – both circumstances that are more or less absent in the case of an American educated middle class. For the problem of a comparison between the German *Bildungsbürgertum* and the American professions see T. Goebel, 'The Children of Athena: Chicago Professionals and the Creation of a Credentialed Social Order, 1870–1920', University of Chicago Ph.D. thesis, 1993, 424–68. For an overview on the debates about the German *Bürgertum* see J. Sperber, 'Bürger, Bürgertum, Bürgerlichkeit, Bürgerliche Gesellschaft: Studies of the German (Upper) Middle Class and Its Sociocultural World', *Journal of Modern History*, 69, 1997, 271–97. Unfortunately there has been – with the notable exception of Goebels' study (published in Hamburg in 1996) – little research done on the social history of the middle class(es) in Chicago. See R. Sennett, *Families Against the City: Middle Class Homes of Industrial Chicago, 1872–1890* (Cambridge 1970), did not find many followers, and the most recent study, A. W. Cohen, *The Racketeer's Progress: Chicago and the Struggle for the Modern American Economy, 1900–1940* (Cambridge 2004), focuses on the lower middle class of small businessmen and craft workers.

[7]   This does not mean that 'educated middle class' and 'progressivism' were synonymous: for a discussion about the relationship of professionals and progressivism and especially the shifting loyalties of lawyers between reform and city-hall politics see Goebel, 'Children of Athena', 255 and 268, and R. Hofstadter, *The Age of Reform. From Bryan to F.D.R.* (New York 1955), 154.

[8]   K. Finegold, *Experts and Politicians: Reform Challenges to Machine Politics in New York, Cleveland, and Chicago* (Princeton 1995), 124.

[9]   H. F. Gosnell, *Machine Politics: Chicago Model* (Chicago 1937), VII.

From an educated middle-class point of view the mix of universal male
suffrage, mass immigration, and market-driven urban sprawl seemed to deny
any civic coherence. University of Chicago sociologist Charles Richmond
Henderson claimed at the end of the nineteenth century that 'the city comes
to be a huge aggregation of villages, each with distinct and antagonistic
ideals'. But his conclusion – 'communication becomes difficult' – not only
hinted at the cultural distance between a native-stock middle class and a
foreign-born working class.[10] It pointed to something more than a lack of
civic unity: the problem of effective communication between their own group
and Chicago's political leadership remained a central issue for Henderson
and fellow middle-class progressives. One of the most striking examples of
what Henderson had in mind was that of the progressive social reformers'
fight against unsanitary conditions in working class neighbourhoods:
garbage, filth, and overwhelming smell. After a careful examination of the
franchise system for garbage collection, Hull House founder Jane Addams
submitted a bid for garbage removal in her ward. Her bid was thrown out,
and as a somewhat cynical result, the Mayor appointed the prominent
settlement founder garbage inspector for her ward:

> She kept the job for less than a year (...) The image of the brave little woman
> (...) following the garbage carts to make her neighbourhood safer and cleaner
> established her reputation as a practical and determined reformer (...) But the
> streets did not get much cleaner, and the death rate in the nineteenth ward
> remained one of the highest in the city.[11]

Even more frustrating was the fight against garbage and smell in
Packingtown – the neighbourhood adjacent to the notoriously famous stock
yards. Mary McDowell, since 1894 head resident at a well-known social
settlement in this neighbourhood, was confronted with a devastating problem.
Untreated sewage and garbage were dumped into a branch of the Chicago
River which spanned the northern edge of Packingtown. Because of the
carbolic acid from rotting refuse that bubbled to its surface, this part of the
Chicago River was known as 'Bubbly Creek'. In addition to the disastrous
condition of the Chicago River, Packingtown put up with the biggest
garbage-dump in the whole city. Brick-plant owner and alderman Tom Cary
excavated the clay necessary for making brick, then sold the holes to the city.
In a typical 'Chicago deal', Cary, as owner of the holes, received money from
the city on whose behalf he had decided the deal as an alderman. As a
consequence of ubiquitous garbage and severe air pollution (and bad

---

[10]   C. R. Henderson, *Social Settlements* (New York 1898), 11.
[11]   A. F. Davis, *American Heroine: The Life and Legend of Jane Addams* (New
York 1973), 120–21. See also Addams own account: J. Addams, *Twenty Years at
Hull-House* (New York 1910), 284–9.

Figure 11.1 The University of Chicago, around 1910

The University, opened in 1892 and located in Hyde Park, served as an eminent basis for Chicago's middle class-progressives.

Source: Private courtesy of Marcus Gräser.

politics), Packingtown, in 1900, had one of the highest rates of tuberculosis and infant mortality among Chicago neighbourhoods. One child in three died before it turned two.

This miserable situation caused public uproar. The most prominent objection came from Upton Sinclair, whose novel 'The Jungle' (published in 1906) offered a dramatic portrait of the dreaded life of foreign-born packing-house workers. Sinclair suggested that he reached a national audience's stomach but not their brain. The book might have had some influence on the subsequent meat-packing reform, but it had little impact on living conditions in Packingtown. McDowell was less prominent and acted without a national audience, but for decades she consistently focused on social problems in Packingtown. Because of her fight against garbage and stench by means of petitions, City Hall sit-ins, demonstrations, lawsuits, and committees of investigation, McDowell was known as 'Duchess of Bubbly Creek' and 'The Garbage Lady'. Her success was limited. At the end of her 'tenure' as settlement head resident in 1929, only a quarter of Bubbly Creek had been filled and thus made safe. Over the years, McDowell's initiatives were unable to penetrate an invisible cordon which seemed to encircle decision-makers in City Hall.

And those who did manage to temporarily penetrate that cordon – such as garbage inspector Addams and her assistant – were soon countered by the politicos:

> The cleanliness of the ward was becoming much too popular to suit our all-powerful alderman and, although we felt fatuously secure under the régime of civil service, he found a way to circumvent us by eliminating the position altogether. He introduced an ordinance into the city council which combined the collection of refuse with the cleaning and repairing of the streets, the whole to be placed under a ward superintendent. The office of course was to be filled under civil service regulations but only men were eligible to the examination. Although this latter regulation was afterwards modified in favour of one woman, it was retained long enough to put the nineteenth ward inspector out of office.[12]

Is it correct to describe middle-class reformers as powerless? They were well connected. McDowell and Addams could count on support from an upper-class network. Without the financial support of men such as Julius Rosenwald of Sears and Roebuck, private welfare in Chicago would not have been possible. McDowell's settlement was founded and maintained by the University of Chicago which used the settlement as a laboratory for its Department of Sociology. Upper-class friends funded McDowell's trip to Great Britain and Germany in 1911, where she familiarised herself with modern techniques of waste disposal and with the efficiency of a middle-class dominated municipal governance.[13] McDowell had also supporters in Washington. In the War Department her friend Admiral George Dewey for a moment considered intervening at 'Bubbly Creek'. But he found that the federal government was responsible for navigable rivers only.[14]

While Chicago's middle-class reformers were not isolated socially, they felt isolated from the resources of public administration. They were 'politically' isolated and powerless, at least partially disconnected not only from decision-making but also from important responsibilities in their city – otherwise one would expect that these prominent citizens would have been able to have the garbage taken from their alleys? In the years from 1923 to 1927, during the term of the reform-minded Mayor William Dever, McDowell served as Commissioner of Public Welfare, but even in that

---

[12]   Addams, *Twenty years*, 289.
[13]   For the impact of German municipal reform on the progressives see A. R. Schaefer, *American Progressives and German Social Reform, 1875–1920* (Stuttgart 2000), 79–149, and D. T. Rodgers, *Atlantic Crossings: Social Politics in a Progressive Age* (Cambridge 1998), 112–208.
[14]   For Mary McDowell and her fight against garbage see H. E. Wilson, *Mary McDowell: Neighbor* (Chicago 1928), 140–64; D. L. Miller, *City of the Century: The Epic of Chicago and the Making of America* (New York 1996), 218–20, and M. A. Flanagan, *Seeing with Their Hearts: Chicago Women and the Vision of the Good City, 1871–1933* (Princeton 2002), 96–8.

position she was unable to promote any substantial change in her neighbourhood. That was primarily because her department had no executive functions and served only as a clearing-house for the collection and dissemination of information. The Chicago progressives had long been campaigning for that Department, but its construction resembled a Pyrrhic victory: because of the 'difficulties of communication'. Social reformers had confined themselves to a constant appeal to a somewhat ominous, depersonalised public opinion. They had hoped to reach or stimulate public opinion, which should have played a surrogate role for the non-existence of close ties between middle-class social reformers and the municipal administration.

The reason for this distance between reformers and city politics was that neither the educated middle class nor the bourgeoisie had been able to transform the American city into a synonym for middle-class political hegemony. Mass immigration and the consequent growth of Chicago's population from 500,000 in 1880 to 3.3 Million inhabitants in 1940, quick naturalisation and undisputed general male suffrage resulted in the emergence of a political mass-market and the rise of party machines. Decentralised machine politics was not homogenous but rather fragile and it was based on a delicate balance of factions and local powerhouses. This took place mostly within the two dominant parties which were not self-contained in an ideological or organisational sense. The machine's ensuing flexibility was the reason for its political success. The Democratic Party, which developed the more centralised machine, has dominated the city's political life since 1931. The machine's success was based on patronage and successfully conformed to the expectations of immigrants from the rural, and semi-feudal, areas of southern and eastern Europe. Taking a role similar to a 'commodity upon the market', the vote of the ethnic neighbourhoods had been a power base of machine politics.[15] Precinct committeemen and ward captains served as links between the neighbourhoods and the inner circle of machine bosses. The ward-centred first-past-the-post voting system made a powerful representation for the non-numerous educated middle class in the City Council extremely difficult. Power and success of the party machines rested upon the inclusion of lower middle and working class citizens and even the *Lumpenproletariat*. The machine's long-time success rested not only on corruption, franchise, and the electoral weakness of the middle class; it also resulted from the fragility of socialist parties as well.

Machine politics partially replaced the traditional system of municipal administration which acted simply as a 'co-operative organisation of property owners for the administration of private property'.[16] The machine provided

---

[15] H. W. Zorbaugh, *The Gold Coast and the Slum: A Sociological Study of Chicago's Near North Side* (Chicago 1929), 175.

[16] Simon Sterne, a Reformer from New York, quoted in R. L. Einhorn, 'The Civil War and Municipal Government in Chicago', in M. A. Vinovskis, ed., *Toward a*

goods and service to the neighbourhoods, and voters provided personal and political loyalty in return. The party that captured the City Council and the office of the Mayor regarded appointive public offices and jobs as booty, and distributed them to loyal party followers. This was in striking contrast to German municipal politics in the nineteenth century with its close ties between the middle class, the City Council, and municipal administration. Because of class or property-based franchise restrictions, German municipal politics had been dominated by upper- and middle-class councilmen, and a majority of municipal administrators were recruited from the middle class (*Bürgertum*). Even though Theodore Roosevelt's jeer about 'aldermanic liquorsellers' may be too strong a characterisation, machine-dominated city councils in American cities consisted mostly of representatives of the petty bourgeoisie or the lower middle class in general. With the exception of the short-lived Progressive Party which gathered around Roosevelt's presidential candidacy in 1912 and had a stronghold in Chicago there did not exist in Chicago a middle class or 'bourgeois' political party. Both the Republican Party and to a lesser degree the Democratic Party had bourgeois and educated middle-class 'branches', but they cannot be considered parties of the bourgeoisie or the educated middle class.[17] Both parties had to seek votes in a political mass market which ruled out class-oriented or ideologically charged campaigns. The machine's far-reaching practice of inclusion and the opportunities offered by machine politics to second-generation immigrants deprived the middle class of potential allies.[18] The machine was a product of a democratised voting system and of immigration. It was interested in the 'masses' as long as these masses could be organised to its end. On election day, neither those segments of the population which could not be organised such as bohemians nor those who were educated but insignificant in number such as the 'experts' posed a threat to the machine.

Considering the connection between 'reform success and machine failure' or reform failure and machine success, Chicago's powerful and enduring machine as well as its 'politics of frustration' vis-á-vis the educated middle class may have been unique.[19] But even in Chicago the 'gradations and groupings of urban society were able to negotiate their interrelationships in a

---

Social History of the Civil War: Exploratory Essays (Cambridge 1990), 117–38, esp. 120.

[17]   Goebel, 'Children of Athena', 256.

[18]   For the various attempts of social-reform progressives to build up something like a coalition of educated middle class and 'honest', machine-resistant working class see M. Gräser, 'Arbeiterschaft, Bürgertum und welfare state building. Überlegungen zu einem Vergleich der kommunalen Sozialreform in den USA und in Deutschland 1880–1940', *Mitteilungsblatt des Instituts zur Erforschung der europäischen Arbeiterbewegung*, 22, 1999, 59–84, esp. 82.

[19]   Finegold, *Experts*, 13. For an overview on research and debates about the struggle between reformers and the machine see ibid. 10–13, and Goebel, 'Children of Athena', 253.

very wide variety of ways'.[20] Bourgeois magnates did quite well without a bourgeois party. It was enough to secure 'close ties to organisational politicians who could provide the air raids, franchise grants, and police protection of strike-breakers'.[21] Even progressive social reformers occasionally shied away from a policy of confronting the machine: some co-operated with Anton Cermak, 'founding father' of the multinational Democratic machine and President of the Cook County Board of Commissioners in the 1920s. He used 'political reform (...) as a political tool' and so did social reformers.[22] In the case of the reformed County Bureau of Public Welfare, Cermak could present himself as an able and modern administrator. This was why social reformers got an institution that stimulated the ongoing process of professionalisation in the field of social work.[23]

Successful institution-building as a result of co-operation between reformers and machine politicos, however, was rare. The fact remained that Chicago's 'best men' and also women were not acting as a local 'governing class'.[24] In this context, it is inaccurate to blame 'the better element' for not fulfilling 'its mission'.[25] General male suffrage mercilessly diminished the presence of the educated middle class in the City Council and in urban politics in general. The dominant machine in the city had no interest in a governance made up by professionalised bureaucrats. The educated middle class was therefore blocked from staffing the municipal administration. Machine-dominated administrations usually hired experts – mostly civil engineers – for positions in the water works, the sewer system etc., but this remained a co-optation of individuals, not an inclusion of the educated middle class.

The reason for Chicago's 'administrative nihilism', however, originated not only in machine politics but also in the complicated relationship between Chicago and the State of Illinois.[26] The state and its General Assembly (with a majority of representatives from rural, downstate Illinois) exercised central legislative control over the city. Chicago's administrative competence was small: Illinois had not provided the city with an effective legal machinery for

---

[20]   J. Smith, 'Urban Elites c. 1830–1930 and Urban History', in *Urban History*, 27, 2000, 255–75, esp. 259.

[21]   Finegold, *Experts*, 125.

[22]   P. M. Green, 'Anton Cermak: The Man and His Machine', in P. M. Green and M. G. Holli, eds, *The Mayors: The Chicago Political Tradition* (Carbondale 1987), 99–110, esp. 103. Cook County consisted of the City of Chicago and just a few suburbs.

[23]   W. S. Reynolds, 'Cook County Comes to Order', *The Survey*, 56, 1926, 244–5.

[24]   J. Bryce, *The American Commonwealth* (New York 1888), cit. after Hammack, 'Problems', 329.

[25]   M. Ostrogorski, *Democracy and the Organization of Political Parties,* 2 vols. (New York 1902), vol. 2, 433.

[26]   W. D. P. Bliss, *The New Encyclopedia of Social Reform* (New York 1908), 8.

home rule. The progressive charter movement of 1906 and 1907 had attempted to bring home rule to the city. A charter was drafted from a middle-class point of view. It was not only supposed to make Chicago free from state interference, it also tried to establish rules for responsible public spending. But the charter movement failed – for several reasons of which not the least had been a typical urban progressive inability of sound coalition-building.

There was no second chance after 1918. Large segments of the city's middle class migrated to the suburbs, a process which can be described as an escape from the city. This escape made Chicago even more proletarian and even more Catholic than before. Chicago's rapid growth was partly a result of the incorporation of several townships and villages. This process, which had helped spur Chicago's industrial development by providing open space, came to an abrupt halt in 1893. Having grown to its limits, the city was unable to talk an adjoining town (suburb) into joining the metropolis and to give up independence. Most of the suburbs were a functional appendix of their big neighbour. Confronted with the prospect of being swallowed up by Chicago, these towns became stubborn and came to see the advantages of being autonomous. Having escaped the city, the middle class was unwilling to give up what they had secured for themselves in suburbia: an efficient, cheap and clean municipal administration. The congruence between middle-class interests and political will, of course, helped stabilise suburban social homogeneity. Chicago with its mix of widespread corruption, its badly reputed administration, and its restricted financial manoeuvrability was unable to offer incentives to its suburban neighbours. For the twentieth century, the metropolis was accordingly confined to the area between the lake in the east and a hostile suburban belt in all other directions. Progressivism had lost its inner city basis for good.[27] 'Legally, Chicago is an infant', the political scientist Albert Lepawsky concluded in 1935, and its municipal competence remained small.[28]

Is it possible to detect a correlation between the politically disconnected middle class and the puny size of the city's public bureaucracy? From a comparative point of view, especially from a German point of view, the connection between an early bureaucratisation and a belated democratisation seems evident. The American example suggests a coupling of an early success of democratisation, a middle class that could therefore not count, like its German counterpart, on some class or property-based franchise restrictions, which would have helped to establish upper- and middle-class political hegemony. In most European countries the middle class with its capital of education and expert knowledge staffed the bureaucracy. This

---

[27] For the weird situation of suburban residents who still claimed to be Chicago reformers see Zorbaugh, *Gold Coast*, 269, and A. R. Hirsch, *Making the Second Ghetto: Race and Housing in Chicago 1940–1960* (Chicago 1998), 135.

[28] A. Lepawsky, *Home Rule for Metropolitan Chicago* (Chicago 1935), 1.

seems to suggest that a bureaucratisation that antedates democratisation strengthens the middle class and, as a kind of compensation for denied political rights, even the organised segments of the working class. Step by step, both a middle class and a working class transformed German (municipal) bureaucracies into agents, not for democracy, but for social reform. After the democratisation of the municipal franchise in 1918, the middle class in Germany could recover some of its former political strength because of the indisputable position of middle-class professionals in local bureaucracies. The American way of early democratisation with ensuing bureaucratic nihilism seems to sustain upper-class and business interests of unrestricted access to markets, on the one hand, and the patronage-minded parts of the petty bourgeoisie and of a foreign born working class, on the other.

Limited administrative competence was in the interest of the machine: politics based on patronage needed a non-professionalised administration and low profile jobs for its clientele. Bureaucratic progress was not part of its design. For Chicago's long-time Mayor Carter Harrison II 'as for most politicians of the period, expertise was inferior to practical experience'.[29] 'The expert', Harrison told the Conference of Mayors in 1914, 'fails to take into consideration the human equation'.[30] Governmental fragmentation, a negligence of expertise and experts and the rise of machine politics out of party fragmentation complemented each other: Chicago's 'jumble of boards and districts' with 'independent powers and separate accounts' served as a useful basis for patronage and for the mayor's divide-and-conquer policy.[31] It also allowed rival politicians to maintain their organisations even when they were out of power at the top.[32] The weakness of the municipal bureaucracy and that of the educated middle class thus complemented each other. The educated middle class cultivated a strong anti-bureaucratic sentiment, because they knew very well that once democratisation had taken place it required political power to staff and to control a bureaucracy.[33]

The lack of an efficient municipal bureaucracy and of administrative control techniques even came to affect the life of a wealthy bourgeoisie. It was unable to protect the social exclusiveness of their neighbourhoods. Since the middle of the nineteenth century, industrialised European cities had been socially segregated. But in Chicago, the dividing line between class and neighbourhood was much more in flux. The most famous upper-class

---

[29]   Finegold, *Experts*, 135.
[30]   Cit. after ibid.
[31]   Ibid. 29, and Ostrogorski, *Democracy*, 172.
[32]   Finegold, *Experts*, 29.
[33]   See M. Gräser, 'Demokratie versus Bürokratie. Bildprogramm und Politik der settlement-Bewegung in Chicago am Ende des 19. Jahrhunderts', in M. Gräser et. al., eds, *Staat, Nation, Demokratie. Traditionen und Perspektiven moderner Gesellschaften. Festschrift für Hans-Jürgen Puhle* (Göttingen 2001), 115–28.

residential area in the late nineteenth century – the Prairie Street – lost its appeal in the first three decades of the twentieth century. The City of Chicago's zoning ordinances were put in place too late to prevent the opening of brothels and cheap nursing homes. The social homogeneity and stability in upper- and middle-class residential areas, which in most European cities was based on the political power of its residents and efficient zoning ordinances, which regulated patterns of utilisation of land resources and inner city districts, remained absent from Chicago. Some zoning policy was introduced in 1923 but was ultimately less efficient. If the wealthy bourgeoisie was unable to protect the social cohesion of their neighbourhoods, what about its leverage in city politics? It made sense to attribute the relative failure of urban zoning ordinances in America to 'the lack of an enlightened public or official opinion in support of some of the broad social purposes of zoning'.[34] This absence of an 'enlightened public' was due to the restricted access to the municipal administration by that segment of the middle class (and an upper class) which was educated and considered itself to be 'enlightened'.

Was it impossible to defeat the machine? In the heyday of Chicago progressivism, between 1900 and 1917, the educated middle class and its political associations, particularly the Municipal Voters' League and the City Club, scored successes in the fight against the plebeian machine. Corrupt aldermen were stigmatised in public and beaten in elections. And during the reform-oriented administrations of Mayors Edward Dunne (1905–1907) and William Dever (1923–1927) prominent progressives were appointed to public office. Addams served as a member of the School Board, and McDowell held office as a Commissioner of Public Welfare. But these reform administrations were short-lived. The mayors were not re-elected and they left no legacy. The Chicago progressives never took the city. They never had a popular progressive Mayor like Hazen Pingree in Detroit, or Tom Johnson in Cleveland, or Samuel Jones and Brand Whitlock in Toledo. Significantly, the candidacy of Charles E. Merriam for mayor in the general election of 1911 and in the Republican primary of 1919 failed – not only because 'University-trained experts were (...) unpopular' but also because his campaign was, especially in its 'ethnocultural attitudes', quite traditional and hence not very successful in building a coalition between native stock reformers and foreign stock ethnic groups.[35]

The political will of the educated middle class thus had to confine itself to associations and clubs, hence to organisations which in contrast to a party did not seek to win a majority at the poll and offices for its members. Instead, they tried to influence public opinion and set up their own private political

---

[34]   R. Whitten, 'Zoning', in E. R. A. Seligman, ed., *Encyclopedia of the Social Sciences*, vol. 15 (New York 1935), 538–9.
[35]   Finegold, *Experts*, 161–3.

Figure 11.2 The Art Institute of Chicago, around 1930

The institute was one the finest achievements of Chicago's bourgeoisie and its educated middle class: Two lions are protecting the Art Institute against the rough city and its 'politicians'.

Source: Private courtesy of Marcus Gräser.

sphere. These clubs and associations overlapped little with the governing bodies which were responsible for political decisions. Certainly, middle-class associations and middle-class money filled gaps left by the not-so-competent municipal administration: most of the city's welfare activities were undertaken or sponsored by private institutions or associations, and major cultural institutions like the Art Institute or the Chicago Symphony Orchestra were founded and supported by private individuals. The impact of these institutions, however, was limited to the upper and middle class itself. The main thrust of these institutions was not to gain cultural control but to set cultural standards for their own kind.[36] Much like a neighbourhood machine alderman, the middle class focused 'on the fragment rather than the whole'.[37]

---

[36]   See S. Beckert, *The Monied Metropolis: New York City and the Consolidation of the American Bourgeoisie, 1850–1896* (Cambridge and New York 2001), 256.

[37]   J. C. Teaford, *The Unheralded Triumph: City Government in America, 1870–1900* (Baltimore 1984), 25. For a critique of Teafords optimistic portrait of the American city and its administrators see M. Gräser, 'Chicago 1880–1940: Urbanisierung ohne administrative Kompetenz?', *ZENAF Arbeits- und Forschungsberichte*, 1, 2001, 5–6.

Was it true, as one famous machine politician once said, that Chicago 'ain't ready for reform yet'?[38] In fact, some change occurred, but it was prompted from the outside. In the early 1930s the Great Depression hit Chicago with tremendous force. In 1932 the city was bankrupt, with 30 per cent of all men and 24 per cent of all women unemployed. The municipal election in 1931 was a sea change. As a consequence of the Democratic Party's victory, decentralised machine politics was replaced by a more centralised political machine. From now on, the mayor could act as a key figure in linking administration and machine. This in itself would not have bridged the gap between state laws and city needs. Once again, help came from outside. Franklin Delano Roosevelt's New Deal established an unprecedented link between big cities and the federal government. Central legislative control by the state lost much of its relevance because it could now be bypassed via Washington. Mutual interests were involved. Roosevelt needed the electorate in the big cities, and without federal help the cities could not have overcome the effects of the depression. Federal money, emergency relief for the unemployed, massive funds for public employment programs, housing projects, as well as the Social Security Act of 1935 changed the face of the cities, and forced them to establish bureaucracies, which were viewed as agencies of the evolving welfare state. The middle class and its professionals were now making headway. But they no longer sought to cause change as a political collective. Instead, they were needed as experts. In this way, the municipal politics of the New Deal were quite different from the old style machine politics. But the old machine and the New Deal had something in common: both favoured big numbers, and both liked organised interests. The educated middle class, of course, fit neither of these categories.

An analysis of this situation, in which no single group had exclusive access to the city's power, as 'pragmatic pluralism' might successfully characterise a 'politics without hegemony'.[39] It has to be added, however, that access to political power inside the political framework provided by state constitution and city charter was unequally distributed. It is important to keep in mind this uneven distribution of power *within* pragmatic pluralism when trying to explain the 'collective failure to institutionalise the exercise of pragmatic pluralism'.[40] The de-facto exclusion of the educated middle class from political decision-making significantly distinguished Chicago as well as other American cities from northern and western European cities. As a consequence, many progressives became even more doubtful about mass

---

[38]   W. J. Grimshaw, 'Is Chicago Ready for Reform? – or, a New Agenda for Harold Washington', in M. G. Holli and P. M. Green, eds, *The Making of the Mayor: Chicago 1983* (Grand Rapids 1984), 141–65, esp. 141.

[39]   B. A. Ruble, *Second Metropolis: Pragmatic Pluralism in Gilded Age Chicago, Silver Age Moscow, and Meji Osaka* (Cambridge 2001), 319–55.

[40]   Ibid. 357.

democracy. Their scepticism had much to do with their peculiar situation outside of machine politics and, in fact, little in common with a Jeffersonian longing for a pre-industrial society and a less complex social order; most of the progressives remained optimists about an urban and industrialised society. The discomfort with urban, machine-style democracy did not lead to an anti-democratic political attitude. In order to improve the role of the educated middle class within a democratised political sphere it was necessary to build coalitions with the 'masses' and to engage in education and social welfare. Progressivism was progressive to the extent that the fight for political power by an educated middle class did result in a strengthened democracy.

CHAPTER TWELVE

Patrician Elites and Power in Nineteenth-Century Montreal and Quebec City

Brian Young

A pair of vignettes helps introduce this exploration of patrician power in two North American cities. In 1871, two judges, prominent members of the families we meet below, were among 211 individuals who contributed to the City of Quebec Agricultural Society's annual exhibition. Judge Jean-Thomas Taschereau paid two Dollars for his annual membership and gave five Dollars to the exhibition prize fund. More parsimonious, his fellow judge Thomas McCord contributed thirty cents for exhibition prizes.[1] In 1789, almost a century earlier, the Society had been founded and among the 'eight English and eight Canadian gentlemen' chosen as directors were members of the same families: Gabriel-Élzéar Taschereau and a McCord ancestor, George Davidson. The exhibition had two goals that remained constant over a century: judging showcase stock produced on gentlemen estates and, for the popular classes, the 'encouragement of Agriculture in all of its branches in this district'.[2] Over 8,000 people a day attended the 1871 exhibition on the garrison cricket field, visiting an industrial display in the nearby skating and curling rinks, a regatta in the harbour, and a dog show, reputedly the first ever held in Quebec.

The second event occurred six years later and just a few blocks away when workmen in the basement of the Quebec Basilica discovered the remains of Monsigneur François de Laval, first bishop of Quebec, who had died in 1708. Archbishop Elzéar-Alexandre Taschereau, grandson and brother of the Taschereau mentioned above, took charge of organising re-burial of the bishop's remains, this time in the Seminary of Quebec, an institution founded by the Bishop in 1663 and the bedrock of Catholicism in Quebec. Although the Seminary is part of an ecclesiastical compound shared by the Basilica, a circuitous procession through the upper city was chosen

---

[1]   Canadian Institute for Historical Microreproductions (CIHM), A01816, *City of Quebec Agricultural Society, 1871.*
[2]   CIHM, A01816, *The Centenary Volume of the Literary and Historical Society of Quebec 1824–1924* (Quebec City 1924), 128–9.

that allowed thousands to view a spectacle 'unlike anything the city had ever seen'.[3] With its advance punctuated with salutes from garrison cannon, the procession was headed by Archbishop Taschereau, followed by the Papal envoy, the Archbishop of St. Boniface who had travelled from western Canada, the Premier of Quebec (a Protestant), and government, judicial, and native representatives.[4] Symbolic stops at St. Patrick's Church and at the chapels of the Ursulines, Jesuits, and Hôtel Dieu hospital permitted recognition of several constituencies: Irish Catholics, the Jesuits recently readmitted to Canada, the city's most prominent nunnery with its model of female virtues, and national societies like the St. Jean Baptiste Society.

How do an agricultural exhibition, the re-burial of a seventeenth-century bishop, and the sustained presence of two families contribute to an understanding of power in Montreal and Quebec? In fact, adjudicating the teeth of horses, determining place, costumes, and symbolic noise in a procession, and honouring the bones of an eighteenth-century bishop are, in a city landscape not transformed by department stores, mass transit, factories, and Olmstedian public parks, important elements in the establishment of a civic legitimacy and hegemony. Certainly, a dog show, the convent chapel, and a thirty-cent contribution for prizes, have little in common with traditional treatments of power in Canadian cities, which, until the last decade, were usually situated in what David Harvey aptly calls the 'maelstrom of capitalist progress'.[5] Classics in Canadian historiography such as Harold Innis's 'Fur Trade in Canada', Arthur Lower's 'Great Britain's Woodyard', and Donald Creighton's 'Commercial Empire of the St. Lawrence' integrate Montreal and Quebec into the Laurentian thesis. Assuming a certain uniformity in the metropolitan condition, this interpretation gives centrality to merchant capitalism and to imperial (as opposed to local) conditions.[6] Gerald Tulchinsky's study of Montreal merchants and George Bervin's equivalent study in Quebec along with the multiple works of Michael Bliss form part of an entrepreneurial historiographical tradition that gives primacy to individual acts, to a certain geographic determinism, and to the centrality of commercial activity along the St. Lawrence. Inevitably, these interpretations focus on the merchants and other capitalists, often Scots, who exercised what one historian called 'raw power': from this perspective, ethnicity and identity are easily simplified to ethnic determinism or to a Canadian reworking of the religion and rise of

---

[3]   This event is drawn from R. Rudin, *Founding Fathers: Celebration of Champlain and Laval in the Streets of Quebec, 1878–1908* (Toronto 2003), 12.

[4]   Ibid. 44–6.

[5]   D. Harvey, *Paris: Capital of Modernity* (London 2003), 295.

[6]   For the Laurentian thesis see W. L. Morton, 'Clio in Canada: The Interpretation of Canadian History', in C. Berger, ed., *Approaches to Canadian History* (Toronto 1967), 42–9.

capitalism debate.[7] Even Western Canada, well outside the St. Lawrence nexus, had what Alan Artibise characterised for Winnipeg as a 'city-building process' in which a business elite dominated.[8] Probably the most influential historian of Montreal in his generation, Paul-André Linteau can be situated in this tradition. Describing Montreal as one of the 'great cities of the continent' and the main 'foyer' of Francophones in America, he emphasises promoters, 'Two Montreals' and the central place of the Anglophone bourgeoisie, and the 'tacit accord' between that dominant group and its collaborating Francophone counterpart:

> The grande bourgeoisie [of Montreal at the turn of the twentieth century] largely consisted of businessmen who formed the financial elite of the country, although a few big business lawyers, doctors, judges or university professors occupying a dominant position in their profession and who could show important wealth, slipped in. Wealth in effect was the most visible characteristic of this group.[9]

A final characteristic of this historiography is the emphasis on the abrupt, watershed effect of industrialism. In his atlas, Jean-Claude Robert describes how 'in Montreal, as in the majority of North American cities of the period, industrialisation completely upset social relations' built around institutions such as family or church.[10]

Writing on these subjects in the 1970s from a Marxist perspective, I too had a 'watch their hands' economic-history bias in which I emphasised English-speaking capitalists, a collaborative French-Canadian bourgeoisie, and the monied wealth of the Roman Catholic Church in Montreal. In early studies, I placed promoters, their capital accumulation and the power of

---

[7]   Ch. Moore, 'Interpreting History', *The Beaver*, February/March 2000, 85; G. J. J. Tulchinsky, *The River Barons: Montreal businessmen and the growth of industry and transportation* (Toronto 1977), and M. Bliss, *Northern Enterprise: Five Centuries of Canadian Business* (Toronto 1987). For the development of urban history in Canada see G. Stelter and A. F. J. Artibise, *The Canadian City: Essays in Urban History* (Ottawa 1977), especially the article by Gilbert Stelter. See also the *Urban History Review/Revue d'histoire urbaine*, particularly the special issue on Montreal in the nineteenth century (*Urban History Review/Revue d'histoire urbaine*, 31, No. 1, Fall 2002). Fernand Ouellet has been the most persistent in relating ethnicity to nationalism and economic conditions. See F. Ouellet *Lower Canada 1791–1840: Social Change and Nationalism* (Toronto 1980).

[8]   A. Artibise, *Winnipeg: a social history of urban growth 1874–1914*, 2 vols. (Montreal 1975), vol. 1, 36.

[9]   P.-A. Linteau, *Brève histoire de Montréal* (Montreal 1992), 7; P.-A. Linteau, *Histoire de Montréal depuis la Confédération* (Montreal 1992), 48, and 166–7. See also P.-A. Linteau, *Maisonneuve ou comment des promoteurs fabriquent une ville, 1883–1918* (Montreal 1981).

[10]   J.-C. Robert, 'Montréal 1821–71. Aspects de l'urbanisation', École des hautes études, Paris, Doctorat de 3e cycle, 1977, 305.

Figure 12.1 Montreal from the mountains, around 1870

This view of Montreal emphasizes the persistent physical pre-industrial characteristics of the city in the late nineteenth century. In the foreground is the campus of McGill University while in the background church spires and the courthouse dome dominate the horizon.

Source: Alexander Henderson photograph, National Archives of Canada, No. 147423.

steam and rail as defining features of the histories of both Montreal and Quebec: bled of significant gender or cultural content, the bourgeois family in those studies was reduced to educational advantage, money, and international business and professional networks.

Labour, cultural and gender history, the social history expounded by 'History Workshop', and debate over the place of discourse and modernity in the urban experience have changed the writing of Canadian urban history. The works of Leonore Davidoff, Catherine Hall and Mary Ryan have given centrality to family, to the place of women as 'hidden investments', to the significance of religion as a cultural phenomenon, and to the presence of women in public space.[11] As I began to grapple with issues of moral landscapes, museums, bourgeois memory, and the writing of history, I was

---

[11]   L. Davidoff and C. Hall, *Family Fortunes: Men and women of the English middle class 1780–1850* (London 1987), 272; C. Hall, *White, Male and Middle Class: Explorations in Feminism and History* (London 1992), and M. Ryan, *Cradle of the Middle Class: The Family in Oneida County, New York, 1790–1865* (Cambridge 1981).

particularly struck by Bonnie Smith's insistence on the political conservatism of many bourgeois women.[12] And, in the muddy waters of post-modernism and post-colonialism, David Harvey has been provocative in broadening his focus on land rents and class structure to a larger culturalist interpretation of urban power that encompasses art and literature, Honoré Balzac's Paris, and 'moments' like the uprisings of 1848 or the construction of Sacre-Cœur on Montmartre. A host of intellectuals, mostly European, have helped Canadian urban historians re-think the implications of public space, material culture, institutions, and the relationship of culture, class, and urban power: Philip Corrigan and Derek Sayer, Carl Schorske, Jürgen Habermas, and John Berger have been of particular importance to me. Robert J. Morris and Peter Clark, using British examples, have shaped our understanding of urban civil society, voluntarism, and bourgeois identity.[13] Writing on the Cape Colony, Robert Ross has been influential in showing how cultural phenomena such as domestic relations, body language, food, and funerals are at the intersections of race, gender, and social and economic power.[14]

Of course, I have not invented the wheel in asking these questions in a central Canadian context. Louise Dechêne, a former colleague at McGill University and author of the classic on pre-industrial Montreal, always insisted on the centrality of feudal European institutions in Montreal and their 'drag' in the face of frontier and new North American conditions.[15] In an underestimated article, Paul-André Linteau and Jean-Claude Robert pointed the way, arguing for the power of landed property in Montreal, much of it held by Francophone patricians, in some of the ways suggested below. In multiple works, historical geographer Sherry Olson has shown the relationship of ethnicity, social change, and neighbourhood.[16] As early as 1992, Cecelia Morgan, Lykke de la Cour, and Mariana Valverde were contesting traditional Canadian interpretations of power such as the Laurentian thesis, what they called 'the masculinisation of public power', and in the same volume Ian Radforth and Allan Greer suggested that power in

---

[12]   B. Smith, *Ladies of the Leisure Class: The Bourgeoisies of Northern France in the Nineteenth Century* (Princeton 1981), 8–9.

[13]   R. J. Morris, 'Voluntary Societies and British Urban Elites', *Historical Journal*, 26, 1983, 95–118; and R. J. Morris, 'Clubs, Societies and Associations', in F. M. L. Thompson, ed., *The Cambridge Social History of Britain, 1750–1950*, vol. 3: *Social Agencies and Institutions* (Cambridge 1990), 395–443, and P. Clark, *British Clubs and Societies 1580–1800: The Origins of an Associational World* (Oxford 2000).

[14]   R. Ross, *Status and Respectability in the Cape Colony 1750–1870: A Tragedy of Manners* (Cambridge 1999). See also K. M. Brown, *Good Wives, Nasty Wenches and Anxious Patriarchs: Gender, Race, and Power in Colonial Virginia* (Chapel Hill 1996).

[15]   L. Dechêne, *Habitants et marchands de Montréal au XVIIe siècle* (Paris 1974).

[16]   See for example, her work with David Hanna on rents in Montreal in the easily accessible L. Dechêne and D. Hanna, *Historical Atlas of Canada: The Land Transformed*, 3 vols. (Toronto 1993), vol. 2, plate 49.

Canada was 'coming to be a central preoccupation of the historian'.[17] From quite different viewpoints, Canadian colleagues Keith Walden, Ronald Rudin, and H. V. Nelles have brought the cultural history insights of Jackson Lears, Roger Chartier, and Lynn Hunt to the study of Canadian cities.[18] Two recent works provide nuance for the concept of urban landed wealth and forms of bourgeois power. Richard Rodger's 'Transformation of Edinburgh' (2001) is path-finding for Quebec studies in showing how feudal forms of landholding and of institutional property ownership determined land use, affected social relations, and contributed to perpetuating ecclesiastical and patrician power.[19] Finally, the work of Brian Lewis is important in showing varieties of power as exercised by different layers in the bourgeoisie. Using Lancashire, he demonstrates a disunited bourgeoisie whose incoherence 'was a sign of strength, not of weakness' in the establishment of bourgeois hegemony.[20]

In this contribution, I briefly treat examples of patrician power in the two most important cities on the St. Lawrence River, a major gateway to the North American interior. As a social construction, patricians are characterised more by family, birth, status, and respectability than by enormous capitalist wealth: given the lack of a formal aristocracy in post-conquest Canada, their roots may have been professional or merchant but their social instincts were shaped by seigniorial privilege, inherited landed wealth, position in Anglican or Roman Catholic hierarchies, local status (as opposed to international recognition) and forms of power filtered through honours, profession, militia, or voluntary associations. Although urban in the context studied here, their discourse and actions retained a feudal resonance that emphasised respect, authority, honours, and the application of historic legal, landed, and religious privileges.

Three elements provide comparative points with other contributions in this volume. First are the ethnic and religious characteristics of Montreal and Quebec. These are given human and patrician face here in the McCords, Ulster Scot in origin and rooted first in Quebec and then in Protestant Montreal, and the Taschereau – Catholic, French and bastions of the patrician community in Quebec. Second is the persistence of pre-industrial legal, religious, and seigniorial institutions in mid-nineteenth century St. Lawrence cities. I like David Harvey's term 'feudal residuals'.[21] This permitted

---

[17]   A. Greer and I. Radforth, *Colonial Leviathan: State Formation in Mid-Nineteenth Century Canada* (Toronto 1992), 163 and 9.

[18]   K. Walden, *Becoming Modern in Toronto: the Industrial Exhibition and the Shaping of a Late Victorian Culture* (Toronto 1997); H. V. Nelles, *The Art of Nation Building* (Toronto 1998); Rudin, *Founding Fathers.*

[19]   R. Rodger, *The Transformation of Edinburgh: Land, Property and Trust in the Nineteenth Century* (Cambridge 2001), esp. 69–122.

[20]   B. Lewis, *The Middlemost and the Milltown: Bourgeois Culture and Politics in Early Industrial England* (Palo Alto 2001), 249.

[21]   D. Harvey, *The Urban Experience* (Baltimore 1989), 91.

extended power to an elite rooted in the culture and privileges of these institutions. New France was built on the seventeenth and eighteenth centuries ancien-regime model of its metropolis. This included banal mills, seminaries integrated to their Parisian mother houses, an official state church, and a customary legal system. Despite hesitations after the conquest (1763) and continuing contestation from British merchants, Westminster respected the integrity of these institutions, theoretically separating the French-settled St. Lawrence region from areas being settled by English-speakers in which freehold tenure and common law were applied. Their dismantling would await the assumption of political power by a Canadian elite after 1840. This feudal drag occurred in two cities which, by the mid nineteenth century were marked by early industrialisation, the transportation revolution, heavy Irish immigration, and state modernisation in forms like universal education, registry offices, and elected municipal governments. These phenomena occurred in the same time-window as the collapse of British mercantilism and disengagement of the metropolis from British North America.

A final theme is insistence on the importance of comparative urban studies. While old hat to European urban historians raised on the mother's milk of comparisons of cities like Budapest and Vienna, comparative studies of Canadian cities are few. Sister cities in their history and structures and always treated as integral to a Quebec national state, Montreal and Quebec were (and still are) engaged in furious interurban competition. Pre-industrial institutions may have persisted with greater strength in Quebec, climaxing only late in the nineteenth century with the dismantling of seigniorialism (two decades later than in Montreal), with construction of a direct railway between Quebec and the interior (a quarter century after Montreal had its Grand Trunk to both the Atlantic and American midwest), and with the delay by decades in building a bridge over the St. Lawrence (similar to that built at Montreal in 1860). Although by-passed as federal capital in favour of Ottawa, Montreal was the financial and industrial capital of the pan-Canadian state. One possible result of these structural differences was that the patrician elite retained influence longer in Quebec. With energy, the Taschereau produced Canada's first cardinal, Canada's first French Canadian chief justice of the Supreme Court, and, in the twentieth century, a provincial premier. In Montreal, the magnitude of insurance, tobacco, and railway fortunes, expansion of the popular classes and populism, consumerism, and the non-conformist Protestant churches, dwarfed traditional forms of patrician power in which pew, bench, friendship association, and male and female leadership in voluntary associations had been hallmarks of power. After a run stretching back to the conquest and expiry in 1892–1893 of its 99-year seigniorial leases on an urban fief, the McCord family of Montreal lapsed into effeteness and ultimate extinction.

Urban situations

Some 1,000 kilometres from the Atlantic, Quebec's magnificent site straddles
a promontory which dominates the narrowing of the St. Lawrence estuary.
Tides facilitate shipping, port activities, and shipbuilding on the flats along
the river while cliffs protect the citadel and fortifications of the upper town.[22]
From its establishment in 1608, Quebec served as a trade centre both with the
metropolis and in triangular exchanges of furs, rum, and manufactured goods
with France, the West Indies, and the French-controlled interior. It was the
centre of nineteenth-century shipbuilding in Canada as well as of the timber
trade. Until late in the nineteenth century, Quebec was the principal port for
British North America with dock, warehousing, and shipbuilding activities
spread along its fifteen-kilometre shoreline. Under both French and British
regimes, Quebec also served as political and religious capital of the colony.
One measure of its geo-political importance across the colony is the
Séminaire de Québec, which had a 177-year monopoly on the training of
priests until a competing theological college was opened in Montreal in 1840.
Nomination of a first bishop in 1658 gave the bishop's palace in Quebec
ecclesiastical power over French North America, a power only ceded with the
conquest and then establishment of the diocese of Montreal in 1836. On the
Protestant side, the Anglican diocese of Quebec, established in 1793, retained
control until the founding of the diocese of Toronto in 1839 and Montreal in
1850. Finally, Quebec's strategic site ensured it primacy as the principal
French fortress in North America. Indeed, it was on the plains just outside the
city walls that New France's destiny was played out. French defeat in 1759
did not alter the city's military importance, however, and the British military
presence remained a critical social and economic reality over the next
century: an annual average of 1,900 men, officers, and their families were
lodged in the Quebec garrison from 1814 to 1840.[23]

More than three hundred kilometres upstream from Quebec at the break-
of-bulk point at the foot of the Lachine Rapids, Montreal was established in
1642 as a religious mission. While Quebec was retained by the crown,
Montreal was, by 1663, part of a seigniory held by the Seminary of Saint-
Sulpice. This seventeenth-century union of parish, religious community, and
seigniory remained central to power relationships in Montreal. Indeed, within
the city walls some 20 per cent of urban space was controlled by religious

---

[22]   S. Courville and R. Garon, *Atlas historique du Québec. Québec ville et
capitale* (Sainte-Foy 2001), 9.
[23]   For the history of Quebec see D. T. Ruddel, *Quebec City 1765–1832: The
evolution of a colonial town* (Hull 1991), and Courville and Garon, *Atlas historique*.
For the British military presence see Claudette Lacelle, *La garnison britannique dans
al ville de Québec d'après les journaux de 1764 à 1840* (Ottawa 1976), 41.

communities.[24] In the industrialising city two centuries later, the Seminary was still far from a spent economic force: construction of schools and social institutions, their increasingly valuable suburban seigniorial domains, their purchasing and employment, their double strength as seignior and parish priest, and their investments of capital in municipalities and private companies, gave them urban power that far surpassed the spiritual and social effects one might anticipate in a North American urban church. Although the city's fortifications were demolished in the early nineteenth century, Montreal, like Quebec, had an important British military presence until 1871. In the decades following the conquest, Montreal's strategic economic position allowed it to compete with the Hudson's Bay Company for control of the continental trade in furs. The commercial influence of its entrepreneurs, largely English-speaking and often Scot, only expanded as the inauguration of banks and canals and then railways and manufactures gave the city increasing strength.

The two cities had comparable populations of some 22,000 in 1825, and in 1851 Quebec's population of 45,940 was still competitive with Montreal's 57,715. It was in the second half of the century that Montreal totally surpassed Quebec with its population of 267,730, dwarfing Quebec's 68,840. Ethnic demographics also changed radically with Quebec's English-speaking population declining from 40 per cent of the city's population in 1861 to 16 per cent in 1901. The English-speaking population of Montreal declined more slowly from a majority position in 1861 to 33 per cent in 1901.[25] As gateway ports and places of work, both cities were deeply marked by immigration in the nineteenth century. In critical years like 1832, 60,000 immigrants passed through the port of Quebec; in 1911 some 16 per cent of the Montreal population was born outside of Canada with five per cent of the city population neither French nor British in origin.[26]

These two urban realities ceated differing conditions for senior elites like the patricians. Readers with an interest in bourgeois culture will not be surprised that Law was the favoured male profession in both families, with the McCords counting a magistrate, police inspector, sheriff, several judges and the secretary of the civil-law codification commission among its members. The Taschereau are arguably Canada's most prominent legal family, with three members acceding from Quebec law practises to seats on the Supreme Court of Canada. Clerical and lay religious leadership is particularly critical in cities with such divided populations. The nomination of Elzéar-Alexandre Taschereau as cardinal must not overwhelm a broader leadership of patrician men and women in public space and urban moral geographies, particularly as both cities became increasingly segregated along

---

[24]   J.-C. Robert, *Atlas historique de Montréal* (Montreal 1994), 52.

[25]   Courville and Garon, *Atlas historique*, 172, 177, and Robert, *Atlas historique de Montréal*, 177; Linteau, *Histoire de Montréal*, 160–62.

[26]   Ruddel, *Quebec City*, 40, and Linteau, *Histoire de Montréal*, 161.

class lines.[27] And the presence of seignior Louis-Alexandre Taschereau as provincial premier (1920–1936) suggests flagrant exceptions to the apparent given that patricians simply ceded political power to professionals in the modern state. The Universities – English-language and Protestant McGill in Montreal and the French and Catholic *Université Laval* in Quebec – were, like the Literary and Historical Society of Quebec or Montreal's Natural History Society, intellectual institutions with sustained patrician input. Leaving these for longer treatment elsewhere, we will restrict ourselves here to three readily demonstrable examples of patrician influence: landed influence, the volunteer militia, and voluntarist associations and honours.

Landed influence

In both cities, clerical institutions and bourgeoisie retained an important landed presence that was rooted in seigniorial privilege. As seigniors of the island of Montreal, the Seminary of Montreal continued to collect *cens et rentes*, *lods et ventes*, and only abandoned their banal mills under merchant pressure in the early nineteenth century. Part of the seigniory had been ceded by the Seminary as fiefs to female religious orders whose social and religious missions depended on these seigniorial revenues. The McCord family wealth was rooted in two ninety-nine year leases for the Nazareth Fief accorded to them in 1792–1793 by the Sisters of Hôtel-Dieu and the Congregation of Notre Dame.[28] This fief, on the city's southwestern outskirts, was strategically located. From its agricultural origins, it became the site of early shipyards and slaughter houses and then rapid urbanisation as the Lachine Canal was built nearby. With the right to subdivide lots on the fief, the McCords benefited enormously: in 1840, the fief was valued at 27,616 English pounds and two McCord brothers were sharing land rents from 247 individuals. The fief continued to be of great value in the 1840s and 1850s as rents began to be converted from feudal to capitalist forms.

In Quebec, seigniorial power exercised by both clergy and grande bourgeoisie was equally prominent. The city's most powerful intellectual and landed institution, the Seminary of Quebec had several seigniories, all outside

---

[27]   See R. Trigger, 'Protestant Restructuring in the Canadian city: Church and Mission in the Industrial Working-Class District of Griffintown, Montreal', *Urban History Review/Revue d'histoire urbaine*, 31, No. 1, Fall 2002, 5–18.

[28]   McCord intermarriage with the Ross family gave them an alliance with one of the most important propertied families in Lower Canada. In 1825 David Ross was the seventh largest property-holder in the city. The Ross family also held St. Gilles de Beaurivage, a large Quebec City area seigniory that was listed as nineteenth in value ($100,412) in Quebec in 1863. See Canada, *Cadastres abrégés des seigneuries du district de Québec* (Montreal 1863), cited in J. Benoit, 'La Question Seigneuriale au Bas-Canada, 1850–1867', Université Laval, M. A. thesis, 1978, 206.

the city and indeed across the St. Lawrence region. For their part, the Ursulines' large upper-town fief just outside the fortifications gave conventual voice which, along with that of military proprietors, could be determinant in establishing landscape and land use in the upper city. Among the most prominent Ursuline superiors was Marie-Anne-Louise Taschereau who headed the convent 1793–1799, 1805–1811, and 1815–1819.[29] Seminaries in both cities headed the seigniorial palmares. In 1863, the Seminary of Quebec was Lower Canada's most important seigniorial proprietor ($788,575), followed in second place by the Seminary of Montreal ($674,740), while the Ursulines were twenty-third ($88,698).[30] Like the Seminary of Quebec, the Taschereau were essentially urbanites in profession and abode while drawing wealth from their rural seigniory of *La Nouvelle Beauce*. Located along both sides of the Chaudière River, the seigniory was granted to the Taschereau family in 1736 and remained a source of family wealth across the nineteenth and early twentieth centuries.[31] While liberalism was the predominant discourse of urban professionals, patricians preferred to speak of feudal entitlement. Jean-Thomas Taschereau, seignior, Quebec lawyer, and later judge of the Supreme Court of Canada, told a seigniorial enquiry in 1842 'ours are vested rights, (...) rights guaranteed to us by the public faith and by immemorial prescription', and warned authorities not to be 'more unjust towards them than towards the poorest member of society'.[32] Seigniorial land was in fact only opened to conversion to capitalist forms in the mid nineteenth century and compensation for seigniors was generous.

What actual power did this landed wealth bring in the industrialising city? In urban environments of wars, bankruptcies, shipwrecks, bourgeois mobility, and declining English-speaking demographics, the significance of the stability of this form of wealth for the clergy, to which it represented mortmain, and to patrician families who could readily transmit it, should not be underestimated. Members of the Taschereau family members still reside in the seigniorial manor – even if it has a bed-and-breakfast vocation – while the McCords' ninety-nine year lease gave urban sustenance to three generations. Patricians generally dispensed this wealth with discretion and an eye to taste: a classical estate on Mount Royal, education in Europe for sons, a summer home on the lower St. Lawrence, visits to a spa, and fruit trees imported from England. Sons, grandsons, and great grandsons on the bench, in the episcopacy, or with military commissions, and daughters of succeeding

---

[29] S. Prince, 'Marie-Anne-Louise Taschereau named Saint-François Xavier', *Dictionary of Candian Biography* (Toronto 1987), vol. 6, 751–2.

[30] Canada, *Cadastres abrégés des seigneuries du district de Québec; de Montréal; des Trois-Rivières* (Desbarats and Derbyshire 1863) cited in Benoit, 'La Question', 204–207.

[31] *Titles and Documents relating to the Seigneurial Tenure... 1851* (Montreal 1852), 243–4.

[32] *Journals*, Legislative Assembly of Canada, vol. 3, Appendix F.

generations with marriages into peer families or alternatively, with access to careers in a most prestigious convent, represent the fundamental exercise of power and privilege.

Alongside this private privilege, land ownership gave control over urban land use. Concerned with land values and the moral setting surrounding their new college and seminary in the 1860s, the Seminary of Montreal used domain land to offer a site to the Grey Nuns and to lay out respectable adjoining neighbourhoods in which housing types, building materials, and landscaping standards were tightly regulated: uses like factories or slaughterhouses were specifically prohibited in sales contracts. In the popular neighbourhoods developing on their fief, the McCords used their seigniorial rights and municipal lobbying to influence street layouts, market locations, and the mix of industry and housing; Anglicans themselves and concerned with working-class morals, they offered a site for the local Anglican chapel. This canal-side landscape was diametrically opposed to the bourgeois ideal they envisaged for their family and community on the slopes of Mount Royal. In the late 1830s, they built their estate, drawing its name Temple Grove from poet William Wordsworth, and integrating it into a segregated Protestant environment that included Christ Church Cathedral, McGill University, and Mount Royal Cemetery. If flooding, epidemics, ethnic confrontation, immigrant sheds, poverty, and overcrowding characterised life on their fief, a romantic and genteel vision of life on the urban fringe held sway on the mountain.

Volunteer militia

Families like the McCords and Taschereau had perennial connections with the British military. An ever-present force in both cities, its arms were used to control civil disobedience while it acted as a powerful force in local economies: its purchases of supplies like beef, flour, firewood, and hay represented 70 to 80 per cent of public expenses in Lower Canada.[33] Like the seigniorial landlords, the military had an often decisive voice on urban landscapes through constructing or deconstructing fortifications, opening spaces and improving parade grounds, or building gates, warehouses, or docks. Troops from the Quebec garrison did road work, building for example, the Craig Road which began on the Ross seigniory at St. Giles.

Beside this physical and economic presence, colonial troops represented a powerful physical and ideological presence linking History, Trafalgar, Race,

---

[33] G. Bervin, *Québec au XIXe siècle. L'activité économique des grand marchands* (Septentrion 1991), 187 and 181. For the military in Montreal see E. Senior, *British Regulars in Montreal: An Imperial Garrison, 1832–1854* (Montreal 1981). For military property in Quebec see C. Lacelle, *Military Property in Quebec City, 1760–1871* (Parks Canada 1982).

and Empire to public and private imagination. Was it coincidence that eleven years after the Battle of Trafalgar, the Garrison Library, established in Quebec in 1816 to provide 'rational entertainment', was modelled on its counterpart at Gibraltor: ladies in the families of 'officers' or 'gentlemen' were admitted to its reading room. Members of patrician French-Canadian families like Colonel Thomas-Pierre-Joseph Taschereau were among the library's early members.[34] For their part, patricians like John Samuel McCord preferred to minimise their grandfather John McCord's support for the Americans in the revolutionary war, dissipating this memory by an active presence in the social life of the Montreal garrison, its parades, balls, and military excursions.

Joan Scott and Linda Colley have shown the role of gender in establishing, legitimatising, and transmitting concepts of power; here again the example of Trafalgar is useful.[35] Anne Ross, wife of John Samuel McCord, recounted to her children the great impact in her childhood imagination of the erection of the Nelson Monument in 1808, the inscription of which reminded Montrealers that 'ENGLAND EXPECTS EVERY MAN WILL DO HIS DUTY'. One of Anne Ross's first diary entries as a thirteen-year old was a tribute to the British dead in the Napoleonic Wars.[36]

Supplements to British garrisons, Volunteer forces had crucial civil functions in colonial cities like Quebec and Montreal that were without professional police until the 1840s.[37] Volunteers came to prominence in Britain in the 1790s with the danger of French invasion, and after the Napoleonic Wars they were used to control unrest in hotspots like Manchester and Peterloo.[38] In Canada, the Volunteers showed their importance in the War of 1812 between Britain and the United States. As deputy adjutant-general of the Lower Canadian militia, Major Jean-Thomas Taschereau was second only to the adjutant-general. In the district of Montreal, David Ross, seignior in his own right and future father-in-law of John Samuel McCord, was promoted captain in the Montreal Incorporated

---

[34]   *Regulations and Catalogue of the Quebec Garrison Library* (Quebec 1824), and *Quebec Directory or Strangers' Guide in the City for 1826* (Quebec 1826).

[35]   L. Colley, *Bitrons Forging the Nation 1707–1837* (London 1994), 253, and J. Scott, *Gender and the Politics of History* (Cambridge 1988), 48.

[36]   McCord Museum Archives, vol. 1007, A. Ross-McCord, *Book of Collected Poems.* Unpublished Ms.; full inscription of the monument in Newton Bosworth, *Hochelaga Depicta or the Early History of Montreal, 1839* (Montreal 1839), 155–7.

[37]   A. Greer, 'The Birth of Police in Canada', in A. Greer and I. Radforth, *Colonial Leviathan: State Formation in Mid-Nineteenth Century Canada* (Toronto 1992), 17–49.

[38]   E. P. Thompson, *The Making of the English Working Class* (Vintage 1963), 276, 454 and 685. See also H. Cunningham, *The Volunteer Force: A Social and Political History* (Archon 1975).

Volunteers.[39] As ethnic relations deteriorated, the Volunteers were directed against their fellow citizens of nationalist bent. Armed with six-pound cannon and authorised to call up 2,000 men, they were despatched to keep peace in the streets of Montreal during the rebellions of 1837–1838. In the 1840s, their presence was felt at sites of unrest across the Montreal area: against Irish strikers at Beauharnois in 1843, at the Lachine locks in 1844, and keeping the peace in Griffintown, part of the McCord's Nazareth Fief, during the elections of 1844.

As with the regulars, the Volunteers in both cities were powerful vehicles of masculinity, of brotherhood and discipline, and of class position. Purged of French Canadians in moments of ethnic crisis, they also brought symbolic colour and physicality to the British connection, what one officer called 'a bond of union which unites "all" Britons – tories, whigs, and radicals'.[40] Military dress, the sword, boot, and cape, like the costumes of judge and cardinal worn by their brothers and sons, provided vivid images of traditional urban hierarchies. And, whatever its longterm fate in the urban environment, the horse, the preserve of the officer and cavalry, accorded patrician seating, height, resplendency, and sexual power.

John Samuel McCord followed the military tradition of his father-in-law, father, brother, and brother-in-law, joining the militia at age nineteen and commanding the Montreal Volunteer Brigade during the rebellions of 1837–1838. Training, arming, and commanding the troops allowed men like McCord to unite civil and martial authority. Once the Riot Act had been read, and McCord apparently kept a folded copy in his uniform, his troops could fire on the mob, occupy houses, and deploy cannon. Military power extended to private life. Obedience was expected off the parade ground and volunteers agreed not to marry without their captain's permission.[41]

In Quebec, the Taschereau had not been part of the military aristocracy of New France.[42] They were however, active supporters of British authority during the American Revolution with Gabriel-Elzéar Taschereau, accompanying the army of Burgoyne as paymaster. In revenge for this loyalism, the Taschereau seigniory was sacked by passing American troops. Gabrie-Elzéar's seigniorial heir Thomas-Pierre-Joseph Taschereau (1775–1826) began his military career with the 'Royal Canadian Volunteers' commanding

---

[39]   L. Homfray Irving, *Canadian Military Institute: Officers of the British Forces in Canada during the War of 1812–15* (Welland 1908), 100, 164.

[40]   McCord Museum Archives, vol. 735, Major H. Driscoll to J. S. McCord, 24 April 1838. See also B. Young, 'The Volunteer Militia in Lower Canada, 1837–50', in T. Myers et al., eds, *Power, Place and Identity: Historical Studies of Social and Legal Regulation in Quebec* (Montreal 1998), 37–54.

[41]   McCord Museum Archives, vol. 780, 'Standing Orders Ermatinger Troop', 1844.

[42]   Thomas-Jacques Taschereau (1680–1749) did not apparently serve in the French forces and only one of his sons, a young Charles-Antoine, (1741–1820), was active in the campaigns in the 1850s leading to the Conquest. See R. Legault, *Une élite en déroute. Les militaires canadiens après la Conquête* (Athena 2002), 11.

the Fourth Quebec Batallion in the War of 1812.[43] Notwithstanding the straining of ethnic relations in the mid-nineteenth century, the Taschereau maintained their strong military connection, culminating in 1884 with the publication by Joseph Ernest de Montarville Taschereau, ex-lieutenant in the Canadian Artillery Regiment, of a *Petit Code à l'usage des officiers*. Translating much of the Volunteers Army Act of 1883 into a 'code', Taschereau explained that his intention was to show 'the exactitude of the military code which governs us' and its importance 'from the standpoint of our dear and good old French language'.[44]

Voluntary associations and honours

English Montreal and Quebec are easily identifiable as part of what Peter Clark calls the 'associational world'.[45] Rudimentary, state formation in Canada was often distrusted by patricians who preferred to maintain elite control of institutions. Until the 1840s, Montreal and Quebec remained administered by justices of the peace. Organised forms of reading, political debate, and shared scientific and learned news depended on private initiatives. The formalisation of professions led to bar and medical associations, while heavy immigration brought both destitute countrymen, ethnic frictions, and a need for national solidarity that was recognised in the establishment of English, Scot, Irish, and French national societies. Family dispersal, epidemics, and urban roughness gave urgency to institutions for orphans, the broken, the sick, and the aged. As a young man, John Samuel McCord was active in a drinking club, the Brothers in Law. Marriage marked his passage to more serious voluntary associations. As an active militia officer, judge and fief-holder, he was a Mason, a member of the first council of the Art Association of Montreal, secretary of the Natural History Society of Montreal, a prominent layman in Christ Church Cathedral, and a member of the Anglican Church Society, a body which planned church expansion.[46] Three generations of McCord women – Jane Davidson Ross, Anne Ross, and Anne McCord – served as secretary of the Protestant Orphan Asylum. They were also active in the Women's Auxiliary and Missionary Society of their church.

---

[43]   P.-G. Roy, *La famille Taschereau* (Levis 1901), 27 and 49. See also F. Ouellet, 'Militia Officers and Social Structure', in F. Ouellet, ed., *Economy, Class, and Nation in Quebec: Interpretative Essays* (Toronto 1991), 87–120.

[44]   *Petit Code à l'usage des officiers* (Coté 1884), 6.

[45]   Clark, *British Clubs*, 94–140.

[46]   These should be compared to the examples cited in R. J. Morris, *Class, Sect and Party: The Making of the British Middle Class, Leeds 1820–1850* (Manchester 1990), and in David Blackbourn's discussion of voluntary associations in D. Blackbourn and G. Eley, eds, *The Peculiarities of German History: Bourgeois Society and Politics in Nineteenth-Century Germany* (Oxford 1984), 190–205.

At this writing, the role of volunteerism in Catholic society is less clear. A list of Taschereau membership in voluntary associations is suggestive that voluntary associations were more prevalent in Protestant that in Catholic society. In the latter, the church played a central role in collecting tithes, providing social venues, instigating philanthropic measures under direct clerical control, and ensuring cross-class coherence. The sectarianism of Protestantism may have forced more diverse organisations. Or perhaps the Taschereau felt less compulsive as joiners. Certainly, many of the clubs to which they belonged originated in the English-speaking community:

Table 12.1 Clubs to which Taschereau belonged

Literary and Historical Society of Quebec (2)
Institut Canadien de Québec (6)
Société Charitable des Dames catholiques de Québec (1)
Cercle catholique de Québec (1)
Quebec Gun Club (1)
Quebec Garrison Library (1)
Quebec Garrison Club (2)
Union Club of Quebec (1)
Société de géographie de Quebec (3)
Quebec Agricultural Society (3)
Société des bons livres de la paroisse de Québec (2)

Source: Author's investigation.

Voluntary activities and their accompanying sense of public duty merge with honours as largely symbolic ways of expressing authority and of marking identity and hierarchy. Thomas Mann's Johann Buddenbrook put it aptly: 'A proper man, a gentleman / A man of splendid poses.'[47]

Often associated with feudalisation, titles, honorary degrees, chancellor-ships, and positioning in ceremonies formed an integral part of patrician cul-ture, particularly on a continent marked by republicanism and egalitarianism. The seigniorial pew, the fief-holder's coach, and militia leadership, all patrician means of separating themselves from other bourgeois ranks were supplemented by a multitude of honours and awards that conferred respect, seniority, seriousness, and recognition from Monarch or Episcopate.[48] John

---

[47]   Th. Mann, *Buddenbrooks: The Decline of a Family* (New York 1994, orig. 1900), 52.

[48]   See for example, D. Blackbourn, 'The German bourgeoisie: an introduction', in D. Blackbourn and R. J. Evans, eds, *The German Bourgeoisie: Essays on the social history of the German middle class from the late eighteenth to the early twentieth century* (London 1991), 14.

McCord accepted the honorific position of Chancellor of the University of Bishop's College, an Anglican institution and part of his judicial circuit in the Eastern Townships. Writing from India where his son-in-law was serving with British forces, Justice of the Supreme Court Henri-Elzéar Taschereau successfully lobbied the Prime Minister of Canada and Queen Victoria that Supreme Court justices be knighted and in 1903 he proudly accepted the honour.

Burial sites can serve as a litmus test of honorific power since, as wags put it, 'all men are buried six feet under'! The urban poor of Quebec and Montreal, whatever their religion, were buried in unmarked graves. For their part, the Taschereau, although usually urbanites in schooling, profession, and residence, regularly exercised their right to be buried in the crypt of their parish church of *Ste Marie de Beauce*: here they lie 'opposite the pew of the captains of militia' or 'under the seigniorial pew'. Long widowhoods may have drawn Taschereau women in another direction. With the seigniory often in the hands of sons, widows apparently lived out their lives in Quebec and five, forsaking place beside their husbands, used family rank to be buried in the Ursuline crypt, steps from their homes and the classrooms where they had studied as girls.[49]

Family togetherness in the tomb seems to have held more importance for the McCords, and in Protestant tradition the wife invariably followed husband to his family plot. Three generations of McCords were active in the affairs of the Protestant burial grounds and John Samuel McCord presided over construction of the new Mount Royal Cemetery which opened in 1852. His position gave him right to the choice of a secluded and prestigious site. Adjoining that of their Ross in-laws, the McCord burial lot acted to unite the religious, financial, industrial, and intellectual bourgeoisie. Their lot is adjacent to that of the Bishop of Montreal, the President of the Bank of Montreal, a prominent city brewer, a railway president, and the principal of McGill University.

The slower advance of industrial capitalism in Quebec may have permitted its patrician group to persist more effectively using anchors in the church, militia, justice, and land-owning sectors. The rapid decline of the English-speaking community, particularly merchants and other capitalists, may also have contributed to the persistence of pre-industrial seigniorial, religious, and military institutions. While the Taschereau enjoyed apparent stability, fruitfulness, and social recognition, an entire generation of McCords in Montreal died childless witnessing the sale of the family estate and collapse of family finances. In Montreal, and here parallels with German studies seem apt, the patricians were superceded by the finance and industrial capitalists who moved to economic power in the city in the late nineteenth

---

[49]   Canadian Institute of Historical Microfilms, 24470, Sir Henri Elzéar Taschereu, 'Branche ainé de la famille Taschereau en Canada'.

century.[50] The older group's romanticism, its pre-Darwinian science, its marginality to new technologies, and its preference for British over American culture, seems to have alienated it from this new elite. Certainly, the landed wealth of families like the Viger, Papineau, or McCords was completely overshadowed by new forms of capitalist wealth. This brief study suggests the importance of ongoing comparative research into broad aspects of urban power that include gender, cultural and ethnic identity, and pre-industrial institutions.

---

[50] See for example, J. Sperber, 'Bürger, Bürgertum, Bürgerlichkeit, Bürgerliche Gesellschaft: Studies of the German (Upper) Middle Class and Its Sociocultural World', *Journal of Modern History*, 69, 1997, 271–97.

Bibliography

Introduction: Who Ran the Cities?
Ralf Roth and Robert Beachy

Beckert, S., *The Monied Metropolis. New York City and the Consolidation of the American Bourgeoisie, 1850–1896* (Cambridge and New York 2001).

Best, H., *Die Männer von Besitz und Bildung. Struktur und Handeln parlamentarischer Führungsgruppen in Deutschland und Frankreich 1848/49* (Düsseldorf 1990).

Blackbourn, D., and Eley, G., *The Peculiarities of German History: Bourgeois Society and Politics in Nineteenth-Century Germany* (Oxford and New York 1984).

Clark, P., *British Clubs and Societies, 1580–1800. The Origins of an Associational World* (Oxford 2000).

Dreitzel, H. P., *Elitebegriff und Sozialstruktur. Eine soziologische Begriffsanalyse* (Stuttgart 1962).

Gall, L., 'Bismarck und Bonapartismus', *Historische Zeitschrift*, 223, 1976, 618–37.

Habermas, J., *Strukturwandel der Öffentlichkeit. Untersuchungen zu einer Kategorie der bürgerlichen Gesellschaft* (Frankfurt am Main 1962).

Herzog, D., *Politische Führungsgruppen. Probleme und Ergebnisse der modernen Elitenforschung* (Darmstadt 1982).

Herzog, D., *Politische Karrieren. Selektion und Professionalisierung politischer Führungsgruppen* (Opladen 1975).

Jeske, R., 'Kommunale Amtsinhaber und Entscheidungsträger – die politische Elite', in L. Gall, ed., *Stadt und Bürgertum im Übergang von der traditionalen zur modernen Gesellschaft* (Munich 1993), 273–94.

Lamprecht, K., 'Der Ausgang des geschichtswissenschaftlichen Kampfes', *Die Zukunft*, 31 Juli 1897.

Lamprecht, K., 'Halbwahrheiten', in K. Lamprecht, ed., *Zwei Streitschriften den Herren H. Oncken, H. Delbrück, M. Lenz zugeeignet* (Berlin 1897), 39–77.

Looz-Corswarem, C. v., 'Die politische Elite Kölns im Übergang vom 18. zum 19. Jahrhundert', in H. Schilling and H. Diederiks, eds, *Bürgerliche Eliten in den Niederlanden und in Nordwestdeutschland. Studien zur Sozialgeschichte des europäischen Bürgertums im Mittelalter und in der Neuzeit* (Cologne and Vienna 1985), 421–44.

Maentel, Th., 'Reputation und Einfluß – die gesellschaftlichen Führungsgruppen', in L. Gall, ed., *Stadt und Bürgertum im Übergang von der traditionalen zur modernen Gesellschaf* (Munich 1993), 295–314.

Marx, K., 'Der achtzehnte Brumaire des Louis Bonaparte', in Marx-Engels Werke, vol. 8 (Berlin 1975), 111–207.

Mayer, K. U., 'Struktur und Wandel der politischen Eliten in der Bundesrepublik', in R. Lasserre et al., eds, *Deutschland – Frankreich, Bausteine zu einem Strukturvergleich* (Stuttgart 1980), 165–95.

Morris, R. J., 'Clubs, societies and associations', in F. M. L. Thompson, ed., *The Cambridge Social History of Britain*, vol. 3: *Social Agencies and Institutions* (Cambridge 1990), 395–443.

Morris, R. J., 'The middle class and British towns and cities of the Industrial Revolution, 1780–1870', in D. Fraser and A. Sutcliffe, eds, *The pursuit of Urban History* (London 1983), 286–306.

Nagle, J. D., *System and succession. The social bases of political recruitment* (Austin 1977).

Nipperdey, Th., 'Verein als soziale Struktur in Deutschland im späten 18. und frühen 19. Jahrhundert', in H. Heimpel, ed., *Geschichtswissenschaft und Vereinswesen im 19. Jahrhundert* (Göttingen 1972), 1–44.

Nipperdey, Th., *Deutsche Gesellschaft 1800–1866. Bürgerwelt und starker Staat* (Munich 1983).

Parsons, T., 'Evolutionäre Universalien der Gesellschaft', in W. Zapf, ed., *Theorien des sozialen Wandels* (Königstein/Ts. 1979), 75–94.

Pflanze, O., 'Bismarcks Herrschaftstechnik als Problem der gegenwärtigen Historiographie', *Historische Zeitschrift*, 234, 1982, 562–99.

Poulantzas, N., *Politische Macht und gesellschaftliche Klassen*, 2. ed. (Frankfurt am Main 1975).

Roth, R., *Stadt und Bürgertum in Frankfurt am Main. Ein besonderer Weg von der ständischen zur modernen Bürgergesellschaft 1760 bis 1914* (Munich 1996).

Schäfer, M., *Bürgertum in der Krise. Städtische Mittelklassen in Edinburgh und Leipzig 1890 bis 1930* (Göttingen 2003).

Scheuch, E. K., 'Continuity and Change in German Social Structure', *Historical Social Research* 46, 1988, 31–121.

Schmuhl, H.-W., *Die Herren der Stadt. Bürgerliche Eliten und städtische Selbstverwaltung in Nürnberg und Braunschweig vom 18. Jahrhundert bis 1918* (Gießen 1998).

Schulz, A., 'Wirtschaftlicher Status und Einkommensverteilung – die ökonomische Oberschicht', in: L. Gall, ed., *Stadt und Bürgertum im Übergang von der traditionalen zur modernen Gesellschaft* (Munich 1993), 249–71.

Schumann, H.-G., 'Die soziale und politische Funktion lokaler Eliten', in B. Kirchgässner and J. Schadt, eds, *Kommunale Selbstverwaltung – Idee und Wirklichkeit* (Sigmaringen 1983), 30–38.

Siewert, H.-J., *Lokale Elitensysteme. Ein Beitrag zur Theoriediskussion in der Community-Power-Forschung und ein Versuch zur empirischen Überprüfung* (Tübingen 1979).

Stammer, O., and Weingart, P., *Politische Soziologie* (Munich 1972).

Stone, L., 'Prosopographie – englische Erfahrungen', in K. Jarausch, ed., *Quantifizierung und Geschichtswissenschaft. Probleme und Möglichkeiten* (Düsseldorf 1976), 64–97.

Wehler, H.-U., 'Theorieprobleme der modernen deutschen Wirtschaftsgeschichte', in H.-U. Wehler, ed., *Historische Sozialwissenschaft und Geschichtsschreibung. Studien zu Aufgaben und Traditionen deutscher Geschichtswissenschaft* (Göttingen 1980), 106–25.

Wehler, H.-U., *Das Deutsche Kaiserreich 1871–1918*, 5. ed. (Göttingen 1983).

Welsh, W. A., *Leaders and Elites* (New York 1979).

Weyrauch, E., 'Zur sozialen und wirtschaftlichen Situation Kitzingens im 16. Jahrhundert', in I. Bátori and E. Weyrauch, eds, *Die bürgerliche Elite der Stadt Kitzingen. Studien zur Sozial- und Wirtschaftsgeschichte einer landesherrlichen Stadt im 16. Jahrhundert* (Stuttgart 1982), 27–90.

Elite and Pluralist Power in Eighteenth-Century English Towns:
A Case Study of King's Lynn
Emi Konishi

Borsay, P., *English Urban Renaissance: Culture and Society in the Provincial Town, 1660–1820* (Oxford 1989).

Bradfer-Lawrence, H. L., 'The Merchants of Lynn', in C. Ingleby, ed., *A Supplement to Blomfield's Norfolk* (Norwich 1929), 145–203.

Clark, P., *British Clubs and Societies c. 1580–1800: The Origins of an Associational World* (Oxford 2000).

Commission for inquiring into the state of the several municipal corporation in England and Wales, *Report on the Borough of King's Lynn* (London 1835).

Corfield, P. J., *Power and the Professions in Britain, 1700–1850* (London 1995).

Davidoff, L., and Hall, C., *Family Fortunes: Men and Women of the English Middle Class, 1780–1850* (London 1987).

Habermas, J., *The Structural Transformation of the Public Sphere: An Inquiry into a Category of Bourgeois Society*, translated by T. Burger (Cambridge 1989).

Konishi, E., 'Change and Continuity of Local Administrative Bodies: Special Reference to King's Lynn in the Long Eighteenth Century', *The Comparative Urban History Review*, 22, No. 2, 2003, 41–58 (in Japanese).

Konishi, E., 'Local Administration and Community in Long-Eighteenth-Century England: Special Reference to the King's Lynn Paving Commission', in Study Group of British Urban and Rural Communities and Tohoku University Economic and Business History Group, eds, *The Studies of British Urban History* (Tokyo 2004), 193–220 (in Japanese).

Konishi, E., 'The Age of Pluralist Power: The Urban Elite and the Public Sphere in King's Lynn, 1750–1835', Keio University Ph.D. thesis, 2000.

Martin, M. C., 'Women and Philanthropy in Walthamstow and Leyton, 1740–1870', *London Journal*, 19, 1995, 119–50.

Norfolk and Norwich Archaeological Society, ed., *A Calendar of Freemen of Lynn 1292–1836* (Norwich 1913).

Richards, P., *King's Lynn* (Chichester 1990).

Richards, W., *History of Lynn* (King's Lynn 1812).

Sweet, R., *The English Town, 1680–1840: Government, Society and Culture* (London 1999).

Thew, J. D., *Personal Recollections* (King's Lynn 1891).

Vickery, A., 'Golden Age to Separate Sphere? A Review of the Categories and Chronology of English Women's History', *Historical Journal*, 36, 1993, 383–414.

Webb, S. and B., *English Local Government*, 5 vols. (London 1908).

Urban Power, Industrialisation and Political Reform:
Swansea Elites in the Town and Region, 1780–1850
Louise Miskell

Alban, J. R., *Calendar of Swansea's Freemen's Records from 1760* (Swansea 1982).

Alban, J. R., *Portreeves and Mayors of Swansea* (Swansea 1982).

Boorman, D., *The Brighton of Wales. Swansea as a Fashionable Seaside Resort, c. 1780–1830* (Swansea 1986).

Bowen, E. G., 'Carmarthen: an urban study', *Archaeologia Cambrensis*, 17, 1968, 1–7.

Bush, G., *Bristol and its Municipal Government, 1820–1851* (Bristol 1976).

Cadogan, P., *Early Radical Newcastle* (Consett 1975).

Carter, H., *The Towns of Wales. A Study in Urban Geography* (Cardiff 1965).

Clark, P., and Houston, R., 'Culture and leisure, 1700–1840', in P. Clark, ed., *The Cambridge Urban History of Britain*, vol. 2: *1540–1840* (Cambridge 2000), 577–8.

Crouzet, F., *The First Industrialists. The Problem of Origins* (Cambridge 1985).

Daunton, M. J., *Coal Metropolis. Cardiff 1870–1914* (Leicester 1977).

Davies, J., *Cardiff and the Marquesses of Bute* (Cardiff 1981).

Evans, N., 'Urbanisation, elite attitudes and philanthropy: Cardiff, 1850–1914', *International Review of Social History*, 27, 1982, 290–323.

Grant, R., *The Parliamentary History of Glamorgan, 1542–1976* (Swansea 1978).

Hallesy, H. L., *The Glamorgan Pottery Swansea, 1814–38* (Llandysul 1995).

Harris, J. R., *The Copper King. A Biography of Thomas Williams of Llanidan* (Liverpool 1964).

Jenkins, P., 'Tory industrialism and town politics: Swansea in the eighteenth century', *Historical Journal*, 28, 1985, 102–23.

John, A. H., 'Introduction. Glamorgan, 1700–1750', in G. Williams and A. H. John, eds, *Glamorgan County History*, vol. 5: *Industrial Glamorgan* (Cardiff 1980), 1–46.

Jones, H. M., *Llanelli Lives* (Llandybie 2000).

Jones, W. H., *History of the Port of Swansea* (Carmarthen 1922).

Jones, W., 'Robert Morris, the Swansea friend of John Wilkes', in *Glamorgan Historian*, vol. 11 (Barry 1975), 126–36.

A List of the Names and Residences of the High Sheriffs of Glamorgan from 1541–1966 (Cardiff 1966).

Miskell, L., 'Civic leadership and the manufacturing elite: Dundee, c.1820–1850', in L. Miskell, C. A. Whatley and B. Harris, eds, *Victorian Dundee. Image and Realities* (East Linton 2000), 51–69.

Miskell, L., 'The making of a new "welsh metropolis": science, leisure and industry in early nineteenth-century Swansea', *History*, 88, 2003, 32–52.

Morgan, N., and Trainor, R. H., 'The dominant classes', in W. H. Fraser and R. J. Morris, eds, *People and Society in Scotland*, vol. 2: *1830–1914* (Edinburgh 1990), 103–37.

Morris, R. J., 'Voluntary societies and British urban elites, 1780–1850: an analysis', *Historical Journal*, 26, 1983, 95–118.

Newell, E., '"Copperopolis": the rise and fall of the copper industry in the Swansea district, 1826–1921', *Business History*, 32, 1990, 75–97.

Nicholson, G., *The Cambrian Traveller's Guide* (Stourport 1808).

O'Gorman, F., 'Campaign rituals and ceremonies: the social meaning of elections in England 1780–1860', *Past and Present*, 135, 1992, 79–115.

Prest, J., *Liberty and Locality. Parliament, Permissive Legislation and Ratepayers' Democracies in the Nineteenth Century* (London 1990).

Price, W. W., *Biographical Index of W. W. Price* (Aberystwyth 1981).

Randall, H. J., and Rees, W., eds, 'Diary of Lewis Weston Dillwyn', in *South Wales and Monmouth Record Society*, vol. 5 (Newport 1963), 15–98.

Rees, J. C. M., 'Evolving patterns of residence in a nineteenth century city: Swansea 1851–1871', University of Wales Swansea Ph.D. thesis, 1983.

Reynolds, P. R., 'Industrial development', in G. Williams, ed., *Swansea. An Illustrated History* (Swansea 1990), 29–55.

Ridd, T., 'Gabriel Powell: the uncrowned king of Swansea', in *Glamorgan Historian*, vol. 5 (Cowbridge 1968), 152–60.

Ridd, T., 'The development of municipal government in Swansea in the nineteenth century', University of Wales Swansea M. A. thesis, 1955.

Roberts, R. O., 'The White Rock copper and brass works near Swansea, 1736–1806', in *Glamorgan Historian,* vol. 12 (Barry 1981), 136–51.

Rubinstein, W. D., *Elites and the Wealthy in Modern British History. Essays in Social and Economic History* (Brighton 1987).

Smith, J., 'Urban elites c.1830–1930 and urban history', *Urban History*, 27, 2000, 255–75.

Temple Patterson, A., *A History of Southampton, 1700–1914*, vol. 1: *An Oligarchy in Decline, 1700–1835* (Southampton 1966).

Thomas, W. S. K., 'Municipal government in Swansea, 1485–1640', in S. Williams, ed., *Glamorgan Historian,* vol. 1 (Cowbridge 1963), 27–36.

Toomey, R. R., *Vivian and Sons, 1809–1924. A Study of the Firm in the Copper and Related Industries* (London 1985).

Trainor, R. H., 'The elite', in W. H. Fraser and I. Maver, eds, *Glasgow*, vol 2: *1830–1912* (Manchester 1997), 227–64.

Trainor, R. H., *Black Country Elites. The Exercise of Authority in and Industrial Area, 1830–1900* (Oxford 1993).

Williams, J., *Digest of Welsh Historical Statistics*, vol. 1 (Cardiff 1985), 318–31.

Who Really Ran the Cities?
Municipal Knowledge and Policy Networks
in British Local Government, 1832–1914
James Moore and Richard Rodger

Allan, C. M., 'The Genesis of British Urban Redevelopment with Special Reference to Glasgow', *Economic History Review*, 17, 1965, 598–613.

Ashton, T. S., *Economic and Social Investigations in Manchester, 1833–1933* (London 1934).

Baugh, G. R., 'Government Grants in Aid of the Rates in England and Wales 1889–1950', *Bulletin of the Institute of Historical Research*, 1992, 215–37.

Bell, Q., *The Schools of Design* (London 1963).

Bellamy, C., *Administering Central-Local Relations 1871–1919* (Manchester 1988).

Bentham, J., *Introduction to the Principles and Morals of Legislation* (1789).

Bentley, M., *Politics without Democracy, 1815–1914* (Oxford 1985).

Best, G. F. A., 'Another part of the island', in H. J. Dyos and M. Wolff, eds, *The Victorian City: Images and Realities*, 2 vols. (London 1978), vol. 2, 389–411.

Bosanquet, H., *The Poor Law Report of 1909* (London 1909).

Brebner, J. B., 'Laissez-faire and state intervention in nineteenth century Britain', *Journal of Economic History*, 8, 1948, 59–73.

Briggs, A., 'The background to the English parliamentary reform movement in three English cities', *Cambridge Historical Journal*, 10, 1952, 293–317.

Briggs, A., *Victorian Cities* (Harmondsworth 1990, orig. London 1963).

Brodrick, G. C., 'Local government in England', in J. W. Probyn, ed., *Local Government and Taxation* (London 1875), 6.

Butler, B. N., *Victorian Aspirations: the Life and Labour of Charles and Mary Booth* (London 1972).

C., T. S., 'Sir Henry Littlejohn', *Edinburgh Medical Journal*, 13, 1914, 404–7.

Cannadine, D., ed., *Patricians, Power and Politics in Nineteenth Century Towns* (Leicester 1982).

Cherry, G., *Pioneers in British Planning* (London 1981).

City of Edinburgh, *Report on the Common Good* (Edinburgh 1905).

Clarke, P. F., *Lancashire* (Cambridge 1971).

Cullen, M. J., *The Statistical Movement in Early Victorian Britain: the Foundations of Empirical Research* (New York 1975).

Daunton, M. J., *Trusting Leviathan: the Politics of Taxation in Britain 1799–1914* (Cambridge 2001).

Davis, J., 'Central government and the towns', in M. J. Daunton, ed., *The Cambridge Urban History of Britain*, vol. 3: *1840–1950* (Cambridge 2000), 261–72.

Dennis, R., 'Modern London', in M. J. Daunton, ed., *The Cambridge Urban History of Britain*, vol. 3: *1840–1950* (Cambridge 2000), 101–4.

Doig, A., *Corruption and Misconduct in Contemporary British Politics* (Harmondsworth 1984).

Doyle, B. M., 'The changing function of urban government: councillors, officials and pressure groups', in M. J. Daunton, ed., *The Cambridge Urban History of Britain*, vol. 3: *1840–1950* (Cambridge 2000), 287–313.

Eastwood, D., *Government and the Community in the English Provinces* (Basingstoke 1997).

Ewen, S. D., 'Power and administration in two Midland cities c. 1870–1938', unpublished University of Leicester Ph.D. thesis, 2003.

Feldman, D., and Jones, G. S., eds, *Metropolis – London. Histories and Representation since 1800* (London 1989).

Finer, S. E., *The Life and Times of Edwin Chadwick* (London 1952).

Finlayson, G. B. M. A., 'The Municipal Corporation Commission and Report 1833–1835', *Bulletin of the Institute of Historical Research*, 36, 1963, 36–52.

Fraser, D., ed., *Municipal Reform and the Industrial City* (Leicester 1982).

Fraser, D., *Power and Authority in the Victorian City* (Oxford 1979).

Fraser, D., *Urban Politics in Victorian England* (Leicester 1976).

Garrard, J., 'The Salford Gas Scandal of 1887', *Manchester Region History Review*, 2, 1988–1989, 2–6.

Garrard, J., and Parrott, V., 'Craft, professional and middle-class identity', in A. Kidd and D. Nicholls, eds, *The Making of the British Middle Class? Studies of Regional and Cultural Diversity since the Eighteenth Century* (Stroud 1998), 148–68.

Garrard, J., *Democratisation in Britain* (Basingstoke 2002).

Garrard, J., *Leadership and Power in Victorian Industrial Towns, 1830–1880* (Manchester 1983).

Gaskell, S. M., *Building Control: National Legislation and the Introduction of Local Byelaws in Victorian England* (London 1986).

Glasgow Municipal Commission on the Housing of the Poor, *Report and Evidence* (Glasgow 1904).

Gunn, S., *The Public Culture of the Victorian Middle Class* (Manchester 2000).

Haskell, F., *The Ephemeral Museum* (New Haven 2000).

Headrick, T. E., *The Town Clerk in English Local Government* (London 1962).

Hennock, E. P., 'Central/local government relations', *Urban History Yearbook*, 1982, 38–49.

Hennock, E. P., 'Finance and politics', *Historical Journal*, 6, 1963, 212–15.

Hennock, E. P., *Fit and Proper Persons – Ideal and Reality in Nineteenth Century Urban Government* (London, 1973).

Hietala, M., *Services and Urbanization at the Turn of the Century* (Helsinki 1987).

Hill, J., 'Manchester and Salford politics and the early development of the Independent Labour Party', *International Review of Social History*, 26, 1981, 171–201.

Hobsbawm, E. J., *Industry and Empire* (Harmondsworth 1968).

Holdsworth., W., *A History of English Law*, vol. 15 (London 1965).

Hollis, P., *Ladies Elect: Women in English Local Government, 1865–1914* (Oxford 1987).

Innes, J., and Rogers, N., 'Politics and government 1700–1840', in P. Clark, ed., *The Cambridge Urban History of Britain*, vol. 2: *1540–1840* (Cambridge 2000), 529–74.

Joyce, P., 'The factory politics of Lancashire in the later nineteenth century', *Historical Journal*, 18, 1975, 525–53.

Kearns, G., 'Town Hall and Whitehall: Sanitary Intelligence in Liverpool, 1840–63', in S. Sheard and H. Power, eds, *Body and City: Histories of Urban Public Health* (Aldershot 2000), 89–108.

Keith-Lucas, B., and Richards, P. G., *A History of Local Government in the Twentieth Century* (London 1978).

Keith-Lucas, B., *The Unreformed Local Government System* (London 1980).

Kellett, J. R., 'Municipal socialism, enterprise and trading in the Victorian city', *Urban History Yearbook*, 1978, 36–45.

Kidd, A. J., '"Outcast Manchester": voluntary charity, poor relief and the casual poor 1860–1905', in A. J. Kidd and A. W. Nicholls, eds, *City, Class and Culture* (Manchester 1985), 48–73.

Kitson-Clark, G., *An Expanding Society: Britain 1830–1900* (Cambridge 1967).

Lambert, R., *Sir John Simon 1816–1904 and English Administration* (London 1963).

Lancaster, W., *Radicalism, Co-operation and Socialism: Leicester Working-Class Politics 1860–1906* (Leicester 1987).

Laxton, P., 'Fighting for public health: Dr Duncan and his adversaries 1847–1863', in S. Sheard and H. Power, eds, *Body and City: Histories of Urban Public Health* (Aldershot 2000), 59–88.

Littlejohn, H. D., *Report on the Sanitary Condition of the City of Edinburgh* (London 1865).

Loughlin, M., *Legality and Locality* (Oxford 1996).

MacDonald, S., *The History and Philosophy of Art Education* (London 1970).

McCrone, D., and Elliott, B., *Property and Power in a City: the Sociological Significance of Landlordism* (London 1989).

Meller, H., *Patrick Geddes. Social Evolutionist and City Planner* (London 1990).

Meller, H., 'Philanthropy and public enterprise: international exhibitions and the modern town planning movement, 1889–1913', *Planning Perspectives*, 10, 1995, 295–310.

Meller, H., *Towns, Plans and Society in Modern Britain* (Cambridge 1997).

Miller, M., *Raymond Unwin. Garden Cities and Town Planning* (Leicester 1992).

Millward, R., 'The political economy of urban utilities', in M. J. Daunton, ed., *The Cambridge Urban History of Britain*, vol. 3: *1840–1950* (Cambridge 2000), 315–49.

Mitchell, B. R., and Deane, P., *Abstract of British Historical Statistics* (Cambridge 1971).

Moore, J., 'Progressive pioneers: Manchester Liberalism, the Independent Labour Party, and local politics in the 1890s', *Historical Journal*, 44, 2001, 989–1013.

Moore, J., The transformation of urban Liberalism, unpublished University of Manchester Ph.D. thesis, 1999.

Morris, R. J., *Class, Party and Sect: the Making of the British Middle Class: Leeds, 1820–1850* (Manchester 1990).

Mullen, B., *The Royal Museum and Libraries, Salford* (Salford 1899).

Offer, A., *Property and Politics 1870–1914: Landownership, Law, Ideology, and Urban Development in England* (Cambridge 1981).

Ostrogorski, M., *Democracy and the Organisation of Political Parties*, vol. 1 (London 1902).

An outline of the Parish and District Councils Bill (London 1893).

Owen, D., *The Government of Victorian London 1855–1889: The Metropolitan Board of Works, the Vestries and the City Corporation* (Cambridge, MA 1992).

Parry, J., *The Rise and Fall of Liberal Government in Victorian England* (Yale 1993).

Pennybacker, S., *A Vision for London 1889–1914: Labour, Everyday Life and the LCC Experiment* (London 1995).

Phillips, J. A., *The Great Reform Bill in the Boroughs: English Electoral Behaviour 1818–1841* (Oxford 1992).

Phillips, W. R. F., 'The "German example" and the professionalization of American and British city planning at the turn of the century', *Planning Perspectives*, 11, 1996, 167–83.

Pryde, G. S., *Central and Local Government in Scotland since 1707* (London 1960).

Pugh, M., *The Making of Modern British Politics, 1867–1939* (Oxford 1993).

Purbrick, L., ed., *The Great Exhibition of 1851* (Manchester 2001).

Redford, A., *The History of Local Government in Manchester*, vol. 2 (London 1939).

Redlich, F., and Hirst, F. W., *Local Government in England*, 2 vols. (London 1903).

Robertson, E., *Glasgow's doctor: James Burn Russell, MOH* (East Linton 1997).

Rodger, R., 'The Common Good and civic promotion: Edinburgh, 1860–1914', in R. Colls and R. Rodger, eds, *Cities of Ideas: Civil Society and Urban Governance in Britain 1800–2000* (Aldershot 2004), 144–77.

Roebuck, J., *Urban Development in Nineteenth Century London: Lambeth, Battersea and Wandsworth 1838–1888* (Chichester 1979).

Scott, J., *Leaves from the Diary of a Citizens Auditor* (Manchester 1884).

Simey, T. S., *Charles Booth Social Scientist* (Westport 1980).

Simon, E. D., *A City Council From Within* (London 1926).

Smellie, K. B., *A History of Local Government* (London 1969).

Smith, J. B., The governance of Wolverhampton elite c. 1840–1880, unpublished University of Leicester Ph.D. thesis, 2001.

Smith, J. B., 'Certified correct: the great Wolverhampton Council fraud 1900–1918', in J. Moore and J. B. Smith, eds, *Corruption in Urban Politics and Society, Britain 1780–1950* (Aldershot forthcoming 2007).

Snell, K. D. M., *Annals of the Labouring Poor* (Cambridge 1985).

Steffel, R. V., 'The Boundary Street Estate: An Example of the Urban Redevelopment by the London County Council, 1890–1914', *Town Planning Review*, 47, 1976, 161–73.

Sutcliffe, A., *Toward the Planned City: Germany, Britain, the United States and France, 1780–1914* (Oxford 1981).

Sweet, R., *The English Town 1680–1840* (Harlow 1999).

Taylor, A. J., *Laissez-faire and State Intervention in Nineteenth Century Britain* (Basingstoke 1972).

Taylor, P., *Popular Politics in Early Industrial Britain: Bolton 1825–50* (Keele 1995).

Thornhill, W., ed., *The Growth and Reform of English Local Government* (London 1971).

Trainor, R., *Black Country Elites: the Exercise of Authority in an Industrial Area 1830–1900* (Oxford 1993).

Turner, M. J., *British Politics in an Age of Reform* (Manchester 1999).

Turner, M. J., *Reform and Respectability* (Manchester 1995).

Waller, P. J., *Town, City and Nation: England 1850–1914* (Oxford 1983).

Webb, B., and Webb, S., *English Local Government – English Poor Law History*, part II, vol. 1 (London 1929 private edition).

Whitaker, P., The growth of Liberal organisation in Manchester from the 1860s to 1903, unpublished University of Manchester Ph.D. thesis, 1956.

Woods, R., and Shelton, N., *An Atlas of Victorian Mortality* (Liverpool 1997).

Yelling, J. A., *Slums and Slum Clearance in Victorian London* (London 1986).

Running an Unregulated Town: Strategies of Lincoln's Municipal Elite, 1860–1910

Denise McHugh

Anderson, C. H. J., *The Lincoln Pocket Guide* (London 1880).

Barber, B., 'Municipal Government in Leeds', in D. Fraser, ed., *Municipal Reform and the Industrial City* (Leicester 1982), 61–108.

Beckwith, I., *The Book of Lincoln* (Buckingham 1990).

Bellamy, C., *Administering Central-Local Relations, 1871–1919: The Local Government Board in its Fiscal and Cultural Context* (Manchester 1988).

Brabner, J. F. H., ed., *The Comprehensive Gazetteer of England and Wales* (London 1894).

Briggs, A., *Victorian Cities* (London 1963).

Briscoe, R., English, J. S., and Melrose, E. A., *The Typhoid in Lincoln* (Lincoln 1980).

Cannadine, D., ed., *Patricians, Power and Politics in Nineteenth-Century Towns* (Leicester 1982).

Cook's Lincoln Directory, 1885 (Lincoln 1885).

Cook's Lincoln Directory, 1897 (Lincoln 1897).

Crossick, G., 'The emergence of the lower middle class in Britain', in G. Crossick, ed., *The Lower Middle Class in Britain 1870–1914* (London 1977), 9–39.

Doyle, B. M., 'The changing functions of urban government: Councillors, officials and pressure groups', in M. J. Daunton, ed., *The Cambridge Urban History of Britain*, vol. 3: *1840–1950* (Cambridge 2001), 287–313.

Fraser, D., *Urban Politics in Victorian England: The Structure of Politics in Victorian Cities* (Leicester 1976).

Fraser, H., 'Municipal socialism and social policy', in R. J. Morris and R. Rodger (eds), *The Victorian City, A Reader in British Urban History 1820–1914* (London 1993), 258–81.

Garrard, J., *Leadership and Power in the Victorian Industrial Towns 1830–1880* (Manchester 1983).

Gatrell, V. A. C., 'Incorporation and the pursuit of Liberal hegemony in Manchester 1790–1839', in D. Fraser, ed., *Municipal Reform and the Industrial City* (Leicester 1982), 15–55.

Giles, G., *Report made to the Sanitary Committee of the Corporation of Lincoln* (Lincoln 1849).

Hennock, E. P., *Fit and Proper Persons: Ideal and Reality in Nineteenth-Century Urban Government* (London 1973).

Hill, F., *Victorian Lincoln* (Cambridge 1974).

Hoppen, K. T., *The Mid-Victorian Generation 1846–1886* (Oxford 1998).

Kelly's Directory of Lincolnshire (London 1896).

Kelly's Directory of Lincolnshire (London 1906).

Kelly's Directory of Lincolnshire (London 1909).

Forgotten Lincoln (Lincoln 1898).

Lincoln Pocket Guide (Lincoln 1874).

McHugh, D., 'Remaking the Victorian County Town 1860–1910' unpublished University of Leicester Ph.D. thesis, 2002.

Morris, R. J., *Class, Sect and Party: The Making of the British Middle Class, Leeds 1820–1850* (Manchester 1990).

Olney, R. J., *Rural Society and County Government in Nineteenth Century Lincolnshire* (Lincoln 1979).

Payne, P. L., 'Iron and steel manufactures', in D. H. Aldcroft, ed., *The Development of British Industry and Foreign Competition 1875–1914: Studies in Industrial Enterprise* (London 1968), 71–100.

Perkin, H., *The Rise of Professional Society. England Since 1880* (London 1989).

Pollard, S., *Britain's Prime and Britain's Decline: The British Economy 1870–1914* (London 1989).

Prest, J., *Liberty and Locality: Parliament, Permissive Legislation and Ratepayers' Democracies in the Nineteenth Century* (Oxford 1990).

Priestley, J. B., *English Journey* (London 1934).

Riley, G. R., *The Rise of Industrial Lincoln 1800–1959* (unpublished manuscript).

Ruddock's Lincoln Directory (Lincoln 1903).

Saul, S. B., 'The engineering industry', in D. H. Aldcroft, ed., *The Development of British Industry and Foreign Competition 1875–1914: Studies in Industrial Enterprise* (London 1968), 186–238.

Smith, D., *Conflict and Compromise, Class Formation in English Society 1830–1914: A Comparative Study of Birmingham and Sheffield* (London 1982).

Smith, J., 'Urban elites c. 1830–1930 and urban history' *Urban History*, 27, 2000, 255–75.

Sweet, R., *The English Town 1680–1840: Government, Society and Culture* (Oxford 1999).

Thompson, D. M., 'Historical survey 1750–1949', in D. Owen, ed., *A History of Lincoln Minster* (Cambridge 1994), 252–62.

Waller, P. J., *Town, City and Nation, England 1850–1914* (Oxford 1983).

White, W., *White's History, Gazetteer and Directory of Lincolnshire 1872* (Sheffield 1872).

White, W., *White's History, Gazetteer and Directory of Lincolnshire 1882* (Sheffield 1882).

Wiener, M. J., *English Culture and the Decline of the Industrial Spirit 1850–1980* (Cambridge 1981).

Wright, N. R., *Lincolnshire Towns and Industry, 1700–1914* (Lincoln 1982).

The Challenge of Urban Democracy: Municipal Elites in Edinburgh and Leipzig, 1890–1930
Michael Schäfer

Adam, T., *Arbeiterbewegung und Arbeitermilieu in Leipzig 1871–1933* (Cologne 1999).

Atkinson, M., *Local Government in Scotland* (Edinburgh 1904).

Buchan, D. D., *Edinburgh in its Administrative Aspect* (Edinburgh 1908).

'Citizens' Representative Tscharmann, 18 February 1914', in *Verhandlungen der Stadtverordneten zu Leipzig* 1913/14 (Leipzig 1914), 91.

Daunton, M. J., *Home and House in the Victorian City: Working-Class Housing 1850–1914* (London 1983).

Dawson, W. H., *Municipal Life and Government in Germany* (London 1914).

Doyle, B. M., 'The structure of elite power in early twentieth century Norwich, 1900–1935', *Urban History*, 24, 1999, 179–99.

Engeli, C., 'Städte und Stadt in der Weimarer Republik', in B. Kirchgässner and J. Schadt, eds, *Kommunale Selbstverwaltung – Idee und Wirklichkeit* (Sigmaringen 1983), 163–81.

Fox, R. A., *Members of the Labour Party Elected to Edinburgh Town Council 1909–1917* (Edinburgh 1971).

Fraser, D., ed., *Municipal Reform and the Industrial City* (Leicester and New York 1982).

Gall, L., ed., *Stadt und Bürgertum im 19. Jahrhundert* (Munich 1990).

Gall, L., ed., *Stadt und Bürgertum im Übergang von der traditionalen zur modernen Gesellschaft* (Munich 1993).

Goetz, H., 'Die ausländischen Gemeinden im Vergleich zu den deutschen, in H. Peters, ed., *Handbuch der kommunalen Wissenschaft und Praxis*, 3 vols. (Berlin 1956–1959), vol. 1, 597–603.

Gordon, G., 'Working class housing in Edinburgh, 1837–1974', *Wirtschaftsgeographische Studien*, 3, 1979, 75–8.

Gray, R. Q., *The Labour Aristocracy in Victorian Edinburgh* (Oxford 1986).

Häpe, G., 'Königreich Sachsen', in *Verfassung und Verwaltungsorganisation der Städte*, 7 vols. (Leipzig 1905–1908), vol. 4/1, 41–5.

Hennock, E. P., *Fit and Proper Persons. Ideal and Reality in Nineteenth Century Urban Government* (London 1973).

Hoffmann, W., *Zwischen Rathaus und Reichskanzlei. Die Oberbürgermeister in der Kommunal- und Staatspolitik des Deutschen Reiches von 1890 bis 1933* (Stuttgart 1974).

Hofmann, W., 'Aufgaben und Strukturen der kommunalen Selbstverwaltung in der Zeit der Hochindustrialisierung', in K. G. A. Jeserich et al., eds, *Deutsche Verwaltungsgeschichte*, 6 vols. (Stuttgart 1983–88), vol. 3, 606–12.

Holford, J., *Reshaping Labour. Organisation, Work, and Politics – Edinburgh in the Great War and after* (London 1988).

Keith-Lucas, B., and Richards, P. G., *A History of Local Government in the Twentieth Century* (London 1978).

Knox, E., 'Between Capital and Labour: The petite bourgeoisie in Victorian Edinburgh', University of Edinburgh Ph.D. thesis, 1986.

Krabbe, W. R., *Die deutsche Stadt im 19. und 20. Jahrhundert* (Göttingen 1989).

Krabbe, W. R., *Kommunalpolitik und Industrialisierung: Die Entfaltung der städtischen Leistungsverwaltung im 19. und frühen 20. Jahrhundert* (Stuttgart 1985).

Lapp, B., *Revolution from the Right: Politics, Class and the Rise of Nazism in Saxony, 1919–1933* (Atlantic Heights 1997).

Liebmann, H., *Zweieinhalb Jahre Stadtverordnetentätigkeit der USP in Leipzig* (Leipzig 1921). 101–10.

Ludwig-Wolf, L., 'Leipzig', in *Verfassung und Verwaltungsorganisation der Städte*, 7 vols. (Leipzig 1909), vol. 4/1, 136–9.

McCrone, D., and Elliott, B., *Property and Power in a City. The Sociological Significance of Landlordism* (Basingstoke and London 1989).

Midwinter, A., 'A return to ratepayer democracy? The reform of local government finance in historical perspective', *Scottish Economic and Social History*, 10, 1990, 61–8.

Morris, R. J., *Class, Sect and Party: The Making of the British Middle Classes: Leeds, 1820–1850* (Manchester 1990).

O'Carroll, A., 'The influence of local authorities on the growth of owner occupation before the Second World War', *Urban History*, 24, 1997, 221–41.

Paulus, J., *Kommunale Wohlfahrtspolitik in Leipzig 1930 bis 1945. Autoritäres Krisenmanagement zwischen Selbstbehauptung und Vereinnahmung* (Cologne 1998).

Reulecke, J., 'Bildungsbürgertum und Kommunalpolitik', in J. Kocka, ed., *Bildungsbürgertum im 19. Jahrhundert*, 4 vols. (Stuttgart 1985–93), vol. 4, 122–45.

Reulecke, J., *Geschichte der Urbanisierung in Deutschland* (Frankfurt am Main 1985).

Rodger, R. G., 'Crisis and confrontation in Scottish housing, 1880–1914', in R. G. Rodger, ed., *Scottish Housing in the Twentieth Century* (Leicester 1989), 25–46.

Rudloff, M., and Adam, T., *Leipzig – Wiege der deutschen Sozialdemokratie* (Berlin 1996).

Schäfer, M., 'Bürgertum, Arbeiterschaft und städtische Selbstverwaltung zwischen Jahrhundertwende und 1920er Jahren im deutsch-britischen Vergleich', *Mitteilungsblatt des Instituts zur Erforschung der europäischen Arbeiterbewegung*, 20, 1998, 192–5.

Schäfer, M., 'Die Burg und die Bürger. Stadtbürgerliche Herrschaft und kommunale Selbstverwaltung in Leipzig 1889–1929', in W. Bramke and U. Hess, eds, *Wirtschaft und Staat in Sachsen im 20. Jahrhundert* (Leipzig 1998), 275–9.

Schäfer, M., *Bürgertum in der Krise. Städtische Mittelklassen in Edinburgh und Leipzig von 1890 bis 1930* (Göttingen 2003).

Schmuhl, H.-W., 'Bürgertum und Stadt', in P. Lundgreen, ed., *Sozial- und Kulturgeschichte des Bürgertums* (Göttingen 2000), 224–48.

Seger, F., *Dringliche Reformen. Einige Kapitel Leipziger Kommunalpolitik* (Leipzig 1912).

Sheppard, M. G., 'The effects of franchise provisions on the social and sex compositions of the municipal electorate, 1882–1914', *Bulletin of the Society for the Study of Labour History*, 14, 1982, 19–23.

Siegert, R., *Das Verhältnis der Gemeindeverordneten zum Gemeinderat nach der Sächsischen Gemeindeordnung* (Leipzig 1927). 16–28.

Smellie, K. B., *A History of Local Government* (London 1968).

Smith, P. J., 'Planning as environmental improvement: Slum clearance in Victorian Edinburgh', in A. Sutcliffe, ed., *The Rise of Modern Urban Planning* (London 1980), 99–133.

Thamer, H.-U., and Kaiser, J. C., 'Kommunale Wohlfahrtspolitik zwischen 1918 und 1933 im Vergleich (Frankfurt/Leipzig/Nürnberg)', in J. Reulecke, ed., *Die Stadt als Dienstleistungszentrum* (St. Katharinen 1995), 325–70.

Trainor, R., 'Urban elites in Victorian England', *Urban History Yearbook*, 1985, 1–17.

Zimmermann, C., *Von der Wohnungsfrage zur Wohnungspolitik* (Göttingen 1991).

Governing Trondheim in the Eighteenth Century:
Formal Structures and Everyday Life
Steinar Supphellen

Bull, I., 'City merchants as structuring element in the Norwegian region Trøndelag', in H. Th. Gräf and K. Keller, eds, *Städtelandschaft – Réseau Urbain – Urban Network* (Vienna 2004), 171–84.

Bull, I., 'Merchant households and their networks in eighteenth-century Trondheim', *Continuity and Change*, 17, 2002, 213–31.

Bull, I., *De trondhjemske handelshusene på 1700-tallet: slekt, hushold og forretning* (Trondheim Merchant Houses in the Eighteenth Century: Family, Household and Business), Trondheim Studies in History, No. 26 (Trondheim 1998).

The History of Trondheim 997–1997, vol. 2 (Trondheim 1997).

Sandnes, J., et. al., eds, *Trondheims historie 977–1997*, 6 vols. (Trondheim 1997).

Supphellen, S., 'Byadministrasjon I Noreg på 17.h.' (The Administration of Towns in Norway in the Eighteenth Century), in B. Ericsson, ed., *Stadsadministrasjon i*

Norden på 1700-talet (The Administration of Towns in the Nordic Countries in the Eighteenth Century) (Trondheim 1982), 115–72.

Supphellen, S., ed., *Urban history. The Norwegian Tradition in a European Context*, Trondheim Studies in History, No. 25 (Trondheim 1998).

300 years with Cicignon (Trondheim 1981).

German Urban Elites in the Eighteenth and Nineteenth Centuries
Ralf Roth

Adam, Th., *Arbeitermilieu und Arbeiterbewegung in Leipzig 1871–1933. Demokratische Bewegungen in Mitteldeutschland* (Cologne et al. 1999).

Adler, F., *Freies Deutsches Hochstift. Seine Geschichte erster Teil 1859–1885* (Frankfurt am Main 1959).

Ballenthin, S., 'Ein Gothaer Unternehmer zwischen privaten Geschäften, städtischem Engagement und nationalen Reformversuchen. Ernst Wilhelm Arnoldi', in H.-W. Hahn, W. Greiling and K. Ries, eds, *Bürgertum in Thüringen. Lebenswelt und Lebenswege im frühen 19. Jahrhundert* (Rudolstadt and Jena 2001), 231–52.

Blackbourn, D., 'The German bourgeoisie: An introduction', in D. Blackbourn and R. J. Evans, eds, *The German Bourgeoisie. Essays on the social history of the German middle class from the late eighteenth to the early twentieth century* (London and New York 1991), 1–45.

Blackbourn, D., and Eley, G., *The Peculiarities of German History. Bourgeois Society and Politics in Nineteenth-Century Germany* (Oxford and New York 1984).

Boblenz, F., '"Bete und arbeite für König und Vaterland". Zur Biographie des Industriellen Johann Nicolaus von Dreyse', in H.-W. Hahn, W. Greiling and K. Ries, eds, *Bürgertum in Thüringen. Lebenswelt und Lebenswege im frühen 19. Jahrhundert* (Rudolstadt and Jena 2001), 201–29.

Boch, R., *Grenzenloses Wachstum? Das rheinische Wirtschaftsbürgertum und seine Industrialisierungsdebatte 1814–1857* (Göttingen 1991).

Bourdieu, P., 'Structure, Habitus, Power: Basis for a Theory of Symbolic Power', in N. B. Dirks, et. al., eds, *A Reader in Contemporary Social Theory* (Princeton 1994), 155–99.

Burkhardt, F., 'Zeugschmidtmeister, Ziegeleibesitzer und Stadtbürger. Zum politischen Karriereprofil des Jenaer Handwerkers Johann David Böhme', in H.-W. Hahn, W. Greiling and K. Ries, eds, *Bürgertum in Thüringen. Lebenswelt und Lebenswege im frühen 19. Jahrhundert* (Rudolstadt and Jena 2001), 303–33.

Conze, W., and Kocka, J., eds, *Bildungsbürgertum im 19. Jahrhundert*, 2 vols. (Stuttgart 1979).

Daniel, U., 'Kulturgeschichte – und was sie nicht ist', in U. Daniel, *Kompendium Kulturgeschichte. Theorien, Praxis, Schlüsselwörter* (Frankfurt am Main 2001), 7–25.

Dann, O., 'Die bürgerliche Vereinsbildung in Deutschland und ihre Erforschung', in É. François, ed., *Sociabilité et société bourgeoise en France, en Allemagne et en Suisse* (Paris 1986), 43–52.

Eley, G., 'Nations, Publics, and Political Cultures: Placing Habermas in the Nineteenth Century', in N. B. Dirks, et. al., eds, *A Reader in Contemporary Social Theory* (Princeton 1994), 297–335.

Engelhardt, U., *Bildungsbürgertum. Begriffs- und Dogmengeschichte eines Etiketts* (Stuttgart 1986).

Frevert, U., 'Bürgertumsforschung. Ein Projekt am Zentrum für interdisziplinäre Forschung (ZiF) der Universität Bielefeld', *Jahrbuch der Historischen Forschung*, 1986, 36–40.

Gaethgens, Th. W., 'Wilhelm Bode und seine Sammler', in E. Mai and P. Paret, eds, *Sammler, Stifter und Museen. Kunstförderung in Deutschland im 19. und 20. Jahrhundert* (Cologne 1993), 153–72.

Gall, L., 'Stadt und Bürgertum im 19. Jahrhundert. Ein Problemaufriß', in L. Gall, ed., *Stadt und Bürgertum im 19. Jahrhundert* (Munich 1990), 1–18.

Gall, L., 'Stadt und Bürgertum im Übergang von der traditonalen zur modernen Gesellschaft', in L. Gall, ed., *Stadt und Bürgertum im Übergang von der traditionalen zur modernen Gesellschaft* (Munich 1993), 1–12.

Gall, L., 'Vom alten zum neuen Bürgertum. Die mitteleuropäische Stadt im Umbruch 1780–1820', in L. Gall, ed., *Vom alten zum neuen Bürgertum. Die mitteleuropäische Stadt im Umbruch 1780–1820* (Munich 1992), 1–18.

Ginzburg, C., 'Der Inquisitor als Anthropologe', in Ch. Conrad and M. Kessel, eds, *Geschichte schreiben in der Postmoderne. Beiträge zur aktuellen Diskussion* (Stuttgart 1994), 203–18.

Gramsci, A., *Philosophie der Praxis. Eine Auswahl* (Frankfurt am Main 1967).

Grasskamp, W., 'Die Einbürgerung der Kunst. Korporative Kunstförderung im 19. Jahrhundert', in E. Mai and P. Paret, eds, *Sammler, Stifter und Museen. Kunstförderung in Deutschland im 19. und 20. Jahrhundert* (Cologne 1993), 104–13.

Häfen, W. v., 'Zwischen Fürstendienst und bürgerlicher Selbständigkeit. Der Mediziner und Verleger Ludwig Friedrich von Froriep', in H.-W. Hahn, W. Greiling and K. Ries, eds, *Bürgertum in Thüringen. Lebenswelt und Lebenswege im frühen 19. Jahrhundert* (Rudolstadt und Jena 2001), 53–80.

Hahn, H.-W., *Altständisches Bürgertum zwischen Beharrung und Wandel. Wetzlar 1689–1870* (Munich 1991).

Hansert, A., *Städelscher Museums-Verein Frankfurt am Main* (Frankfurt am Main 1994).

Hein, D., 'Badisches Bürgertum. Soziale Struktur und kommunalpolitische Ziele im 19. Jahrhundert', in L. Gall, ed., *Stadt und Bürgertum im 19. Jahrhundert* (Munich 1990), 65–96.

Hein, D., 'Die Kultur der Geselligkeit. 200 Jahre Harmonie-Gesellschaft Mannheim', in *200 Jahre von der Tradition zur Zukunft. Harmonie-Gesellschaft von 1803* (Mannheim 2003), 27–72.

Hein, D., 'Kunst und bürgerlicher Aufbruch. Das Karlsruher Vereinswesen und der Kunstverein im frühen 19. Jahrhundert', in J. Dresch and W. Rößling, eds, *175 Jahre Badischer Kunstverein. Bilder im Zirkel* (Karlsruhe 1993), 25–35.

Hein, D., 'Soziale Konstituierungsfaktoren des Bürgertums', in L. Gall, ed., *Stadt und Bürgertum im Übergang von der traditionalen zur modernen Gesellschaft* (Munich 1993), 151–81.

Hein, D., 'Stadt und Bürgertum in Baden. Karlsruhe und Mannheim vom Ancien Régime bis zur Revolution 1848/49', unpublished Johann Wolfgang Goethe-University Habil. thesis, 1995.

Heinsohn, K., *Politik und Geschlecht. Zur politischen Kultur bürgerlicher Frauenvereine in Hamburg* (Hamburg 1997).

Herzog, D., *Politische Führungsgruppen. Probleme und Ergebnisse der modernen Elitenforschung* (Darmstadt 1982).

Hoppe, P., 'Zum Luzerner Patriziat im 17. Jahrhundert', in K. Messmer and P. Hoppe, eds, *Luzerner Patriziat. Sozial- und wirtschaftsgeschichtliche Studien zur Entstehung und Entwicklung im 16. und 17. Jahrhundert* (Luzern 1976), 217–416.

Huber-Sperl, R., *Organisiert und engagiert. Vereinskultur bürgerlicher Frauen im 19. Jahrhundert in Westeuropa und den USA* (Königstein/Ts. 2002).

Jeske, R., 'Kommunale Amtsinhaber und Entscheidungsträger – die politische Elite', in L. Gall, ed., *Stadt und Bürgertum im Übergang von der traditionalen zur modernen Gesellschaft* (Munich 1993), 273–94.

Kanngießer, O., *Frankfurts Gegenwart und nächste Zukunft. Eine Denkschrift* (Frankfurt am Main 1892).

Kill, S., *Das Bürgertum in Münster 1770–1870* (Munich 2001).

Klausmann, Ch., *Politik und Kultur der Frauenbewegung im Kaiserreich. Das Beispiel Frankfurt am Main* (Frankfurt am Main 1997).

Klee, W., *Preußische Eisenbahngeschichte* (Stuttgart 1982).

Kluke, P., *Die Stiftungsuniversität Frankfurt am Main 1914–1932* (Frankfurt am Main 1972).

Koch, R., *Grundlagen bürgerlicher Herrschaft. Studien zur bürgerlichen Gesellschaft in Frankfurt am Main 1612–1866* (Wiesbaden 1983).

Kocka, J., 'Obrigkeitsstaat und Bürgerlichkeit. Zur Geschichte des deutschen Bürgertums im 19. Jahrhundert', in W. Hardtwig and H.-H. Brandt, eds, *Deutschlands Weg in die Moderne. Politik, Gesellschaft und Kultur im 19. Jahrhundert* (Munich 1993), 107–21.

Krabbe, W., 'Munizipalsozialismus und Interventionsstaat. Die Ausbreitung der städtischen Leistungsverwaltung im Kaiserreich', *Geschichte in Wissenschaft und Unterricht*, 30, 1979, 265–83.

Kramer, H., 'Die Anfänge des sozialen Wohnungsbaus in Frankfurt am Main 1860–1914', *Archiv für Frankfurts Geschichte und Kunst*, 56, 1978, 123–90.

Kühl, U., 'Le débat sur le socialisme municipal en Allemagne avant 1914 et la municipalisation de l'électricité', in U. Kühl, ed., *Der Munizipalsozialismus in Europa* (Munich 2001), 81–100.

Langewiesche, D., 'Stadt, Bürgertum und "bürgerliche Gesellschaft" – Bemerkungen zur Forschungsentwicklung', *Informationen zu Modernen Stadtgeschichte*, 1, 1991, 2–5.

Leiser, W., 'Die Einwohnergemeinde im Kommunalrecht des Großherzogtums Baden', in B. Kirchgässner and J. Schadt, eds, *Kommunale Selbstverwaltung. Idee und Wirklichkeit* (Sigmaringen 1983), 39–55.

Lenger, F., 'Bürgertum, Stadt und Gemeinde zwischen Frühneuzeit und Moderne', *Neue Politische Literatur*, 40, 1995, 14–29.

Lenger, F., 'Bürgertum und Stadtverwaltung in rheinischen Großstädten des 19. Jahrhunderts. Zu einem vernachlässigten Aspekt bürgerlicher Herrschaft', in L. Gall, ed., *Stadt und Bürgertum im 19. Jahrhundert* (Munich 1990), 97–169.

Lerner, F., *Bürgersinn und Bürgertat. Geschichte der Frankfurter Polytechnischen Gesellschaft 1816–1966* (Frankfurt am Main 1966).

Lips, M. A., *Die Nürnberg-Fürther Eisenbahn in ihren nächsten Wirkungen und Resultaten* (Nuremberg 1836).

Liste der 212 Mitglieder des Casino (Frankfurt am Main 1810).

Liste der effectiven und 10 supernumerären Mitglieder erster Klasse des Casino für das Jahr 1816/17 (Frankfurt am Main 1817).

Looz-Corswarem, C. v., 'Die politische Elite Kölns im Übergang vom 18. zum 19. Jahrhundert', in H. Schilling and H. Diederiks, eds, *Bürgerliche Eliten in den Niederlanden und in Nordwestdeutschland. Studien zur Sozialgeschichte des europäischen Bürgertums im Mittelalter und in der Neuzeit* (Cologne 1985), 421–44.

Lutzer, K., *Der Badische Frauenverein 1859–1918. Rotes Kreuz, Fürsorge und Frauenfrage* (Stuttgart 2002).

Maentel, Th., 'Reputation und Einfluß – die gesellschaftlichen Führungsgruppen', in L. Gall, ed., *Stadt und Bürgertum im Übergang von der traditionalen zur modernen Gesellschaft* (Munich 1993), 295–314.

Mettele, G., *Bürgertum in Köln 1775–1870. Gemeinsinn und freie Assoziation* (Munich 1998).

Möller, F., *Bürgerliche Herrschaft in Augsburg 1790–1880* (Munich 1998).

Müller, B., *Stiftungen für Frankfurt am Main* (Frankfurt am Main 1958).

Nachama, A., *Ersatzbürgertum und Staatsbildung. Zur Zerstörung des Bürgertums in Brandenburg-Preußen* (Frankfurt am Main 1984).

Nipperdey, Th., 'Verein als soziale Struktur in Deutschland im späten 18. und frühen 19. Jahrhundert', in H. Heimpel, ed., *Geschichtswissenschaft und Vereinswesen im 19. Jahrhundert* (Göttingen 1972), 1–44.

Nipperdey, Th., *Deutsche Gesellschaft 1800–1866. Bürgerwelt und starker Staat* (Munich 1983).

Reulecke, J., *Geschichte der Urbanisierung in Deutschland* (Frankfurt am Main 1985).

Reuter, D., 'Das Heilbronner Bürgertum und seine Führungsgruppen 1770 bis 1880', unpublished Johann Wolfgang Goethe-University Ph.D. thesis, 1993.

Reuter, D., 'Der Bürgeranteil und seine Bedeutung', in L. Gall, ed., *Stadt und Bürgertum im Übergang von der traditionalen zur modernen Gesellschaft* (Munich 1993), 75–92.

Roth, R., '"... denn die Eisenbahn war es, die nunmehr den Anlaß zu einer Kolonisation der Heide gab ... ". Die Eisenbahnen und das rheinisch-westfälische Industriegebiet', in *Rheinisch-westfälische Zeitschrift für Volkskunde*, 47, 2002, 101–38.

Roth, R., '"Bürger" and Workers, Liberalism and the Labor Movement in Germany, 1848 to 1914', in D. E. Barclay and E. D. Weitz, eds, *Between Reform and Revolution. German Socialism and Communism from 1840 to 1990* (Oxford 1998), 113–40.

Roth, R., '"Der Toten Nachruhm". Aspekte des Mäzenatentums in Frankfurt am Main (1750–1914)', in J. Kocka and M. Frey, eds, *Bürgerkultur und Mäzenatentum im 19. Jahrhundert* (Berlin 1998), 99–127.

Roth, R., 'Das Vereinswesen in Frankfurt am Main als Beispiel einer nichtstaatlichen Bildungsstruktur', *Archiv für Frankfurts Geschichte und Kunst*, 64, 1998, 143–211.

Roth, R., 'Die Frankfurter Bürger auf der Suche nach ihrer Geschichte', *Mitteilungen des Oberhessischen Geschichtsvereins Gießen*, 88, 2003, 159–80.

Roth, R., 'Die Geschichte der Frankfurter Gesellschaft für Handel, Industrie und Wissenschaft 1920 bis 1995', in L. Gall, ed., *Frankfurter Gesellschaft für Handel, Industrie und Wissenschaft – Casinogesellschaft von 1802* (Frankfurt am Main 1995), 37–82.

Roth, R., 'Die Stadt der Paulskirche als Modell einer selbstverwalteten Republik', in B. Heidenreich, ed., *Deutsche Hauptstädte – von Frankfurt nach Berlin* (Wiesbaden 1998), 53–68.

Roth, R., 'Kaufleute als Werteproduzenten', in H.-W. Hahn and D. Hein, eds, *Bürgerliche Werte und Wertevermittlung um 1800* (Jena 2005), 95–118.

Roth, R., 'Von Wilhelm Meister zu Hans Castorp. Der Bildungsgedanke und das bürgerliche Assoziationswesen im 18. und 19. Jahrhundert', in D. Hein and A. Schulz, eds, *Bürgerkultur im 19. Jahrhundert. Bildung, Kunst und Lebenswelt* (Munich 1996), 121–39.

Roth, R., *Gewerkschaftskartell und Sozialpolitik in Frankfurt am Main. Arbeiterbewegung vor dem Ersten Weltkrieg zwischen Restauration und liberaler Erneuerung* (Frankfurt am Main 1991).

Roth, R., *Das Jahrhundert der Eisenbahn. Die Herrschaft über Raum und Zeit 1800 – 1914* (Ostfildern 2005).

Roth, R., *Stadt und Bürgertum in Frankfurt am Main. Ein besonderer Weg von der ständischen zur modernen Bürgergesellschaft 1760 bis 1914* (Munich 1996).

Rüschemeyer, D., 'Bourgeoisie, Staat und Bildungsbürgertum. Idealtypische Modelle für die vergleichende Erforschung von Bürgertum und Bürgerlichkeit', in J. Kocka, ed., *Bürger und Bürgerlichkeit im 19. Jahrhundert* (Göttingen 1987), 101–20.

Sarasin, Ph., *Stadt der Bürger. Bürgerliche Macht und städtische Gesellschaft Basel 1846–1914*, 2nd edn. (Göttingen 1997).

Schambach, K., 'Geselligkeit und wirtschaftlicher Wandel. Zur Entwicklung des Vereinswesens in Dortmund im 19. Jahrhundert', *Beiträge zur Geschichte Dortmunds und der Grafschaft Mark*, 87, 1997, 117–33.

Schambach, K., *Stadtbürgertum und industrieller Umbruch. Dortmund 1780–1870* (Munich 1996).

Schmuhl, H. W., 'Bürgerliche Eliten in städtischen Repräsentativorganen', in J. Puhle, ed., *Bürger in der Gesellschaft der Neuzeit. Wirtschaft – Politik – Kultur* (Göttingen 1991), 178–98.

Schmuhl, H. W., *Die Herren der Stadt. Bürgerliche Eliten und städtische Selbstverwaltung in Nürnberg und Braunschweig vom 18. Jahrhundert bis 1918* (Gießen 1998).

Schulz, A., 'Wirtschaftlicher Status und Einkommensverteilung – die ökonomische Oberschicht', in L. Gall, ed., *Stadt und Bürgertum im Übergang von der traditionalen zur modernen Gesellschaft* (Munich 1993), 249–71.

Schulz, A., *Vormundschaft und Protektion. Eliten und Bürger in Bremen 1750–1880* (Munich 2002).

Schumann, H.-G., 'Die soziale und politische Funktion lokaler Eliten', in B. Kirchgässner and J. Schadt, eds, *Kommunale Selbstverwaltung – Idee und Wirklichkeit* (Sigmaringen 1983), 30–38.

Siegrist, H., ed., *Bürgerliche Berufe. Zur Sozialgeschichte der freien und akademischen Berufe* (Göttingen 1988).

Siewert, H.-J., *Lokale Elitensysteme. Ein Beitrag zur Theoriediskussion in der Community-Power-Forschung und ein Versuch zur empirischen Überprüfung* (Tübingen 1979).

Sobania, M., 'Rechtliche Konstituierungsfaktoren des Bürgertums', in L. Gall, ed., *Stadt und Bürgertum im Übergang von der traditionalen zur modernen Gesellschaft* (Munich 1993), 131–50.

Sobania, M., 'Vereinsleben. Regeln und Formen bürgerlicher Assoziationen im 19. Jahrhundert', in D. Hein and A. Schulz, eds, *Bürgerkultur im 19. Jahrhundert. Bildung, Kunst und Lebenswelt* (Munich 1996), 170–90.

Söllner, A., *Geschichte und Herrschaft. Studien zur materialistischen Sozialwissenschaft* (Frankfurt am Main 1979).

Speitkamp, W., 'Geschichtsvereine – Landesgeschichte – Erinnerungskultur', *Mitteilungen des Oberhessischen Geschichtsvereins Gießen*, 88, 2003, 181–204.

Sperber, J., 'Bürger, Bürgertum, Bürgerlichkeit, Bürgerliche Gesellschaft: Studies of the German (Upper) Middle Class and Its Sociocultural World', *Journal of Modern History*, 69, 1997, 271–97.

Tenfelde, K., 'Stadt und Bürgertum im 20. Jahrhundert', in K. Tenfelde and H.-U. Wehler, eds, *Wege zur Geschichte des Bürgertums* (Göttingen 1994), 317–53.

Tiessen, H., *Industrielle Entwicklung, gesellschaftlicher Wandel und politische Bewegung in einer württembergischen Fabrikstadt des 19. Jahrhunderts. Esslingen 1848–1914* (Sigmaringen 1982).

Wachsmuth, R., *Die Gründung der Frankfurter Universität* (Frankfurt am Main 1929).
Wehler, H.-U., 'Bürger, Arbeiter und das Problem der Klassenbildung 1800–1870. Deutschland im internationalen Vergleich', in J. Kocka, ed., *Arbeiter und Bürger im 19. Jahrhundert. Varianten ihres Verhältnisses im europäischen Vergleich* (Munich 1986), 1–28.
Wehler, H.-U., 'Die Geburtsstunde des deutschen Kleinbürgertums', in H.-J. Puhle, ed., *Bürger in der Gesellschaft der Neuzeit. Wirtschaft – Politik – Kultur* (Göttingen 1991), 199–209.
Wehler, H.-U., *Deutsche Gesellschaftsgeschichte*, 4 vols. (Frankfurt am Main 1987–2003).
Weichel, Th., 'Die Kur- und Verwaltungsstadt Wiesbaden 1790–1822', in L. Gall, ed., *Vom alten zum neuen Bürgertum. Die mitteleuropäische Stadt im Umbruch 1780–1820* (Munich 1992), 317–56.
Weichel, Th., *Die Bürger von Wiesbaden. Von der Landstadt zur 'Weltkurstadt' 1780–1914* (Munich 1997).
Weyrauch, E., 'Zur sozialen und wirtschaftlichen Situation Kitzingens im 16. Jahrhundert', in I. Bátori and E. Weyrauch, eds, *Die bürgerliche Elite der Stadt Kitzingen. Studien zur Sozial- und Wirtschaftsgeschichte einer landesherrlichen Stadt im 16. Jahrhundert* (Stuttgart 1982), 27–90.
Wogawa, F., '"Zu sehr Bürger...?" Die Jenaer Verleger- und Buchhändlerfamilie Frommann im 19. Jahrhundert', in H.-W. Hahn, W. Greiling and K. Ries, eds, *Bürgertum in Thüringen. Lebenswelt und Lebenswege im frühen 19. Jahrhundert* (Rudolstadt and Jena 2001), 81–107.
Zerback, R., *München und sein Stadtbürgertum. Eine Residenzstadt als Bürgergemeinde 1780–1870* (Munich 1997).

Voluntary Society in Mid-Nineteenth-Century Pest: Urbanisation and the Changing Distribution of Power
Árpád Tóth

Alt, R., and Sandmann, X., Festöi Megtekintések Budára és Pestre. – Malerische Ansichten von Ofen und Pest (Vienna 1851).
Bácskai, V., 'Pest társadalma és politikai arculata 1848-ban', *Tanulmányok Budapest múltjából*, 19, 1972, 283–326.
Bácskai, V., and Nagy, L., 'Market Areas, Market Centres and Towns in Hungary in 1828', *Acta Historica Academiae Scientiarum Hungaricae*, 26, 1990, 1–25.
Bácskai, V., and Nagy, L., *Piackörzetek, piacközpontok és városok Magyarországon 1828-ban* (Budapest 1984).
Barta, I., 'Az 1831. évi koleramozgalom', *Tanulmányok Budapest múltjából*, 13, 1961, 445–70.
A Nemzeti Casino alapszabályai (Pest 1829).
A Pesti Casino tagjainak A.B.C. szerint való feljegyzése és annak alapjai (Pest 1828).
Corfield, P., *The Impact of English Towns, 1700–1800* (Oxford 1982).
Csizmadia, A., *A magyar városi jog* (Kolozsvár 1941).
Czoch, G., 'A városi polgárság nemzeti hovatartozásának kérdése Magyarországon a 19. század közepén', in C. Fedinec, ed., *Nemzet a társadalomban* (Budapest 2004), 51–67.
Gergely, A., ed., *19. századi magyar történelem, 1790–1918* (Budapest 1998).
Gorsky, M., 'Mutual aid and civil society: friendly societies in nineteenth-century Bristol', *Urban History*, 5, issue 3, 1998, 302–22.

Ilk, M., *A Nemzeti Casinó százéves története, 1827–1926* (Budapest 1927).

Isoz, K., 'A Pest-Budai Hangászegyesület és nyilvános hangversenyei, 1836–1851', *Tanulmányok Budapest múltjából*, 3, 1934, 165–79.

Kontler, L., *Milleneum in Central Europe. A History of Hungary* (Budapest 1999).

Mályusz, E., 'A magyarországi polgárság a francia forradalom korában', *A Bécsi Magyar Történeti Intézet Évkönyve*, 1, 1931, 225–82.

Morris, R. J., 'Voluntary societies and British urban elites 1780–1850: an analysis', in Peter Borsay, ed., *The Eighteenth Century Town. A Reader in English Urban History, 1688–1820*, 2nd edn. (London 1990), 338–66.

Nagy, L., *Budapest története a török kiűzésétől a márciusi forradalomig* (Budapest 1975).

Oszetzky, D., *A hazai polgárság társadalmi problémái a rendiség felbomlásakor* (Budapest 1935).

Pajkossy, G., 'Egyesületek a reformkori Magyarországon', *História*, 2, 1993, 6–8.

Pajkossy, G., 'Egyesületek Magyarországon és Erdélyben 1848 előtt', *Korunk*, 4, 1993, 103–9.

Scheiben-Schützen-Almanach für das Schützen-Jahr 1830 (Pest 1830).

Shani, D'Cruze, 'The middling sort in eighteenth-century Colchester: independence, social relations and the community broker', in J. Barry and Ch. Brooks, eds, *The Middling Sort of People. Culture, Society and Politics in England, 1550–1800* (Macmillan 1994), 181–207.

Silber, M. K., 'A zsidók társadalmi befogadása Magyarországon a reformkorban. A "kaszinók"', *Századok*, 126, issue 1, 1992, 113–41.

Sobania, M., 'Vereinsleben. Regeln und Formen bürgerlicher Assoziationen im 19. Jahrhundert', in D. Hein and A. Schulz, eds, *Bürgerkultur im 19. Jahrhundert. Bildung, Kunst und Lebenswelt* (Munich 1996), 176–81.

Szöcs, S., *A városi kérdés az 1832–1836-os országgyűlésen* (Budapest 1996).

Szvoboda-Dománszky, G., 'A Pesti Műegylet, 1839–1867', Hungarian Academy of Sciences Ph.D. thesis, 1994.

Tóth, A., 'A társadalmi szerveződés polgári és rendi normái. A Pesti Jótékony Nőegylet fennállásának első korszaka, 1817–1848', *FONS*, 45, 1998, 411–79.

Tóth, A., 'Önsegélyezés és önszerveződés. Temetkezési és betegsegélyező egyletek a reformkori Pesten', *Korall*, 2, issue 5/6, 2001, 49–71.

Tóth, A., *Önszervező polgárok. A pesti egyesületek társadalomtörténete a reformkorban* (Budapest 2005).

Tóth-Könyves, K., *Budapest Székesfőváros közjótékonysági, szociálpolitikai és közművelődési közigazgatásának kézikönyve* (Budapest 1930).

Vasquez, Carlo, *Buda és Pest Szabad Királyi Várossainak tájleírása* (Vienna 1837).

Verfassung der wohlthätige Frauenvereine in Ofen und Pesth (Pest 1817).

Running 'Modern' Cities in a Patriarchal Milieu:
Perspectives from the Nineteenth-Century Balkans
Dobrinka Parusheva

Anastassiadou, M., *Salonique, 1830–1912. Une ville ottomane à l'âge des Réformes* (Leiden, New York and Cologne 1997).

Beograd u prošlosti i sadašnosti. Povodom 500–godišnjce smrti Despota Stevana, 1389–1427 (Belgrade 1927).

Çelik, Z., *The Remaking of Istanbul. Portrait of an Ottoman City in the Nineteenth Century* (Seattle and London 1986).

Djordjevic, D., 'Foreign Influences on Nineteenth-Century Balkan Constitutions', in K. Shangriladze and E. Townsend, eds, *Papers for the V Congress of Southeast European Studies, Belgrad, September 1984* (Columbus, Ohio 1984), 72–102.

Hadzhijski, I., *Bit i dushevnost na nashija narod* (Material and spiritual life of our people) (Sofia 1995).

Hristov, Hr., 'Obshtinite i bulgarskoto natzionalno Vazrazhdane' (*Obshtina* and the Bulgarian National Revival), in K. Kosev et al., eds, *Bulgaria 1300. Institutzii i durzhavna traditzia* (Bulgaria 1300. Institutions and state tradition), vol. 1 (Sofia 1981), 271–91.

Hristov, Hr., *Bulgarskite obshtini prez Vazrazhdaneto* (Bulgarian *obshtina* during the National Revival) (Sofia 1973).

Iliou, Ph., 'Luttes sociales et mouvement de Lumières à Smyrne en 1819', in Association Internationale d'études du Sud-est européen, ed., *Structure sociale et développement culturel des villes sud-est européennes et adriatiques aux XVIIe-XVIIIe siècles: Actes du Colloque interdisciplinaire de l'Association Internationale d'études du Sud-est européen* (Bucharest 1975), 295–315.

Jubilejna kniga na grad Sofia, 1878–1928 (Jubilee Book of the City of Sofia, 1878–1928) (Sofia 1928).

Lerner, D., *The Passing of Traditional Society: Modernizing the Middle East* (Glencoe, Ill. and London 1964).

Mazower, M., *The Balkans* (London 2001).

Mishkova, D., 'The nation as zadruga: Remapping nation-building in nineteenth-century Southeast Europe', in M. Dogo and G. Franzinetti, eds, *Disrupting and Reshaping. Early Stages of Nation-building in the Balkans* (Ravenna 2002), 103–16.

Mooney, G., 'Urban "disorders"', in St. Pile, Chr. Brook and G. Mooney, eds, *Unruly Cities? Order/Disorder* (London and New York 1999), 53–102.

Morris, R. J., 'The middle class and British towns and cities of the Industrial Revolution, 1780–1870', in D. Fraser and A. Sutcliffe, eds, *The pursuit of Urban History* (London 1983), 286–306.

Parusheva, D., 'Political Elites in the Balkans, nineteenth and early twentieth century: Routes to Career', *Etudes balkaniques*, 4, 2001, 69–79.

Paskaleva, V., 'Za samoupravlenieto na bulgarite prez Vazrazhdaneto' (On the self-government of the Bulgarians during the National Revival), *Izvestija na Instituta po istorija*, 14/15, 1964, 73–112.

Rapportu din partea Consiliului Communal facut conformu art. 59 din legea communelor şi votat şi aprobat în siedintiele de la 5, 6 si 9 februariu 1870 (Bucharest 1870).

Shishkov (Chichcof), St., *Plovdiv v svoeto minalo i nastojashte. Istoriko-etnografski i politiko-ekonomicheski pregled / Plovdiv dans son passé et son présent. Aperçu historico-ethnographique et politico-économique* (Plovdiv 1926).

Simic, A., *The peasant urbanites: a study of rural-urban mobility in Serbia* (New York 1973).

Siupiur, E., 'Les intellectuels roumains du XIXe siècle et la réorganisation de la classe politique et du système institutionnel', *Revue Roumaine d'Histoire*, 1–2, 1995, 75–95.

Sundhaussen, H., *Historische Statistik Serbiens 1834–1914. Mit europäischen Vergleichsdaten* (Munich 1989).

Tankova, V., *Kogato Plovdiv ne e veche stolitza* (When Plovdiv was not a capital anymore) (Sofia 1994).

Todorov, N., *The Balkan City, 1400–1900* (Seattle and London 1983).

Tsonev, St., *Kum vaprosa za razlozhenieto na esnafskite organizatsii u nas prez perioda na Vazrazhdaneto* (To the question of decline of the guilds during the period of National Revival) (Sofia 1956).

Vucinich, W., 'Some Aspects of the Ottoman Legacy', in Ch. and B. Jelavich, eds, *The Balkans in Transition. Essays on the Development of Balkan Life and Politics Since the Eighteenth Century* (Berkeley and Los Angeles 1963), 81–114.

Yerasimos, St., 'À propos des réformes urbaines des Tanzimat', in P. Dumont and Fr. Georgeon, eds, *Villes Ottomanes à la fin de l'Empire* (Paris 1992), 17–32.

Class and Politics: The Case of New York's Bourgeoisie
Sven Beckert

Almond, G. A., *Plutocracy and Politics in New York City* (Boulder 1998).

Beard, Ch. A., and Beard, M. R., *The Rise of American Civilization*, vol. 2: *The Industrial Era* (New York 1937).

Beckert, S., 'Contesting Suffrage Rights in Gilded Age New York', *Past & Present*, 20, February, 2002, 116–57.

Beckert, S., 'Die Kultur des Kapitals: Bürgerliche Kultur in New York und Hamburg im 19. Jahrhundert', *Vorträge aus dem Warburg-Haus*, 4, 2000, 139–73.

Beckert, S., *The Monied Metropolis: New York City and the Consolidation of the American Bourgeoisie* (Cambridge and New York 2001).

Bridges, A., 'Another Look at Plutocracy in Antebellum New York City', *Political Science Quarterly*, 97, 1982, 57–71.

Burnham, W. D., 'The System of 1896: An Analysis', in P. Kleppner et al., eds, *The Evolution of American Electoral Systems*, (Westport 1981), 147–202.

Cohen, L., *Making a New Deal: Industrial Workers in Chicago, 1919–1939* (New York 1990).

Conniff, M. L., *Latin American Populism in Comparative Perspective* (Albuquerque 1982).

Dawley, A., *Class and Community: The Industrial Revolution in Lynn* (Cambridge, Mass. 1976).

Department of the Interior, Census Office, *Statistics of the Population of the United States at the Tenth Census, June 1, 1880* (Washington 1883).

Fink, L., 'The New Labor History and the Powers of Historical Pessimism: Consensus, Hegemony, and the Case of the Knights of Labor', *The Journal of American History*, 75, June 1988, 115–36.

Foner, Ph., *Business and Slavery: The New York Merchants and the Irrepressible Conflict* (Chapel Hill 1941).

Frisch, M. H., and Walkowitz, D. J., *Working-Class America: Essays on Labor, Community, and American Society* (Urbana 1983).

Goodwyn, L., *The Populist Moment* (New York 1978).

Gronowicz, A. B., 'Revising the Concept of Jacksonian Democracy', University of Pennsylvania Ph.D. thesis, 1981.

Gutman, W., *Work, Culture, and Society in Industrializing America: Essays in American Working-Class and Social History* (New York 1976).

Hofstadter, R., *The American Political Tradition and the Men Who Made it* (New York 1948).

Ionescu, G., and Gellner, E., *Populism: Its Meaning and National Characteristics* (London 1969).

Katz, I., *August Belmont; A Political Biography* (New York 1968).

Katznelson, I., and Zolberg, A., eds, *Working-Class Formation: Nineteenth Century Patterns in Western Europe and the United States* (Princeton 1986).

Keller, M., *Affairs of State: Public Life in Late Nineteenth-Century America* (Cambridge, Mass. 1977).

Laurie, B., *Artisans Into Workers: Labor in Nineteenth-Century America* (New York 1989).

Long, C. D., *Wages and Earnings in the United States, 1860–1890* (Princeton 1960).

Mandelbaum, S., *Boss Tweed's New York* (New York 1965).

Montgomery, D., *The Fall of the House of Labor: The Workplace, the State, and American Labor Activism, 1865–1925* (New York 1987).

Moore, B., *Social Origins of Dictatorship and Democracy: Lord and Peasant in the Making of the Modern World* (Boston 1966).

Nevins, A., and Milton, H. Th., eds, *The Diary of George Templeton Strong*, vol. 4 (New York 1974).

Oestreicher, R., 'Two Souls of American Democracy', in G. R. Andrew and H. Chapman, eds, *The Social Construction of Democracy, 1870–1990* (New York 1995), 118–31.

Report of the Commission to Devise a Plan for the Government of Cities in the State of New York: Presented to the Legislature, March 6th, 1877 (New York 1877).

Twentieth Annual Report of the Corporation of the Chamber of Commerce of the State of New–York for the Year 1877 – 1878 (New York 1878).

Sklar, M. J., *The Corporate Reconstruction of American Capitalism, 1890–1916: The Market, The Law, and Politics* (New York 1989).

Sproat, J. G., *The Best Men: Liberal Reformers in the Gilded Age* (New York 1968).

Stedman Jones, G., *Languages of Class: Studies in English Working-Class History, 1832–1932* (Cambridge 1983).

Tella, T. Di, 'Populism and Reform in Latin America', in C. Veliz, ed., *Obstacles to Change in Latin America* (London 1965), 47–74.

Tilden, S., '"Municipal Reform Message" Address to the Legislature, Albany, 11 May 1875', in J. Bigelow, ed., *The Writings and Speeches of Samuel J. Tilden*, vol. 2 (New York 1885), 119–37.

Townsend, R., *Mother of Clubs: Being the History of the First Hundred Years of the Union Club of the City of New York, 1836–1936* (New York 1936).

Trachtenberg, A., *The Incorporation of America: Culture and Society in the Gilded Age* (New York 1982).

Wallace, A. C., *Rockdale: The Growth of an American Village in the Early Industrial Revolution* (New York 1972).

Wiebe, R., *The Search for Order* (New York 1967).

Wilentz, S., *Chants Democratic: New York City and the Rise of the American Working-Class* (New York 1984).

Williams, P., '"The Horrors of the Commune": Urban Politics and Suffrage Restriction in Post-Reconstruction Texas'. Unpublished manuscript, 2001.

A 'Jeffersonian Skepticism of Urban Democracy'?
The Educated Middle Class and the Problem of Political Power in Chicago, 1880–1940
Marcus Gräser

Addams, J., *Twenty Years at Hull-House* (New York 1910).

Beckert, S., *The Monied Metropolis: New York City and the Consolidation of the American Bourgeoisie, 1850–1896* (Cambridge and New York 2001).

Bliss, W. D. P., *The New Encyclopedia of Social Reform* (New York 1908).

Bryce, J., *The American Commonwealth* (New York 1888).

Cohen, A. W., *The Racketeer's Progress: Chicago and the Struggle for the Modern American Economy*, 1900–1940 (Cambridge 2004).

Davis, A. F., *American Heroine: The Life and Legend of Jane Addams* (New York 1973).

Diner, S. J., *A City and Its Universities: Public Policy in Chicago, 1892–1919* (Chapel Hill 1980).

Einhorn, R. L., 'The Civil War and Municipal Government in Chicago', in M. A. Vinovskis, ed., *Toward a Social History of the Civil War: Exploratory Essays* (Cambridge 1990), 117–38.

Finegold, K., *Experts and Politicians: Reform Challenges to Machine Politics in New York, Cleveland, and Chicago* (Princeton 1995).

Flanagan, M. A., *Seeing with Their Hearts: Chicago Women and the Vision of the Good City, 1871–1933* (Princeton 2002).

Goebel, T., 'The Children of Athena: Chicago Professionals and the Creation of a Credentialed Social Order, 1870–1920', University of Chicago Ph.D. thesis, 1993.

Gosnell, H. F., *Machine Politics: Chicago Model* (Chicago 1937).

Gräser, M., 'Arbeiterschaft, Bürgertum und welfare state building. Überlegungen zu einem Vergleich der kommunalen Sozialreform in den USA und in Deutschland 1880–1940', *Mitteilungsblatt des Instituts zur Erforschung der europäischen Arbeiterbewegung*, 22, 1999, 59–84.

Gräser, M., 'Chicago 1880–1940: Urbanisierung ohne administrative Kompetenz?', *ZENAF Arbeits- und Forschungsberichte*, 1, 2001, 5–6.

Gräser, M., 'Demokratie versus Bürokratie. Bildprogramm und Politik der settlement-Bewegung in Chicago am Ende des 19. Jahrhunderts', in M. Gräser et. al., eds, *Staat, Nation, Demokratie. Traditionen und Perspektiven moderner Gesellschaften. Festschrift für Hans-Jürgen Puhle* (Göttingen 2001), 115–28.

Green, P. M., 'Anton Cermak: The Man and His Machine', in P. M. Green and M. G. Holli, eds, *The Mayors: The Chicago Political Tradition* (Carbondale 1987), 99–110.

Grimshaw, W. J., 'Is Chicago Ready for Reform? – or, a New Agenda for Harold Washington', in M. G. Holli and P. M. Green, eds, *The Making of the Mayor: Chicago 1983* (Grand Rapids 1984), 141–65.

Hammack, D. C., 'Problems in the Historical Study of Power in the Cities and Towns of the United States, 1800–1960', *American Historical Review*, 83, 1978, 323–49.

Hammack, D. C., *Power and Society: Greater New York at the Turn of the Century* (New York 1982).

Henderson, C. R., *Social Settlements* (New York 1898).

Hirsch, A. R., *Making the Second Ghetto: Race and Housing in Chicago 1940–1960* (Chicago 1998).

Hofstadter, R., *The Age of Reform. From Bryan to F.D.R.* (New York 1955).

Lepawsky, A., *Home Rule for Metropolitan Chicago* (Chicago 1935).

Miller, D. L., *City of the Century: The Epic of Chicago and the Making of America* (New York 1996).

Ostrogorski, M., *Democracy and the Organization of Political Parties, 2* vols. (New York 1902).

Park, R. E., 'Community Organization and the Romantic Temper', in R. E. Park et al., eds, *The City* (Chicago 1925), 113–25.

Reynolds, W. S., 'Cook County Comes to Order', *The Survey*, 56, 1926, 244–5.

Rodgers, D. T., *Atlantic Crossings: Social Politics in a Progressive Age* (Cambridge 1998).

Ruble, B. A., *Second Metropolis: Pragmatic Pluralism in Gilded Age Chicago, Silver Age Moscow, and Meji Osaka* (Cambridge 2001).

Schaefer, A. R., *American Progressives and German Social Reform, 1875–1920* (Stuttgart 2000).

Sennett, R., *Families Against the City: Middle Class Homes of Industrial Chicago, 1872–1890* (Cambridge 1970).

Smith, J., 'Urban Elites c. 1830–1930 and Urban History', in *Urban History*, 27, 2000, 255–75.

Sperber, J., 'Bürger, Bürgertum, Bürgerlichkeit, Bürgerliche Gesellschaft: Studies of the German (Upper) Middle Class and Its Sociocultural World', *Journal of Modern History*, 69, 1997, 271–97.

Teaford, J. C., *The Unheralded Triumph: City Government in America, 1870–1900* (Baltimore 1984).

Weber, M., *Wirtschaft und Gesellschaft* (Tübingen 1985).

Whitten, R., 'Zoning', in E. R. A. Seligman, ed., *Encyclopedia of the Social Sciences*, vol. 15 (New York 1935), 38–9.

Wilson, H. E., *Mary McDowell: Neighbor* (Chicago 1928).

Zorbaugh, H. W., *The Gold Coast and the Slum: A Sociological Study of Chicago's Near North Side* (Chicago 1929).

Patrician Elites and Power in Nineteenth-Century Montreal and Quebec City
Brian Young

Artibise, A., *Winnipeg: a social history of urban growth 1874–1914*, 2 vols. (Montreal 1975).

Benoit, J., 'La Question Seigneuriale au Bas-Canada, 1850–1867', Université Laval, M. A. thesis, 1978.

Bervin, G., *Québec au XIXe siècle. L'activité économique des grand marchands* (Septentrion 1991).

Blackbourn, D., 'The German bourgeoisie: an introduction', in D. Blackbourn and R. J. Evans, eds, *The German Bourgeoisie: Essays on the social history of the German middle class from the late eighteenth to the early twentieth century* (London 1991), 1–14.

Blackbourn, D., and Eley, G., eds, *The Peculiarities of German History: Bourgeois Society and Politics in Nineteenth-Century Germany* (Oxford 1984).

Bliss, M., *Northern Enterprise: Five Centuries of Canadian Business* (Toronto 1987).

Bosworth, N., *Hochelaga Depicta or the Early History of Montreal, 1839* (Montreal 1839).

Brown, K. M., *Good Wives, Nasty Wenches and Anxious Patriarchs: Gender, Race, and Power in Colonial Virginia* (Chapel Hill 1996).

The Centenary Volume of the Literary and Historical Society of Quebec 1824–1924 (Quebec City 1924), 128–9.

Clark, P., *British Clubs and Societies 1580–1800: The Origins of an Associational World* (Oxford 2000).

Petit Code à l'usage des officiers (Coté 1884).

Colley, L., *Bitrons Forging the Nation 1707–1837* (London 1994).

Courville, S., and Garon, R., *Atlas historique du Québec. Québec ville et capitale* (Sainte-Foy 2001).

Cunningham, H., *The Volunteer Force: A Social and Political History* (Archon 1975).

Davidoff, L., and Hall, C., *Family Fortunes: Men and women of the English middle class 1780–1850* (London 1987).

Dechêne, L., and Hanna, D., *Historical Atlas of Canada: The Land Transformed*, 3 vols. (Toronto 1993).

Dechêne, L., *Habitants et marchands de Montréal au XVIIe siècle* (Paris 1974).

Greer, A., 'The Birth of Police in Canada', in A. Greer and I. Radforth, *Colonial Leviathan: State Formation in Mid-Nineteenth Century Canada* (Toronto 1992), 17–49.

Greer, A., and Radforth, I., *Colonial Leviathan: State Formation in Mid-Nineteenth Century Canada* (Toronto 1992).

Hall, C., *White, Male and Middle Class: Explorations in Feminism and History* (London 1992).

Harvey, D., *Paris: Capital of Modernity* (London 2003).

Harvey, D., *The Urban Experience* (Baltimore 1989).

Irving, L. Homfray, *Canadian Military Institute: Officers of the British Forces in Canada during the War of 1812–15* (Welland 1908).

Lacelle, C., *La garnison britannique dans al ville de Québec d'après les journaux de 1764 à 1840* (Parks Canada 1976).

Lacelle, C., *Military Property in Quebec City, 1760–1871* (Ottava 1982).

Legault, R., *Une élite en déroute. Les militaires canadiens après la Conquête* (Athena 2002).

Lewis, B., *The Middlemost and the Milltown: Bourgeois Culture and Politics in Early Industrial England* (Palo Alto 2001).

Linteau, P.-A., *Brève histoire de Montréal* (Montreal 1992).

Linteau, P.-A., *Histoire de Montréal depuis la Confédération* (Montreal 1992).

Linteau, P.-A., *Maisonneuve ou comment des promoteurs fabriquent une ville, 1883–1918* (Montreal 1981).

Mann, Th., *Buddenbrooks: The Decline of a Family* (New York 1994, orig. 1900).

Moore, Ch., 'Interpreting History', *The Beaver*, February/March 2000, 85.

Morris, R. J., 'Clubs, Societies and Associations', in F. M. L. Thompson, ed., *The Cambridge Social History of Britain, 1750–1950*, vol. 3: *Social Agencies and Institutions* (Cambridge 1990), 395–443.

Morris, R. J., 'Voluntary Societies and British Urban Elites', *Historical Journal*, 26, 1983, 95–118.

Morris, R. J., *Class, Sect and Party: The Making of the British Middle Class, Leeds, 1820–1850* (Manchester 1990).

Morton, W. L., 'Clio in Canada: The Interpretation of Canadian History', in C. Berger, ed., *Approaches to Canadian History* (Toronto 1967), 42–9.

Nelles, H. V., *The Art of Nation Building* (Toronto 1998).

Ouellet, F., 'Militia Officers and Social Structure', in F. Ouellet, ed., *Economy, Class, and Nation in Quebec: Interpretative Essays* (Toronto 1991), 87–120.

Ouellet, F., *Lower Canada 1791–1840: Social Change and Nationalism* (Toronto 1980).

Prince, S., 'Marie-Anne-Louise Taschereau named Saint-François Xavier', *Dictionary of Candian Biography* (Toronto 1987), vol. 6, 751–2.

Quebec Directory or Strangers' Guide in the City for 1826 (Quebec 1826).

Regulations and Catalogue of the Quebec Garrison Library (Quebec 1824).

Robert, J.-C., 'Montréal 1821–71. Aspects de l'urbanisation', École des hautes études, Paris, Doctorat de 3ᵉ cycle, 1977.

Robert, J.-C., *Atlas historique de Montréal* (Montreal 1994).

Rodger, R., *The Transformation of Edinburgh: Land, Property and Trust in the Nineteenth Century* (Cambridge 2001).

Ross-McCord, A., *Book of Collected Poems* (unpublished Ms.).

Ross, R., *Status and Respectability in the Cape Colony 1750–1870: A Tragedy of Manners* (Cambridge 1999).

Roy, P.-G., *La famille Taschereau* (Levis 1901).

Ruddel, D. T., *Quebec City 1765–1832: The evolution of a colonial town* (Hull 1991).

Rudin, R., *Founding Fathers: Celebration of Champlain and Laval in the Streets of Quebec, 1878–1908* (Toronto 2003).

Ryan, M., *Cradle of the Middle Class: The Family in Oneida County, New York, 1790–1865* (Cambridge 1981).

Scott, J., *Gender and the Politics of History* (Cambridge 1988).

Senior, E., *British Regulars in Montreal: An Imperial Garrison, 1832–1854* (Montreal 1981).

Smith, B., *Ladies of the Leisure Class: The Bourgeoisies of Northern France in the Nineteenth Century* (Princeton 1981).

Sperber, J., 'Bürger, Bürgertum, Bürgerlichkeit, Bürgerliche Gesellschaft: Studies of the German (Upper) Middle Class and Its Sociocultural World', *Journal of Modern History*, 69, 1997, 271–97.

Stelter, G., and Artibise, A. F. J., *The Canadian City: Essays in Urban History* (Ottawa 1977).

Thompson, E. P., *The Making of the English Working Class* (Vintage 1963).

Trigger, R., 'Protestant Restructuring in the Canadian city: Church and Mission in the Industrial Working-Class District of Griffintown, Montreal', *Urban History Review/Revue d'histoire urbaine*, 31, No. 1, Fall 2002, 5–18.

Tulchinsky, G. J. J., *The River Barons: Montreal businessmen and the growth of industry and transportation* (Toronto 1977).

Walden, K., *Becoming Modern in Toronto: the Industrial Exhibition and the Shaping of a Late Victorian Culture* (Toronto 1997).

Young, B., 'The Volunteer Militia in Lower Canada, 1837–50', in T. Myers et al., eds, *Power, Place and Identity: Historical Studies of Social and Legal Regulation in Quebec* (Montreal 1998), 37–54.

Index